Financial Inclusion Law and Over-Indebtedness

The book addresses the current challenges faced by financial consumers in the context of enormous technological developments. This edited collection covers safeguarding financial consumers, encompassing topics such as financial inclusion, data protection, and consumer over-indebtedness. Addressing specific issues related to vulnerable consumer groups and the increasing digitisation of financial services, it grapples with the emerging challenge demanding that consumers possess technological literacy.

The book offers a distinct new perspective, going beyond the traditional understanding of financial inclusion, which typically only considers the possession of a bank account. Instead, it explores new dimensions, including the obstacles consumers face in obtaining credit, establishing a credit history, and coping with issues such as being blacklisted. The book explores diverse strategies for enhancing financial inclusion, such as leveraging data, and open banking. It also scrutinises the pursuit of credit fairness and examines methods to either mitigate or effectively address over-indebtedness, a persistent and formidable challenge for financial consumers.

The book will be of interest to researchers, practitioners, and governmental organisations in the field of finance law and the law of emerging technologies.

Duygu Damar-Blanken completed her LLB and LLM studies in Istanbul, Turkey. After the completion of her LLB study, she was a teaching and research assistant at Istanbul Bilgi University. She was awarded with a Dr. iur. title in 2011 after the completion of her PhD study at the University of Hamburg, Germany. From 2011 to 2018, she was senior research fellow at the Max Planck Institute for Comparative and International Private Law. She also held lectures at the University of Hamburg. Currently, she is working on her post-doc thesis on the "Prohibition of Discrimination in German and US-American Contract Law." Since 2020, she has worked as research associate at the Institute for Responsible Finance. Since October 2024, she has been a member of the Financial Services User Group at the European Commission. Her fields of expertise are private international law, comparative law, antidiscrimination law, contract law, commercial law, and law of financial services.

Michelle Kelly-Louw is a professor of banking law and head of the Department of Commercial Law at the University of Cape Town, South Africa. Her publications have been cited by various high courts, including the South African Supreme Court of Appeal, the Constitutional Court, and High Court of Namibia, Main Division, Windhoek. For her research, she has received five research awards. Throughout her career, she has been involved in various law reform initiatives and legislative drafting projects. She has held visiting fellowships at international universities. She is the immediate past president of the International Association of Consumer Law (IACL), a member of the International Academy of Commercial and Consumer Law (IACCL), a member of the Academy of Science of South Africa (ASSAf), and an ex-comember of the International Academy of Financial Consumers (IAFICO). She serves on the Specialist Law Committee of the South African National Rating System and was re-appointed to the adjudication panel of the South African Women-in-Science-Awards.

Routledge Research in Finance and Banking Law

Regulation and Governance of Mutual Funds
United Kingdom and United States of America Perspectives on Investor Protection
Mohammed Khair Alshaleel

Regulation of Debt Collection in Europe
Understanding Informal Debt Collection Practices
Cătălin-Gabriel Stănescu

The Regulation of Megabanks
Global Systemically Important Banks and their Legal Frameworks
Katarzyna M. Parchimowicz

Regulating Open Banking
Comparative Analysis of the EU, the UK and Taiwan
Chang-Hsien Tsai and Kuan-Jung Peng

The Law of ESG Derivatives
Risk, Uncertainty and Sustainable Finance
Ligia Catherine Arias-Barrera

Financial Technology Regulation in Africa
Iwa Salami

Foreign Direct Investment and International Law
Liberalization and Economic Sovereignty
Adaeze Agatha Aniodoh

Financial Inclusion Law and Over-Indebtedness
Edited by Duygu Damar-Blanken and Michelle Kelly-Louw

For more information about this series, please visit: www.routledge.com/Routledge-Research-in-Finance-and-Banking-Law/book-series/FINANCIALLAW

Financial Inclusion Law and Over-Indebtedness

Edited by Duygu Damar-Blanken and Michelle Kelly-Louw

Routledge
Taylor & Francis Group
LONDON AND NEW YORK

First published 2026
by Routledge
4 Park Square, Milton Park, Abingdon, Oxon OX14 4RN

and by Routledge
605 Third Avenue, New York, NY 10158

Routledge is an imprint of the Taylor & Francis Group, an informa business

British Library Cataloguing-in-Publication Data
A catalogue record for this book is available from the British Library

ISBN: 978-1-032-81297-7 (hbk)
ISBN: 978-1-032-83642-3 (pbk)
ISBN: 978-1-003-51040-6 (ebk)

DOI: 10.4324/9781003510406

Typeset in Times New Roman
by Apex CoVantage, LLC

Contents

Figures

Tables

Contributors

Izzah Khalif Raihan Abidin

Izzah Khalif Raihan Abidin holds a bachelor of laws (SH) degree from Faculty of Law, Universitas Airlangga, Surabaya, Indonesia, after graduating in 2021. She also obtained her master of laws (MH) degree from Faculty of Law, Universitas Airlangga, Surabaya, Indonesia in March 2024. She works at Universitas Airlangga Hospital as the legal staff, and she is active in conducting scientific research with her lecturer and team on health law and other legal topics. She also actively participates in one of student activities, namely Student Association of Postgraduate Law School Universitas Airlangga as media and information division staff.

Rizky Amalia

Rizky Amalia is a member of the Private Law Department, Faculty of Law, Universitas Airlangga, Indonesia. Amalia obtained her bachelor's and master's degree both from Faculty of Law Universitas Airlangga. She is currently serving as the secretary of Master Program of Faculty of Law Universitas Airlangga and also part of the Directorate of Career Development, Business Incubation, and Alumni (DPKKA) Universitas Airlangga. Apart from teaching, researching, and doing law-related projects, she is also member of Indonesian Private Law Lecturer Association (APHK).

Joana Farrajota

Joana Farrajota is a professor of private law at NOVA School of Law in Lisbon, Portugal, as well as vice-dean for research and quality and founder and director of the NOVA Centre on Financial Markets at NOVA Law School. She is the coordinator of the Master in Law and Financial Markets program, the result of a partnership between NOVA School of Law and NOVA Information Management School, the first edition of which opened in September 2015. As an academic, she has taught several subjects and published on various private law topics, with a particular focus on contract law. Her main areas of legal practice are civil and commercial law. She currently teaches Law of Obligations (undergraduate), Banking Law and Introduction to Mediation classes. She is of counsel at a law office in Lisbon, providing legal advice in the areas of arbitration and litigation, as well as banking and finance. Between 2011 and 2015, she worked as an advisor for the Minister of Agriculture and the Sea, as well as to the Secretary of State for Internal Affairs. She was admitted to the Portuguese Bar Association between 2002 and 2007.

Weronika Herbet-Homenda

Weronika Herbet-Homenda is a PhD candidate at the Department of Commercial Law, Faculty of Law and Administration of the University of Warsaw, Poland. She specialises in competition, consumer protection, and company law, focusing her research on issues located on the borderline of these areas. In 2020, she completed her masters studies at the University of Warsaw (summa cum laude) and undertook doctoral studies. Her project, concerning piercing the corporate veil and antitrust liability has received a grant of the Polish National Center of Science (2024–2025) and a scholarship of the Max Planck Institute for Comparative and International Private Law (2024). Besides her academic background, she has been affiliated with BWHS law firm since 2017, where she currently holds an associate position.

Anu Kaup

Anu Kaup completed her LLB and LLM studies in Tartu University. In addition to her master's degree in law, she has a master's degree in public administration. From 2008 to 2019, she worked in the Estonian Bar Association. Currently, she works as a quality and legal manager in the Estonian National Metrology Institute AS Metrosert.

Helena Kordasiewicz

Helena Kordasiewicz is a fifth year law student at the Faculty of Law and Administration and student at the Faculty of Physics at the University of Warsaw, Poland. She has participated in research projects on the digital exclusion of the elderly in the financial sector and sustainability within corporate law. Her research interests include contract law, competition law, and legal theory. She has gained professional experience in the digital banking sector and capital markets regulatory at an international law firm. Kordasiewicz has been a visiting researcher at the Max Planck Institute for Comparative and International Private Law in Hamburg, Germany, and at the Department of Innovation and Digitalisation in Law at the University of Vienna, Austria.

Ulrich Krüger

Ulrich Krüger is a professor of law at the Bremen University of Applied Sciences in Germany. He studied law at the Universities of Marburg and Munich, Germany, followed by the legal clerkship (partly at the Environmental Protection Agency in Chicago, USA). He did the second state exam in Hamburg. As a scholarship holder of the Deutsche Forschungsgemeinschaft (DFG), he did his PhD in law at the University of Bremen. He was legal counsel for the Institute for Responsible Finance in Hamburg (*iff*) and lawyer at the Oberlandesgericht

Hamburg. Since 2003, he has been a professor of business law at the Hochschule Bremen, director of the international double degree program "Business/International Management," guest lecturer in France, and research fellow at the Universidad Valencia/Spain and associate dean. Since 2021, he has been the co-editor of the consumer law journal *Verbraucher und Recht*. His fields of expertise are (international) business law, banking law, insolvency law, compliance, and business ethics.

Faizal Kurniawan

Faizal Kurniawan holds a bachelor of laws (SH) degree from the Faculty of Law, Universitas Airlangga, Surabaya, Indonesia (2005), majoring on business law. He earned his master of laws (MH) from the Universitas Airlangga (2007) and also an LLM degree from the Utrecht University in the Netherlands (2011). Currently, he is a lecturer and a researcher at the Faculty of Law, Universitas Airlangga, Indonesia. He obtained his doctoral degree at Faculty of Law, Universitas Airlangga in 2019. His dissertation is about unjust enrichment as legal basis for restitution. Kurniawan's area of expertise are contract law, public procurement law, law of obligation, government contract, public private partnership, and construction law. He also obtained a certified qualification as an arbitrator (ACIArb) awarded by The Chartered Institute of Arbitrators in 2021.

Marc Lacoursière

Marc Lacoursière has been a professor of business law at Université Laval's Faculty of Law since 2000 and a member of the Quebec Bar since 1993. He received his doctorate in banking law from Osgoode Hall Law School, York University, Toronto, Canada, in 2001, and his master's thesis from Université Laval, Quebec City, Canada, in 1996. In addition to his law degree, he holds a bachelor's degree in business administration (Université Laval). His projects focus on banking, consumer protection, and e-commerce. He is the author of *Droit de la consommation* (2024) and the co-author (with Professor Nicole L'Heureux) of *Droit bancaire* (2017). He has been a member of the consumer protection advisory committees of the Financial Consumer Agency of Canada since 2018 and of the Autorité des marchés financiers since 2023. Since 2021, he has been the co-chair of Université Laval's cross-faculty research ethics committee.

Maradona

Maradona earned his bachelor of law (LLB) from Airlangga University's Faculty of Law, Indonesia, in 2005. He pursued a master of law (LLM) specialising in criminal law and criminology at Groningen University, the Netherlands, in 2010, and completed his doctor of law (SH) degree at Erasmus School of Law, Erasmus University, Rotterdam, in 2018. Currently serving as Vice Dean III for Research, Publication, Community Development, and Cooperation at Airlangga University's Faculty of Law, he has been a lecturer there since 2006. Maradona specialises in criminal law, economic criminal law, anti-corruption law, corporate criminal law, victimology, and criminology. He is an active member of the

Indonesian Criminal Law and Criminology Society since 2007 and conducts research at the Center for Anti-Corruption and Criminal Policy and the Center for Health Law at Airlangga University's Faculty of Law.

Claudia Lima Marques

Claudia Lima Marques is the dean of and full professor at the Law School of the Federal University of Rio Grande do Sul, Porto Alegre, Brazil, current president of the International Association of Consumer Law (IACL) since 2023, chair of the ILA Committee on international protection of consumers, and director of the CDEA-Center for European and German Studies (supported by the DAAD) at UFRGS-PUCRS. She was the general rapporteur of the Federal Senate to update the Brazilian Consumer Protection Code (Act 14.181/2021) and is a member of the Senate Committee of Jurists responsible for reviewing and updating the Brazilian Civil Code and the Artificial Intelligence Framework Law. She holds a doctor *honoris causa* from Giessen, Germany, and Savoie Mont-Blanc, France. She holds a PhD from Heidelberg University, a LLM from Tübingen University and a Diploma in European Integration from the Saarland University, all in Germany.

Jagna Mucha

Jagna Mucha is an assistant professor at the Department of Transnational Law at Faculty of Law and Administration of the University of Warsaw, Poland. After completion of her doctoral studies there, in 2017, Mucha was awarded a PhD in law *summa cum laude* based on the PhD thesis on *Alternative dispute resolution for consumer disputes in the EU*. Her academic interests revolve around EU and transnational law, different methods of consumer law enforcement, and the problem of access to justice. She conducted several studies in this field, among others at the Harvard Law School, University of Oxford, and Ludwig-Maximilians University in Munich. She is also a grantholder of the Foundation for Polish Science (FNP), DAAD, and Kościuszko Foundation. Currently, Mucha is a principal investigator in the project "Public enforcement of consumer collective interests in Poland in the context of the EU law" – funded by the Polish National Science Centre (decision no. 2020/39/D/HS5/01115).

Dinda Ajeng Puspanita

Dinda Ajeng Puspanita earned her bachelor of laws (LLB) equivalent degree from the International Undergraduate Programme (IUP), Faculty of Law, Universitas Airlangga, Indonesia in 2022. She pursued her master of laws (MH) at the same university, graduating in 2024 with a focus on international business law, driven by her strong passion for business law and human rights. Currently, Puspanita is a secretary officer and assistant lecturer at the Faculty of Law, Universitas Airlangga. She actively participates in international legal forums and earned the Best Paper award in privacy and cyber law at Universiti Kebangsaan, Malaysia, in October 2023. She also serves as an assistant editor for *YURIDIKA*, the Faculty of Law's journal.

Hilda Yunita Sabrie

Hilda Yunita Sabrie is a member of the Private Law Department, Faculty of Law, Universitas Airlangga, Indonesia. Sabrie obtained her bachelor's and master's degree both from Faculty of Law Universitas Airlangga. She is currently serving as the secretary of the Centre for Development of Research, Community Service and International Publication (UP4I) Faculty of Law Universitas Airlangga and also part of the Center of Communication and Public Information (PKIP) Universitas Airlangga. Apart from teaching, researching, and doing law-related projects, she is also member of Indonesian Private Law Lecturer Association (APHK).

Karin Sein

Karin Sein is a professor of civil law in the Faculty of Law of the University of Tartu, Estonia. She completed her LLM degree in 1999 at the University of Freiburg, Germany, and her Dr. iuris degree in 2007 at the University of Tartu. She has published extensively in the areas of domestic and European contract law, consumer law, data protection, and digital law, her latest book being *Data Protection, Privacy and New Technologies* (Routledge 2024). During 2018–2021, she led a scientific project funded by the Estonian Research Council concentrating on consumer contract law in the Digital Single Market and is currently involved in a research project at Oslo University on consumer eID. In addition to the academic publications, she has provided expertise for the Estonian Supreme Court and advised the Estonian Ministry of Justice on implementing European consumer protection directives into Estonian law. During the Estonian EU presidency in 2017, she chaired the Council's working group on contract law.

Harven Filippo Taufik

Harven Fillipo Taufik holds a bachelor's degree in law from the Faculty of Law, Universitas Airlangga, Indonesia. His area of expertise lies in business law, with a particular focus on contract law, corporate law, and commercial dispute resolution. He also excels in legal debating and academic writing, has emerged as the champion in several law debate competitions, and has written numerous legal articles that have been published in national and international journals. Furthermore, he has gained valuable experience as the judge and reviewer for Universitas Airlangga's delegation in various law debate competition.

Noah Vardi

Noah Vardi is a professor of comparative law at the Roma Tre University Law School, Italy. She graduated *summa cum laude* in law at the Roma Tre University and obtained her PhD in European private law at the University of Verona, Italy. She was Fulbright Visiting Scholar at the Yale Law School, USA, and Visiting Scholar at the Max Planck Institute for Comparative and International Private Law in Hamburg, Germany. She is currently Deputy Member of the

Italian Banking and Financial Ombudsman (Rome Panel) and Member of the Expert Group of the Roma Tre Law Department, winner of the European Parliament Tender for the provision of external expertise on technical, regulatory and policy issues in the field of Bank Resolution. Vardi's research topics and publications focus mainly on European private law, financial markets, banking and payment systems, and the law of money.

Anne-Marie Weber

Anne-Marie Weber is an assistant professor at the Department of Commercial Law, Faculty of Law and Administration of the University of Warsaw, Poland. She holds two master's degrees in the field of law (University of Warsaw and Berkeley Law School, USA) and defended her PhD thesis *summa cum laude* at the University of Warsaw. She specialises in company law and financial market regulation. She is an associated researcher of the European Banking Institute, a fellow of the European Law Institute as well as an academic member of the European Corporate Governance Institute. Weber is a recipient of scholarships and research grants funded, amongst others, by the Max Planck Institute for Comparative and International Private Law in Hamburg, the Polish-German Science Foundation, the Polish Agency of Academic Exchange, and the French Government. Her projects "Combatting financial exclusion of the elderly in the digital era – a regulatory roadmap" and "The role of sustainable corporate governance for EU climate policy" have received grants from the Polish National Center of Science.

Preface

The International Association of Consumer Law (IACL) was created in Brazil in the early 1990s by a group of idealistic law scholars, all then very influential scholars in their respective countries, ranging from Argentina, Belgium, Brazil, Canada, England, Finland, France, Germany, Malaysia, Portugal and the United States of America, amongst others. The IACL developed out of a series of different conferences held in Brazil, (1990, 1991, and 1992) Argentina (1993), and Toronto (1995) and became a formal association after the Malaysian conference in Kuala Lumpur in 1997 and was registered in accordance with Belgian law in 1997.

The main objective of the IACL is to develop education and research in all fields of consumer law and aims to distribute international high-level information concerning the rights and protection of consumers. It is a forum in which law scholars, public servants, policymakers, regulators, and practitioners in consumer law from around the world can come together to understand each other's jurisdiction, explain and reflect on their own jurisdiction, and engage in productive comparison for the development of consumer protection globally. The IACL also assists in developing consumer law and building a network of international consumer experts from all countries.

The IACL advances consumer law development, particularly for the financial consumer, while simultaneously assisting different countries to renew their own legal system to face new challenges, many of which are associated with new developments in the consumer-credit market. Despite the great differences between countries and systems, it is apparent that financial consumer law scholars, practitioners, and jurists throughout the world are grappling with many comparable problems and the same growing international need for more protection for the financial consumer.

In the last 30 years, the IACL has successfully been organising international conferences in different parts of the world, such as Brazil, Canada, Belgium, Finland, Greece, New Zealand, Malaysia, South Africa, India, England, Australia, the Netherlands, the United States of America, Germany, and, with the 2025 conference, Argentina. Since the IACL's inception, it has managed to find willing national hosts for its major international conferences, traditionally held every second year. The only period one conference had to be postponed with was during the COVID pandemic, when travel and other restrictions prevailed.

The most recent conference, the 18th Conference of the IACL, was hosted and sponsored by the German Institute for Responsible Finance and was held in Hamburg, Germany, from 19 to 21 July 2023. The main theme of the 2023 conference was "Challenges and Unanswered Questions of Consumer Law." Some of the papers presented at this conference dealing specifically with financial inclusion, credit fairness, and over-indebtedness form the foundation of some of the chapters in this book, while other chapters on related and similar topics are not based on papers presented but on novel ideas formed at the conference by the authors of the respective chapters.

The research in this book is justified as it fundamentally focuses on crucial and contemporary aspects of financial consumer protection as well as financial inclusion and addresses selected issues regarding vulnerable consumer groups, increased digitalisation of financial services, processing of personal financial data, and consumer over-indebtedness.

Challenges posed by financial services may have serious results for consumers since they relate to one of the most important resources, namely money. The book contains a distinctive take on the current and often similar challenges a financial consumer faces in the different jurisdictions including Germany, Finland, Estonia, Poland, Portugal, Indonesia, South Africa, Kenya, Canada, Brazil, and the United States of America. The book offers a unique perspective in that it not only looks at financial inclusion in the traditional sense of only considering the inclusion as meaning consumers to have a bank account. But it also looks at other aspects, such as consumers' challenge to obtain credit in the first place, to build a credit score, or to deal with being blacklisted. It looks at different ways of improving financial inclusion, such as, by way of using data, open banking and other artificial intelligence tools and instruments. In addition, the book addresses various issues of financial exclusion, pertaining either to certain consumer groups or due to the design of certain financial services, for example, credit databanks. It also assesses the risk and opportunities of new financial products for financial inclusion such as Central Bank Digital Currencies and open banking. With technologies advancing, it brings with it the new challenge that consumers, in addition to having to be financially literate, nowadays also need to be technologically and digitally literate. Understanding technology poses various challenges, especially for the elderly population and other vulnerable groups, the book deals with issues relating to achieving and aiming for credit fairness. Although an increase in financial inclusion and better access to credit do improve consumers' lives, they also carry the accompanying risk of causing consumers to become over-indebted. Over-indebtedness is a daunting and ever-remaining challenge the financial consumer faces. Therefore, the book in its last chapters addresses not only the practices which may lead to over-indebtedness but also mechanisms to either curb and/or deal with over-indebtedness.

All the chapters in this book constitute new research not published elsewhere. The chapters are written from the premise of different law jurisdictions. To assure quality and originality of the research in this book, all the chapters, except the introduction and conclusion, were subjected to rigorous, double-blind peer-review prior to publication, with the identities of the reviewers not revealed to the authors. The reviewers were completely independent of the publisher and/or authors in question, and the personal details of the authors were removed prior to the peer-review process. The reviewers commented positively on the scholarly merits of each chapter and recommended their publication. Where the reviewers recommended revision and/or improvements to a chapter, the author(s) responded satisfactorily to such recommendations. The bibliography for each chapter and extensive footnotes and other references bear testimony to the main methodological approach and demonstrate the high standard of research ethics that the authors of each chapter observed. The book makes many new contributions to the legal knowledge from high-level intellectual work relating to specialised niches in the relevant field of financial consumer law.

The target audience for this book is national and international lawyers, academics, law researchers, judges, magistrates, postgraduate students, and financial regulators, and it offers advanced/expert legal knowledge in the field of financial consumer law.

THE EDITORS
Duygu Damar-Blanken and Michelle Kelly-Louw

Introduction

Michelle Kelly-Louw and Duygu Damar-Blanken

1. Financial inclusion and access

Financial inclusion is an important instrument for worldwide socio-economic development as it lessens poverty and boosts economic growth. Financial inclusion levels for developed and high-earning countries have greatly increased, but in some African and other less developed countries, generally, they have remained very low despite various African and other governments having initiated many financial literacy programmes. There are various reasons for this, and some include fragmented financial literacy programmes and uncoordinated, duplicated, and unclear financial education policy. Literature acknowledges the undeniable benefits of financial inclusion towards socio-economic development. These include improved financial behaviour and financial attitude, which translate to improved access and usage of financial products and services as well as a stable financial system.

The main tasks of the financial system are facilitating financial transactions, offering means to build assets, and helping households to manage financial shocks and liquidity bottlenecks more effectively, thereby reducing the risk of over-indebtedness and poverty.[1] It is, therefore, of vital importance that all groups and especially all consumer groups are included in it. Consequently, financial inclusion requires that all groups, including low-income and/or vulnerable groups in a society have adequate access to affordable financial products.[2]

Two of the most well-known barriers to financial inclusion are access barriers and usage barriers. Usage barriers are those which can be classified to hinder utilisation of financial products and services. There are usage barriers to financial inclusion, which can be classified as the barriers that hinder the potential users of financial products and services from using services, namely trust. Formal financial institutions are generally regarded with suspicion by the public, especially regarding banking and insurance though they are trusted to keep money safe. Vulnerable and low-income (often those marginalised) consumers feel that they are not the target market for formal financial institutions like banks, insurance companies, and asset managers, therefore perceiving these institutions to serve mainly the affluent or those with formal jobs. Many of these consumers may feel overwhelmed and find it difficult to understand complex financial products and services, particularly where there is a lack of usage of plain language in the relevant documents.

DOI: 10.4324/9781003510406-1

Access barriers, in contrast, are those which can be identified to prevent access to the utilisation of financial products and services. Apart from that, there are access barriers to financial inclusion as a result of pitfalls and shortcomings stemming from the financial system that cause lower income households and vulnerable consumers to not be able to access financial products and services for various reasons. For instance, high transaction charges associated with those products such as minimum balance in transactional accounts, initiation fees in asset management, and administration fees in loan applications are often cited by potential users as a barrier for savings, payments, and transaction products. Another stumbling block for these consumers, particularly marginalised groups, to access financial services is that formal financial institutions often require confirmation of employment, proof of residential address, or a title deed, which are not always readily available for the adult population in some underdeveloped countries (for example, African countries where homelessness and unemployment are rife) as well where micro- and small-sized enterprises are not formally registered. For instance, when opening an account at a bank or asset management company, the institution always requires formal proof of income, which is something that is not readily documented for the informally employed or self-employed consumers, for example, in many African countries, thus resulting in an access barrier to financial services products.

The first entry point to achieve financial inclusion is access. Therefore, the body of law that we call financial inclusion law addresses, first and foremost, barriers in adequate access to affordable financial products. Therefore, the first part of the book is dedicated to access issues in financial services.

Access barriers for the purposes of financial inclusion law go beyond mere physical accessibility issues.[3] As mentioned, costs of financial products such as high payment account fees, hidden costs in standard terms, and high interest rates not only may cause economic barriers but may also result in distrust in financial service providers and financial systems as well as in over-indebtedness. In respect thereof, the first contribution by Jagna Mucha examines unfair terms in foreign currency loans that caused a considerable body of case law at the Court of Justice of the European Union (CJEU). Especially after the COVID-19 pandemic, many consumers had difficulties in fulfilling their repayment duties. This was especially true in Poland where the duty to repay the mortgage loan is occasionally indexed to a foreign currency, which even caused some consumers to lose their houses. The author analyses the case law of the CJEU as to under which circumstances contractual agreements pertaining to price or remuneration might be deemed invalid under the Unfair Contract Terms Directive[4] and reflects, based on the Polish example, on the results of the invalidity of a mortgage contract resulting from the invalidity of a standard term regarding the subject matter of the mortgage credit.

Access barriers may also be caused by factual circumstances. This is especially the case with regard to access to digital financial services. The underlying causes for it can vary from lacking infrastructure, such as the lack of speedy Internet infrastructure in rural areas or the more developed models of smartphones; the lack of trust in digital systems, such as the growing distrust in digital payment systems caused by the increasing number of online banking fraud cases; or the digital affinity – or in other words digital-financial literacy – of certain consumer groups, such as the elderly. Although digital financial services have the great potential of increasing financial inclusion, they also require digital affinity, which is not present in every consumer group. The elderly are, for instance, among the most negatively affected consumer groups in the access to digital financial services. In order to prevent the financial exclusion of the elderly and increase their digital-financial literacy, among others, suitable regulatory measures are necessary. In their contribution, Anne-Marie Weber, Weronika Herbet-Homenda, and Helena Kordasiewicz examine the existing body of legal and empirical research within the European Union (EU) and determine the gaps within, as well as the shortcomings of, the existing research that should lay the basis for regulatory intervention.

Various literature suggests there are numerous drivers of financial inclusion such as: banking services, information and communication technologies, connectivity (Internet) and mobile phones, regulatory framework, political will, and physical infrastructure, but literature also clearly stresses the critical importance of financial education. Financial education may be loosely defined as the way in which a person acquires an understanding of financial products and concepts and through information, instruction, and advice develop skills and confidence to become more aware of financial risks and opportunities to make informed decisions to improve financial security.

However, it is essential for all regulatory authorities in the world not only to educate consumers about financial matters but also to truly promote informed participation of financial consumers. Financial literacy is basically the ability to understand how money works and how one can earn money or make more money.[5] It specifically refers to the set of skills and knowledge that allows a person to make informed and effective decisions with all of their financial resources.[6] Financial literacy is one among a number of strategies directed towards nudging changes in consumer behaviour. It sits between the old regulatory model, which relies on disclosure of information for effective and rational decision-making, and a newer regulatory model, which takes into account individual's perceptions and behavioural biases and may seek to accommodate for these by imposing obligations on financial services providers beyond mere disclosure of information.[7]

The role of disclosure (for example, receiving information beforehand and documents in plain language) is important for financial and credit legislation. The role and value of disclosure is core, but such disclosure to individuals will be ineffective if there are low levels of financial literacy. The focus and reliance of financial and credit legislation generally on disclosure as a tool to protect and educate consumers rather than them also focusing and relying on promoting financial literacy amongst consumers is of concern.[8]

Doubtlessly, financial literacy thus plays a vital role in financial inclusion and in access to financial services. Academic research and efforts in increasing financial literacy, almost without exception (and rightfully so), focus on the financial literacy of consumers. Nevertheless, an additional measure was adopted by the EU legislator in the Mortgage Credit Directive[9] to protect financially illiterate consumers. Article 9 of the Directive requires that staff working in banks and granting mortgage credit to have and to keep up to date an adequate level of knowledge and competence in relation to the manufacturing, offering, or granting of credit agreements. In her contribution, Joana Farrajota questions the effectiveness and adequacy of this requirement from the perspective of consumer protection by reflecting on the Portuguese implementation.

Being a financially included consumer also means to be able to have access to credit. Very few consumers have the means to purchase expensive items like homes and motor vehicles using cash. It is thus natural that most consumers at some point in their life require credit to purchase goods and/or services. A consumer not only needs to be able to afford the credit being granted (affordability test – a simple calculation test) but also needs to be creditworthy. In short, creditworthiness refers to how likely the consumer is to repay the credit by looking at the specific consumer's repayment history of credit. Creditworthiness is more difficult to determine than affordability, and a credit provider traditionally considers a consumer's debt repayment history to determine the consumer's creditworthiness. For the creditworthiness test, the credit reports and scores/rating from credit bureaux, credit registries, and credit-scoring companies are normally used.[10] Credit reports not only show the debt repayment history but also use algorithms to predict the consumer's likely behaviour in repaying the debt. The reality, however, is that many low-income, vulnerable, or unbanked consumers either have no credit score/rating or if they do have one, the credit score is often either lacking, poor, or shows the consumer being blacklisted for non-payment. The accuracy of information and the period of the credit information (particularly negative information) kept by credit bureaux, credit registries, and credit-scoring companies are vital as they may mean the difference between a consumer being financially included (that is, obtaining credit) or excluded.

Anu Kaup and Karin Sein in their contribution consider how credit registries and credit-scoring companies deal with the practices and rules regarding the disclosure of information on payment defaults in credit information registers, even for old and prescribed debts, and their impact on the privacy of consumers. They stress that while information on a consumer's previous payment defaults often provides valuable information about a consumer's payment habits and credibility, blacklisting a consumer in the credit information registers, the information being kept may also cause a consumer's financial exclusion. They examine this issue within the context of the EU and the domestic law of Estonia and Finland (two countries near each other), drawing lessons from these jurisdictions. They point out differences in the approaches taken by different EU Member States as to how they keep and disclose old, prescribed – or also already paid – debts when doing creditworthiness assessments or when made public in the credit registries. Some Member States claim that the publication of defaults for old, prescribed, and already paid debts is fully justified, while others do not and are more consumer-friendly. Kaup and Sein also consider why the disclosure of payment default information of consumers on credit registers is a privacy issue. They conduct a comparative analysis of the rules and practices of Estonia and Finland to determine if Estonia needs to modify their rules and practices to safeguard the privacy of consumers. They also give attention to the application of the EU's General Data Protection Regulation (GPDR)[11] regarding the length of time of storage of payment default when analysing the Estonian rules and practices providing for these periods.

It is well-known that a person needs credit to get credit, but how does a consumer go about building a credit score when the consumer has no credit yet? A consumer without a credit report with a credit score/rating will struggle to meet the test for creditworthiness, even if the consumer is able to meet the affordability test. Building a credit score is often difficult for low-income, unbanked, informally employed consumers, and other vulnerable consumers due to a lack of appropriate information being available, particularly credit information. Ulrich Krüger focuses on the financial exclusion of consumers with no credit scores, the so-called credit invisibles, and those with poor credit scores. The contribution focuses on credit scores and financial exclusion, specifically in the United States of America (USA) and EU (specifically Germany). He correctly points out that credit scores are not only used for credit application but also for other transactions, such as approving a consumer to conclude a rental agreement. Therefore, "[i]f more and more consumers are excluded from financial services because their creditworthiness is poor or non-existent, it is no longer only a personal and social problem but also a problem for all creditors and the economy as a whole." Krüger unpacks how credit scores can lead to financial exclusion and that credit invisibles and consumers with poor credit scores end up paying more money not only for credit, financial services, and consumables but also for more with data. He also scrutinises various strategies in place in the USA and EU for credit building to determine if they truly assist consumers in building credit scores.

2. Increased digitalisation

The second part of the book deals with the increasing digitalisation, prevalent in financial services and the industry. The increase of digitalisation, on the one hand, poses challenges for certain vulnerable consumer groups, such as the elderly as addressed in this book. On the other hand, digitalisation offers new opportunities for alleviating financial exclusion.

Globally, there is vast interest in Central Bank Digital Currencies (CBDCs), particularly retail CBDCs (that is, a version available to ordinary consumers for low-value, high-volume transactions). A CBDC is basically virtual money backed, issued, and regulated by a central or reserve bank of a country. It is the digital form of a country's fiat currency that constitutes a claim on the central or reserve bank.[12] Very few countries have so far accepted CBDCs as legal tender. Generally, legal tender for most countries in the world refers to the coins and notes (cash) issued by the respective country's central or reserve bank. Traditionally only cash is legal tender that a creditor is obligated to accept unless the country has declared CBDCs to also constitute legal tender. Usually, a creditor is only obligated to accept legal tender as payment unless the creditor accepts other methods of payment. So, although money may constitute "legal tender," the concept of "money" may also be much broader and not necessarily also be legal tender. The concepts bear some similarities, but they are distinct from each other. The very short definition of money in the sense of currency is "that which passes freely from hand to hand throughout the community in final discharge of debts."[13] While the term "money" in the strict legal sense

> *refers to all chattels (tangible movable property) which are issued under the authority of the law of the State of issue and which, in terms of that law, are denominated with reference to a unit of account and serve as the universal means of exchange in that State.*[14]

Some countries that have fully embraced retail CBDCs as legal tender include Nigeria, Bahamas, and Jamaica.[15] In contrast, most other countries are more cautious and have opted to first pilot CBDCs, either retail, wholesale (a version to settle high-value, low-volume transactions between institutions), or both types. The objective of piloting them is to, *inter alia*, first determine if they want their respective central or reserve banks to issue them, declare them as legal tender, and have them constitute a payment instrument that will be the electronic equivalent to cash. This includes the EU exploring the possibility of a digital euro. One reason to first pilot CBDCs is that there are various challenges with CBDCs, for instance, consumers may draw too much money out of banks at once by purchasing CBDCs, causing a run on banks. They also carry high operational risks because they are vulnerable to cyber-attacks and thus need to be made resilient against them. To appropriately regulate CBDCs and the technology that underlies them requires a multifaceted and strict regulatory framework that not only focuses on and addresses issues of data privacy but also provides adequate consumer protection. Any legal framework would also have to meet appropriate and stringent anti-money laundering standards. How CBDCs would integrate into the national payment systems of respective countries and exist alongside traditional money such as cash would also need to be carefully assessed and planned. Therefore, there are various factors for a country to consider cautiously before adopting CBDCs and embracing its underpinning technology.

It is, thus, apt that Noah Vardi in her contribution considers CBDCs and explores their risks and opportunities for financial inclusion and access to credit, particularly for vulnerable consumers. She considers the vulnerability of different consumers from a financial inclusion perspective while also addressing the issue of whether the digital euro could provide greater access to credit. Vardi sensibly analyses the risks and opportunities of CBDCs and shows how some of these risks may be overcome. She correctly identifies key issues like data privacy and consumer protection that may be especially of concern for central bankers and other regulators in the EU, contemplating the use of CBDCs for both financial inclusion and expansion of access to credit.

Technological advancements have also meant that large databases with consumer's financial data are possible. Over the years, we have seen the rise of big financial technology companies (BigTechs), and we live in a world where consumer data has become an important commodity with substantial market value for financial institutions and other service providers. Consumer data also advances competition in the financial industry. However, the safekeeping and responsible usage of consumer data and privacy are pivotal. There are various regulations and legislation worldwide aimed at protecting consumers' data and privacy. Consumer data has been the catalyst leading to many new technological innovations emerging, for example, open banking. Open banking basically allows for more personalised banking products for consumers based on collected data about consumers. Banks have a duty to keep personal and financial data concerning their consumers (customers) private; however, where open banking is permitted, it, in essence, entails that banks may open up their consumer data to third-party providers via application programming interfaces (APIs), creating an open ecosystem that permit licensed third-party providers (for instance, financial technology companies (FinTechs)), and even other banks, to use customer financial data to create very customised products and services for consumers. Research on open banking, therefore, naturally centres around data protection and data privacy of consumers generally. Marc Lacoursière deals with the impact of open banking on consumer protection and the legal framework in Canada in his contribution. He scrutinises open banking, the emergence of FinTechs, and how this influences the regulatory model traditionally used for banking in Canada. He explains the transformation in the Canadian banking system and the possibility of regulating open banking and also traces recent development aimed at protecting Canadian consumers whose data is shared with FinTechs.

Digitalisation also facilitates faster transactions and financial investments. Algorithmic systems enable trading of financial instruments with limited or no human intervention. However, as every digital system, algorithmic trading systems are also prone to system errors. In such an event, consumers may be prevented from carrying out transactions, for a short or longer period of time and, thus, suffer damages. Legal conflicts arising from such losses could result in lengthy court processes delaying any remedy for consumers. The contribution of Faizal Kurniawan et al. focuses on online dispute resolution as a subtype of alternative dispute resolution for damages caused by algorithmic trading errors. They first establish the applicable provisions to the liability of financial service providers in Indonesian law and lay down the main substantial issues, including the burden of proof, in algorithmic trading errors. They then examine the pros and cons of online dispute resolution for the settlement of consumer claims in case of algorithmic trading errors. Based on this analysis, they determine the loopholes regarding effective consumer protection and offer solutions.

3. Over-indebtedness

The last part of the book is dedicated to over-indebtedness. Over-indebtedness occurs when a person or a household are not able to meet their due payments over a long period despite reducing their standard of living.[16] Temporary liquidity problems do not necessarily pose over-indebtedness as they can be overcome by borrowing money, also from banks. Credits taken by consumers, *inter alia*, in order to bypass temporary liquidity problems, can contribute to consumer over-indebtedness especially if they are granted on a higher than the average interest rate. According to the empirical research in Germany, for instance, obligations caused by consumer credits (excluding mortgage loans) were the most common type of obligation among over-indebted consumers in 2023 and have been since 2013.[17] In her contribution, Claudia Lima Marques provides an overview of the 2021 reform in the Brazilian Consumer Code, which introduces new mechanisms to protect consumers in credit contracts and to prevent over-indebtedness. The contribution, further, explains the new judicial and extrajudicial proceedings over-indebted consumers can initiate. She critically analyses whether the reform provides effective measures for responsible lending and preventing over-indebtedness, also on the basis of empirical data from the period before and after the reform.

When a consumer defaults on a credit agreement, the consumer may often find him- or herself stuck in the unfortunate position of being able to only pay off the interest and other costs of credit without ever reducing the principal amount borrowed, thus remaining in a debt trap forever. Credit providers often fail to take prompt legal action against consumers, simply leaving consumers to continue to service merely the interest for years without the consumers ever truly having the opportunity to pay off their debt. Some African countries try to counter this situation and attempt to provide consumers with an opportunity to catch up on their arrears and limit the amount owed. Michelle Kelly-Louw in her contribution turns to two African countries, namely South Africa and Kenya, that make use of a rare indirect debt-relief mechanism that regulates and caps the interest rate of defaulting consumers in certain instances.

Similar to other countries, South Africa also has both direct mechanisms, such as debt restructuring or formal bankruptcy procedures, and indirect mechanisms to deal with over-indebtedness. One such indirect debt relief mechanism is found in the South African National Credit Act 34 of 2005. It is a specific rule against the accrual of further unpaid interest and other costs of credit when they equal the outstanding principal debt in terms of a credit agreement. It comes into operation only when a consumer defaults and operates for as long as the consumer remains in default (refer to the *in duplum* rule). This statutory rule is founded on a similar rule that developed under Roman-Dutch law (common-law rule) in South Africa. The South African *in duplum* rule resulted in Kenya also adopting a similar statutory rule. Due to the Kenyan rule being founded on the South Africa rule, South African jurisprudence is often used to interpret the Kenyan rule. The rules in both countries operate as important tools to protect defaulting consumers of credit agreements from, among others, an ever-increasing accumulation of interest. The two rules are similar but also operate in a slightly different manner. Although the rule initially developed in ancient times, Kelly-Louw analyses the operation of the two different rules, albeit in their more "modern" statutory forms, and illustrates how the rules are still useful today and continue to play a vital role in protecting consumers against exploitation from their credit providers.

Finally, digitalisation shows its effect also in over-indebtedness of consumers. According to the debt advice centres in Germany, the number of especially young consumers is increasing who are affected by the debt spirals caused by the so-called

"Buy Now, Pay Later" (BNPL) credits. In her contribution, Duygu Damar-Blanken illustrates the problems caused by the late payment of BNPL credits and how this could affect the lives of young consumers who, based on empirical data, do not perceive the BNPL credits as "credits." Subsequently, she analyses the current lack of any legal safeguards in the EU and questions whether the mechanism of pre-contractual and contractual information duties as well as the duty of the lender to perform a creditworthiness assessment would provide effective safeguards to prevent over-indebtedness caused by BNPL credits.

Notes

1 European Investment Fund, "Financial and Social Inclusion in Europe," 1.
2 Gortsos, "Financial Inclusion," 10.
3 Physical accessibility issues are addressed in several regulations and legislation across the globe, such as the European Accessibility Act (EAA) in the European Union (EU), in the Equality Act of 2010 in the United Kingdom (UK), the Americans with Disabilities Act (ADA) in the United States of America (USA), Disability Discrimination Act of 1992 in Australia, and in the South African National Credit Act 34 of 2005.
4 Council Directive 93/13/EEC of April 5, 1993, on unfair terms in consumer contracts, OJ 1993 L 95/29.
5 Pearson, Stoop, and Kelly-Louw, "Balancing Responsibilities," 2.
6 Pearson, Stoop, and Kelly-Louw, "Balancing Responsibilities," 2–4.
7 Pearson, Stoop, and Kelly-Louw, "Balancing Responsibilities," 4.
8 See, in general, Pearson, Stoop, and Kelly-Louw, "Balancing Responsibilities".
9 Directive 2014/17/EU of February 4, 2014, on credit agreements for consumers relating to residential immovable property, OJ 2014 L 60/34.
10 Kelly-Louw and Stoop, "Alternative," 51–53.
11 Regulation (EU) 2016/679 of the European Parliament and of the Council of April 27, 2016, on thc protection of natural persons with regard to the processing of personal data and on the free movement of such data, and repealing Directive 95/46/EC (General Data Protection Regulation), OJ 2016 L 119/1.
12 See https://www.atlanticcouncil.org/cbdctracker/ and Koonprasert et al., *Central Bank,* 1.
13 Sharrock, *Banking and Payment*, 197 and the authorities relied upon.
14 Sharrock, *Banking and Payment*, 197 and the authorities relied upon.
15 See https://www.atlanticcouncil.org/cbdctracker/.
16 Peters et al., *iff-Überschuldungsreport 2024*, 6.
17 Peters et al., *iff-Überschuldungsreport 2024*, 58.

References

European Investment Fund. "Financial and Social Inclusion in Europe." Working Paper 2021/72. Accessed December 5, 2024. https://www.eif.org/news_centre/publications/eif_working_paper_2021_72.pdf.

Gortsos, Christos. "Financial Inclusion: An Overview of Its Various Dimensions and the Initiatives to Enhance Its Current Level." Working Papers ECEFIL (15). Accessed December 5, 2024. https://papers.ssrn.com/sol3/papers.cfm?abstract_id=2715625.

Kelly-Louw, M., and P.N. Stoop. "Alternative Methods of Validating Unbanked Consumers' Income and Assessing Their 'Creditworthiness' and 'Affordability' of Repayments." In *Magister: Essays vir/for Jannie Otto*, edited by D. Van der Merwe, 50–77. Durban: LexisNexis, 2020.

Koonprasert, Tayo Tunyathon, Shiho Kanada, Natsuki Tsuda, and Edona Reshidi. *Central Bank Digital Currency Adoption: Inclusive Strategies for Intermediaries and Users*. FinTech Notes, Vol. 2024, Issue 005. Washington, DC: International Monetary Fund, September 20, 2024.

Pearson, G., P.N. Stoop, and M. Kelly-Louw. "Balancing Responsibilities – Financial Literacy." *Potchefstroom Electronic Law Journal* 20 (2017): 1–55.

Peters, Sally, Hanne Roggemann, Duygu Damar-Blanken, Ingrid Größl, and Henri Thomas. *iff-Überschuldungsreport 2024 – Überschuldung in Deutschland*. Hamburg, 2024. https://www.iff-hamburg.de/wp-content/uploads/2024/09/ueberschuldungsreport–2024.pdf.

Sharrock, Robert, ed. *The Law of Banking and Payment in South Africa*. Claremont: Juta and Company (Pty) Ltd, 2016.

Part I

Access

1 Protection of financial consumers in the EU against unfair contract terms in foreign currency loans*

Jagna Mucha

1. Introduction

Protection against unfair contract terms has constituted a core element of EU consumer law[1] for 30 years already. Drafting legislative framework in this area was as a huge challenge due to the very diverse approaches of the Member States towards the concept of unfairness.[2] As a matter of consensus reached at the EU level, the Unfair Contract Terms Directive[3] (UCTD) was adopted. Heated discussions and controversies related to the scope of this piece of legislation resulted in its narrow shape. Thus, UCTD is focused on consumer contracts based on standard forms only, and it does not cover individual terms which have been individually negotiated, however, with the reservation that these terms are expressed in a plain intelligible language.[4] The EU legal framework for consumer protection is based on the assumption that the consumer is the weaker party to the contract. At the same time, however, superior knowledge and experience of a specific consumer does not disqualify such person from being a 'consumer' for the purposes of the UCTD.[5] The Directive follows a minimum harmonization standard, which means that Member States may provide a higher standard of protection than the one regulated at the EU level.[6] Thirty years after its introduction, the UCTD is still considered as one of the most effective tools of the EU law.[7] Due to its significant practical value, the UCTD was widely applied by national courts referring many preliminary questions to the Court of Justice of the European Union (CJEU), which, in turn, gave a rise to the complex case law in this respect.

The consumer-friendly approach of the CJEU allowed it to find solutions for many problems faced by consumers over the years, with the prominent example of its case law which addressed the foreign currency loan crisis in Europe. The crisis started in the early 2000s when banks encouraged people to take loans in foreign currency, mostly denominated or indexed in Swiss francs in order to benefit from lower interest rates in Switzerland, which, in a short term, was beneficial. Due to the fact that the source of their income was mostly in the domestic currency, consumers were exposed to the risk connected to an unfavourable change in interest rate. As a result of the financial crisis in 2008 and after the Swiss franc was unpegged from the euro in 2015, the instalments increased dramatically. The situation of borrowers was only worsened by the COVID-19 pandemic when many

DOI: 10.4324/9781003510406-3

consumers affected by the crisis suffered financial difficulties, including those with the timely payment of their commitments. Since the majority of loans was secured by mortgages, consumers started to lose their homes, which heated the debate on how the law can contribute to the protection of the right to housing.[8]

The aforementioned problem was addressed differently in particular Member States.[9] Some of them implemented a broad range of support measures with the aim of easing the challenges faced by borrowers.[10] These measures included, among others, so-called payment holidays providing for a payment relief for obligors affected by the COVID-19 pandemic by allowing suspension or postponement of payments within the specific period of time. At the EU level, the European Banking Authority (EBA) published guidelines on legislative and non-legislative moratoria on loan repayments applied in the light of the COVID-19 crisis.[11]

Unfortunately, unlike most EU Member States, in Poland no legislative measures have been taken in order to sufficiently assist consumers affected by the foreign currency loan crisis.[12] At the same time, the scale of the problem was massive – it was estimated that approx. 550.000 borrowers in Poland were affected.[13] As a result, consumers started court actions against the banks. According to data presented by the financial ombudsman, in 2021, there were approximately 70.000 lawsuits in Swiss franc cases pending before the court of first instance and about 4.000 cases on appeal.[14] The debate on the borrowers' rights was particularly heated due to a very strong banking lobby, supported by the Polish Financial Supervision Authority. The main argument voiced in the public discussion was that foreign currency loans were not, as such, forbidden in consumer contracts in Poland and that the borrowers must have been aware of the risk associated with the change of the foreign currency and variable interest rate. On the other hand, consumers invoked that the loan contract terms are unfair due to the fact that the indexing mechanism allowed the bank to arrange the exchange rate at its discretion. The national courts were supposed to evaluate whether the terms included in consumer loans shall be assessed in line with requirements specified in the UCTD and, consequently, in case of the breach of the fairness requirement, to adjudicate on relevant remedies.

2. The EU concept of unfairness

The concept of unfairness provided in Article 3(1) of UCTD relates to the contractual term that has not been individually negotiated with consumers.[15] Such a term is unfair if, contrary to the requirement of good faith, it causes a significant imbalance in the parties' contractual rights and obligations, to the detriment of the consumer. Assessment of fairness does not apply to the terms relating to the definition of the main subject matter of the contract and to the adequacy of the price and remuneration. At the same time, however, these terms must comply with the principle of transparency, namely be drafted in plain, intelligible language. In case of doubt about the meaning of a term, the interpretation most favourable to the consumer should prevail. As a consequence of the breach of the fairness requirement, the unfair terms are not binding for the consumer. Since the provisions of the UCTD are general and rather imprecise, national courts were struggling in the process of interpretation of the national law consistently with EU law.[16] It was, therefore, the significant role of the CJEU to specify the rules on application of this UCTD in practice.[17] In relation to the foreign currency loan contracts, the key questions referred by the national courts related to the issues whether the indexing mechanism constitutes the essence of the contract, what the consequences of unfairness are, and how to understand the principle of transparency.

The first vital issue to be addressed is whether the indexing mechanism used for the purpose of loan repayment should be considered as the essence of the contractual relationship. Such qualification is important in view of the possibility of continuing the contract after finding the term unfair. The CJEU did not provide a clear answer to the question at first but gave some guidelines to the national courts who should examine this issue in relation to the specific case. In *Kásler*, the CJUE stated that it is the role of the national court to

> *determine, having regard to the nature, general scheme and the stipulations of the loan agreement and its legal and factual context, whether the term setting the exchange rate for the monthly repayment instalments constitutes an essential element of the debtor's obligations, consisting in the repayment of the amount made available by the lender.*[18]

The position of the CJEU evolved over the years. In its recent judgment in the case of *Dziubak*,[19] the Court held expressly that terms relating to the exchange risk define the subject matter of a loan contract. This obviously weakened the level of consumer protection since it implied that in principle, the indexation clause is excluded from assessment of fairness provided in the UCTD. Nevertheless, the requirement of transparency still applies. It follows from Article 4(2) of the UCTD that all terms of consumer contract must comply with the principle of transparency. If the term is not plain and intelligible, the court may review the unfairness even if the term refers to the main subject matter of the contract.

Secondly, if the national court recognizes that the contract term is unfair, such term is not binding for the consumer, whereby the contract should continue to be binding for the parties only if it is capable of continuing in existence without the unfair term. In view of this, it is of utmost importance for the national court to decide on the consequences of unfairness. If the court decides that the contract should be annulled, the parties are obliged to reimburse the payments and therefore the consumer may be exposed to particularly unfavourable consequences.[20] In *Dziubak*, the Polish court was wondering how to uphold the contract. It was not sure whether it was possible to replace provisions considered unfair solely on the basis of the national provisions of general nature. The CJUE answered this question negatively.[21] The justification given was based on the assumption that the possibility of substitution derogates from the general rule that the contract at issue can remain binding on the parties only if it can continue in existence without the unfair terms it contains. By way of exception, the gap could be filled only by the supplementary provisions of the national law or those which are applicable where parties so agree.[22] However, the national courts are not entitled to fill the gap of the contract solely on the national provisions of general nature.[23] It must be noted at this point that the wish of the consumer is decisive when it comes to the annulment of the contract due to the unfair term. If, as a consequence of the removal of the unfair term, the contract would not continue to exist, the consumer may decide that the unfair contract term remains binding.[24] This is justified in view of the fact that in case of the annulment of the contract, the consumer would be obliged for immediate repayment of the loan (minus installments), which can be particularly unfavourable.

Thirdly, the EU concept of fairness implies that all contractual terms included in consumer contracts must be written in plain, intelligible language. The UCTD provides that in case of doubts, the interpretation most favourable to consumers should prevail. If the unfair term is not plain and intelligible, the court may review the unfairness even if the term refers to the main subject matter of the contract. The CJEU referred to the principle of transparency many times in its case law[25] underlying its importance in view of the weaker position of the consumer vis-à-vis seller or supplier as regards both bargaining power and level of knowledge. As a starting point, the requirement of transparency should be understood as requiring that the contractual term must be formally and grammatically intelligible to the consumer. Further, it means that an average consumer, who is reasonably well informed and reasonably observant and circumspect, must be in a position to understand the specific functioning of the term and thus evaluate, on the basis of clear intelligible criteria, the potentially significant economic consequences of such term for his or her financial obligations.[26] In the context of foreign currency loan agreements, the principle of transparency plays a vital role. It requires the bank to draft a contract in a way which enables an average consumer to estimate, in particular, the total cost of the loan,[27] which as will be demonstrated in what follows, has significant consequences in practice.

3. Application of the principle of transparency in practice

The EU concept of unfairness is being tested in judicial practice very frequently. One of the recent judgments which comprehensively addresses all of the key problems discussed before is the Polish case of *M.P. i B.P* against *Bank 'A'*.[28] This decision provides some important guidelines for the national courts adjudicating the claims related to foreign currency loan contracts. The CJEU explains steps which national courts should take while applying national law in line with the UCTD. The decision also shows the reluctant attitude of some national courts, including the Polish Supreme Court, towards the Swiss loan crisis in Poland.[29] In spite of the fact that the CJUE clearly stated that an unfair clause of the contract cannot be replaced by the provision of the general nature,[30] in the case at hand the Polish referring court was still searching for national provisions that could substitute the unfair term.[31]

The case concerned consumers who concluded in 2008 with a Polish bank 'A' a mortgage loan agreement indexed to Swiss franc in an amount of approximately 100.000 euros. The consumers signed a statement to the effect that they were aware of the exchange rate risk and that they were informed about loan instalments being expressed in foreign currency, however, the repayment being required in Polish zloty. According to the general conditions, the funds were to be released in Polish zloty at a rate not lower than the buying rate, under the table in force at the time of their release. In 2013, the consumers signed a rider saying that they will repay the loan in Swiss francs without having recourse to exchange transactions carried by the bank. The effect of fluctuations in the exchange rate between Polish zloty and the Swiss franc between 2008–2014 resulted in that consumers were obliged to repay approximately 6.700 euros more than the sum that they would have repaid if the loan had been denominated in Polish zloty. The consumers took the view that the clause indexing the loan was unfair on the ground that it did not specify the method implied by the bank when determining the exchange rate. They brought an action against the bank claiming approximately 11.000 euros.

The key problem here was that the parties to the contract understood the indexation clause differently. For the bank, that clause provided that the exchange rate for the currency of the loan was to be determined in relation to the market rate, as set out daily in the bank exchange rate table. On the other hand, the borrowers interpreted the clause as providing that the currency's exchange rate is to be set on the basis of an objective rate, such as that set by the National Bank of Poland. The referring court found it questionable whether the bank fulfilled its transparency obligations specified in the UCTD due to the fact that the indexation was included in general terms. It was also particularly doubtful in view of the fact that neither the indexation clause nor the general condition of the contract specified all the factors taken into account by the bank when setting the exchange rate. Therefore, the referring court characterized the indexation clause less by ambiguous wording than by a failure to indicate the method for determining the exchange rate that was applied by the bank to calculate the repayment instalments.[32] On the other hand, it was uncertain whether the UCTD required the bank to draft the indexation clause in such way as to enable consumers to determine the rate independently at a given time due to the fact that the loan was concluded for 40 years and the exchange rate changes constantly over time. Having this in mind, the referring court asked whether, in such circumstances, it is possible to formulate a more general wording of the contact term that refers to the market value of the foreign currency.

The first issue examined by the CJUE in the case of *M.P. i B.P* against *Bank 'A'* was the application of the principle of transparency. Following its *Dziubak* judgment, the Court stated that the indexation clause in question included in general terms does not constitute the main subject matter of the contract nor refers it to the adequacy of price and remuneration.[33] Having said so, the Court referred solely to the principle of transparency, which is applicable to the whole consumer contract. In the context of foreign currency consumer loans, it is of utmost importance to determine whether the contract sets out transparently the reason for and the specific features of the mechanism for converting the foreign currency. It is on the basis of that information that the consumer decides whether he or she wants to become contractually bound to the bank.

In order to fulfill the requirement of transparency, the contractual term should satisfy two conditions: linguistic and grammatical intelligibility and economic transparency.[34] It follows from the Court's case law that the consumer must be put in the position to understand, on the basis of clear, intelligible criteria, the economic consequences for him or her which derive from it.[35] The CJUE obliged the national court to verify in light of all the relevant facts whether

> *an average consumer, who is reasonably well informed and reasonably observant and circumspect, may not only be aware of the existence of the variations in exchange rates generally observed on the foreign exchange market, but also assess the potentially significant economic consequences for him or her resulting from the application of the selling rate of exchange for the calculation of the repayments for which he or she will ultimately be liable and, therefore, estimate the total cost of the loan.*[36]

Having this in mind, it became clear that in line with Article 5 of UCTD, an indexation clause must enable a consumer to understand, on the basis of clear and intelligible criteria, the way in which the rate used to calculate the amount of repayment instalments is set.[37] The failure to mention the relevant criteria set by the bank cannot be justified by the fact that foreign currency exchange rate changes in the long term. Unlike the referring court, the CJEU had no doubts that the consumer must be able to determine himself the exchange rate at any time.

4. Consequences of unfairness of the contract term

Consequences of the breach of transparency requirement in consumer contracts are tremendous. Lack of transparency must be taken into account by the national court in assessment of whether the term is unfair.[38] The unfair term is not binding for the consumer, whereby the contract should continue to be binding for the parties only if it is capable of continuing in existence without the unfair term. In view of this, another problem addressed by the national courts dealing with the foreign currency loan crisis related to the possibility of a supplement of the agreement in order to remedy the unfair contract clause. This issue was not new, and in view of the clear interpretation given by the CJEU in the *Dziubak* case,[39] it was quite surprising that the national court referred this question again to the CJEU. In the *Bank A* case, the referring court was looking for the possibility to substitute the unfair contract term. For this aim, the Polish court presented an idea to recourse to the general concept of the market value of the foreign currency and argued that such interpretation would correspond to the common intention of the parties to the agreement. According to Article 65 of the Polish Civil Code,[40] it would be possible to remedy the lack of transparency by giving the interpretation of the unfair term corresponding to the common intention of the parties.

In order to clarify the concerns of the Polish court, in the *Bank A* case, the CJEU comprehensively explained how the EU concept of unfairness provided in UCTD should be applied in practice.[41] These guidelines referred to (i) requirements for assessment whether the contractual term is unfair and (ii) consequences of assessment of unfairness: annulment of the contract being uncapable of continuing in existence without unfair terms (as a general rule) or upholding the contract under certain conditions only (as an exception).

Firstly, the national court should assess whether the contractual term is unfair. For this aim, it is necessary to determine whether the bank failed to observe the requirement of good faith and examine the possible existence of the significant imbalance to the detriment of consumer. In the case at hand, the referring court stated that the bank cannot be regarded as having acted in bad faith; therefore, this issue was not further explored by the Court. The focus was put on the examination of the second requirement, namely verification whether there is a significant imbalance in the parties' rights and obligations arising under the agreement, to the detriment of the consumer. The CJEU provided some guidance in this respect and specified that

> *such an examination cannot be limited to a quantitative economic evaluation based on a comparison between the total value of the transaction which is the subject of the contract, on the one hand, and the costs charged to the consumer under that clause, on the other. A significant imbalance may result from a sufficiently serious impairment of the legal situation in which the consumer, as a party to the contract in question, is placed under the relevant national provisions, whether this be in the form of a restriction of the rights which, in accordance with those provisions, he or she enjoys under the contract, or a constraint on the exercise of those rights, or the imposition on him or her of an additional obligation not envisaged by the national rules.*[42]

It is up to the national court to decide whether the legal situation of borrowers was impaired or their rights were restricted.

The second step to be taken by the national court is to adjudicate the legal consequences for the parties to the loan agreement in case the contract term is unfair. As a general rule, an unfair term should not be binding for consumers, and the contract should continue to bind the parties only if it is capable of continuing in existence without the unfair term. What are the options to remedy the problem of unfairness? The first solution would be recourse to the national legislation allowing to provide the contract term substituting the unfair clause. According to the CJEU, this legislation must respect the requirements specified in the UCTD,[43] which means that a new contract term cannot have the result of weakening the protection guaranteed to consumers. It was already mentioned that in Poland, however, no legislative measures were undertaken in order to solve the problem of Swiss francs crisis.[44] As a consequence, the national courts were forced to handle the problem without having an appropriate legal instrument in hand. Therefore, unsurprisingly, the courts were looking for solutions in existing law. In the *Bank A* case, in view of the lack of any supplementary provisions, the referring court was searching for the possibility to supplement the contract by the provisions of the general nature. At this point, the Court was very clear that this is not an option and that the national court cannot modify the contract by revising the content of that term. The possibility of such modification will make the sellers or suppliers tempted to use unfair contract terms in knowledge that, even if they were declared invalid, the contract could nevertheless be modified by the national court.[45]

Having said so, is it possible at all to supplement an agreement with unfair contract terms? The CJEU stated that only if the invalidity of the unfair contract term were to require the national court to declare the contract invalid in its entirety, thereby exposing consumers to particularly unfavourable consequences, then the national court might replace that term with the supplementary provision of the national law.[46] However, the Court reminded that the UCTD precludes the national court to fill the gap in the contract solely on the provisions of the general nature. In view of this, it became clear that the national court is precluded from interpretation of the unfair contract term even if that interpretation would correspond to the common intention of the parties.

5. Consequences of invalidity of the contract

The practice shows that consumers wish to exercise their rights for protection against unfair contract terms granted by the UCTD. As a result of the consumer-friendly interpretation of the CJEU case law, the national courts in the majority of individual cases tend to declare the loan contracts invalid on the ground of unfairness of the contract terms.[47] This tendency is very painful for the banking sector, suffering severe financial losses as a result. In order to recover from losses, the banks started claims against consumers on the ground of unjust enrichment and undue performance. National courts adjudicating these cases were confused – should consumers pay for the use of the capital to the banks if the latter violated consumer law by use of unfair contract terms? An argument presented in this discussion referred to the so-called 'free loans' problem. Once the court confirmed the invalidity of the loan contract, consumers used the borrowed capital free of charge often for more than several years. This was obviously not welcomed by the banks, surprisingly supported by the president of the Financial Supervision Authority in Poland saying that the stability of the financial markets will be threatened if the banks were not allowed to seek compensation from consumers. It also provoked heated discussion amongst other borrowers having loan contracts in national currency. In the public opinion in Poland, the ridiculous argument was voiced that consumers having their loans in Polish zloty are discriminated against by the ones having loans in foreign currency.

Does the EU law provide a solution for this problem? The UCTD does not govern the consequences of the invalidity of the contract after the excision of unfair contact terms; therefore, it is up to the Member States to determine such consequences. However, national rules in this respect must be compatible with EU law, including the UCTD which, amongst others, aims at deterrence. One of the most urgently awaited CJEU judgments clarifying this issue was rendered as a result of a claim brought against a bank by one of the Polish activists.[48] He had concluded a mortgage loan agreement in foreign currency including an unfair contact term which thus was deemed invalid. According to Polish law, in such a case, where the parties have performed certain services, they may claim reimbursement for undue performance. It was clear for the national court that in this situation, the borrower should repay the equivalent of the principal loan granted by the bank and that the bank should repay the equivalent of monthly instalments and expenses paid by the consumer. However, the national court was not sure whether in addition to those payments, parties may claim the payment of other amounts on account of the use of funds over a certain period without any legal basis. The national court was of the opinion that neither the bank nor the consumer should have any additional claims. On the one hand, the bank should not have any profits from the invalidity of the loan agreement since the invalidity results from the conduct of the bank which used the unfair contract term(s). On the other hand, however, allowing consumers to claim payment in respect of the use without a legal basis of the amount of the instalments would impose a disproportionate penalty to the bank.[49]

The CJEU took a different view. It stated that the possibility by the consumer to assert claims that go beyond the reimbursement of monthly instalments and paid expenses does not undermine the objectives of the UCTD, quite to the contrary, it supports its deterrent effect. As opposed to the assumptions of the national court, the Court stated that payment of such restitution is not contrary to the principle of legal certainty since it constitutes a practical implementation of the prohibition of unfair contract terms provided by UCTD.[50] Moreover, such payment would also be proportionate as long as it is necessary to restore the situation in which the consumer would have been if the contract had not existed.[51] On the other hand, the Court clearly confirmed that the bank cannot seek from consumer compensation going beyond the capital paid. For the Court, it was clear that the bank cannot derive economic advantages from its unlawful conduct or be compensated for the disadvantage caused by such conduct.[52] It was not persuaded by the argument relating to the stability of financial market since it is not relevant in the context of UCTD, which aims to protect consumers.[53] Indeed, the effectiveness of consumer protection would be undermined if consumers were exposed to the risk of paying compensation since it would be more advantageous for the consumers to continue to perform the contract with unfair contract term rather than to exercise the rights under the UCTD.[54]

The judgment in the *Bank A* case was widely discussed in Poland. The banking lobby was threatened that consumers will massively go to court and start proceedings against financial institutions. However, although in theory such a scenario is possible, it seems to be very unlikely in practice. The goal of the consumers is to confirm the invalidity of the loan agreements, to return the borrowed capital and simply to get out of any obligations towards banks. Apart from the group of activists, consumers in general are not very litigious and they are not willing to pursue their claims. The situation of credit Swiss loan contracts was exceptional because the value of the claim was significant. But, if the goal is achieved and the loan contract is invalid, there is a very little possibility that consumers will start other proceedings just to recover some minor compensation.

6. Conclusions

The interpretation of the UCTD by the CJEU is clearly consumer friendly. There is no doubt that principles relating to the mechanism of indexation of the loan to the foreign currency must be clear, transparent and understandable for the consumer, who, at any time, should be able by him- or herself to assess the costs of the loan. In order to satisfy the requirement of transparency, it is not enough to refer to the market value or to other general clauses. The CJEU upholds its position regarding the consequences of the unfair clauses and states that the main sanction for the banks which use the unfair clause is that such term is not binding for the consumer. It is possible to substitute the unfair clause only if: (i) due to the unfair clause, the contract cannot continue to bind the parties, (ii) invalidity of the contract exposes the consumer to particularly unfavourable consequences and (iii) there exist specific national supplementary provisions tailored to remedy the problem of unfairness which can be used in order to replace the unfair clause. These requirements must be satisfied jointly. If the national court could revise the content of the unfair term included in a contract, such power would contribute to the elimination of the dissuasive effect of the UCTD. Banks would still be tempted to use those unfair terms with the knowledge that even if the term will be declared invalid, the contract can nevertheless be modified by the court.

Further, the CJEU recognizes the significance of the wishes of the consumers. The national courts are not entitled to remove unfair contract terms, and such terms may be still applicable if the consumer, after having been informed by the courts, does not intend to assert its unfair or non-binding status. If, as a consequence of unfairness, the contract is to be declared invalid, the consumers would be obliged for immediate repayment of all the remaining amount of the loan, which can be particularly unfavourable. Therefore, after being advised, consumers should have the possibility to decide whether they want the contract to be invalid or not. Although it is nice to have such a choice, practice shows that consumers wish to exercise their right to be protected against unfair contract terms and claim that the loan contracts are invalid. In this sense, the UCTD is used as a tool to release consumers from the obligation towards banks to pay high interest rates.

Importantly, in cases where the loan contract is invalid since it cannot continue in existence after removal of the unfair contract terms, the financial institutions are entitled to claim the reimbursement of the capital and interests at the statutory rate from the date on which notice for payment is served. There is no doubt that banks are not entitled to claim any compensation beyond such reimbursement. This is a very important safeguard for consumers which should encourage them to pursue their claims and enforce their rights granted under the UCTD. As a consequence of the invalidity of the loan agreement, the situation should be restored in which the consumer would have been if the contract had not existed. For this aim, consumers may seek from the bank compensation beyond reimbursement of the monthly instalments and expenses paid in respect of the performance of that agreement. In such a case, it is up to the national court to decide whether such a claim is proportionate. However, it is unlikely that consumers will massively start such proceedings having in mind that they are reluctant towards litigation, courts are very cautious as regards payment of compensation and proceedings are very lengthy. The main goal of consumer claims is to be released from the obligations towards the bank regarding payment of high interests and simply to repay the capital borrowed.

Notes

* This chapter constitutes a part of the research: "Public enforcement of consumer collective interests in Poland in context of the EU law – the clash between 'the law in books' and 'the law in action', no. 2020/39/D/HS5/01115 funded by Polish National Science Center (*Narodowe Centrum Nauki*).
1 Dean, "Unfair Contract Terms," 581.
2 Howells, "Unfair Contract Terms," 133.
3 Council Directive 93/13/EEC of 5.04.1993 on unfair terms in consumer contracts, OJEC L 95, p. 29 ("UCTD").
4 Article 5 UCTD.
5 European Commission, Guidance on interpretation and application of Council Directive 93/13/EEC on unfair terms in consumer contracts, 2019/C 323/04, OJEU C 323, p. 10.
6 Klamert, "Harmonisation," 367.
7 At the same time however, it is argued that since UCTD was not modernised over the years, it does not meet challenges of the digital age, see Durovic and Poon, "Consumer Vulnerability," 420; Loos and Luzak, *Update the Unfair Contract Terms Directive.*
8 Domurath and Mak, "Private Law and Housing," 1189.
9 Regulatory responses to the challenges of loan contracts indexed to foreign currency in particular Member States are discussed in several contributions in Tereszkiewicz and Golecki, *Protecting Financial Consumers in Europe.*
10 Regulatory responses to the challenges of loan contracts indexed to foreign currency in particular Member States are discussed in several contributions in Tereszkiewicz and Golecki, *Protecting Financial Consumers in Europe.*
11 European Banking Authority, *Guidelines on Legislative and Non-Legislative Moratoria on Loan Repayments Applied in the Light of the COVID-19 Crisis*, consolidated version as of 2.12.2020. Accessed March 10, 2024. https://www.eba.europa.eu/guidelines-legislative-and-non-legislative-moratoria-loan-repayments-applied-light-covid-19-crisis.
12 In 2011 the so called "Anti-Spread Act" was adopted enabling consumers to pay installments in foreign currency (Act of 29 July 2011 amending the Act of 29 August 1997-Banking Act and other acts, Journal of Laws 2011, No. 165, item 984). However, this act did not address the problem of unfair terms included in loan contracts.
13 Golecki and Tereszkiewicz, "Complex Mortgage Loans," 19.
14 Rzecznik Finansowy, "Analiza aktualnych zagadnień dotyczących kredytów frankowych 2021."
15 Busch and Lehmann, *Unfair Terms in Banking and Financial Contracts*, 26.
16 Miščenić, Tereszkiewicz, and Infantino, "The Interplay Between the CJEU and National Courts," 353.
17 Tereszkiewicz, "Foreign Currency Loans," 248; Lapuente, "Control of Price Related Terms," 67.
18 Judgment of the CJEU of 30.04.2014, C-26/13 Kásler and Káslerne Rásbai, EU:C:2014:282, para 51; on the exclusion of so called core-terms from unfairness test see: Rott, "Unfair Contract Terms," 293; Fazekas, "The Consumer Credit Crisis," 104; Feher, "From Kásler to Dunai," 291.
19 Judgment of the CJEU of 3.10.2019, C-260/18, *Dziubak and others* against *Raiffeisen Bank International*, ECLI:EU:C:2019:819, para 44.
20 Judgment of the CJEU, C-26/13 Kásler, para 83.
21 Critical on the reasoning of the CJUE see Esposito, "Dziubak," 542.
22 Judgment of the CJEU, C-26/13 *Kásler*, para 81.
23 Judgment of the CJEU, C-260/18, *Dziubak*, para 62.
24 Judgment of the CJEU, C-260/18, *Dziubak*, para 56; see also Ziemblicki and Lewandowski, "Legal Consequences of Unfair Contract Terms," 360.

25 Judgment of the CJEU of 3.03.2020, C-125/18 *Gómez del Moral Guasch*, EU:C:2020:138, para 52.
26 Judgment of the CJEU of 10.06.2021, C-776/19 do C-782/19 *BNP Paribas Personal Finance*, EU:C:2021:470, para 64.
27 Judgment of the CJEU of 10.06.2021, C-776/19 do C-782/19 *BNP Paribas Personal Finance*, EU:C:2021:470, para 67.
28 Judgment of the CJEU of 18.11.2021, C-212/20, M.P., B.P. against bank 'A', ECLI:EU:2021:934.
29 Wiewiórowska-Domagalska, "Unfair Contract Terms," 210.
30 Judgment of the CJEU, C-260/18, *Dziubak*, para 62.
31 For the critical remarks see Węgrzynowski, "Przejrzystość i wykładnia."
32 Judgment of the CJEU, C-212/20, para 48.
33 Judgment of the CJEU, C-212/20, para 37.
34 Loos, "Crystal Clear?" 285.
35 Judgment of the CJEU, C-212/20, para 49; in relation to other CJEU case law in this respect see Loos, "Transparency of Standard Terms," 187; Junuzovic, "Transparency of (pre-) contractual Information," 77.
36 Judgment of the CJEU, C-212/20, para 50.
37 Judgment of the CJEU, C-212/20, para 55.
38 Judgment of the CJEU, C-212/20, para 58: see Loos, "Crystal Clear?," 293.
39 Wiewiórowska-Domagalska, "Unfair Contract Terms," 211.
40 Act of 23.04.1964 – Civil Code, Journal of Law 1964 no. 16 item 93 with amendments.
41 Mucha, "Wymóg zrozumiałości i przejrzystości," 50–58.
42 Mucha, "Wymóg zrozumiałości i przejrzystości," para 66.
43 Mucha, "Wymóg zrozumiałości i przejrzystości," para 61.
44 See Wiewiórowska-Domagalska, "Prawo z tektury"; Mroczkowski, "Legal Effects of Unenforceability," 1.
45 Judgment of the CJEU, C-212/20, para 69.
46 See Serafin, "The Court of Justice on Unfair Terms," 154.
47 According to statistics, in Poland in 96% of cases won by consumers, the latter claimed the invalidity of the contract due to the unfair contract term; see Parkiet, "Lawina wyroków w sprawach umów kredytów frankowych"; for Hungary see Király, "The Invalidity of Foreign Currency Loans," 60.
48 Judgment of the CJEU of 15.06.2023, C-520/21, *Arkadiusz Szcześniak* against *Bank Millenium*, ECLI:EU:C:2023:478.
49 Judgment of the CJEU of 15.06.2023, C-520/21, *Arkadiusz Szcześniak* against *Bank Millenium*, ECLI:EU:C:2023:478, para 28.
50 Judgment of the CJEU of 15.06.2023, C-520/21, *Arkadiusz Szcześniak* against *Bank Millenium*, ECLI:EU:C:2023:478, para 72.
51 Judgment of the CJEU of 15.06.2023, C-520/21, *Arkadiusz Szcześniak* against *Bank Millenium*, ECLI:EU:C:2023:478, para 73.
52 For critical remarks see: Bresci, "Transparency Claims," 406; Grundmann and Badenhoop, "Foreign Currency Loans," 18.
53 Judgment of the CJEU, C-520/21, para 80.
54 Judgment of the CJEU, C-520/21, para 79.

References

Bresci, Catherina. "Transparency Claims, Intellectual Services and Consumer Contracts: A Case of Consumer Over-Protection and Under-Protection?" *European Review of Contract Law* 19, no. 4 (2023): 394–421. https://doi.org/10.1515/ercl-2023-2023.

Busch, Danny, and Matthias Lehmann. *Unfair Terms in Banking and Financial Contracts*. Oxford University Press, 2023.

Cámara Lapuente, Sergio. "Control of Price Related Terms in Standard Form Contracts in the European Union: The Innovative Role of the CJEU's Case-Law." In *Control of*

Price Related Terms in Standard Form Contracts, edited by Yesim M. Atamer and Pascal Pichonnaz. Springer, 2020.

Cardone-Riportella, Clara, and Myriam García-Olalla. "Changes to the Regulation and the Declaration of Unfair Terms in Mortgage Agreements: An Event Study Approach to the Spanish Banking Industry." *European Journal of Law and Economics* 51 (2021): 157–81. https://doi.org/10.1007/s10657-020-09678-y.

Dean, Meryll. "Unfair Contract Terms: The European Approach." *The Modern Law Review* 56, no. 4 (1993): 581–90. https://doi.org/10.1111/j.1468-2230.1993.tb01890.x.

Domurath, Irina, and Chantal Mak. "Private Law and Housing Justice in Europe." *The Modern Law Review*, 83, no. 6 (2020): 1188–220. https://doi.org/10.1111/1468-2230.12557.

Durovic, Mateja, and Joseph Poon. "Consumer Vulnerability, Digital Fairness, and the European Rules on Unfair Contract Terms: What Can Be Learnt from the Case Law Against TikTok and Meta?." *Journal of Consumer Policy* 46 (2023): 419–43. https://doi.org/10.1007/s10603-023-09546-7.

Esposito, Fabrizio. "*Dziubak* Is a Fundamentally Wrong Decision: Superficial Reasoning, Disrespectful of National Courts, Lowers the Level of Consumer Protection: Judgment of the Court of Justice (Third Chamber) of 3 October 2019, *Kamil Dziubak, Justyna Dziubak* v *Raiffeisen Bank International AG* (Case 260/18)." *European Review of Contract Law* 16, no. 4 (2020): 538–51. https://doi.org/10.1515/ercl-2020-0030.

Fazekas, Judith. "The Consumer Credit Crisis and Unfair Contract Terms Regulation-Before and After Kásler." *Journal of European Consumer and Market Law* 6, no. 3 (2017): 99–106.

Feher, Miklos Zoltan. "From Kásler to Dunai. A Brief Overview of Recent Decisions of the CJEU in Hungarian Cases Concerning Unfair Contract Terms in Consumer Contracts." *Hungarian Yearbook of International and Law and European Law* 7, no. 1 (2019): 289–302. https://doi.org/10.5553/HYIEL/266627012019007001017.

Golecki, Mariusz, and Piotr Tereszkiewicz. "Complex Mortgage Loans as a Case Study for Consumer Law and Economics." In *Consumer Law and Economics*, edited by Klaus Mathis and Avishalom Tor. Springer, 2021.

Grundmann, Stefan, and Nikolai Badenhoop. "Foreign Currency Loans and the Foundations of European Contract Law – A Case for Financial and Contractual Crisis?" *European Review of Contract Law* 19, no. 1 (2023): 1–36. https://doi.org/10.1515/ercl-2023-2002.

Howells, Geraint. "Unfair Contract Terms." In *Rethinking EU Consumer Law*, edited by Geraint Howells, Christian Twigg-Flesner, and Thomas Wilhelmsson. Routledge, 2017.

Junuzović, Mia. "Transparency of (Pre-)Contractual Information in Consumer Credit Agreements: Is Consistency the Missing Key?" *Croatian Yearbook of European Law & Policy* 14, br. 1 (2018): 69–98. https://doi.org/10.3935/cyelp.14.2018.310.

Király, Péter Bálint. "The Invalidity of Foreign Currency Loans in the Hungarian Judicial Practice." *Public Governance, Administration and Finances Law Review* 2 (2017): 60–66. https://doi.org/10.53116/pgaflr.2017.2.4.

Klamert, Marcus. "What We Talk About When We Talk About Harmonization." *Cambridge Yearbook of European Legal Studies* 17 (2015): 360–79. https://doi.org/10.1017/cel.2015.12.

Lapuente, Cámara. "Control of Price Related Terms in Standard Form Contracts in the European Union: The Innovative Role of the CJEU's Case-Law." In *Control of Price Related Terms in Standard Form Contracts*, edited by Y.M. Atamer and P. Pichonnaz. Springer, 2020.

Loos, Marco B.M. "Crystal Clear? The Transparency Requirement in Unfair Terms Legislation." *European Review of Contract Law* 19, no. 4 (2023): 281–99. https://doi.org/10.1515/ercl-2023-18.

Loos, Marco B.M. "Transparency of Standard Terms Under the Unfair Contract Terms Directive and the Proposal for a Common European Sales Law." *European Review of Private Law* 23, no. 2 (2015): 179–93.

Loos, Marco B.M., and Joasia Luzak. *Update the Unfair Contract Terms Directive for Digital Services. Study Requested by European Parliament*. European Union, 2021.

https://www.europarl.europa.eu/RegData/etudes/STUD/2021/676006/IPOL_STU (2021)676006_EN.pdf.
Mišćenić, Emilia, Piotr Tereszkiewicz, and Marta Infantino. "The Interplay Between the CJEU and National Courts in the Case Law on Unfair Contract Terms in Foreign Currency Loans: A Comparative Overview." *European Review of Contract Law* 19, no. 4 (2023): 346–74. https://doi.org/10.1515/ercl-2023-2021.
Mroczkowski, Rafal. "Legal Effects of Unenforceability or Invalidity of an Agreement for a Denominated in or Indexed to a Foreign Currency Mortgage Loan in The Light of Judicial Decisions." *Financial Law Review* 24, no. 4 (2021): 1–23. https://doi.org/10.4467/22996834FLR.21.029.14654.
Mucha, Jagna. "Wymóg zrozumiałości i przejrzystości w umowie kredytu hipotecznego oraz brak możliwości zmiany treści nieuczciwego warunku umownego przez sąd krajowy – wprowadzenie i wyrok Trybunału Sprawiedliwości z 18.11.2021 r., C-212/20, M.P. i B.P. przeciwko 'A.', prowadzącemu działalność za pośrednictwem 'A.' S.A." *Europejski Przegląd Sądowy* 6 (2022): 50–58.
Parkiet. "Lawina wyroków w sprawach umów kredytów frankowych." Accessed March 1, 2024. https://www.parkiet.com/banki/art39453151-lawina-wyrokow-w-sprawach-umow-kredytow-frankowych.
Rzecznik Finansowy. *Analiza aktualnych zagadnień dotyczących kredytów frankowych 2021*. Warszawa, 2022. https://rf.gov.pl/baza-wiedzy/analizy-i-raporty.
Rott, Peter. "Unfair Contract Terms." In *Research Handbook on EU Consumer and Contract Law*, edited by Christian Twigg-Flesner. Edward Elgar, 2016.
Serafin, Riccardo. "The Court of Justice on Unfair Terms and Supplementation of the Contract: How Far Is Too Far?" *Journal of European Consumer and Market Law* 12, no. 4 (2023): 150–58.
Tereszkiewicz, Piotr. "Foreign Currency Loans and Directive 93/13: The CJUE as a Legal Architect." In *Protecting Financial Consumers in Europe. Comparative Perspectives and Policy Choices*, edited by Piotr Tereszkiewicz and Mariusz Golecki. Brill, 2022.
Vandenberghe, Ann-Sophie. "The Law on Unfair Terms in Standard Form Contracts in Europe." In *Consumer Law and Economics*, edited by Klaus Mathis and Avishalom Tor. Springer, 2020.
Węgrzynowski, Łukasz. "Przejrzystość i wykładnia umowy kredytu frankowego z perspektywy dyrektywy 93/13. Glosa do wyroku TS z dnia 18 listopada 2021 r., C-212/20." LEX/el., 2021. https://sip.lex.pl/komentarze-i-publikacje/glosy/przejrzystosc-i-wykladnia-umowy-kredytu-frankowego-z-perspektywy–386286371.
Wiewiórowska-Domagalska, Aneta. "Prawo z tektury. Państwo mogło zapobiec problemom frankowiczów." *Gazeta Prawna*, August 6, 2019. https://serwisy.gazetaprawna.pl/finanse-osobiste/artykuly/1424985,rola-panstwa-w-kryzysie-frankowym.html.
Wiewiórowska-Domagalska, Aneta. "Unfair Contract Terms in CHF Mortgage Loans. Case C-260/28 Dziubak – Where Do We Go from Here?" *Journal of European Consumer and Market Law* 9 (2020): 206–12.
Ziemblicki, Bartosz, and Mateusz Lewandowski. "The Legal Consequences of Unfair Contract Terms in Consumer Loan Agreements Valorized with Foreign Currency: Considerations with Respect to the Judgment of the CJEU in the Dziubak Case (C-260/18)." *Review of Central and East European Law* 46 (2021): 346–73. https://doi.org/10.1163/15730352-bja10055.

2 Unveiling digital-financial exclusion among the elderly

Gaps in knowledge and methodology[1]

Anne-Marie Weber, Weronika Herbet-Homenda, and Helena Kordasiewicz

1. Introduction

In the past decades, the concept of financial inclusion has gained considerable traction across various policy and academic domains. More recently, discussions regarding the rationale behind adopting Central Bank Digital Currencies have underscored the high priority of financial inclusion on global, regional, and national policy agendas.[2] This growing emphasis is further solidified by an emerging consensus advocating for the recognition of a "right to financial inclusion" as a fundamental human right.[3] Aligned with the methodology of the largest dataset on financial inclusion provided by the World Bank, financial inclusion typically encompasses access to financial services, such as owning an account and utilising it for withdrawals and payments as well as access to savings accounts and credit.[4] Financial inclusion also refers to financial resilience, signifying the ability to access money in emergencies and "financial worrying" that reflects the stress experienced in relation to financial circumstances.[5] Additionally, financial literacy is widely regarded as a crucial indicator for financial inclusion.[6]

The discourse on financial inclusion is increasingly nuanced, recognising that the reasons, forms, and solutions for financial exclusion vary across different demographic groups.[7] Particularly, against the backdrop of the ageing population phenomenon,[8] there is a growing interest in addressing financial exclusion among the elderly, (i.e., people of at least 60 years of age).[9] This is partly due to the strain on social security systems and the systemic risks associated with the lack of financial resilience among seniors.

Although the drive towards financial inclusiveness is global in scope, further consideration should be focused mainly of the European Union and its current or former member states. In this respect, the issue of financial exclusion among the elderly intersects with another current EU policy focus, namely the digital transformation of modern economy.[10] As the digital landscape evolves, financial services are progressively provided electronically and online. This trend has been accelerated by the COVID-19 pandemic, which, for instance, hastened the closure of bank branches.[11] Hence, accessing basic financial services now often requires the use of digital tools or entails the burden of travelling to the nearest branch. Although an

DOI: 10.4324/9781003510406-4

expanding body of literature acknowledges digitalisation and, particularly, FinTech solutions as a potential catalyst for advancing financial inclusion,[12] there is a concurrent observation of associated risks and regulatory challenges.[13] Among these concerns, there is a growing awareness of potential exclusionary effects concerning elderly individuals.[14] The digitalisation of the economy may inherently marginalise elderly individuals, whose absence in the digital world leads to a particular (i.e., digital) social exclusion.[15] Although witnessed in various aspects, digital exclusion stands out as particularly severe within the financial services domain. The access to financial services is indispensable for conducting transactions for goods and services that fulfill essential needs across all facets of the elderly's societal engagements.[16] Financial inclusion is, therefore, currently regarded as a basic human right.[17] Thus, given the dynamically changing landscape for financial service provision, there is an increased urgency to scrutinise the extent to which elderly individuals are integrated into this digital financial paradigm. Empirical evidence of digital exclusion, particularly highlighting age as a significant demographic determinant, underscores the urgency of the matter.[18] This raises the question of whether the effects of rapid market-driven digitalisation in financial services on the elderly should be addressed through legislative interventions.

To address financial exclusion in an ageing society, the Organisation for Economic Cooperation and Development (OECD) and the Global Partnership on Financial Inclusion developed the G20 Fukuoka Policy Priorities on Aging and Financial Inclusion, which were endorsed by the G20 finance ministers and central bank governors in 2019.[19] The general well-being of older people is embedded in Goal 3 of the 17 Sustainable Development Goals in the UN Agenda 2030.[20] Strategic, yet non-binding, commitments also emerged at the national level in the form of national financial education strategies, targeting older people as a particularly vulnerable demographic group,[21] as well as guidance by financial market regulators directed to supervised market actors regarding specific actions that have exclusionary effects on the elderly.[22] However, while the issue of financial exclusion among the elderly is clearly recognised in public policy, it has only recently begun to be examined through the lens of legal scholarship. Consequently, the literature lacks an assessment of the need and potential modalities of legislation that could remedy the diagnosed problem.

In this chapter, we argue that the overlapping dynamics of digital and financial exclusion necessitate a targeted research effort in legal scholarship. We contend that there is a need to assess potential regulatory responses that would specifically address the vulnerabilities of the elderly. However, an interdisciplinary, evidence-driven analysis of regulatory pathways requires data obtained through rigorous study design. This, in turn, necessitates preconceiving adequate avenues for legislative intervention that would effectively channel empirical research efforts. The aim of this chapter is, therefore, to unveil gaps in knowledge and methodology regarding financial exclusion occurring at the intersection with the exclusionary effects of digitalisation. In elucidating the challenges faced by elderly individuals in navigating the digital financial landscape, our aim is not only to enrich academic discourse but also to inform policy interventions and practical initiatives geared towards fostering financial inclusion and equity for the elderly. While we acknowledge the global scope of the analysed problem, we focus our attention on the European Union.

The chapter consists of five sections. Following this introduction, Section 2 delineates the current legal state of play regarding the protection of the elderly against digital-financial exclusion. Based on this assessment, we outline potential legislative avenues that, in our view, should inform and guide the design of empirical research. Section 3 presents a review of the literature and available data relevant to the digital-financial exclusion of the elderly. In light of the regulatory options (Section 2) and the reviewed literature and data (Section 3), Section 4 explains the gaps in knowledge and methodology that we identify. Finally, Section 5 summarises our findings.

2. Legal landscape

The legal framework governing the rights of the elderly and the risks they face is shaped by two primary regulatory streams: anti-discrimination and consumer protection law. Despite their shared goal of safeguarding vulnerable social groups that are particularly prone to certain inequalities and abuses, each of these streams employs its own tactics in addressing vulnerability, regulatory methods, legal instruments, and justifications for protection.

Anti-discrimination law is grounded in primary EU law,[23] which prohibits unfair disparate treatment based on characteristics such as gender, religion or belief, disability, sexual orientation, and age (Article 21 EChFR). Age discrimination is considered to violate the fundamental rights of human dignity, equality of treatment, and respect.[24] Therefore, the adoption of regulations that prohibit unjustified age discrimination and offer effective remedies for its victims is considered a crucial element of an effective equality strategy and one of the EU's priorities.[25]

Despite the pervasive nature of the problem, in secondary EU law, age discrimination and its adverse social implications are mainly acknowledged and addressed by specific regulations in the context of employment.[26] Secondary legislation notably lacks detailed measures ensuring equal access to the financial market for various stakeholders, including those particularly vulnerable to inequalities stemming from the adverse effects of digitalisation and the dynamic evolution of new technologies. One may argue that the inequalities arising in this context should not fall under the purview of anti-discrimination law, as they do not stem from discriminatory practices but rather from the vulnerability of certain individuals to market phenomena. Conversely, one could speculate that certain forms of positive discrimination might effectively bolster the position of specific consumer groups, such as the elderly, who are at risk of financial exclusion in the increasingly digitised and complex financial services market. However, under the current legal framework (consisting in particular of consumer law legislation, including Unfair Commercial Practices Directive,[27] and sectoral financial market regulation, including Consumer Credit Directive[28] or Payment Services Directive),[29] the elderly are treated equally to other market participants. Consequently, the quest for identifying regulatory instruments aimed at addressing the issue of digital-financial exclusion of the elderly must shift towards EU consumer protection law.

While shaping the standards of conduct, EU consumer law is based on the model of the so-called average consumer, defined as one who is well-informed, reasonably observant, and circumspect. According to the UCPD, market practices may be considered abusive if they impair the ability of such a consumer to make an informed decision (Article 5.2(b) UCPD). However, as an exception to this concept, consumer legislation defines vulnerable consumers as those who require additional protection due to mental or physical infirmity, age, or credulity (Article 5 UCPD). Additional protections are granted to vulnerable consumers against commercial practices that are likely to materially distort their economic behaviour (Article 5.3 UCPD).

Despite some lack of clarity and emerging criticism,[30] the notion of vulnerability may be a valid concept for future developments and a useful legal tool for the protection of the elderly, albeit only if contextualised. Different markets possess distinct characteristics that influence who is perceived as a vulnerable consumer and why. For instance, elderly consumers may navigate freely in the largely unchanged food market yet encounter significant barriers in the financial market due to its high complexity and ubiquitous digitalisation.[31] Therefore, the protection of consumers vulnerable in a given context requires targeted rather than one-size-fits-all legal solutions. Despite the declaration of prioritising the protection of particularly vulnerable consumer groups in the new consumer agenda adopted in 2020,[32] no specific legal arrangements have been established regarding the elderly. As a result, current financial sector-specific legislation lacks dedicated measures for protecting seniors as particularly vulnerable consumers. On the other hand, recent legislation provides examples of specific legal instruments designed to protect selected consumer groups, distinguished due to their age and particular vulnerability (e.g., minors).[33]

The assessment of the current legal landscape leads to the conclusion that on EU level, the existing state of play does not adequately address the unique vulnerabilities of older individuals within the highly digitalised financial market. Further research on potential legislative interventions must build upon a thorough empirical diagnosis of the phenomenon that is supposed to be cured. However, the design of that research requires some preliminary reflections on the potential regulatory pathways.

The legislative interventions that we envision can be divided into two categories. The first category encompasses legislation aimed at either initiating or directly imposing obligations on financial institutions providing (or expected to provide) essential financial services crucial for the financial inclusion of the elderly. The second category consists of regulatory measures that introduce institutional or procedural solutions primarily geared towards addressing the effects of digital-financial exclusion and providing ex-post remedies.

The first category of potential legislative avenues is grounded in the premise that achieving digital-financial inclusion for the elderly necessitates intervention in the legal relationship between financial institutions and elderly consumers. Such intervention could manifest as a form of admissible positive discrimination, as it would entail providing elderly consumers with "special treatment" by financial institutions. The most comprehensive legislative option would involve adopting a definition of elderly consumers tailored to the specific market context of financial services. Such a definition could impact various aspects of financial institutions' operations and serve as the foundation for establishing a standard of conduct that addresses the challenges typically faced by the elderly when participating in financial markets. This may include obligations related to in-person service provision, such as operating stationary temporary service points or mobile service points or implementing specific communication channels.[34] Additionally, legislative measures within this category could include customised disclosure requirements applicable solely to interactions with the elderly. Such disclosures would entail, for example, information on the nearest contact point or additional instructions and assistance in converting to online banking services. Legal obligations of financial institutions towards the elderly could also encompass providing legal education, which is currently only carried out through voluntary and *ad hoc* initiatives.[35]

The institutional measures contained in the second category of potential legislative avenues could include the establishment of a public authority or a unit within an existing public authority tasked with overseeing the financial market participation of the elderly or vulnerable consumers in general. In addition to monitoring financial institutions' policies and practices, such an institution could be endowed with specialised enforcement powers (e.g., to request detailed information, issue binding recommendations, or sanction possible violations). Furthermore, this category may involve amendments to existing administrative or judicial consumer protection enforcement mechanisms to better accommodate the specific vulnerabilities and challenges faced by the elderly in safeguarding their rights related to financial services. These amendments could involve granting public authorities the right to participate in such proceedings as observers or even to initiate them *ex officio*.

3. Literature review

In the context of EU law, the attempt at a comprehensive examination of the potential legislative interventions outlined previously involves several layers of legal analysis. Key doctrinal inquiries include assessing the legal basis in the Treaties for adopting secondary legislation and evaluating any proposal against the principles of subsidiarity and proportionality. Importantly, the pursuit of any of the available regulatory options must be informed by interdisciplinary empirical research unveiling the patterns of digital-financial exclusion.

The current body of literature on the digital-financial exclusion of the elderly is constantly evolving and results from both policy and academic research efforts. Since the topics of both digital and financial inclusion bear significance for policymaking, the different approaches to the topic deliver potentially relevant informational output. The multitude of sources on the subject stems from the recognition that the identified phenomenon is of concern to a diverse range of academic disciplines, including psychology, public health, law, computer science, and economics.[36] Consequently, the research output is variegated in its assumptions, methodologies, and geographical scope. All these factors contribute to the multi-faceted nature of the literature, posing a challenge for academic and policy-driven efforts to connect various outcomes into a coherent body of knowledge in which comparisons are performed and developments are observed based on methodologically corresponding research outcomes. While this review attempts to structure the literature according to themes, it is important to acknowledge the "patchwork rug" of evidence related to digital-financial exclusion and embrace its complexity.

Our review incorporates both quantitative and qualitative research alongside select articles offering comprehensive overviews of the topic by summarising findings from previous studies.[37] The analysed literature is not confined to recent publications; rather, a comparative analysis spanning older and newer studies enables a nuanced understanding of the evolving approaches to the subject matter over time. Older studies frequently address issues such as physical infrastructure inadequacies, perceived minimal necessity for Internet usage, and general attitudes;[38] in contrast, contemporary research increasingly emphasises deficiencies in necessary skills or a cautious reluctance towards adopting new technologies.[39]

An important focus of contemporary research lies in identifying the primary factors influencing the utilisation of digital technologies and the encountered barriers among elderly users. Studies have highlighted the paramount importance of user-friendliness and usefulness as well as the user's attitude.[40] Notwithstanding its subjective nature, two elements have been identified as having the most universal influence on this attitude: the "perceived ease of use" and the "perceived usefulness"[41] – with an emphasis on the *perception* part. Hence, it is evident that feelings of inclusion and skill levels vary considerably when navigating in the digital environment.

Simultaneously, the literature presents a divergence of perspectives regarding the general self-perception of the elderly. On one hand, a study conducted among individuals over 65 years of age revealed that some senior respondents, who classified themselves as "non-users" of the Internet, devalued their competences due to comparisons with those of their children or grandchildren.[42] This study also documented the lived experience of exclusion, with interviewees expressing feelings of isolation and a sense of being "old" or even "like a dinosaur" in this digital context.[43] To move beyond the dichotomy between mere usage and non-usage of the Internet, the research categorised different approaches of the elderly interviewees towards technology into: (i) avoidance practices (the interviewees actively avoided using digital technologies through, for example, finding alternative sources of information to the Internet); (ii) usage practices (in which the interviewees used digital technologies for certain purposes, yet without recognising it as "real" technology use); (iii) appropriation practices (through which the senior respondents learned digital technologies from courses, manuals, or family members); and (iv) subjectivation practices (in which the interview partners integrated their alleged non-use of digital technologies into their self-perception of being an "older non-user").[44]

On the other hand, other studies have demonstrated that even the elderly with low levels of IT skills and those who rarely use digital technologies do not *feel* excluded or have a problem with the state of the matter. A study of Polish elderly, who were chosen among those attending senior clubs and support groups,[45] has shown that 70% of the responders did not consider themselves excluded.[46] This perception may stem from a lack of sufficient knowledge of what the use of digital technologies may offer them or purely a lack of perceived need to participate in this segment of the economy.

Given this backdrop, a strong argument emerges that the elderly should not be regarded as a homogeneous group. Drawing upon the stratification of Internet usage among senior citizens across different age brackets, a body of research underscores the necessity of categorising seniors into various subgroups to effectively ascertain the factors influencing their circumstances in the digital era. However, this division between those affected by the grey digital divide[47] remains understudied;[48] therefore, the concept of further categorisation of elderly consumers requires further research and, above all, precise definition of criteria for such subdivision. According to one of the hypotheses, the relevant circumstances can be divided into individual-level ("human capital such as education, motivation, technical interest, economic capital (income), health, age and sex") and social-context ("marital status, social capital (support and encouragement by social network members) and Internet use within one's social network").[49] The results of this interview-based research have shown that the last of the social-context factors is not as important as previously thought, but the positive effect of encouragement by peer group has also been demonstrated. This understanding of the impact of networks is challenged by studies focused on the context of online banking,[50] which will be discussed further.

The importance of attitude has also been demonstrated by another UK-based study of the perception of digital technologies by the elderly,[51] conducted in focus groups of persons between 54 and 85 years of age. It has been demonstrated that even when the "initial fear of breaking the technology" is overcome or alleviated, some seniors have replaced it with a new anxiety related to security and "the vulnerability of both themselves and the technology."[52] Conversely, researchers from the Centre of Aging at the University of Miami highlight that "older people are not 'technophobic' and are willing and able to use technology such as computers," but their declining cognitive abilities can pose a barrier to effectively utilising technology.[53] This study has also highlighted that while the elderly are receptive to using modern technologies, they oftentimes have high levels of anxiety connected to their ability to use them efficiently. The key role of non-material aspects of digital exclusion has been further confirmed.[54]

Eventually, a UK-based study has characterised the elderly's approach to digital technologies as "ambivalent."[55] Some of the participants of this study have described keeping up to date with modern technologies as too difficult and not useful. In contrast, others belonging to the "younger" elderly have been using computers to "prepare for the old age,"[56] meaning that they have seen how online solutions may help them preserve bigger parts of their independence later in life (e.g., online shopping, e-health, online banking).

The correlation between maintaining independence and digital inclusion of the elderly has also been studied in China.[57] Although the scope of this literature review is generally limited to the EU area, this study appears relevant as far as it points out the differences between high- and medium-income countries. More importantly, it shows that the elderly, as a vulnerable part of modern populations, may strongly benefit from access to the Internet, as it decreases their likelihood of functioning dependently.

Another significant stream of research pertains to the vulnerability of senior consumers amidst diverse market dynamics. While literature and policy widely acknowledge the particular vulnerability of the elderly due to their advanced age,[58] some studies examining consumer capabilities across various markets argue that older individuals are not inherently more exposed to consumer vulnerability than others.[59] Given such inconclusive findings, research focusing on specific markets while assessing the position and vulnerability of seniors active within them appears to be the most desirable approach.

Such demand for contextualisation is met by studies within the third herein distinguished area of research, which is specifically narrowed to the financial market and concentrates on the barriers restricting the accessibility of financial services for senior customers. By drawing on accessible data, two main groups of factors contributing to the exclusion (both financial and digital in nature) of the elderly can be identified. The first one consists of barriers emerging on the part of seniors, such as (i) lack of sufficient financial skills (so-called financial illiteracy); (ii) lack of IT skills, and reluctance to use digital tools (as in the case of general research outlined before); and (iii) poverty and low income.[60] The second one unveils the barriers created by the market itself, including (iv) a lack of products and services dedicated to senior customers or (v) a lack of customer education programs. However, despite their apparent relevance, the following literature review demonstrates that the research addressing these factors remains broadly inconclusive.

The current literature offers inconsistent descriptions of the impact of age on financial literacy. On one hand, certain studies demonstrate that financial capabilities tend to increase with age.[61] Financial capabilities are defined here as a "combination of financial literacy and desirable financial behaviours."[62] The researchers have looked at both the subjective and objective literacy, both of which turned out to be positively correlated with age and peaking in the age group 65–69, but it may decrease after the age of 80. Conversely, other studies have suggested literacy will start to diminish around the age of 65.[63]

Regarding the barriers posed by the digitalisation of commercial banking services, some research indicates that elderly individuals who do not utilise online banking abstain from it due to fear and their perception of difficulty.[64] Other studies demonstrate that it *is* primarily the lack of skills that prohibits the elderly from using online banking.[65] Eventually, some research questions the existence of a problem of the inaccessibility of modern commercial banking to the elderly. In a Polish study, almost 60% of the seniors declared no problems whatsoever in the context of banking, and 80% of them confirmed they use online banking.[66] However, it is important to stress that this study was performed online, meaning that already only those of the elderly who have sufficient IT skills to fill out an online questionnaire could have participated, which has an obvious bearing on the implications of this study for the issue of digital exclusion.

In the "When I'm 84"[67] study, not only the elderly have been interviewed but also their informal carers. Considering the previously described discrepancies between the perception of seniors of their Internet usage and skills and the actual extent to which they rely on online technologies, it provides an important insight from those who support the senior citizens in their daily lives and help in managing their finances.

As regards the demand side of the financial market, the demand of the elderly for various types of financial services is thought of as being primarily determined by their level of income; other important factors include age, education, and the declared financial situation.[68] In the same study, it has been stressed that a unified treatment of the elderly can lead to a deeper financial exclusion, which poses an obvious detriment to both the consumers and financial institutions.

On the one hand, it is being highlighted that there is a lack of products dedicated to senior consumers,[69] which may be one of the leading causes of financial exclusion[70] and an insufficient focus on this segment of the market.[71] However, in a study prepared by the Polish Banks' Association (*Związek Banków Polskich*), merely 16% of the respondents expressed that the offer is unsatisfactory.[72]

Another study focused on the issue of access to loans and found that the age of loan applicants influences lending practices, especially as bank branch closures hinder access to advice for older borrowers.[73] Decreased income in retirement and increased mortality risk contribute to lower repayment probabilities with age.[74] Mandatory residual debt insurance and age limits exacerbate age-related disadvantages.[75] Furthermore, standardisation in credit lending, driven by digitalisation, may lead to older individuals being rejected without individual assessment.[76]

While assessing the banks' approach towards senior customers, apart from the product range, the elderly respondents point out the lack of dedicated education programs, which they believe should be provided by the financial institutions.[77] In their view, such training should cover both digital skills and financial literacy. This study was conducted online, with the study group of persons over 60 years of age. In this case, the online nature of the survey appears to be of little relevance since the study offers important and quite universal insight into how the elderly who do use online banking find the encounter and what could be done to elevate their experience.

In the *discussion* section of numerous papers, conclusions for the market have been formulated. The most vivid example is a Polish study that claims that even if the aspect of social responsibility is not convincing for financial institutions to broaden their offer dedicated to the elderly, the "pragmatic (economical)"[78] reasons ought to push them in this direction. Others have focused on fostering a "strong corporate culture that emphasises developing the network scale and network density of senior customers",[79] which could include establishing cultural organisations for senior consumers and maintaining a proper business culture. This ought to be done in order to obtain more elderly consumers, as the study has shown the network effect in the process of selection of banks by seniors.[80] It has also been emphasised that financial inclusion can be increased by financial institutions through the use of modern technologies in a way that is also accessible and readable for seniors.[81] Adjusting the digital infrastructure to meet the needs of senior consumers seems particularly appealing in view of the continuous closure of bank branches. An example of a proposed solution for the problem of the high technical entry barrier, which may be unattainable for the elderly, is the utilisation of biometric identification instead of a set of passwords. This approach can alleviate concerns related to forgotten passwords or difficulty in typing for individuals with limited manual skills.

4. Gaps in knowledge and methodology

Our extensive examination of the literature and data substantiates the increasing acknowledgment of digital-financial exclusion among the elderly within academic circles and policymaking spheres. However, notwithstanding this recognition, the current state of research lacks the foundation for conducting an informed analysis of potential regulatory interventions aimed at mitigating this issue. Our assessment elucidates several critical knowledge gaps and methodological shortcomings present within the existing body of research.

The prevailing policy paradigm regarding digital exclusion, which advocates for inclusivity in the digital revolution, notably influences the discourse on addressing digital-financial exclusion among the elderly. The underlying objective epitomised by the slogan of "leaving no one behind," explains a narrow focus on promoting digital skills and literacy among the elderly as the primary solution to digital-financial exclusion. This exclusive focus on augmenting digital capabilities often assigns blame solely to the elderly for their exclusion, thereby disregarding broader societal forces underpinning the phenomenon.

Our proposed regulatory pathways offer an alternative perspective, shifting away from this technology-centric approach. By detaching from the sole objective of integrating the elderly into digital technologies, these pathways prompt a reconsideration of how to ensure financial inclusion in the face of persistent digital exclusion. Indeed, by reassessing the foundational assumptions, we broaden the scope of discourse to consider alternative avenues for achieving financial inclusion despite ongoing digital exclusion. Consequently, within the context of investigating legislative responses to digital-financial exclusion among the elderly, a critical reassessment of these deeply ingrained assumptions becomes imperative.

To facilitate the future analysis of potential legislative avenues, a fundamental shift in research design is warranted. This "second-generation research" on digital-financial exclusion should not only aim to elucidate the causes of the phenomenon but also adopt a solution-driven approach. Central to this approach is the overarching question: "What interventions could effectively address digital-financial exclusion?" This entails formulating research hypotheses grounded in specific regulatory proposals, as outlined in this chapter, while also considering additional strategies that may emerge from ongoing scholarly and policy discussions.

The prevailing assumption that digital-financial exclusion should primarily be addressed by bridging the digital divide has led to a strong emphasis on enhancing digital skills among the elderly to align with established market practices. A revised assumption, however, suggests that elderly individuals deserve financial inclusion even in the absence of digital inclusion, prompting inquiries into how market practices might be adapted to ensure their financial inclusion. Consequently, research on digital-financial exclusion should draw from longstanding themes in the consumer protection law discourse, which explore adjustments in service provision to safeguard consumer rights (e.g., information obligations towards elderly consumers could be valuable). Currently, practitioners and academics in consumer law debate the efficacy of information provided to consumers across various markets, including the financial sector. Therefore, to propose substantive solutions aimed at mitigating financial exclusion among the elderly, it is essential to ascertain whether senior citizens engage with the information provided by entrepreneurs and whether the manner and format of such information (oral, written) are relevant to them, including considerations such as font size and language used.

Another significant category of identified weaknesses in the current body of research pertains to methodological issues. It is evident that studies relying solely on online tools to measure the digital engagement of respondents offer limited informational value. Such studies often only provide insights into the specific services used by individuals who are already digitally included. The same shortcoming applies to the financial education programs, the vast majority of which are available online, thereby significantly limiting their target group.[82]

Another notable methodological flaw is the measurement of attitudes and perceived skills rather than the actual testing of digital competencies. While such studies might be relevant in the fields of sociology or psychology, they cannot precisely inform legal research on regulatory options.

Further, the examined studies have revealed large inconsistencies as to the definition of the elderly and old age that determine the group of respondents. While some studies include participants as young as 50,[83] others focus on individuals above the age of 80.[84] Apart from the researcher's perspective, the lack of common understanding of the term "elderly" also negatively impacts both business and regulatory practices.[85] Therefore, for the purpose of evaluating regulatory options, narrowing down the age brackets would be appropriate to exclude respondents whose occupations require regular use of digital technologies, as they may distort the research outcome. Moreover, a stronger focus on "the older elderly" would likely provide a more precise account of the correlation between age and cognitive abilities. This refined approach would offer valuable insights into the specific challenges faced by the oldest segments of the elderly population in navigating digital-financial services, contributing to a more nuanced understanding of the issue and informing targeted regulatory interventions.

The analysis of the collected literature also indicates a tendency to treat seniors as a homogenous group despite various differentiating features. For the purposes of designing adequate legislative responses to the problem, one should thus explore whether financial literacy and vulnerability to financial exclusion are correlated with the factors such as: (i) education (higher, secondary, primary); (ii) place of residence (big city, small city, village); (iii) family situation (single v. living with spouse/children/grandchildren); (iv) assets condition/financial capability (sources of income, savings); (v) type of bank used (commercial, cooperative); and (vi) extra-occupational activity (voluntary work, senior citizens' clubs). In order to strengthen the credibility of the research and the tangibility of its results, future empirical studies should thus include respondents belonging to various subgroups distinguished due to these listed features.

Furthermore, in terms of methodology, research designs targeting elderly individuals could enhance their efficacy by including their caregivers and families as additional respondents. This approach would offer an external perspective, enriching the comprehension of digital-financial exclusion among the elderly and providing insights into the broader socio-economic context within which these individuals interact with financial services.

5. Conclusions

With an ageing population and the accelerating trend of digitalisation in financial services, the exclusion of elderly individuals from the digital-financial realm poses a pressing concern. While academia and policymaking have visibly recognised this issue, the discourse on regulatory solutions in the field of legal scholarship has been relatively subdued.

The existing literature and data on digital-financial exclusion among the elderly exhibit several weaknesses that impede their utility for informing legislative interventions. In addition to various methodological flaws, our review has revealed that the most significant knowledge gaps are largely attributable to a prevailing policy-driven perception. This policy paradigm asserts that addressing digital-financial exclusion primarily entails bridging the digital divide by providing the elderly with access and skills to participate in the digital revolution, influencing research design accordingly. However, re-evaluating the notion of "leaving no one behind" reveals that not all segments of society necessarily require participation in digital-financial services. This realisation underscores the need for legal tools to safeguard the right to financial inclusion among the elderly. Consequently, a range of regulatory options to address digital-financial exclusion among the elderly should be explored in solution-focused studies to ascertain whether specific legal interventions could effectively remedy the problem.

We argue that addressing the identified knowledge gaps and implementing suggested methodological improvements are essential steps in structuring future empirical research. Such research is critical for informing the subsequent legal analysis of potential legislative avenues aimed at effectively addressing digital-financial exclusion.

Notes

1 The text presents the results of research project no. UMO-2023/51/D/HS5/1563, "Combatting financial exclusion of the elderly in the digital era – a regulatory roadmap," funded by the National Science Center, Poland.
2 Shivani, "Empowering"; Lannquist and Tan, *Central*; Riganti and Weber, "Digital."
3 Queralt, "A Human."
4 Demirgüç-Kunt et al., *The Global*.
5 Demirgüç-Kunt et al., *The Global*.
6 OECD, *OECD/INFE Toolkit*.
7 Demirgüç-Kunt et al., *The Global*; Damar-Blanken et al., *Altersdiskriminierung*.
8 See data included in: United Nations, *Worlds*.
9 OECD, *Financial Consumer*; Financial Conduct Authority, *Ageing*.

10 See e.g., European Commission, *New Consumer Agenda.*
11 Weber et al., "Digitalizing."
12 Buckley et al., "FinTech"; Buckley et al., "FinTech for"; Lee, "Financial."
13 Kern and Karametaxas, "Digital"; Machiavello, *Microfinance*; Chiu, "FinTech."
14 Weber et al., "Digitalizing."
15 Mubarak and Suomi, "Elderly"; Weber et al., "Digitalizing."
16 Riganti and Weber, "Digital."
17 Queralt, "A Human."
18 European Commission, *Digital*, 24; Mubarak and Suomi, "Elderly"; Cooper, *When.*
19 GPFI and OECD, *G20 Fukuoka.*
20 The UN, *The 17.*
21 OECD, *National Strategy.*
22 Financial Conduct Authority, *Finalised.*
23 The term "primary law" refers to the treaties concluded by the EU Member States, including i.a. the Treaty on the Functioning of the European Union and the Charter of Fundamental Rights of the European Union, hereinafter referred as "EChFR." The term "secondary law," on the other hand, encompasses the body of law in the form of regulations, directives, decisions, recommendations, and opinions. See also Syrpis, "The Relationship."
24 Fredman, "The Age."
25 European Commission, *Age Discrimination*, 5.
26 See also European Commission, *Age Discrimination*; European Commission, *Age and*; AGE Platform Europe, *The Right*; Freeland and Vickers, "Age"; Numhauser-Henning, "Ageism"; Numhauser-Henning and Rönnmar, *Age.*
27 Directive 2005/29/EC of the European Parliament and of the Council of 11 May 2005 concerning unfair business-to-consumer commercial practices in the internal market and amending Council Directive 84/450/EEC, Directives 97/7/EC, 98/27/EC and 2002/65/EC of the European Parliament and of the Council and Regulation (EC) No 2006/2004 of the European Parliament and of the Council ('Unfair Commercial Practices Directive'), hereinafter referred as "UCPD."
28 Directive 2008/48/EC of the European Parliament and of the Council of 23 April 2008 on credit agreements for consumers and repealing Council Directive 87/102/EEC.
29 Directive 2015/2366 of the European Parliament and of the Council of 25 November 2015 on payment services in the internal market, amending Directives 2002/65/EC, 2009/110/EC and 2013/36/EU and Regulation (EU) No 1093/2010, and repealing Directive 2007/64/EC.
30 See e.g., Waddington, "Vulnerable"; Kaprou, "The Current."
31 European Parliamentary Research Service, *Vulnerable*, 5.
32 European Commission, *New Consumer Agenda.*
33 See, e.g., recitals 40, 46, 71, Articles 14(3) and 28 of the Regulation (EU) 2022/2065 of the European Parliament and of the Council of 19 October 2022 on a Single Market For Digital Services and amending Directive 2000/31/EC (Digital Services Act).
34 Weber et al., "Digitalizing," 104.
35 See e.g., The OECD International Network on Financial Education. Accessed August 13, 2024. https://www.oecd.org/en/networks/infe.html.
36 To grasp the variety of approaches, see e.g., Hill, Betts, and Gardner, "Older"; Lu, Yao, and Jin, "Digital"; Fredman, "The Age."
37 Lu, Yao, and Jin, "Digital."
38 See e.g., Asmi and Ishaya, "Understanding"; Selwyn, "The Information."
39 See e.g., Msweli and Tendani, "Enablers"; Solarz and Adamek, "Determinants."
40 See: Msweli and Tendani, "Enablers."
41 Asmi and Ishaya, "Understanding."
42 Gallistl et al., "Doing."
43 Gallistl et al., "Doing."

44 Gallistl et al., "Doing."
45 Such a selection may not prove extendable to different subgroups – other research has shown the influence of the support of a peer group in the situation of the elderly when using digital technologies. Due to the selection of a specific (and thus on a larger scale unrepresentative) research group, the result of this study thus appears as hardly universal.
46 Potyrańska and Hajduk-Stelmachowicz, "Wykluczenie."
47 Mubarak and Suomi, "Elderly."
48 Friemel, "The Digital."
49 Friemel, "The Digital."
50 See: Cui and Xu, "Understanding."
51 Hill, Betts, and Gardner, "Older."
52 Hill, Betts, and Gardner, "Older."
53 Czaja and Lee, "The Impact."
54 Berry, *Older.*
55 Selwyn, "The Information."
56 Selwyn, "The Information."
57 Lu, Yao, and Jin, "Digital."
58 E.g., European Parliamentary Research Service, *Vulnerable*; United Nations, *Older.*
59 Berg, "Consumer Vulnerability," 9.
60 Financial Watch, *A Wrinkle.*
61 Xiao, Chen, and Sun, "Age."
62 Xiao, Chen, and Sun, "Age."
63 Lusardi, Mitchell, and Curto, "Financial."
64 Lusardi, Mitchell, and Curto, "Financial."
65 Solarz and Adamek, "Determinants."
66 Związek Banków Polskich, "Infosenior."
67 Cooper, *When.*
68 Czerwiński, "Zachowania."
69 See: Matejczuk and Łakoma, "Dostęp."
70 Marcinkowska, Ziemba, and Świeszczak, "Wykluczenie."
71 Guido, Amatulli, and Sestino, "Elderly."
72 Związek Banków Polskich, "Infosenior."
73 Damar-Blanken et al., *Altersdiskriminierung.*
74 Damar-Blanken et al., *Altersdiskriminierung.*
75 Damar-Blanken et al., *Altersdiskriminierung.*
76 Damar-Blanken et al., *Altersdiskriminierung.*
77 Senior.Hub, *Cyfrowe.*
78 Marcinkowska, Ziemba, and Świeszczak, "Wykluczenie."
79 Cui and Xu, "Understanding."
80 Cui and Xu, "Understanding."
81 Cichowicz, "The Use."
82 OECD, *Financial Literacy*, 45.
83 E.g., Marcinkowska, Ziemba, and Świeszczak, "Wykluczenie"; Barnes et al., *The Social.*
84 E.g., Cooper, *When.*
85 See: Matejczuk and Łakoma, "Dostęp."

References

AGE Platform Europe. *The Right to Work in Old Age. How the EU Employment Framework Directive Still Leaves Older Workers Behind.* Brussels, 2021. https://social.un.org/ageing-working-group/documents/AGE%20Platform%20Europe_The%20right%20to%20work%20in%20old%20age.pdf.

Asmi, Fahad, and Tanko Ishaya. "Understanding the Behavior of the Elderly Towards Internet Banking in the UK." *Proceedings of the Second International Conference on Social Eco-Informatics (SOTICS)*, 100–6. SOTICS, 2012.

Barnes, Matt, Annalies Blom, Kate Cox, and Carli Lessof. *The Social Exclusion of Older People: Evidence from the First Wave of the English Longitudinal Study of Ageing (ELSA), Final Report*. London: Office of the Deputy Prime Minister, 2006.

Berg, Lisbet. "Consumer Vulnerability: Are Older People More Vulnerable as Consumers Than Others?." *International Journal of Consumer Studies*, 39, no. 4 (2015): 284–93.

Berry, Richard. *Older People and the Internet: Towards a System Map of Digital Exclusion*. London: International Longevity Centre-UK, 2011.

Buckley, Ross R., A. Zetzsche Dirk, and W. Arner Douglas. "FinTech for Financial Inclusion: Designing Infrastructure for Financial Transformation." In *Sustainable Development Goals – Harnessing Business to Achieve the SDGs Through Finance, Technology and Reform*, edited by Julia Walker, Alma Pekmezovic, and Gordon Walker, 179–214. Hoboken: Wiley & Sons, 2019.

Buckley, Ross R., A. Zetzsche Dirk, W. Arner Douglas, and Robin Veidt. "FinTech, financial Inclusion and the UN Sustainable Development Goals." In *Routledge Handbook of Financial Technology and the Law*, edited by Iris H.-Y. Chiu and Gudula Deipenbrock, 247–72. Oxon: Routledge, 2021.

Chiu, Iris H.-Y. "FinTech and Disruptive Business Models in Financial Products, Intermediation and Markets – Policy Implications for Financial Regulators." *Journal of Technology Law and Policy*, no. 21 (2016): 55–112.

Cichowicz, Ewa. "The Use of Modern Technology by Financial Institutions in Combating Financial Exclusion." *Annales Etyka W Życiu Gospodarczym* 21, no. 5 (2018): 109–19. https://doi.org/10.18778/1899-2226.21.5.09.

Cooper, Hillary. *When I'm 84: Locking the Door on the Older Old: The Challenge Facing Britain's Banks*. Cambridge: The Finance Foundation, 2016.

Cui, Xiaolei, and Jing Xu. "Understanding the E-Banking Channel Selection Behavior of Elderly Customers." *Journal of Organizational and End User Computing* 34, no. 6 (2022): 1–21. https://doi.org/10.4018/joeuc.300765.

Czaja, Sara J., and Chin Chin Lee. "The Impact of Aging on Access to Technology." *Universal Access in the Information Society*, no. 4 (2006): 341–49. https://doi.org/10.1007/s10209-006-0060-x.

Czerwiński, Bogumił. „Zachowania seniorów z Polski Północnej na rynku usług finansowych w świetle wyników badań." *Handel Wewnętrzny*, no. 3 (2016): 76–87.

Damar-Blanken, Duygu, Helena Klinger, Hanne Roggemann, Sally Peters, Ingrid Größl, and Daniel Daneshian. *Altersdiskriminierung bei der Kreditvergabe. Abschlussbericht*. Institut für Finanzdienstleistungen, 2023, e.V. https://www.iff-hamburg.de/2023/09/26/altersdiskriminierung-bei-der-kreditvergabe/

Demirgüç-Kunt, Asli, Leora Klapper, Dorothe Singer, and Dorothe Ansar. *The Global Findex Database 2021: Financial Inclusion, Digital Payments, and Resilience in the Age of COVID-19*. Washington, DC: World Bank, 2022. https://doi.org/10.1596/978-1-4648-1897-4.

European Commission. *Digital Economy and Society Index (DESI)*, 2022.

European Commission, Communication from the Commission to the European Parliament and the Council. "New Consumer Agenda: Strengthening Consumer Resilience for Sustainable Recovery." 2020. https://eur-lex.europa.eu/legal-content/EN/TXT/?uri=CELEX%3A52020DC0696.

European Commission, Directorate-General for Employment, Social Affairs and Equal Opportunities, O'Cinneide, Colm. *Age Discrimination and European Law*. Luxembourg: Office for Official Publications of the European Communities, 2005.

European Commission, Directorate-General for Justice, Beale Anna, O'Dempsey Declan. *Age and Employment*. Publications Office, 2011.

European Parliamentary Research Service. *Vulnerable Consumers*, 2021. https://www.europarl.europa.eu/RegData/etudes/BRIE/2021/690619/EPRS_BRI(2021)690619_EN.pdf.

Financial Conduct Authority. "Ageing Population and Financial Services." Occasional Paper 2017/31. https://www.fca.org.uk/publication/occasional-papers/occasional-paper–31.pdf.

Financial Conduct Authority. *Finalised Guidance FG 22/6, Branch and ATM Closures or Conversions*, 2022. https://www.fca.org.uk/publications/finalised-guidance/fg22-6-branch-and-atm-closures-or-conversions.

Financial Watch. *A Wrinkle in the Process: Financial Inclusion Barriers in an Ageing Europe*. Financial Watch, 2021.

Fredman, Sandra. "The Age of Equality." In *Age as an Equality Issue: Legal and Policy Perspectives*, edited by Sandra Fredman and Spencer Sarah, 21–70. Oxford and Portland: Hart Publishing, 2003.

Freeland, Mark, and Lucy Vickers. "Age Discrimination and EU Labour Rights Law." In *Research Handbook on EU Labour Law*, edited by Alan Bogg, Cathryn Costello, and A.C.L. Davies, 527–46. Edward Elgar Publishing, 2016.

Friemel, Thomas N. "The Digital Divide Has Grown Old: Determinants of a Digital Divide Among Seniors." *New Media & Society* 18, no. 2 (2014): 313–31. https://doi.org/10.1177/1461444814538648.

Gallistl, Vera, Rebekka Rohner, Lisa Hengl, and Franz Kolland. "Doing Digital Exclusion – Technology Practices of Older Internet Non-users." *Journal of Aging Studies* 59 (2021): 100973. https://doi.org/10.1016/j.jaging.2021.100973.

Guido, Gianluigi, Cesare Amatulli, and Andrea Sestino. "Elderly Consumers and Financial Choices: A Systematic Review." *Journal of Financial Services Marketing* 25, no. 3–4 (2020): 76–85. https://doi.org/10.1057/s41264-020-00077-7.

Hill, Rowena, Lucy R. Betts, and Sarah E. Gardner. "Older Adults' Experiences and Perceptions of Digital Technology: (Dis)Empowerment, Wellbeing, and Inclusion." *Computers in Human Behavior*, no. 48 (2015): 415–23. https://doi.org/10.1016/j.chb.2015.01.062.

Kaprou, Eleni. "The Current Legal Definition of Vulnerable Consumers in the UCPD: Benefits and Limitations of a Focus on Personal Attributes." In *Vulnerable Consumers and the Law: Consumer Protection and Access to Justice*, edited by Christine Riefa and Saintier Séverine. Oxon: Routledge, 2020.

Kern, Alexander, and Xenia Karametaxas. "Digital Transformation and Financial Inclusion." In *Routledge Handbook of Financial Technology and the Law*, edited by Iris H.-Y. Chiu and Gudula Deipenbrock, 273–87. Oxon: Routledge, 2021.

Lannquist, Ashley, and Brandon Tan. *Central Bank Digital Currency's Role in Promoting Financial Inclusion*. International Monetary Fund, FinTech Notes, 2023.

Lee, Emily. "Financial Inclusion: A Challenge to the New Paradigm of Financial Technology, Regulatory Technology and Anti-Money Laundering Law." *Journal of Business Law*, no. 6 (2017): 473–98.

Lu, Xinran, Yao Yao, and Yinzi Jin. "Digital Exclusion and Functional Dependence in Older People: Findings From Five Longitudinal Cohort Studies." *EclinicalMedicine*, no. 54 (2022): 101708. https://doi.org/10.1016/j.eclinm.2022.101708.

Lusardi, Annamaria, Olivia S. Mitchell, and Vilsa Curto. "Financial Literacy Among the Young." *Journal of Consumer Affairs* 44, no. 2 (June 1, 2010): 358–80. https://doi.org/10.1111/j.1745-6606.2010.01173.x.

Machiavello, Eugenia. *Microfinance and Financial Inclusion: The Challenge of Regulating Alternative Forms of Finance*. Oxon: Routledge 2018.

Marcinkowska, Monika, Marika Ziemba, and Krzysztof Świeszczak. „Wykluczenie finansowe osób 50+ w kontekście dostępnej oferty bankowej." *FINANSE Czasopismo Komitetu Nauk o Finansach PAN*, no. 1 (7) (2014): 145–70.

Matejczuk, Grzegorz, Łakoma, Katarzyna. „Dostęp osób starszych do rynku usług finansowych w świetle skarg wpływających do Biura Rzecznika Praw Obywatelskich. "In *Osoby starsze na rynku usług finansowych*, Analiza i zalecenia. Biuro Rzecznika Praw Obywatelskich, 2013.

Msweli, Nkosikhona Theoren, and Mawela Tendani. "Enablers and Barriers for Mobile Commerce and Banking Services Among the Elderly in Developing Countries: A Systematic

Review." In *Lecture Notes in Computer Science*, 319–30. 2020. https://doi.org/10.1007/978-3-030-45002-1_27.

Mubarak, Farooq, and Reima Suomi. "Elderly Forgotten? Digital Exclusion in the Information Age and the Rising Grey Digital Divide." *Inquiry* (January–December 2022). https://doi.org/10.1177/00469580221096272.

Numhauser-Henning, Ann. "Ageism, Age Discrimination and Employment Law in the EU." In *Ageing, Ageism and the Law*, edited by Israel Doron and Nena Georgantzi, 98–115. Edward Elgar Publishing, 2018.

Numhauser-Henning, Ann, and Mia Rönnmar. *Age Discrimination and Labour Law: Comparative and Conceptual Perspectives in the EU and Beyond*. Wolters Kluwer Law & Business, 2015.

Organisation for Economic Co-operation and Development. *Financial Consumer Protection and Ageing Populations*. Paris: Secretary-General of the OECD, 2020. https://web-archive.oecd.org/2020-07-23/559600-Financial-Consumer-Protection-and-Ageing-Populations.pdf.

Organisation for Economic Co-operation and Development. *National Strategy for Financial Education for Poland*. Paris: Secretary-General of the OECD, 2023. https://www.oecd.org/daf/fin/financial-education/National-strategy-financial-education-poland.pdf.

Organisation for Economic Co-operation and Development. *OECD/INFE Toolkit for Measuring Financial Literacy and Financial Inclusion 2022*. Paris: Secretary-General of the OECD, 2022. www.oecd.org/financial/education/2022-INFE-Toolkit-Measuring-Finlit-Financial-Inclusion.pdf.

Organisation for Economic Co-operation and Development and Global Partnership for Financial Inclusion. *G20 Fukuoka Policy Priorities on Aging and Financial Inclusion, 8 Key Steps to Design a Better Future*, 2019. http://www.gpfi.org/sites/gpfi/files/documents/G20%20Fukuoka%20Policy%20Priorities%20on%20Aging%20and%20Financial%20Inclusion.pdf.

Organisation for Economic Co-operation and Development, OECD Business and Finance Policy Papers. *Financial Literacy in Germany: Supporting Financial Resilience and Well-Being*. Paris: Secretary-General of the OECD, 2024. https://doi.org/10.1787/bf84ff64-en.

Potyrańska, Paulina, and Marzena Hajduk-Stelmachowicz. „Wykluczenie finansowe osób w wieku 60+ na rynku usług finansowych." *Problemy Nauk Stosowanych*, no. 10 (2019): 215–28.

Queralt, Jahel. "A Human Right to Financial Inclusion." In *Studies in Global Justice*, 77–92. Springer, 2016. https://doi.org/10.1007/978-3-319-41430-0_5.

Riganti, Federico, and Anne-Marie Weber. "Digital Euro and Financial Inclusion: Considerations on Trust, The Digital Divide and Financial Literacy." In *Central Bank Digital Currency – The Birth of the Digital Euro*, edited by Filippo Annunziata, Christos Hadjiemmanuil, and Bart Joosen. London: Palgrave Macmillan, 2024.

Selwyn, Neil. "The Information Aged: A Qualitative Study of Older Adults' Use of Information and Communications Technology." *Journal of Aging Studies* 18, no. 4 (2004): 369–84. https://doi.org/10.1016/j.jaging.2004.06.008.

Senior.Hub. *Cyfrowe Usługi Finansowe a Seniorzy*, 2021.

Shivani, Inder. "Empowering the Unbanked: The Intersection of Financial Inclusion and CBDC." In *The Framework for Resilient Industry: A Holistic Approach for Developing Economies. Emerald Studies in Finance, Insurance, and Risk Management*, edited by Narinder Kumar, Kiran Sood, Ercan Özen, and Simon Grima, 65–74. Leeds: Emerald Publishing Limited, 2024.

Solarz, Małgorzata, and Jacek Adamek. "Determinants of Digital Financial Exclusion as a Barrier to the Adoption of Mobile Banking Services in Poland." *Ekonomia I Prawo* 21, no. 2 (June 30, 2022): 503–25. https://doi.org/10.12775/eip.2022.028.

Syrpis, Phil. "The Relationship Between Primary and Secondary Law in the EU." *Common Market Law Review* 52, no. 2 (2015): 461–87.

United Nations, Department of Economic and Social Affairs. *The 17 Goals*. https://sdgs.un.org/goals.

United Nations, Department of Economic and Social Affairs. *Worlds Social Report 2023: Leaving No One Behind in An Ageing World*. New York: UN, 2023. https://desapublications.un.org/publications/world-social-report-2023-leaving-no-one-behind-ageing-world.

United Nations, Economic Commission for Europe. "Older Persons as Consumers." UNECE Policy Brief on Ageing No. 3, 2009. https://unece.org/DAM/pau/_docs/age/2009/Policy_briefs/Policy-brief-Old_persons.pdf.

Waddington, Lisa. "Vulnerable and Confused: The Protection of 'Vulnerable' Consumers Under EU Law." *European Law Review* 38, no. 6 (2013): 757–82.

Weber, Anne-Marie, Anne-Christin Mittwoch, Weronika Stefaniuk, and Weronika Herbet-Homenda. "Digitalizing the Commercial Banking Business Model – Vanishing Bank Branches and the Risks of Financial Exclusion of the Elderly." In *Commercial Banking in Transition*, edited by Marco Bodellini, Gabriella Gimigliano, and Dalvinder Singh, 87–107. London: Palgrave Macmillan, 2024.

Xiao, Jing Jian, Cheng Chen, and Lei Sun. "Age Differences in Consumer Financial Capability." *International Journal of Consumer Studies* 39, no. 4 (June 8, 2015): 387–95. https://doi.org/10.1111/ijcs.12205.

Związek Banków Polskich. "Infosenior." 2020. https://www.zbp.pl/getmedia/76a9cdd8-a2da-4195-b5e1-b9d5f2c5adc0/ZBP_InfoSenior_2020_POPR4.

3 Knowledge and competence requirements in the Mortgage Credit Directive

An adequate protection of financially illiterate consumers?

Joana Farrajota

1. Introduction

The 2008 financial crisis had the benefit of bringing to light a staggering lack of knowledge and competence of agents operating in financial markets.

It was against this backdrop that, after 2008, with the goal of ensuring that the mistakes of the past were not repeated, abundant legislation was drafted and enacted imposing an increased number of duties on financial institutions regarding their staff's knowledge and competence requirements. One of the goals of such initiatives was to ensure that natural persons having contact with clients were well-equipped to provide information and clarification to clients, in particular consumers, and, ultimately, positively impact clients' financial behaviour.[1] Article 25 of Directive 2014/65/EU on markets in financial instruments (MiFID II) is a clear example of this effort, when determining that

> *Member States shall require investment firms to ensure and demonstrate to competent authorities on request that natural persons giving investment advice or information about financial instruments, investment services or ancillary services to clients . . . possess the necessary knowledge and competence to fulfil their obligations.*[2]

In what concerns core banking activities, such as lending, one of the central provisions is contained in the Mortgage Credit Directive (MCD).[3] Article 9 of the MCD, under the title "Knowledge and competence requirements for staff," creates a duty for Member States (MS) to ensure a certain level of knowledge and competence (K&C) of the staff, that is "any natural person working for the creditor, or credit intermediary who is directly engaged in the activities" covered by the MCD or "who has contacts with consumers in the course of activities" covered by the MCD (Article 4, paragraph 11) (Staff). It is left to each MS to define the minimum K&C requirements, with the guidance of the set of principles set out in Annex III to the Directive. This provision, as well as Annex III, seem not to have been the subject of discussion within the context of revision of the MCD.[4]

DOI: 10.4324/9781003510406-5

This chapter addresses the relevance of K&C requirements in the context of mortgage lending as an instrument of consumer protection and questions the effectiveness and adequacy of the legislative choices made in the setting of MS duties regarding K&C requirements set forth in Article 9 of the MCD, having recourse to the Portuguese case as an example.

The relevance of K&C requirements as an instrument of consumer protection in a context of high financial illiteracy will be addressed in section 1, before analyzing Art. 9 of the MCD (section 2) and the evaluation of its implementation as well as the on-going review process of the MCD (section 3). Finally, in the last section, the application of the K&C requirements will be illustrated having recourse to the example of the Portuguese legal system (section 4).

2. The relevance of consumer protection in the mortgage credit market

The relevance of consumer protection in the mortgage credit market stems from a number of factors, two of which will be highlighted: the significance of the right to housing, both at a social as well as at an economic level, and the low levels of financial literacy of the average consumer.

2.1 The social and economic relevance of housing: housing as a fundamental right

The global aim of the MCD is "to ensure that consumers entering into credit agreements relating to immovable property benefit from a high level of protection" (MCD, recital 15). The MCD, as a separate set of rules from general consumer credit agreements rules, regulating credit granting for the purpose of acquisition of immovable property, is a reflection of the recognition at the EU level of the relevance of the right to housing. A right engrained in Article 8 of the European Convention on Human Rights and Fundamental Freedoms (November 4, 1950) and benefiting from an explicit legal protection in a wide array of other international conventions, such as the Universal Declaration of Human Rights (December 12, 1948, Article 25); the International Covenant on Economic, Social and Cultural Rights (December 16, 1966, Article 11); the Convention on the Elimination of All Forms of Discrimination Against Women (December 18, 1979, Article 14, paragraph 2, subparagraph h); the Declaration on the Right to Development (December 4, 1986, Article 8); the Convention on the Rights of the Child (November 20, 1989, Article 16); and the International Convention on the Elimination of All Forms of Racial Discrimination (December 29, 1994, Article 5, subparagraph e, indent iii), to name a few.

The social relevance of housing, paired with its economic relevance at an individual as well as at a market level, makes it a relevant and delicate area of regulation. At an individual level, in the vast majority of cases, buying a house is the most significant financial investment of a lifetime. Mortgage borrowing is the main component of household indebtedness.[5] According to the survey carried out from March through April 2023 in the 27 MS, 20% of the respondents have had a mortgage or home loan in the last two years.[6]

The recent and steep increases of interest rates and their impact on household debt levels only added to the relevance of the regulation of this market.

2.2 A financially illiterate consumer

Financial literacy encompasses both a basic *knowledge* of economics, finance and numeracy, as well as the ability to *apply* such knowledge in financial behaviour.[7] Both components go hand-in-hand. As widely agreed, there is a strong correlation between financial education and the ability of individuals to avoid deception and over-indebtedness, as there is a strong correlation between financial education and financial planning. It is evident today that more financial literacy translates into better financial decisions and an increase of wellness not only at the individual but at a supra-individual level. Financial literacy has a positive impact on the economy as a whole, contributing to markets' stability.[8] As made clear by the 2007/08 financial crisis, the more financially literate individuals are, the better they can navigate an economic crisis.[9] That is also true, as is already observable, in the current financial crisis.

The importance of financial literacy has been recognised for about two decades at an international level and, more recently, at a national level. At an international level, the OECD is one of the entities that has been in the forefront of financial literacy policy since 2002 and has, since then, produced a series of works, guidelines and actions in this area, from which the creation in 2008 of the International Network on Financial Education (OECD/INFE) is perhaps the most symbolic. At an international level, the role of the World Bank,[10] as well as the role of the International Organization of Securities Commissions and that of the Economic and Financial Affairs Council, should also be mentioned. At the European level, several initiatives have been taking place, of which I would highlight the 2007 report on "A single market for 21st century Europe", issued by the European Commission, where financial education was presented as an essential component of the efforts to ensure the Single Market, and the creation in 2008 of an *Expert Group on Financial Education*. From a legislative standpoint, abundant instruments on consumer protection related to financial services were issued. I will also draw attention to the role of the European Banking Authority (EBA) and, finally, that of the European Banking Federation (EBF). At a national level, taking the example of Portugal, financial literacy has been a competence of the National Council of Financial Supervisors (NCFS), composed of the three Portuguese financial supervisors (the Portuguese Central Bank, the Portuguese Securities Market Commission and the Portuguese Insurance and Pension Funds Supervisory Authority). In 2011, the NCFS launched the Portuguese National Plan for Financial Education.[11] Other entities at a national level have also invested significantly in financial literacy, such as the Portuguese Banks' Association.

The increasing development of initiatives directed at raising financial literacy levels was in part a side (and positive) effect of the 2008 financial crisis, which had a relevant role in generating an accrued interest in the matter.[12] As a result, the promotion of financial literacy has been the subject of a multitude of initiatives by supervisory bodies, financial institutions and other agents in civil society at a national and *supra*national level.

However, despite all efforts and actions, financial literacy remains *low*, in general, and low in Portugal, in particular. What could be more concerning when analyzing financial literacy data is the fact that in some cases, close to no evolution occurred in the last years, *v.g.* between 2020 and 2023. Those are the conclusions of the OECD/INFE 2023 International Survey of Adult Financial Literacy (2023 Survey):

> *Results indicate that in many participating countries and economies, some areas of basic financial knowledge are particularly weak and have remained so since previous assessments (OECD, 2016; OECD, 2020), namely simple and compound interest as well as applying inflation in a real life context.*[13]

Within the 39 sampled economies, the average financial literacy score across all participating countries and economies is 60 out of 100 points. Furthermore, when analyzing the literacy financial scores of adults in all participating countries, only 34% of adults reached the minimum target score on financial literacy, defined as scoring at least 70%. The heterogeneity of scores in general and within EU countries is striking: in Germany 75% of adults scored more than 70%, whereas in Portugal only 37% did and in Italy 17%.[14]

Comparison between the 2020 and 2023 surveys' results, although tempting, has to be made carefully as the toolkit used to perform the surveys was not the same. Accordingly, some subjects of the 2023 survey were not "assessed" in 2020. Also the number of countries (from 26 to 39) and the countries that participated varied significantly. Only 14 countries participated in both studies. Nevertheless, in some areas comparison is possible, for instance, in what concerns assessment of knowledge on interest and compound interest. In the 2020 survey, the conclusion was the following:

> *Understanding both simple and compound interest, however, has proven to be a very challenging concept. Only about one-third of the respondents (26.3% average for the entire sample; 28.8% across OECD member countries participating in the survey) were able to show understanding of both.*[15]

In 2023, the conclusion was the following:

> *Less than one-third of adults across participating countries and economies correctly understood both simple and compound interest calculations.*[16]

For the sake of clarity as to the complexity of the three questions presented to respondents, to assess their level of knowledge regarding simple and compound interest rates, the questions were the following: "You lend $25 to a friend one evening and he gives you $25 back the next day. How much interest has he paid on this loan?"; "Imagine that someone put $100 into a tax-free savings account with a guaranteed interest rate of 2% per year. They don't make any further payments into this account, and they don't withdraw any money. How much would be in the account at the end of the first year once the interest payment is made?"; "How much would be in the account at the end of five years?"[17]

In light of these examples, it is accurate to state that even in what concerns "basic financial knowledge", essential for any individual with savings or credit products, knowledge remains particularly weak.[18]

For the reasons mentioned before, it is more challenging to compare the average financial literacy score, that in 2020 was 61%[19] and in 2023 was 60%. Bearing in mind the aforementioned *caveats*, based on the average financial scores of countries that participated in the two surveys, the conclusion is that only in five countries was there an increase of the score – in two cases, a significant increase of 10 points, for Germany, and 18 for Malta – whereas in two it decreased and in five remained virtually the same. One question that needs to be addressed relates to the causes of this stagnation of financial literacy levels.

3. The requirements of K&C set forth by the MCD

One of the instruments chosen by the MCD to protect consumers was the imposition of requirements of minimum levels of Staff's K&C. Such choice was based on the assumptions that Staff with higher K&C will provide better information to consumers, thus leading to an increased protection of the latter.[20]

As a result of the MCD, K&C requirements were introduced or reinforced by the EU and national legislators. Duties were imposed on banks to safeguard that "relevant staff of creditors, credit intermediaries and appointed representatives possess an adequate level of knowledge and competence in order to achieve a high level of professionalism" (MCD, recital 32).

In the MCD, the core provision pursuing this goal is contained in its Article 9. Under the title "Knowledge and competence requirements for staff," it creates a duty for MS to ensure a certain level of K&C of the staff. MS have a duty to ensure creditors

> *require their staff to possess and to keep up-to-date an appropriate level of knowledge and competence in relation to the manufacturing, the offering or granting of credit agreements . . . . Where the conclusion of a credit agreement includes an ancillary service, appropriate knowledge and competence in relation to that ancillary service shall be required.*
>
> (Article 9, 1 of the MCD)

The term 'Staff' has the meaning given in Article 4, paragraph 11, of the MCD, including any outsourced personnel as well as employees, and it also includes both front-desk and back-office, including management (recital 32, MCD). MS are also bound to

> *ensure that compliance with the requirements . . . is supervised by the competent authorities, and that the competent authorities have powers to require creditors, credit intermediaries and appointed representatives to provide*

such evidence as the competent authority deems necessary to enable such supervision.

(Article 9, 4 of the MCD)

It is left to each MS to define the minimum K&C requirements, with the guidance of the set of principles set out in Annex III to the Directive.[21] Annex III of the MCD identifies a minimum set of areas in regard to which Staff are required to have an adequate level of K&C, related, broadly, to the execution of MCAs. Such areas of knowledge range from consumer protection laws to land registry procedures, ethics and market knowledge. The definition of the "appropriate level of knowledge and competence" shall be made on the basis of: professional qualifications or professional experience. The professional experience can be defined as a minimum number of years working in areas related to the origination, distribution or intermediation of credit products. The possibility to assess the adequacy of K&C solely based on experience of the Staff, something that was foreseen in order to allow Staff members that were working at the institutions for a long period and did not possess the academic qualifications that are now typically required, was temporary – a transition period that ended on March 21, 2019. Currently, the determination of the appropriate level of knowledge and competence has to be based on both elements, that is, professional qualification and experience.

In 2020, the European Banking Authority (EBA) issued a set of Guidelines on loan origination and monitoring which, similarly to the MCD, provides for very general guidelines in what concerns K&C requirements,[22] in particular when compared, for example, with the guidelines issued by the European Securities Market Authority in 2017, specifying the criteria for the assessment of K&C required under Article 25, paragraph 1, of MiFID II (Guidelines for the assessment of knowledge and competence).[23]

4. The evaluation of the implementation of Article 9 and the review of the MCD

4.1 Evaluation of the implementation

The EU Commission, in compliance with Articles 44 and 45 of the MCD ("Review clause" and "Further initiatives on responsible lending and borrowing," respectively), conducted an evaluation of the MCD's implementation in order to understand its level of effectiveness and relevance. The assessment was performed via three methods: mystery shopping, stakeholder consultation and a consumer survey. The report on the results was published in November 2020.[24] In the Report from the Commission to the European Parliament and the Council on the review of the MCD, the conclusions on the effectiveness of the implementation of Article 9 are (very) positive.[25]

I find it difficult to draw from the analysis of the results obtained the same conclusions as the Commission did. In fact, results of the consumer survey and the mystery shopping seem difficult to reconcile, in that they convey contradictory perceptions of consumers regarding the same issue.

The participants subject to the consumer survey were questioned whether they agreed that the staff working for mortgage credit providers and intermediaries held an appropriate degree of K&C. The outcome was that 80% of consumers believe Staff possesses the sufficient level of K&C to advise them (of which 54% somewhat agree and 24% strongly agree). Thirteen percent of the consumers feel like Staff lacked appropriate K&C, mainly due to insufficient training. Some customers even claimed that the employees are untrustworthy, often found to be lying and hiding things.[26]

The mystery-shopping phase was only executed in seven MS thought to represent the reality across the EU. The mystery shopping was done in two separate phases as a result of the COVID-19 pandemic: a first one carried out online and by telephone, and a second one essentially carried out face-to-face. A strong disparity between results drawn from each phase is shown. In mystery shopping, sub phase 1, only 50% considered the Staff to be knowledgeable and competent, 42% considered the Staff to be somewhat knowledgeable and 8% considered the Staff to be not knowledgeable and/or competent. Within these aggregate results, one should be pointed out: in Spain, no creditor was viewed as knowledgeable and competent and, in Germany, only 20% of respondents considered them so.[27] In sub phase 2, the vast majority of consumers, 88%, considered creditors to be very knowledgeable and competent, 11% considered them to be somewhat knowledgeable and only 1% considered them not knowledgeable and/or competent.[28] In Germany, 100% saw the Staff as very knowledgeable and competent. In Spain, 90% saw the Staff as very knowledgeable and competent.

Reconciling results from both sub phases seems quite difficult, if not an impossible task. However, no mention of such contradictions is made in the report, much less discussed. An obvious question remains unanswered: what justifies such differences in the results?

In addition to these examples, conclusions regarding the impact of the MCD on the K&C of Staff can also be drawn from the analysis of answers to questions not directly related to the evaluation of Article 9 of the MCD. One element should be highlighted: the fact that the main problems existing prior to the implementation of the MCD are the ones that persist after its enactment. And these are the difficulty in understanding information presented and the inadequacy of explanations provided.[29] That is another point where a serious reflection from the Commission is necessary.

An additional element should be considered in the analysis of the results of implementation of the MCD: the 2023 Survey requested by the European Commission, Directorate-General for Financial Stability, Financial Services and Capital Markets Union, and coordinated by the Directorate-General for Communication. The survey, although encompassing a far more comprehensive analysis of the markets, not restricting itself to the universe of mortgage credit agreements, nor to banks, contains at least one element that should be taken into account. And that is clients' level of confidence in the advice offered by banks, insurers or financial advisors. According to the data retrieved from the survey, "[a] larger number, however, report feeling not confident (31% 'not too confident' and 14% 'not at all confident')."[30] Variations within the same MS should also be taken into account.

The proportion feeling 'very' or 'somewhat confident' about investment advice being primarily in their best interest ranges from about one in five respondents in Cyprus (19%) and Greece (20%) to six in ten respondents in Finland (60%). In other countries, the proportion not feeling too confident or not confident at all varies from less than a third in Finland (30%), Czechia (31%) and Portugal (32%) to six in ten respondents in Latvia and Slovenia (both 60%).[31]

The survey did not make a distinction in the questionnaire between the different agents providing advice or the products regarding which advice was offered, making it impossible to isolate banks or advice regarding MC.

4.2 The revised version

The revised version of the MCD, which is currently still on hold, does not (at this point) foresee amendments to Article 9 as well as Annex III to the Directive. It should be noted that the consultation addressed to stakeholders did not specifically address the matter of K&C. Despite that, the European Banking Association, for instance, proposed a revision of the requirements on Staff's K&C involved in the commercialization of mortgage credit with the goal of strengthening such requirements.[32]

5. The implementation of K&C requirements in the Portuguese legal system

5.1 Portugal's financial literacy levels

The systematic assessment of the general population's level of financial literacy began in Portugal in 2010, with a survey from the Bank of Portugal. Three other surveys ensued, in 2015, 2020 and 2023, conducted by the National Council of Financial Supervisors. The council was created in 2010 to carry out co-ordination competences between the supervisory authorities of the financial system – Securities Market Commission, Insurance and Pension Funds Supervisory Authority and Bank of Portugal – and advisory functions with the Bank of Portugal. It occupies a central position in the definition and implementation of the country's financial literacy policy. The core instrument of the policy is the financial literacy plan, drafted and put in place by the Council every five years. The first one dates from 2011. Currently, the third Plan (2020–2025) is in execution.

Whereas the first questionnaire was drafted by the Bank of Portugal, the following surveys were based on the questionnaires drafted by the OECD/INFE and in the context of the surveys carried out by the OECD/INFE in 2016, 2020 and 2023.[33/34]

According to the results of the OECD/INFE 2023 Survey, Portugal scored an average financial literacy score – a sum of financial knowledge, behaviour and attitude scores – of 62.7%,[35] meaning that the minimum score of 70%, representing the "minimum target score", was again not attained. What is more discouraging is not the result itself but the fact that the score on the 2020 survey was virtually the same: 61.8%.[36] Evolution was close to zero. Reference could also be made to the evolution of the position Portugal occupied amongst the other sampled economies: In 2023, Portugal was ranked amongst the 39 sampled economies in 13th, whereas in 2020, amongst 26 economies, Portugal ranked 7th.[37] In respect of such positions, attention should be drawn to the fact that the number of sampled economies, as already mentioned, varied significantly between 2020 and 2023.

Evidence of the low financial literacy levels of the Portuguese population in general was confirmed by the European Central Bank in 2018.[38] In an analysis of 19 MS, Portugal was placed in last, with only 25% of the Portuguese public answering three out of five questions correctly, compared to the 65% obtained in Germany and in the Netherlands. The questions ranged from questions related with risk diversification, inflation and compound interest, among others. More recently, according to the survey carried out from March through April 2023 in the 27 Member States, "Monitoring the level of financial literacy in the EU,"[39] Portugal had an overall financial literacy score of 11, that is, 7 points below the EU's average, placing it in the last position.

It is thus safe and accurate to conclude that Portugal still cannot quite reach that basic level of comprehension in what regards financial concepts and their practical exercise, meaning that most citizens are ill-equipped to make adequate financial choices.

5.2 Portugal's mortgage credit market

As a rule and contrary to other MS, mortgage interest rates in Portugal were in the vast majority variable and made of two components: a reference index, most commonly Euribor 6 or 12 months, and a spread (margin). In January 2022, 85.8% of MCAs had variable interest rates, only 7.5% mixed interest rates and 6.8% fixed interest rates. After the sudden hike of Euribor interest rates, there was a shift in the MCA market, with a tendency – more significant from December 2022 onwards – to abandon variable interest rates for mixed interest rates. Accordingly, in February 2024, the percentage of mixed interest rate is 72.2%, 24% variable and 3.8% fixed.[40]

Mortgage credit is, by far, also in Portugal, the most significant component of household debt. Its relevance has increased significantly with the spike of Euribor interest rates and is expected to gain a more balanced relevance with the lowering of index rates. In 2023, from the 29,224 million euros of household debt, 21,660 corresponded to mortgage credit.[41]

5.3 Portugal's mortgage credit regulation

The MCD was *partially* transposed into the Portuguese legal system, more than one year after the deadline was completed, by Decree-Law 74-A/2017 of June 23, 2017 (Decree-Law) and entered into force on January 1, 2018 (Article 47). The transposition is a partial one as the Portuguese legislator decided to regulate in a different legal instrument the activities carried out by credit intermediation and financial advisory services. Decree-Law 81-C/2017 of July 7, 2017, sets the requirements for access to and exercise of the activity of credit intermediaries and the provision of advisory services in relation to credit contracts. On the other hand, Decree-Law 74-A/2017 has a broader scope than the MCD as it applies to all mortgage credit – as well as to credit guaranteed by other form of immovable collateral, regardless of whether or not the property is intended for housing purposes – and applies also to financial leasing agreements of immovable assets intended for housing purposes (Article 2, paragraph 2).

The preamble of the Decree-Law contains a statement of an intention of consolidation in a single legal instrument of the existing rules, scattered throughout various legislative acts directed at consumer protection in the context of mortgage credit. Two notes on this statement should be mentioned.

Portugal had, before the Directive, an existing corpus of provisions directed at protecting the consumer when executing a mortgage credit agreement. That is not to say that the Directive was not relevant or that it did not develop the legal framework of execution of MCAs.

The second note is that the consolidation was not absolute. A number of rules survived the effort. As a result, the provisions contained in the Decree-Law have to be read and interpreted together with pre-existing legislation on mortgage credit, such as the ones contained in Decree-Law 349/98 of November 11, 1998, which establishes the regime for credit granting for the acquisition, construction and execution of works in permanent, secondary or leasehold housing as well as for the acquisition of land for the construction of owner-occupied housing.

In Portugal, mortgage loan agreements are long-term contracts executed between a natural person and a lender. The lender has to be either a credit institution or a financial company registered with the Bank of Portugal. Even when a credit intermediary intervenes, the credit is always granted by an authorised institution and the credit agreement is executed with that institution. In 2024, there were, in Portugal, 10 to 15 banks granting mortgage credit. MCAs executed after April 1, 2022, should not, following a recommendation (non-binding instrument) issued by the Bank of Portugal, exceed 40 years in the case of customers aged 30 and under; 37 years in the case of customers aged between 30 and 35; and 35 years in the case of clients aged 35 and over. The immovable property acquired with the capital from the loan typically serves as collateral for the loan.

The Decree-Law is divided into eight chapters and has two annexes. The first chapter contains the general rules regarding its scope of application. Chapter II is mainly concerned with conflict of interests between lender and client, imposing a number of rules on Staff's remuneration policy with the purpose to mitigate such risk. In addition to that, and with a view to protecting the consumer, Article 9 defines the K&C requirements for Staff. Chapter III regulates pre-contractual information duties as well as tying practices. Chapter IV regulates the lender's solvability assessment duty as well as the evaluation procedure of immovable property. Chapter V contains the provisions on loans in foreign currency and variable interest rates. Chapter VI regulates information duties and other rights during and after the execution of the loan agreement (e.g., right to early repayment and renegotiation of the contract). Finally, Chapter VII contains sanctions applicable in case of violation of the provisions, and Chapter VIII the final provisions (e.g., entry into force). Annex I contains the model for the European Standardised Information Sheet and Annex II the calculation of the annual percentage rate of charge.

5.4 K&C requirements for implementation in Portugal

The provision transposing Article 9 of the MCD is Article 6 of the Decree-Law, inserted in its Chapter II ("Conditions applicable to lenders"). The first section of Article 6 roughly corresponds to a direct transposition of the Directive's Article 9: lenders with head offices or branches in Portugal must ensure that their employees have and keep an updated and adequate level of K&C in relation to the preparation, commercialization and execution of credit agreements within the scope of the Decree-Law as well as in relation to any ancillary services that may be included in such agreements.

Paragraph 2 of Article 6 replicates Annex III of the MCD in the definition of the minimum knowledge and competence requirements. An adequate level of K&C requires the mastering of, at least, the following: (a) characteristics of the credit products marketed, as well as of the ancillary services normally proposed in association; (b) legislation applicable to credit agreements, especially in what concerns consumer protection; (c) process of real estate acquisition; (d) assessment of guarantees required for the granting of credit; (e) organisation and functioning of real estate registry; (f) Portuguese mortgage credit market; (g) consumers' creditworthiness assessment; (h) business ethics standards; and, lastly, (i) fundamental notions of economics and finance.

A Staff member should be considered as having the appropriate level of K&C when one of two situations occur (Article 6 of the Decree-Law): (a) the Staff member has the legally defined mandatory schooling and the legally required professional training for this specific purpose and (b) the Staff member holds an academic degree, a higher professional technician diploma or post-secondary training that confers a diploma, provided that the study plan also includes the minimum contents identified in section 2 of Article 6.

A transition period for the implementation of the K&C requirements was foreseen, between January 1, 2018, and March 21, 2019. During that period, K&C qualifications could be assessed based solely on experience. An adequate level of K&C could be determined to exist for Staff members who worked at least three consecutive or interpolated years in a field or exercising any function related to the execution of credit agreements subject to the Decree-Law. After such period the Staff Member would have to comply with either the requirement set forth in (a) or (b) as described before.

The training of Staff, in Portugal, to "sell" MCA is regulated by the Decree-Law and two ordinances: Ordinance 385-C/2017 of December 12, 2017, defining the minimum contents of the training—replicating in Article 6, paragraph 2 of the Decree-Law—and Ordinance 385-D/2017 of December 12, 2017, defining the process of certification of training entities by the Bank of Portugal.

A few elements, particularly relevant for our analysis, regarding the training system implemented in Portugal, should be highlighted. Firstly, the training can be provided either internally by the lender to its Staff or by an external, public or private entity, provided such entity was previously approved by the Bank of Portugal to provide such training. The training is to have a minimum mandatory duration of 25 hours. The number of sessions is not defined. It can be in person or online. Only a single training session is required, that is, lenders are not required by law to regularly or periodically renew the training – contrary to what happens in other MS, such as Spain.

The entity responsible for the training system, to ensure its effectiveness, continuous improvement and supervising the levels of K&C requirements, is the Bank of Portugal. In order to ensure the system's quality, this ordinance defines, in its Article 3, the competencies of the Bank of Portugal as a certifying institution, in terms of the creation, monitoring and control of the certification system. As a result, the Bank of Portugal is responsible for: (a) defining and developing methodologies, instruments and procedures capable of ensuring the proper operation of the certification system of training entities; (b) defining qualitative and quantitative assessment indicators in relation to the performance of certified training entities; (c) cooperating with the required institutions; and (d) managing and processing information related to the certification system of training institutions. It is also a duty of the Bank of Portugal to disclose a general list of certified training entities, pursuant to Ordinance 208/2013 of June 26, 2013. Currently there are eight private entities in Portugal certified by the Bank of Portugal to provide such training. There is no public entity providing such service.

Lenders originating from another European Union country but carrying out their activities in Portugal must ensure that their employees meet the K&C requirements set by their home MS as well as those imposed by subparagraphs b, c, e and f of paragraph 2. Qualifications obtained outside Portugal by nationals of MS of the EU or the European Economic Area are recognised by the Bank of Portugal under Law 9/2009 of March 4, 2009.

According to Article 29 of the Decree-Law, non-compliance with the duty to ensure that employees possess and maintain an adequate level of knowledge and skills, in breach of the provisions of Article 6, is qualified as a serious infringement, punishable by a fine ranging from 3,000 to 1,500,000 euros or from 1,000 to 500,000 euros, depending on whether the fine is imposed on a legal or natural person. In addition, this fine may be accompanied by an ancillary sanction.

6. Conclusion

The right to housing is a fundamental right, recognised and protected both at a national as well as at an international level, as a result of its social and economic relevance, both at an individual as well as at a market level.

The protection of this right has assumed a variety of forms, in particular in the context of the acquisition of immovable property for housing purposes with recourse to credit. The need for protection in this particular context – that is one where the acquisition of a house entails the simultaneous acquisition of a financial product – is all the more pressing as consumers have, in general, a low level of financial literacy, as made clear by the OECD/INFE's surveys.

The Mortgage Credit Directive is the product of such concerns.

Within the several instruments deployed to protect the consumer, the MCD, on the one hand, working on the assumption that agents with direct contact with clients may influence such clients' behaviour and, on the other hand, taking into account the general low levels of financial literacy of the adult population, decided to promote a knowledgeable and competent Staff. That was achieved by means of an imposition of an obligation for MS to ensure that such Staff have an adequate K&C in certain areas of knowledge of particular relevance when selling MCAs. However, a wide margin is left for MS to implement such obligation.

The definition of "minimum knowledge and competence requirements" that can be verified by analysing the professional qualifications and professional experience of a candidate is a relevant step in ensuring that Staff have an appropriate level of K&C. It is *not*, however, sufficient.

Portugal is a good example of the insufficiency of the MCD's provisions. The system of implementation of the K&C requirements put in place allows for Staff to be considered compliant with K&C requirements provided they have completed a single 25-hour training with a certified entity. No additional training is required.

Considering the constant evolution of financial markets, it is necessary to update systematically the training of the *Staff* and *to evaluate* and *measure* K&C consistently throughout the period the Staff member is working. In not imposing such obligations, the provision contained in Article 9 of the MCD does not promote an adequate protection of consumers. It falls short by not imposing on MS the obligation to evaluate and measure K&C consistently throughout the period the Staff member is working, as well as a regular refreshing of the training, thus allowing systems such as the Portuguese one to be in place. A regular and consistent monitoring and evaluation of the Staff's K&C are essential to assess whether normative provisions requiring K&C are effective in ensuring consumers an adequate protection.

Notes

1 A working assumption of this chapter is that clients are influenced in their choice of product by the staff working in the bank. Such assumption is based on indirect data, amongst others, from conclusions of the OECD/INFE 2023 International Survey of Adult Financial Literacy, in particular the fact that "only 26% of adults compare products across providers and only 24% of adults seek advice from independent sources when purchasing a financial product or service." In addition, 21% seek advice from non-independent sources, that is, financial agents, including bank staff (pp. 7 and 24 of the survey, https://www.oecd.org/publications/oecd-infe-2023-international-survey-of-adult-financial-literacy-56003a32-en.htm).

2 See also the Guidelines for the assessment of knowledge and competence issued by the European Securities Markets Authority, March 1, 2017.

3 Directive 2014/17/EU of February 4, 2014 on credit agreements for consumers relating to residential immovable property.
4 The revision process seems to have been suspended after several postponements of the release date for the new version of the Directive.
5 According to the OECD/INFE survey carried out in 2020, in more than two-thirds of the countries/economies participating, over 40% of adults hold credit or mortgage products (p. 31 of the Survey). According to OECD 2017 paper "Resilience in a time of high-debt," mortgages account for the largest share of household debt (p. 63, http://www.oecd.org/economy/outlook/Resilience-in-a-time-of-high-debt-november-2017-OECD-economic-outlook-chapter.pdf). See also, for more recent data retrieved by the OECD, https://www.oecd.org/housing/policy-toolkit/data-dashboard/enhancing-resilience/. For data regarding the relevance of mortgage credit agreements in the household debt, see the reports drafted by the Household Finance and Consumption Network (HFCN), from 2010, 2014, 2017 and 2021, https://www.ecb.europa.eu/stats/ecb_surveys/hfcs/html/index.en.html. See, in particular, the results from 2021: "In 2021 mortgage debt remained by far the most significant component of households' debt portfolio" (p. 22 of the 2021 paper). In 2017, the ECB concluded that "Mortgage debt is the most significant component of households' debt portfolio by far" and "[t]he share of households holding mortgage debt remained unchanged at 23.5%" (p. 16 of the 2017 paper).
6 "Monitoring the level of financial literacy in the EU," conducted by Ipsos European Public Affairs at the request of the European Commission, Directorate-General for Financial Stability, Financial Services and Capital Markets Union, survey results and data, https://europa.eu/eurobarometer/surveys/detail/2953.
7 As per the definition of the Organization for Economic Co-operation and Development (OECD), (see "Recommendation of the Council on Financial Literacy of October 19 2020").
8 See Hogarth and Federal Board, "Financial Education and Economic Development." See also the OECD/INFE 2023 international survey of adult financial literacy: "Higher financial literacy is associated with greater individual financial well-being. Results indicate that adults who reach the minimum target financial literacy level also have significantly higher levels of financial well-being and financial resilience" (p. 56 of the survey, https://www.oecd.org/publications/oecd-infe-2023-international-survey-of-adult-financial-literacy-56003a32-en.htm).
9 See, *inter alia*, Lusardi and Mitchell, "The Economic Importance of Financial Literacy," 5–44; Balloch, Nicolae, and Philip, "Stock Market Literacy," 1925–63. See also the "EBA Financial Education Report 2019/20," 8.
10 See, *inter alia*, the G20 Financial Inclusion Indicators Database powered by the World Bank, https://datatopics.worldbank.org/g20fidata/home.
11 See https://www.apb.pt/educacao_financeira/iniciativas.
12 According, *inter alia*, to Kapper, Lusardi, and Panos, *Financial Literacy and the Financial Crisis*.
13 Survey, https://www.oecd.org/publications/oecd-infe-2023-international-survey-of-adult-financial-literacy-56003a32-en.htm.
14 P. 15 of the 2023 survey, https://www.oecd.org/publications/oecd-infe-2023-international-survey-of-adult-financial-literacy-56003a32-en.htm.
15 P. 19 of the survey, https://www.oecd.org/financial/education/oecd-infe-2020-international-survey-of-adult-financial-literacy.pdf.
16 P. 56 of the survey, https://www.oecd.org/publications/oecd-infe-2023-international-survey-of-adult-financial-literacy-56003a32-en.htm.
17 P. 67 of the survey, https://www.oecd.org/publications/oecd-infe-2023-international-survey-of-adult-financial-literacy-56003a32-en.htm.
18 P. 67 of the survey, https://www.oecd.org/publications/oecd-infe-2023-international-survey-of-adult-financial-literacy-56003a32-en.htm.

19 P. 13 of the 2020 survey:

Individuals across the entire sample on average scored only 12.7 or just under 61% of the maximum financial literacy score, which represents a basic set of knowledge concepts and financially prudent behaviours and attitudes. The average across participating OECD member countries is only marginally higher at 13.0 (62% of the maximum). The highest score achieved by any country or economy was 14.8 by Hong Kong, China, or 71% of the maximum, and a minimum of 11.1 was scored by Italy (53% of the maximum). The majority of economies (15) scored between 12 and 14.

(2020 survey, https://www.oecd.org/financial/education/oecd-infe-2020-international-survey-of-adult-financial-literacy.pdf.)

20 These two premises, according to which advice and information given by Staff has an impact on the consumers' decision and the more K&C the Staff has the more positive the impact will be, will not be challenged and will be accepted as truthful for the purposes of this chapter. The reasons that led to this choice are, on the one hand, of practical nature (space and research limitations) and, on the other hand, the result of the fact that it is possible to affirm that the existing literature on the subject offers good reasons for the acceptance of such premises. See, amongst others, N. Chater, S. Huck, and R. Inderst, *Consumer Decision-Making in Retail Investment Services: A Behavioural Economics Perspective* (European Commission, 2010), in particular 6–10 and 169 and ff. Last accessed August 28, 2024. https://www.dectech.co.uk/behavioural_science/public_research/dectech_research_ec.pdf. For the perception of the Portuguese reality, V. Costa, and C. Lopes, "O Meu Banco Aconselhou-me: A Importância da Confiança nas Escolhas Financeiras," In *Famílias Endividadas: Uma abordagem de economia política e comportamental*, Org. A.C. Santos (Almedina, 2015), in particular 108 and f.

21 Annex III of the MCD states as follows:

1. The minimum knowledge and competence requirements for creditors', credit intermediaries' and appointed representatives' staff referred to in Article 9 and for persons involved in the management of credit intermediaries or appointed representatives referred to in point (c) of Article 29(2) and Article 31(2) need to include at least: (a) appropriate knowledge of credit products within the scope of Article 3 and the ancillary services typically offered with them; (b) appropriate knowledge of the laws related to the credit agreements for consumers, in particular consumer protection; (c) appropriate knowledge and understanding of the immovable property purchasing process; (d) appropriate knowledge of security valuation; (e) appropriate knowledge of organisation and functioning of land registers; (f) appropriate knowledge of the market in the relevant Member State; (g) appropriate knowledge of business ethics standards; (h) appropriate knowledge of the consumer's creditworthiness assessment process or where applicable, competence in assessing consumers' creditworthiness; (i) appropriate level of financial and economic competency." 2. When establishing minimum knowledge and competence requirements Member States may differentiate between the levels and types of requirements applicable to the staff of creditors, the staff of credit intermediaries or appointed representatives and the management of credit intermediaries or appointed representatives. 3. Member States shall determine the appropriate level of knowledge and competence on the basis of: (a) professional qualifications, e.g. diplomas, degrees, training, competency tests; or (b) professional experience, which may be defined as a minimum number of years working in areas related to the origination, distribution or intermediation of credit products. After 21 March 2019, the determination of the appropriate level of knowledge and competence shall not be based solely on the methods listed in point (b) of the first subparagraph.

22 Paragraphs 79 to 81 of the Guidelines, regarding resources and skills of the institutions, state the following:

Institutions should have sufficient resources and staff allocated to credit risk taking and, in particular, credit decision-making, credit risk management and internal control.

The organisational structure should be reviewed periodically to ensure that there are adequate resources, competencies and expertise within the credit risk management functions to effectively manage credit risk. Institutions should ensure that the staff members involved in credit granting, in particular decision-making, risk management and internal control, have an appropriate level of experience, skills and credit-related competence. Staff involved in credit granting, including credit decision-making, credit risk management and internal control, should frequently receive appropriate training, which includes considering changes to the applicable legal and regulatory frameworks. Training should be aligned with the institutions' credit culture and business strategy and should be conducted on a regular basis to ensure that all relevant staff are appropriately skilled and familiar with the institutions' credit policies, procedures and processes.

Available at https://www.eba.europa.eu/sites/default/documents/files/document_library/Publications/Guidelines/2020/Guidelines%20on%20loan%20origination%20and%20monitoring/884283/EBA%20GL%202020%2006%20Final%20Report%20on%20GL%20on%20loan%20origination%20and%20monitoring.pdf).

23 Available at https://www.esma.europa.eu/sites/default/files/library/esma71-1154262120-153_guidelines_for_the_assessment_of_knowledge_and_competence_corrigendum.pdf.

24 Report available in full at https://op.europa.eu/en/publication-detail/-/publication/e4a1db26–2f94–11eb-b27b-01aa75ed71a1.

25 In the "Report from the Commission to the European Parliament and the Council on the review of the Directive 2014/17/EU of the European Parliament and of the Council on credit agreements for consumers relating to residential immovable property," dated May 11, 2021 (COM(2021) 229 final), the conclusion stated by the Commission is the following:

Knowledge and competence of staff. The results of the RPA study indicate that the MCD requirements on knowledge and competence of staff (Article 9 and Annex III) may have led to an increase in the level of competence of creditors' staff, in turn contributing to a higher level of professionalism. Most surveyed consumers believed that the staff employed by creditors and credit intermediaries have a suitable level of knowledge and competence. Industry stakeholders indicated that there had been an increase in training costs as a result of the Directive. In this context, it was noted that creditors are increasingly relying on robo advisers.

26 See p. 213 and f. of the "Evaluation of the Mortgage Credit Directive (Directive 2014/17/EU) Final report – Technical Annexes" ("Report"):

At the EU27 level, 80% of respondents agree that the staff employed by mortgage credit providers (e.g. banks) and intermediaries (e.g. mortgage brokers) have an adequate level of knowledge and competence to advise consumers (54% somewhat agree and further 24% strongly agree). 13% of consumers disagree with this statement, out of which 10% somewhat disagree and 3% strongly disagree. The biggest proportions of consumers who agree with the fact that the staff employed by mortgage credit providers and intermediaries have an adequate level of knowledge and competence are located in Finland (87%), Estonia (86%) and Malta (86%). Large shares of consumers disagree in countries such as Croatia (18%), Austria (17%) and Italy (17%). . . . the most frequently reported reasons among consumers who disagree with the statement that the staff employed by mortgage credit providers and intermediaries have an adequate level of knowledge and competence to advise consumers are the fact that the staff may not have enough relevant knowledge/training. Salespeople with the aim of selling products and unreliability have also been reported frequently by the consumers. Finally, a small number of consumers have indicated that they think that staff are not listening to the clients and that the explanations are not sufficiently clear."

Available at https://op.europa.eu/en/publication-detail/-/publication/80baa5d4–9c04–11eb-b85c-01aa75ed71a1/language-en/format-PDF/source-search.

27 See p. 263 of the Report:

Staff were considered knowledgeable and competent in 50% of cases for creditors and in 62% of cases for credit intermediaries. In Spain and Germany, creditors were much less likely to be viewed as knowledgeable and competent (none of the creditors in Spain, and only 20% in Germany).

Available at https://op.europa.eu/en/publication-detail/-/publication/80baa5d4–9c04–11eb-b85c-01aa75ed71a1/language-en/format-PDF/source-search.

28 See p. 264 of the Report, https://op.europa.eu/en/publication-detail/-/publication/80baa5d4–9c04–11eb-b85c-01aa75ed71a1/language-en/format-PDF/source-search.

29 See p. 194 of the Report:

The main problems encountered prior to implementation of the MCD were associated with the information being difficult to understand and not adequately explained to the consumers. These have also been the most frequently reported issues after the implementation of the MCD.

Available at https://op.europa.eu/en/publication-detail/-/publication/80baa5d4–9c04–11eb-b85c-01aa75ed71a1/language-en/format-PDF/source-search.

30 See p. 19 of the summary of the survey, https://europa.eu/eurobarometer/surveys/detail/2953.

31 Ibidem.

32 See section 77 of the "Opinion of the European Banking Authority on the European Commission request for technical advice on issues related to the Mortgage Credit Directive":

77. The EBA also proposed that the Directive should also strengthen the knowledge and competences requirements of creditors' staff involved in the commercialization of mortgage credit and taking into account consumers' financial education when advertising the product. The EBA is of the view that the revised MCD should also include an adequate provision of debt advisory services in alignment with the corresponding provision of the CCD.

Available at https://www.eba.europa.eu/sites/default/documents/files/document_library/Publications/Opinions/2022/Opinion%20on%20MCD%20review%20%28EBA-Op-2022–07%29/1036068/EBA%27s%20response%20to%20the%20EC%20Call%20for%20advice%20on%20the%20review%20of%20MCD.pdf.

33 OECD (2015) OECD/*INFE Toolkit for Measuring Financial Literacy and Financial inclusion*, and OECD (2018), OECD/INFE *Toolkit for Measuring Financial Literacy and Financial Inclusion*, http://www.oecd.org/financial/education/2018-INFE-FinLit-Measurement-Toolkit.pdf.

34 All reports of the surveys are https://clientebancario.bportugal.pt/pt-pt/publicacao/relatorio-do-inquerito-literacia-financeira-da-populacao-portuguesa–2023.

35 See p. 14 of the survey, https://www.oecd.org/publications/oecd-infe-2023-international-survey-of-adult-financial-literacy-56003a32-en.htm.

36 See p. 14 of the survey, https://www.oecd.org/publications/oecd-infe-2023-international-survey-of-adult-financial-literacy-56003a32-en.htm.

37 See p. 16 of the survey, https://www.oecd.org/financial/education/oecd-infe-2020-international-survey-of-adult-financial-literacy.pdf.

38 See chart 1, "Financial literacy of the general public by Euro area Member State," of the ECB's "Communication with the Wider Public," published as part of the ECB Economic Bulletin, Issue 8/2021. https://www.ecb.europa.eu/press/economic-bulletin/html/eb202108.en.html.

39 Survey results and data, https://europa.eu/eurobarometer/surveys/detail/2953.

40 Data from the Bank of Portugal. https://bpstat.bportugal.pt/dados/series?mode=graphic&svid=4709&series=12710765,12710766,12710767.

41 See data, https://www.pordata.pt/portugal/montantes+de+emprestimos+concedidos+no+ano+a+particulares+total+e+por+tipo+de+finalidade-2844–244811.

References

Balloch, A., A. Nicolae, and D. Philip. "Stock Market Literacy, Trust, and Participation." *Review of Finance* 19, no. 5 (2015): 1925–63.
Hogarth, Jeanne, and Federal Board. "Financial Education and Economic Development." 2006. https://www.oecd.org/finance/financial-education/37742200.pdf.
Klapper L. F., A. Lusardi, and G.A. Panos. "Financial Literacy and the Financial Crisis." National Bureau of Economic Research, Working Paper 2012/17930.
Lusardi, A., and O.S. Mitchell. "The Economic Importance of Financial Literacy: Theory and Evidence." *Journal of Economic Literature* 52, no. 1 (March 2014): 5–44.

4 Blacklisting defaulting consumers in credit information registers – lessons from Estonia and Finland*

Anu Kaup and Karin Sein

1. Introduction

As Advocate General (AG) Pikamäe noted in his opinion for the joined cases C-26/22 and C-64/22, mutual confidence forms the basis for any contractual commitment in a market economy. Therefore, from a business point of view, it is understandable that providers of goods and services wish to know about their clients and the risks inherent in such contractual commitment.[1] Credit-scoring providers and credit registries provide such information either by issuing a credit score or in a less sophisticated way, that is, by disclosing information about consumers' payment defaults in the publicly accessible credit information registers. Publishing such negative information that we can also call 'blacklisting' has a direct impact on a consumer's ability to obtain credit, rent a home, get a mobile phone or Internet subscription, or buy items of high value such as a house or a car. Blacklisting consumers in the credit information registers may, therefore, lead to their financial exclusion.

This chapter discusses the rules and practices regarding the disclosure of information on payment defaults in credit information registers and its impact on consumers' (privacy) rights in two small neighbouring EU Member States with close economic and personal relations – Estonia and Finland. The contribution is structured as follows. It begins by describing the general practices on the disclosure of payment defaults in Estonia and Finland and explains why the publication of these defaults constitutes a (privacy) problem for the consumers (2.). It then describes the Estonian and Finnish specific domestic regulations on payment default disclosure that complement the General Data Protection Regulation[2] (GDPR) (3.). After that, the chapter compares the rules of both countries regarding the disclosure of the payment default information as data processing. More specifically, subchapters (4.) – (6.) compare and assess the periods related to the publication of payment defaults under Estonian and Finnish law. Finally, it is asked whether the Estonian regulation that allows for extremely long publication periods is in conformity with the GDPR (7.). The chapter concludes (8.) that after the recent reform, the Finnish regulation is much more consumer-friendly than the Estonian one and that on the background of the recent case law of the Court of Justice of the European Union (CJEU), the Estonian regulation cannot be considered in conformity with the GDPR.

DOI: 10.4324/9781003510406-6

2. The practice of blacklisting defaulting consumers and why it is a (privacy) problem

A payment default is a failure by the debtor to meet a financial obligation. Information on payment defaults usually includes details about the person of the debtor, the amount of the debt together with any ancillary claims, the time of the default, and the type of the underlying transaction. For consumers, payment default information may also include the debtor's name and date of birth or the personal identification (ID) number. All this information constitutes personal data within the meaning of Article 4(1) of the GDPR. In Estonia and Finland, data on payment defaults is disclosed[3] in credit information registers, or digital databases. Both in Estonia and Finland, these registers are operated by private sector players.

The similarities in the Estonian and Finnish practices can be explained by the strong economic and social links between the two countries: tens of thousands of people have moved either from Estonia to Finland or vice versa, and some people have not moved but have close ties through work, study, or business in another country.[4] In many cases, debts incurred in one country are bought by the debt recovery companies and disclosed by them in the other country. For example, Estonian debt recovery companies have bought unpaid parking fines issued by Finnish parking operators against Estonian consumers and disclosed these payment defaults in Estonian credit information registries.[5] It should be stressed that disclosing payment default data is a growing concern in both countries. In Finland, the number of individuals with at least one payment default has risen steadily since 2010, amounting to 388 000 persons in 2021.[6] In Estonia, more than 65% of debtors had more than one payment default in 2023.[7]

The primary purpose of credit information registries and their publication of payment defaults is to provide information about a person's payment behaviour, enable the assessment of their creditworthiness, and thereby contribute to responsible lending or otherwise raise the reliability of commercial transactions. Whereas the obligation to assess a consumer's creditworthiness[8] is considered an important consumer protection measure under EU consumer law,[9] disclosure of payment defaults is a two-bladed sword as it can also be misused as a coercion measure and lead to the financial exclusion of defaulting consumers. In Estonia, for example, the largest credit-scoring provider's webpage provides a link to the webpage of a credit comparison portal stating that 'It is practically impossible to get a loan in Estonia if you have a blacklisted default payment or a bad credit rating.'[10] Whereas this statement is indeed not true in all cases – numerous case law in the Estonian courts tells about credit providers issuing credit to many non-creditworthy consumers – it still indicates the importance of having a good credit history. Similarly, the Finnish Financial Supervisory Authority stresses that a payment default indicates that a person has a significantly higher credit risk. Based on experience, Finnish credit institutions believe that a person with a payment default should not be granted a loan because of their high credit risk.[11]

Disclosure of payment defaults not only raises the risk of negative creditworthiness assessment but can also lead to a consumer's reputational or even financial loss. A glimpse into the Estonian case law also shows that debt recovery companies often use public pressure and stigmatization to motivate consumers to pay off their debts:[12] in addition to publishing the names of debtors in newspapers or on particular websites, there have been cases where debtors' names were printed on giant posters hanging on the walls of several-story buildings or large posters in the centre of the Estonian capital Tallinn.[13]

3. Discretion left to the member states under the GDPR

3.1 Requirements of the GDPR for domestic provisions

Although the GDPR is a directly applicable EU secondary law and, in principle, Member States are not competent to legislate in matters subject to an EU regulation, under certain conditions, Member States have the discretion to maintain, establish, and specify domestic rules on the processing of personal data. Member States are allowed to introduce national regulations, particularly on issues where the GDPR itself does not provide a clear answer.[14] According to Article 6(2) of the GDPR, Member States may maintain or introduce more specific provisions for the fulfillment of Article 6(1)(c) and (e) of the GDPR, that is, where the processing is necessary for compliance with a legal obligation to which the controller is subject or where the processing is necessary for the performance of a task carried out in the public interest or the exercise of official authority vested in the controller. Article 6(3) of the GDPR specifies that the basis for processing personal data referred to in these points is established either by Union law or by the law of the Member State to which the controller is subject.[15] The specific standards laid down by the Member State must be in accordance with the public interest objective and proportionate to the legitimate aim pursued. When disclosing information on payment defaults, even if there is a legal basis for processing personal data, the disclosure of the data must additionally comply with the principles set out in Article 5(1) of the GDPR, which include verifying the accuracy of the data disclosed, informing the data subject of the disclosure, and collecting as little data as possible.

In the Member States covered in this chapter – Estonia and Finland – data processing related to creditworthiness assessment and disclosure of payment default data has, to varying degrees, been specifically regulated in national law. However, a closer comparison reveals that Finnish legislation is much more consumer- and privacy-friendly after the recent legislative reforms than Estonian legislation. The comparison starts with a general description of the legal situation in both countries and then moves on to analyse its specific details.

3.2 Finnish law

Finnish domestic rules on the protection of personal data related to consumer credit are found in the Finnish Data Protection Act[16] and the Credit Information Act

(CIA).[17] As noted, Finland has recently undergone legislative reforms concerning the disclosure of payment defaults. These reforms included the following changes:

- Alignment of the Credit Information Act with the GDPR;[18] the amendments entered into force in two phases on June 1, 2022, and December 1, 2022;
- Shortening of the publication period for payment defaults;[19] the amendments entered into force on June 1, 2022;[20] and
- Creation of a positive credit information register; the first phase of the reform came into force on August 1, 2022,[21] and the entire reform must be completed by April 1, 2026.[22]

As part of reforming the CIA to bring it into line with the GDPR, its compliance with the requirements of the GDPR and the complementary national Data Protection Act was assessed. The reform aimed to minimise duplication of the provisions of the GDPR.[23] On the other hand, new provisions have been inserted where the previous law was too general. For example, §§ 12 and 13 of the CIA restrict the content of data in credit information registers to limit the content to information relevant to creditworthiness assessment. The law further regulates who and under which conditions may obtain information about data subject's payment defaults: § 10 of the CIA stipulates that a credit information provider may not refuse to supply credit information from a public credit register to a person who is required by law to use the credit information to decide on an individual or an undertaking. However, the person requesting the personal credit information must provide the evidence necessary to establish the legal basis of the disclosure (i.e., data processing).

3.3 Estonian law

In Estonia, the Estonian Data Protection Act (DPA)[24] supplements and specifies the rules of the General Data Protection Regulation on the protection of data subjects.[25] Among other things, it contains a specific provision regulating the processing of personal data concerning payment default and creditworthiness assessment: according to § 10(1) of the DPA, transmission of personal data related to a breach of an obligation to third parties and processing of the transmitted data by a third party is permitted for the purpose of data subject's creditworthiness assessment or any other similar purpose, and only if the data controller has verified the accuracy of the personal data transmitted and the legal basis for transmission of personal data, and has registered the data transmission. According to the explanatory memorandum to the Data Protection Act, the Estonian domestic provision is based on Article 6(1)(e) of the GDPR, which allows Member States to establish a legal basis for the processing of personal data for the performance of a task carried out in the public interest. The explanatory memorandum clarifies that the need for domestic regulation is driven by the aim of ensuring the possibility of assessing the creditworthiness of individuals. The legislator saw the practical need to enable financial institutions and commercial entities to assess the reliability of the other party to a contract: the history of how the other party has performed their contractual obligations should give an important indication of their reliability for the future.[26]

In addition to the creditworthiness assessment, personal data related to the payment defaults may be used for 'other similar purposes.' Examples of other similar purposes given by the legislator are the assessment of a person's reliability when applying for employment or the verification of the solvency of tenants.[27] The explanatory memorandum of the Data Protection Act stresses that disclosure of payment history data to other persons is allowed without the consent of the individual to ensure the reliability of the transaction: the protection of contractual partners outweighs the protection of the debtor's privacy while, at the same time, trying to avoid undue harm to debtors.[28]

The law also foresees certain restrictions for publishing credit history data, that is, payment defaults. First, the person asking for such data must have a legal basis for it. According to the Estonian Data Protection Inspectorate, a legal basis may be a legitimate interest of the third party, such as their specific need to assess the creditworthiness of an individual. Personal data of private individuals cannot be disclosed to the public, that is, to an unspecified number of persons for the abstract purpose of 'evaluating the person' as such an interest is not sufficiently well-defined and specific.[29] When asking for the payment default data, the recipient of the data should briefly describe their legitimate interest, the contract or transaction they wish to conclude with the data subject, the timeframe in which they want to do so, and with what evidence, if any, they can demonstrate their legitimate interest.[30] Whether or not this is the everyday practice of credit information registers cannot be verified at this moment. Presumably, anyone can argue that they are planning to conclude a contract with the data subject without the credit information register being able to verify this.

In addition to the existence of a legal basis of the third party for data processing, the credit information register as the data controller must also verify the accuracy of the personal data transmitted to the third party. In other words, the credit register must check whether the debt existed in the first place. The Supreme Court has stressed the importance of this obligation and clarified that the data controller, or the credit information register, must be able to prove it. Moreover, to verify the data, such as the payment default, it is not sufficient to ask for confirmation from the creditor who originally submitted this data; instead, there must be accurate data confirming the existence of the debt.[31] The Estonian Data Protection Inspectorate argues that while data from public registers can be assumed correct, data on payment defaults from private parties must be verified.[32] Yet, a recent second-instance court decision found the Inspectorate's order for the credit information register to require all underlying documentation from the creditor as unproportionate.[33]

Finally, in some instances, § 10(2) of the DPA[34] forbids collecting and disclosing personal data to third parties for creditworthiness assessment or other similar purposes. First, it is precluded in case special categories of personal data within the meaning of Article 9(1) of the GDPR are processed. More importantly, § 10(2)(4) and (5) of the DPA set forth certain time restrictions related to the disclosure of payment defaults. The next subchapters will take a closer look at these time limits and compare the Estonian and Finnish approaches on how soon payment defaults can be disclosed, how long payment defaults can be disclosed after the debt has been paid, and under what circumstances can already be prescribed (but not paid) debts be disclosed to third parties.

4. How soon can payment defaults be disclosed?

4.1 Finnish law

Finnish law regulates the disclosure of payment default information in § 14 of the CIA. This provision allows the disclosure of payment default information in the credit information register if the credit payment is at least 60 days overdue unless the debtor and the creditor have concluded a new payment agreement after the original due date. In addition, under § 14(2)(2) of the CIA, the publication of information in the register is subject to the condition that the creditor has sent the debtor a written demand for payment, together with a reminder to pay the debt and notice that otherwise the default information will be sent to the credit information default register. This written reminder has to be sent to the debtor at least 21 days before the information is transmitted to the register.

Before June 1, 2022, the Credit Information Act also regulated the notification of the data subject of submitting payment default information to the credit information register. Still, during the reforms, the respective provisions were found to duplicate Articles 12 and 14 of the GDPR and were repealed.[35] The principles stemming from the GDPR are outlined, for example, on the website of the Office of the Finnish Data Protection Commissioner, which, among other things, emphasises that the controller must inform of any rectification of personal data in addition to the notification of the transfer of personal data.[36]

Finally, § 14(2)(1) of the CIA sets forth a specific provision allowing publishing payment defaults arising from a consumer credit agreement. Publishing such defaults is allowed only if the original consumer credit contract contains information about the possibility of submitting the payment default information to the credit information register.

4.2 Estonian law

According to § 10(2)(4) of the DPA, transferring personal data relating to a breach of an obligation to a third party and processing the transferred data by a third party is not permitted if less than 30 days have passed since the breach of contract. Compared to the Finnish law, the Estonian regulation is much less consumer-friendly: whereas in Finland, two months must pass before credit payment defaults can be disclosed, in Estonia, consumers can be blacklisted already when payment is one month overdue.

Furthermore, in contrast to Finnish law, § 10 of the DPA does not provide for an obligation to inform the data subject about the processing of personal data in connection with a breach of an obligation, and thus, there are no specific national rules in this respect. Without such specific rules, the obligation to inform the data subject follows from Articles 12–14 of the GDPR. Since payment default data are not collected from the data subject, as a rule, the obligation to inform the data subject stems from Article 14 of the GDPR. Under Article 14(3)(3) of the GDPR, the creditor must notify the data subject at the latest when he sends the payment default information to the credit information register; contrary to Finnish law, a previous reminder or contractual information about the possibility to disclose such payment default is not required. Moreover, Article 14(5) of the GDPR sets forth exceptions from the information obligation. The obligation to inform the data subject does not apply, for example, where the data subject already has the information or where the provision of information proves impossible or would involve a disproportionate effort.[37] In the opinion of the Estonian Data Protection Inspectorate, these two exceptions may be relevant in the context of the payment default data.[38]

The Inspectorate considers the first exception to be applicable in certain cases, such as where the identities of the creditor and the person disclosing the data (i.e., the credit information register) do not coincide and the creditor has already informed the data subject about the disclosure of the payment default data to the register. However, to fulfill the information requirements, the Inspectorate considers it necessary that the privacy policy of the credit information register accompany such notification of the data subject. Moreover, the notification and the disclosure must have a temporal link, that is, it is not permissible for the initial credit agreement to refer to the possible transmission of data to the credit information register but not to inform the person when the payment default is disclosed as the debtor may not even be aware that he is in default (for example, the invoice might have been sent to a wrong address).[39]

Second, the provision of information may be impossible or require disproportionate efforts within the meaning of Article 14(5)(b) GDPR in situations where the data controller does not have the debtor's contact details. The Inspectorate holds that credit information registers should not collect additional personal data solely to fulfill the information obligation. However, if the register as a data controller has the debtor's contact details, they must be informed of the processing, for example, the disclosure of the payment default.[40] The Estonian Supreme Court has also ruled that if the creditor has not informed the debtor of the disclosure of the default, this must be done by the register.[41] Yet, as the Data Protection Inspectorate has identified in several supervisory proceedings, some credit information registers have pointed out that they do not inform debtors separately about processing their personal data and that the debtors should obtain this information from the privacy policies published on the registers' websites.[42]

5. Disclosing payment defaults after the debt has been paid: when must payment default data be deleted from the register?

5.1 Finnish law

In recent years, Finnish legislator has constantly focused on shortening the disclosure periods for payment default information of natural persons. In 2020, in connection with the Finnish Ministry of Justice initiative to create a positive credit register, the shortening of the disclosure periods of payment default information was envisaged.[43] However, the increased over-indebtedness of consumers resulting from the COVID-19 crisis led the Ministry of Justice to launch a separate study to assess whether it could shorten the disclosure periods for defaulted payments even before introducing a positive credit register.[44]

On the one hand, the Finnish government considered the need for creditors to have access to relevant payment information as the feedback of the stakeholders stressed the need for creditors for the assessment and management of credit risks as lenders have a statutory duty to assess the creditworthiness of the credit applicant.[45] Some experts consulted during the law preparation believed that the one-month retention period proposed by the government was too short. Instead, retention periods of three months, six months, or one year after the debt has been paid were suggested. The proposed longer disclosure periods were justified by the argument that removing the payment default information gives rise to the possibility of new debts which could worsen the debtor's problems.[46] On the other hand, the need to support persons in financial difficulties was considered as well, as some stakeholders argued that in a situation where a one-off default is due to a temporary impediment of the person to pay on time, it would be unfair if the non-payment continues to constitute a default after the debt has been discharged.[47]

Finally, instead of the previous two-year disclosure period of payment defaults after the discharge of the debt, a one-month period was agreed upon: the new § 18 of the CIA foresees that payment default information must be deleted within one month from the date of receipt of information on the settlement of the debt. The new regulation allowing for a 'clean' credit history already within one month after the debt has been paid is applicable in Finland since December 1, 2022.

5.2 Estonian law

According to § 10(2)(5) of the DPA, the transfer of personal data relating to a breach of an obligation to a third party and the processing of the transferred data by a third party is not permitted if more than five years have passed since the end of the breach of the obligation. Consequently, Estonian law allows the disclosure of the payment default for five years after the debt has been paid; only after five years must such data be deleted. It is worth mentioning that before the entry into force of the General Data Protection Regulation and, consequently, the adoption of the new Data Protection Act, payment defaults could be disclosed for up to three years from the end of the breach. Hence, the data subject's situation has worsened compared to the pre-GDPR era. The reasons for extending the period for data disclosure remain unclear, and the explanatory memorandum to the draft Data Protection Act only explains that the period for data processing has been extended and that the time limit has been set at five years.[48]

The Estonian Data Protection Inspectorate stresses that the five-year time limit referred to in § 10(2)(5) of the DPA is a maximum and not an automatic time limit for the disclosure of payment default after the breach of the obligation has ended, that is, after the debt has been paid. According to the Inspectorate, publishing payment default information for a maximum period of five years is only allowed in case of the most severe breaches.[49] Since a short delay in payment may happen for a valid reason, it would be unreasonable to disclose information on a person's payment default for five years if they paid the debt immediately after being reminded of the default. Therefore, a further assessment must be made as to whether the disclosure of the data could excessively prejudice the rights or freedoms of the data subject within the meaning of § 10(2)(3) of the DPA. According to the Data Protection Inspectorate, this assessment should consider all circumstances of the data subject.[50] This includes the number and amounts of the debts, the time of the defaults, and the absence of new debts indicating that the person has changed their payment behaviour. Thus, in the case of a single small amount owed years ago, the interference with the debtor's privacy rights is relatively high, and disclosing such a default would be excessively detrimental to the data subject.[51] The Estonian Supreme Court has also confirmed that when assessing the detriment to the data subject's interests under § 10(2)(3) of the DPA, the amount and circumstances of the occurrence of the debt must be taken into account.[52]

However, the survey carried out by the Estonian Data Protection Inspectorate has shown that, in practice, the credit information registers disclosing the payment defaults do not make such an assessment and only follow the maximum time limit of five years.[53] For example, on the website of the credit information register Julianus Inkasso, it was in 2024 explicitly stated that the creditor has the right to publish debt information for up to five years after the debt has been discharged.[54] The Estonian credit information registers thus fail to assess the seriousness of the debtor's breach and the privacy implications of disclosing the payment default data, putting consumers who have voluntarily paid their debts at a disadvantage compared to those who have made no effort to do so.

6. Disclosing payment defaults in case of prescribed debts

6.1 Finnish law

Another considerable difference in treating consumer's privacy concerns the disclosure of payment defaults in case of prescribed debts. According to § 4 of the Limitation of Debts Act,[55] the general prescription period for contractual claims in Finland is three years. According to §§ 5–6 of the Limitation of Debts Act, the prescription period starts to run from the moment the claim becomes due if a payment deadline has been fixed in advance. If the due date for payment of the purchase price or other consideration is not fixed in advance, the prescription period starts to run from when the seller has delivered the sale's object to the buyer or when the other party has performed its obligation. The general three-year prescription period has been in force in Finland for 20 years – since April 1, 2004. Before that, the general prescription period was 10 years.[56] The maximum prescription period for a claim arising from a contract concluded with a natural person is 20 years.[57]

According to § 14 of the Limitation of Debts Act, the legal consequence of the prescription is the termination of the debtor's obligation to pay. This consequence differs from the German or Estonian solution, where the prescription only gives the debtor a legal ground to refuse payment permanently but does not end the obligation.[58] The Finnish law is, therefore, more debtor-friendly as the debtor does not need to rely upon the prescription in the court proceedings, but rather, the statute of limitation brings about the end of the legal obligation *ipso iure*.

The recovery of prescribed debts in Finland is governed by the Debt Recovery Act,[59] § 4 of which provides that prescribed debts cannot be recovered. More importantly, according to § 31 of the CIA, the payment default must be deleted without undue delay if the debt has been prescribed. Consequently, under Finnish law, prescribed debts may not be published in the credit information register. This means that, as a rule, the data subject will have a 'clean' credit history after three years since the payment was due. As we will see next, this differs considerably from the Estonian situation.

6.2 Estonian law

Whereas the legal situation concerning the publication of prescribed debts is relatively straightforward under Finnish law – as noted previously, Finnish law forbids publishing prescribed debts in the credit information register – the situation is much more complicated in Estonia. The complications derive, first, from the fact that under Estonian law, the statute of limitation does not bring about the termination of the debt but only gives the debtor a permanent defense to refuse payment, and second, from the rather vague and failed wording of the law. Estonian law has no precise regulation regarding how long data on payment default can be disclosed when a debt is outstanding but time-barred. Two different time limits are relevant for disclosing data on payment defaults – the statute of limitations and the time limit for processing personal data. In Estonia, there are different interpretations of the combined effect of these time limits, which the authors will describe in the following.

Similarly to the Finnish regulation, under § 146(1) of the General Part of the Civil Code Act (GPCCA),[60] the general limitation period for contractual claims is three years. Under Estonian law, the legal consequence of prescription is transforming a real obligation into an incomplete obligation: the creditor may claim the performance of an incomplete obligation, and the debtor may also fulfill it but is not obliged to do so.[61] According to § 142(1) of the GPCCA, the debtor may refuse to perform an obligation after the claim has become time-barred. Consequently, it is up to the debtor to choose whether or not to exercise the defense of prescription; the court is not entitled to apply prescription *ex officio*.

This legal consequence of the statute of limitation creates problems in the context of the publication of payment defaults. § 10(2)(5) of the Estonian DPA allows publication of payment default data if no more than five years have passed since the end of the breach of the obligation. The problem is how to interpret the words 'since the end of the breach of the obligation' as, according to the civil law understanding, the statute of limitation does not bring about the end of the obligation. Creditors, debt recovery companies, and credit register providers have, therefore, argued that they are entitled to publish and recover prescribed debts.[62] Indeed, back in 2011, the Supreme Court confirmed that the provision concerns the termination of the breach of the obligation and not the prescription period: according to the Supreme Court, a prescription cannot be considered a ground for ending the breach of an obligation within the meaning of this provision. However, the prescription may be taken into account when considering the harm to the data subject's legitimate interests under § 11(7)(2)[63] of the DPA. The Supreme Court held that the longer the period over which personal data are processed, the more the data subject's fundamental rights, particularly his or her right to privacy, are affected.[64] According to the Supreme Court, publishing payment defaults after 13 years since the claim became due is presumably unduly detrimental to the data subject's legitimate interests, as a breach of contractual obligations is not a long-lasting negative characterisation of a person's credibility.[65] The position of the Supreme Court under the previous Data Protection Act was, hence, a relatively relaxed one and, in essence, only restricted the publication of ancient debts. However, several first-instance courts have recently ruled that publishing prescribed payment defaults for more than five years is disproportionate for the debtor and, therefore, illegitimate under § 10(2)(3) of the DPA.[66] Tallinn District Court recently confirmed the same.[67]

The Estonian Data Protection Inspectorate takes a slightly different stance and argues that if the debt is unpaid but is time-barred according to the three-year limitation period under § 146(1) of the GPCCA, the maximum five-year period under § 10(2)(5) of the DPA applies to the disclosure of the payment default data. This means that the so-called 3+5 rule applies, with the result that, as a maximum, the disclosure of payment default information is allowed for eight years since the prescription period started to run. The Data Protection Inspectorate bases its position on the argument that otherwise unpaid but prescribed debts could be published indefinitely, which would be unproportionate. In addition, the Inspectorate thinks that disclosing prescribed debts is subject to additional requirements, such as active steps taken by the creditor to recover the debt during the prescription period. Otherwise, the disclosure of the payment default would constitute a retaliatory measure to recover the debt without the creditor attempting to use the legal remedies available to him during the prescription period.[68] The Data Protection Inspectorate's interpretation is supported by the position of the Tallinn District Court, according to which the fact that the creditor has actively taken steps to recover the debt during the prescription period is of significant importance in assessing the proportionality of the disclosure of the payment default under § 10(2)(3) of the DPA.[69]

It should be noted that for intentional breaches of contractual claims, § 146(4) of the GPCCA sets forth a specific prescription period of ten years. The burden of proof that the breach was intentional rests with the creditor.[70] According to the Estonian Data Protection Inspectorate, the intentionally breached obligation may be disclosed within ten years plus the five years resulting from § 10(2)(5) of the DPA (10+5 rule). To prove the existence of wilfulness, the data controller must rely on specific facts confirming the intentional breach of the obligation, such as a court judgment.[71] It is worth mentioning that under Estonian case law, it is difficult to prove the intentional breach within the meaning of § 146(4) of the GPCCA.

The Supreme Court has ruled that the debtor's intention cannot be inferred from the mere fact that the creditor has continuously demanded repayment of the loan from the debtor over the years, but the debtor has not fulfilled its obligation. An intentional breach of an obligation within the meaning of § 146(4) of the GPCCA presupposes that the debtor intends to achieve an unlawful result and deliberately acts in bad faith. Therefore, applying the 10-year limitation period presumes that the party has breached its obligation intentionally and in bad faith[72] and can only be considered in rather exceptional cases.

However, the practice of debt recovery companies and credit information registers is the opposite, as they generally apply the 10+5 years rule. For example, the website of the debt recovery company/credit register provider Julianus Inkasso stated still in 2024 that payment default data may be published in the register if the outstanding invoice is not older than 15 years and even claimed that such practice is in line with the General Data Protection Regulation, the Estonian Data Protection Act, and the guidelines of the Estonian Data Protection Inspectorate.[73] This statement contradicts at least the guidelines of the Estonian Data Protection Inspectorate, which clearly state that it is not correct to equate the non-payment of debt with the intentional breach of obligation and thereby justify the publication of the payment default for 15 years.[74]

The Estonian Data Protection Inspectorate has observed that, in practice, debt recovery companies use the publication of payment default data in credit information registers as a coercive mechanism for the payment of smaller overdue debts. For example, the registers deliberately disclose prescribed debts of less than €100, which the consumer may not even be aware of and are obviously not indicative of the consumer's payment behaviour. Such defaults are not disclosed to provide information on creditworthiness but as a means of coercion to recover debts.[75] As to such practices, there is a very interesting recent development in the case law at the level of the second instance court in Tallinn. Namely, Tallinn District Court has ruled at least twice that threatening a person with the publication of a prescribed debt in the credit information register constitutes an intentional act against good morals within the meaning of § 1045(1)(8) of the Law of Obligations Act[76] (LOA) triggering non-contractual liability of the debt recovery company. The Court held that such threats do not constitute a standard debt recovery procedure and violate good morals. Consequently, the debt recovery companies have been held liable for the pre-trial legal costs of the natural person.[77] These decisions have entered into force, which means that they were either not referred to the Supreme Court or that the Supreme Court agreed with the second instance court and saw no need to review it. Until now, there has been no case law on whether such disclosure of prescribed debts or the threatening with it can constitute unfair commercial practices.[78]

7. Is the Estonian law in conformity with the GDPR?

The extended disclosure deadlines of § 10(2) of the Estonian DPA provoke the question about its GDPR conformity. As described before, national legislators enjoy broad discretion under Article 6(2) and (3) of the GDPR to introduce more specific provisions on data processing in their national laws, including in cases where the legal basis for data processing is Article 6(1)(e) GDPR, that is, where processing is necessary for the performance of a task carried out in the public interest. Under Article 6(3) third sentence of the GDPR, these specific domestic provisions may, *inter alia*, concern the storage periods.

Indeed, according to the explanatory memorandum, the Estonian legislator based § 10 DPA on Article 6(1)(e) GDPR, referring to the public interest basis. More specifically, the explanatory memorandum argues that:

> *Financial sector companies clearly have a public task to assess creditworthiness, meaning there is a legal basis for processing personal data under sectoral legislation. . . . In practice, information related to a breach of obligation is used not only to assess creditworthiness but also in other cases, such as to assess a person's credibility when applying for a job or before entering into a contractual relationship with them, as well as to check the solvency of borrowers or tenants. The assessment of creditworthiness is essential and protects the public interest, but the other examples given above are also based on the public interest and, therefore, have the same essential purpose.*[79]

Even when agreeing with the argument that credit information registries perform a public task[80] and, hence, the data processing can be based on the legal basis of Article 6(1)(e) of the GDPR combined with the more specific provisions of national law, these national provisions must still comply with the restrictions under Article 6(3) of the GDPR. In accordance with Article 6(3) of the GDPR, the basis for the processing referred to in Article 6(1)(e) of the GDPR is to be defined by Member State law, which must meet an objective of public interest and be proportionate to the legitimate aim pursued. Finally, the necessity criterion of Article 6(1)(e) of the GDPR should not be forgotten: data processing must be necessary to perform the task in the public interest. It is questionable whether the Estonian legislation, which, at least according to its wording, allows disclosing consumer payment defaults even after they are prescribed and, in some instances, up to 15 years complies with these criteria.

Already, the necessity and public interest criteria are problematic. Whereas creditworthiness assessment and creating mutual confidence when concluding contractual relationships is well in the public interest, it is at least questionable whether disclosing excessive information on consumers' past and already expired debts can contribute to such confidence. In other words, is such disclosure necessary to create mutual confidence in contractual relations and assess consumer's creditworthiness? Does the fact that I failed to pay a parking ticket seven years ago really say anything about my creditworthiness today? Most probably, it does not. Moreover, according to the case law of the CJEU, the concept of 'necessity' must be interpreted narrowly.[81] Under the narrow interpretation, disclosing such payment default data for years after the debt is already paid or even expired is not necessary to carry out a creditworthiness assessment, and this alone renders the Estonian legislation to conflict with Article 6(1)(e) and 6(3) of the GDPR.

The same is true for the proportionality criterion. The Court of Justice has elaborated on the proportionality test of Article 6(3) of the GDPR in case C-184/20, explaining that to assess the proportionality of the data processing, it is necessary to measure the seriousness of the interference with the fundamental rights to respect for private life and to the protection of personal data that that processing involves and to determine whether the importance of the objective of general interest pursued by the processing is proportionate to the seriousness of the interference.[82] In other words, the seriousness of the privacy interference must be weighed against the importance of its aim. To assess the severity of the interference, account must be taken, among other things, of the nature of the personal data at issue, in particular of any sensitivity of those data, and of the nature of, and specific methods for, the processing of the data at issue, in particular of the number of persons having access to those data and the methods of accessing them.[83] Or, as put by AG Pikamäe in his opinion on the SCHUFA case:

> *the more easily accessible the information is to the public, the more serious the interference with the fundamental rights of the data subject. This is particularly so where a large number of users have access to the data of the data subject.*[84]

In Estonia, information on payment defaults can be obtained by almost anyone ready to pay a modest fee for the inquiry and argue that he or she wants to conclude a contract with the data subject. Moreover, the information can be obtained online, which further reduces the barriers. Finally, there is the timeline argument used by the CJEU in the SCHUFA case, although within the context of the legitimate interest test: the Court stated that

> *the longer the data in question is stored by credit information agencies, the greater the impact on the interests and private life of the data subject and the greater the requirements relating to the lawfulness of the storage of that information.*[85]

The extremely long processing deadlines under Estonian law – in many cases up to 15 years – profoundly impact consumers' interests and private lives, not least as they prevent them from re-entering the economic life. Taken together, the seriousness of interference with the right to privacy does not outweigh the importance of the objective of creating mutual confidence when entering business relationships. Consequently, there are good arguments to claim that § 10 of the Estonian DPA as it stands is not in conformity with the GDPR, particularly with its Article 6.

8. Conclusions

The recent judgment of the CJEU in the SCHUFA case illustrates the tension between consumer protection and data protection. On the one hand, to prevent consumers' over-indebtedness, creditors offering consumer credit are obliged to assess consumers' creditworthiness and decline credit to consumers who are unlikely to be able to repay it. Information on a consumer's previous payment defaults often provides valuable information about the person's payment habits and credibility. On the other hand, a disclosed payment default will negatively affect a consumer's creditworthiness and, consequently, their possibility of obtaining credit, and it may also damage their good name. In Finland and Estonia, privately owned credit information registers disclose payment defaults of consumers for their financial reliability assessment. As the GDPR does not set specific time limits for storing and disclosing personal data relating to payment defaults, both countries have enacted specific domestic legislation regulating such data processing.

A comparison between these neighbouring jurisdictions reveals that after the recent legislative reforms, Finnish legislation is much more consumer- and privacy-friendly than Estonian legislation. To start with, under Finnish law, consumer credit payment defaults can only be disclosed if 60 days have passed from the date when the payment became due and if, additionally, a written reminder has been sent to the consumer. By contrast, Estonian law allows disclosure of payment default already after 30 days, and no reminder or additional payment period is required. Whereas the new Finnish law entitles the data subject to a 'clean' credit history already within one month after they have paid the debt, the Estonian law allows the disclosure of the payment default as long as for five years after the debt has been paid. Finally, prescribed debts must not be disclosed under Finnish law. Under Estonian law, the legal situation is quite different: disclosure of prescribed debts is not precluded by the law, and in some instances, payment defaults may be disclosed even up to 15 years.

The extremely long disclosure time limits under Estonian law profoundly impact consumers' privacy and financial interests, not least as they prevent them from re-entering economic life. Taken together, the seriousness of interference with the right to privacy does not outweigh the importance of creating mutual confidence when entering business relationships. Consequently, the Estonian domestic data protection regulation is not in conformity with the GDPR, particularly with the proportionality requirement of Article 6(3). Given the supremacy of EU law, such national legislation would be inapplicable. The recent case law of the Estonian lower instance courts has already started sanctioning the disclosure of prescribed debts. However, to gain legal certainty and compliance with the EU data protection law, the Estonian legislator should take action as soon as possible.

Notes

* This work was supported by the Estonian Research Council grant (PRG2640).

1 Opinion of AG Pikamäe in joined cases C-26/22 and C-64/22, March 16, 2023, *UF* (C-26/22) *and AB* (C-64/22) *v Land Hesse*, ECLI:EU:C:2023:222, para 31. This observation was later confirmed by the Court, see joined cases C-26/22 and C-64/22, December 7, 2023, *UF* (C-26/22) *and AB* (C-64/22) *v Land Hesse*, ECLI:EU:C:2023:958, paras 83–86.

2 Regulation (EU) 2016/679 of the European Parliament and of the Council of April 27, 2016 on the protection of natural persons with regard to the processing of personal data and on the free movement of such data, and repealing Directive 95/46/EC (General Data Protection Regulation), [2016] OJ L 119, 1.

3 Disclosure of personal data constitutes data processing within the meaning of Article 4(2) of the GDPR.

4 Virolainen and Aaviksoo, "Eesti ja Soome tulevikukoostöö raport," 12–13.

5 See eg decision of the Consumer Disputes Committee of March 15, 2022, no 19–1/21–15319–010; Decision of the Consumer Disputes Committe of August 11, 2022, no 19–1/22–05473–013.

6 Uusitalo, "Maksuhäiriömerkinnät poistuvat jatkossa kuukauden kuluttua velan maksamisesta."

7 Rahandusministeerium, "Krediiditeabe jagamise seaduse (nn positiivse krediidiregistri) eelnõu väljatöötamiskavatsus (VTK versioon 2.0)," 7–8; Julianus Inkasso, "Eesti suurim eraisikute maksehäirete analüüs"; Julianus Inkasso, "Statistika: inflatsioon ja hinnatõus on põhjustanud eestlaste keskmise võlasumma kasvu."

8 See Article 18 of the recently adopted Consumer Credit Directive and Article 18 of the Mortgage Credit Directive. Directive (EU) 2023/2225 of the European Parliament and of the Council of October 18, 2023, on credit agreements for consumers and repealing Directive 2008/48/EC [2023] OJ L 2023/2225. Directive 2014/17/EU of the European Parliament and of the Council of February 4, 2014 on credit agreements for consumers relating to residential immovable property and amending Directives 2008/48/EC and 2013/36/EU and Regulation (EU) No 1093/2010 [2014] OJ L 60/34 (Mortgage Credit Directive).

9 See on that, in detail, Cherednychenko, "On the Bumpy Road to Responsible Lending," 251–254; Ferretti, "Peer-to-Peer Lending."

10 Financer (a credit comparison portal). https://financer.com/ee/wiki/krediidiinfo-taustakontroll/.

11 Oikeusministeriö, "Maksuhäiriömerkintöjen säilytysaikojen lyhentäminen, lausuntotiivistelmä 2020:19," 14–16; Finantssivalvonta, "Lausunto: Maksuhäiriömerkintöjen säilytysaikojen lyhentäminen"; Suomen Pankki, "Maksuhäiriömerkintöjen säilytysaikojen lyhentäminen."

12 Sein, "Abusive Debt Recovery Practices in Estonia," 110.

13 This was the case which led to the first privacy-and-debt recovery-related Supreme Court decision in 2010. The names of the debtors were printed on a huge poster with the additional text: 'Persons who do not fulfil their obligations duly.' See the decision of the Supreme Court of December 21, 2010 no 3–2–1–67–10.

14 Feiler, Forgó, and Weigl, *The EU General Data Protection Regulation*, 17.

15 The exact relationship between Article 6(2) and (3) is not entirely yet clarified.

16 Finnish Data Protection Act (Tietosuojalaki), 5.12.2018/1050.

17 Credit Information Act (Luottotietolaki), 11.5.2007/527.

18 Oikeusministeriö, "Luottotietolain yhteensovittaminen EU:n tietosuoja-asetuksen kanssa."

19 Oikeusministeriö, "Maksuhäiriömerkintöjen säilytysaikojen lyhentäminen OM061:00/2020."

20 CIA, 13.5.2022/331.

21 Act on the Positive Credit Register (Laki positiivisesta luottotietorekisteristä), 739/2022.

22 Oikeusministeriö, "Positiivisen luottotietorekisterin valmisteleminen OM022:00/2020."

23 Oikeusministeriö, "Luonnos hallituksen esitykseksi eduskunnalle laeiksi luottotietolain, maksupalvelulain 86 §:n ja rikosrekisterilain 4 a §:n muuttamisesta."

24 Personal Data Protection Act (Isikuandmete kaitse seadus), RT I, 11.03.2023, 11.

25 On some problems of the Estonian Data Protection Act, see Pormeister, "Uus isikuandmete kaitse seadus ja isikuandmed teaduses."

26 Justiitsministeerium, "Isikuandmete kaitse seaduse eelnõu 679 SE seletuskiri."

27 Justiitsministeerium, "Isikuandmete kaitse seaduse eelnõu 679 SE II seletuskiri isikuandmete kaitse seaduse eelnõu teiseks lugemiseks."

28 Justiitsministeerium, "Isikuandmete kaitse seaduse eelnõu 679 SE II seletuskiri isikuandmete kaitse seaduse eelnõu teiseks lugemiseks."

29 Andmekaitse Inspektsioon, "Maksehäirete avaldamine."

30 Andmekaitse Inspektsioon, "Maksehäirete avaldamine," 7.

31 Judgment of the Estonian Supreme Court of March 13, 2019 no 2–17–1026.
32 Andmekaitse Inspektsioon, "Maksehäirete avaldamine," 6.
33 Decision of the Tallinn Administrative Court of February 22, 2024 no 3–22–820.
34 See § 10(2) of the DPA.
35 Oikeusministeriö, "Luonnos hallituksen esitykseksi eduskunnalle laeiksi luottotietolain, maksupalvelulain 86 §:n ja rikosrekisterilain 4 a §:n muuttamisesta," 22.
36 Tietosuojavaltuutetun toimisto, "Tietojen täsmällisyys."
37 See Article 14(5) lit a and b of the GDPR.
38 Andmekaitse Inspektsioon, "Maksehäirete avaldamine," 14.
39 Andmekaitse Inspektsioon, "Maksehäirete avaldamine," 15.
40 Andmekaitse Inspektsioon, "Maksehäirete avaldamine," 15.
41 Judgment of the Estonian Supreme Court of March 13, 2019 no 2–17–1026.
42 Andmekaitse Inspektsioon, "Andmekaitse Inspektsiooni seisukoht ja ettepanek isikuandmete kaitse seaduse paremaks täitmiseks."
43 Oikeusministeriö, "Luonnos hallituksen esitykseksi eduskunnalle laeiksi luottotietolain, maksupalvelulain 86 §:n ja rikosrekisterilain 4 a §:n muuttamisesta," 7.
44 "Hallituksen esitys eduskunnalle laeiksi luottotietolain, maksupalvelulain 86 §:n ja rikosrekisterilain 4 a §:n muuttamisesta," 3.
45 Oikeusministeriö, "Maksuhäiriömerkintöjen säilytysaikojen lyhentäminen, lausuntotiivistelmä," 11–12.
46 Uusitalo, "Maksuhäiriömerkinnät poistuvat jatkossa kuukauden kuluttua velan maksamisesta."
47 Oikeusministeriö, "Maksuhäiriömerkintöjen säilytysaikojen lyhentäminen, lausuntotiivistelmä," 18.
48 Justiitsministeerium, "Isikuandmete kaitse seaduse eelnõu 679 SE seletuskiri," 18.
49 Andmekaitse Inspektsioon, "Maksehäirete avaldamine," 9–10.
50 Andmekaitse Inspektsioon, "Maksehäirete avaldamine," 9–12.
51 Andmekaitse Inspektsioon, "Maksehäirete avaldamine," 12–13.
52 Judgment of the Estonian Supreme Court of March 13, 2019 no 2–17–1026.
53 Andmekaitse Inspektsioon, "Andmekaitse Inspektsiooni seisukoht ja ettepanek isikuandmete kaitse seaduse paremaks täitmiseks," 19–20.
54 Julianus Inkasso, "Millal avaldatakse minu andmed maksehäirete registris?"
55 Limitation of Debts Act (Laki velan vanhetumisesta), 15.8.2003/728.
56 "Taolusvaliokunnan mietintö 28/2002 vp."
57 § 13a of the Limitation of Debts Act.
58 Varul et al., *Tsiviilseadustiku üldosa seadus. Kommenteeritud väljaanne*, 681–85.
59 Debt Recovery Act (Laki saatavien perinnästä), 22.4.1999/513.
60 General Part of the Civil Code Act (Tsiviilseadustiku üldosa seadus), RT I, 06.07.2023, 98.
61 Varul et al., *Tsiviilseadustiku üldosa seadus. Kommenteeritud väljaanne*, 685.
62 Sein, "Abusive Debt Recovery Practices in Estonia," 111.
63 Now § 10(2)(3) of the DPA.
64 Judgment of the Estonian Supreme Court of December 12, 2011, no 3–3–1–70–11.
65 Judgment of the Estonian Supreme Court of December 12, 2011, no 3–3–1–70–11.
66 See e.g., judgments of Harju County Court of October 27, 2020, no 2–20–10157 and Viru County Court of April 16, 2021, no 2–20–16579.
67 Judgment of Tallinn District Court of 23.02.2024 no 2–22–10884.
68 Andmekaitse Inspektsioon, "Maksehäirete avaldamine," 10.
69 Decision of Tallinn District Court of January 18, 2023, no 2–22–6314.
70 Judgment of Harju Country Court of October 27, 2020, no 2–20–10157.
71 Andmekaitse Inspektsioon, "Maksehäirete avaldamine maksehäireregistrites," 23.
72 Decision of the Estonian Supreme Court of September 16, 2009, no 3–2–1–79–09. Also the guidelines of the Estonian Data Protection Inspectorate stress that it is not sufficient that the debtor was aware of the contract and the debt, or that the debtor has received a

reminder to pay the debt. Andmekaitse Inspektsioon, "Maksehäirete avaldamine maksehäireregistrites," 11.
73 Julianus Inkasso, "Millal avaldatakse minu andmed maksehäirete registris?" This statement has been corrected by 2025.
74 Andmekaitse Inspektsioon, "Maksehäirete avaldamine maksehäireregistrites," 11.
75 Andmekaitse Inspektsioon, "Maksehäirete avaldamine maksehäireregistrites," 22–23.
76 Law of Obligations Act (Võlaõigusseadus), RT I, 06.07.2023, 116.
77 Decision of Tallinn District Court of July 26, 2022, no 2–22–3662; judgment of Tallinn District Court of February 2, 2024, no 2–22–10884. The debt recovery company was also obliged to compensate the legal fees of the natural person incurred in the court procedure under the 'loser pays' principle.
78 On abusive debt recovery practices as unfair commercial practices see Stănescu, "Unfair Commercial Practices Directive."
79 Justiitsministeerium, "Isikuandmete kaitse seaduse eelnõu 679 SE II seletuskiri isikuandmete kaitse seaduse eelnõu teiseks lugemiseks," 2.
80 Indeed, recital 45 GDPR allows national law to determine whether the controller performing a task carried out in the public interest should be a public authority or another natural or legal person governed by public law, or, where it is in the public interest to do so, also by private law.
81 For example, in C-13/16 – Rīgas satiksme the CJEU held: 'As regards the condition relating to the necessity of processing personal data, it should be borne in mind that derogations and limitations in relation to the protection of personal data must apply only in so far as is strictly necessary.' CJEU, case C-13/16 of May 4, 2017, Rīgas satiksme, ECLI:EU:C:2017:336, para 30.
82 CJEU, case C-184/20 of August 11, 2022 Vyriausioji tarnybinės etikos komisija, ECLI:EU:C:2022:601, para 98.
83 CJEU, case C-184/20 of August 11, 2022 Vyriausioji tarnybinės etikos komisija, ECLI:EU:C:2022:601, para 99.
84 Opinion of AG Pikamäe in joined cases C-26/22 and C-64/22, March 16, 2023, *UF* (C-26/22) *and AB* (C-64/22) *v Land Hesse*, ECLI:EU:C:2023:222, para 72.
85 CJEU, joined cases C-26/22 and C-64/22 of December 7, 2023, *UF and AB v Schufa*, ECLI:EU:C:2023:958, para 96.

References

Andmekaitse Inspektsioon. "Andmekaitse Inspektsiooni seisukoht ja ettepanek isikuandmete kaitse seaduse paremaks täitmiseks." Published June 1, 2020. https://www.aki.ee/sites/default/files/dokumendid/muu/andmekaitse_inspektsiooni_seisukoht_ja_ettepanek_isikuandmete_kaitse_seaduse_paremaks_taitmiseks_veebis.pdf.

Andmekaitse Inspektsioon. "Maksehäirete avaldamine maksehäireregistrites." Accessed May 21, 2023. https://aastaraamat.aki.ee/aastaraamat-2023/aastaraamat-2023-pdf.

Andmekaitse Inspektsioon. "Maksehäirete avaldamine." Published October 3, 2022. https://www.aki.ee/sites/default/files/dokumendid/maksehairete_avaldamine_2022.pdf.

Andmekaitse Inspektsioon. "Maksehäirete avaldamine." Last modified October 31, 2023. https://www.aki.ee/isikuandmed/juhendid/maksehairete-avaldamise-juhend.

Cherednychenko, Olha. "On the Bumpy Road to Responsible Lending in the Digital Marketplace: The New EU Consumer Credit Directive." *Journal of Consumer Policy*, 47, no. 2 (2024): 241–70.

Decision of the Consumer Disputes Committee of March 15, 2022, no. 19-1/21-15319-010.

Decision of the Consumer Disputes Committee of August 11, 2022, no. 19-1/22-05473-013.

Feiler, Lukas, Nikolaus Forgó, and Michaela Weigl. *The EU General Data Protection Regulation (GDPR): A Commentary*. Surrey: Globe Law and Business, 2018.

Ferretti, Federico. "Peer-to-Peer Lending and EU Credit Laws: A Creditworthiness Assessment, Credit-Risk Analysis or . . . Neither of the Two?" *German Law Journal* 22 (2021): 102–21.

Finantssivalvonta. “Lausunto: Maksuhäiriömerkintöjen säilytysaikojen lyhentäminen.” Published August 18, 2020. https://api.hankeikkuna.fi/asiakirjat/ddc9031d-084f-4a95-b1cd-519d98b7655a/e65616f5-1d08-48e2-95f4-1b3c45e1429c/LAUSUNTO_20200820055449.PDF.

“Hallituksen esitys eduskunnalle laeiksi luottotietolain, maksupalvelulain 86 §:n ja rikosrekisterilain 4 a §:n muuttamisesta.” Published May 12, 2021. https://api.hankeikkuna.fi/asiakirjat/a43db69e-fbc8-4ced-9884-afc1dc9e1f87/067e2a5f-82b3-46bb-bf00-e235bcd4610f/ESITYS_20210512123637.pdf.

Julianus Inkasso. “Eesti suurim eraisikute maksehäirete analüüs: võlgade summa on hüppeliselt kasvamas.” Published December 18, 2023. https://julianus.ee/eesti-suurim-eraisikute-maksehairete-analuus-volgade-summa-on-huppeliselt-kasvamas.

Julianus Inkasso. “Millal avaldatakse minu andmed maksehäirete registris?.” Accessed April 28, 2024. https://julianus.ee/volgnikule/kkk/millal-avaldatakse-minu-andmed-maksehairete-registris/.

Julianus Inkasso. “Statistika: inflatsioon ja hinnatõus on põhjustanud eestlaste keskmise võlasumma kasvu.” Published April 4, 2023. https://julianus.ee/statistika-inflatsioon-ja-hinnatous-on-pohjustanud-eestlaste-keskmise-volasumma-kasvu.

Justiitsministeerium. “Isikuandmete kaitse seaduse eelnõu 679 SE seletuskiri.” Accessed May 21, 2024. https://www.riigikogu.ee/tegevus/eelnoud/eelnou/5c9f8086-b465-4067-841e-41e7df3b95af.

Justiitsministeerium. “Isikuandmete kaitse seaduse eelnõu 679 SE II seletuskiri isikuandmete kaitse seaduse eelnõu teiseks lugemiseks.” Accessed May 21, 2024. https://www.riigikogu.ee/tegevus/eelnoud/eelnou/5c9f8086-b465-4067-841e-41e7df3b95af.

Oikeusministeriö. “Luonnos hallituksen esitykseksi eduskunnalle laeiksi luottotietolain, maksupalvelulain 86 §:n ja rikosrekisterilain 4 a §:n muuttamisesta.” Accessed May 21, 2024. https://www.lausuntopalvelu.fi/FI/Proposal/Participation?proposalId=f351fc33-f8b5-439e-acbd-bc76dc9cd1a6&proposalLanguage=da4408c3-39e4-4f5a-84db-84481bafc744.

Oikeusministeriö. “Luottotietolain yhteensovittaminen EU:n tietosuoja-asetuksen kanssa.” Accessed April 29, 2024. https://oikeusministerio.fi/hanke?tunnus=OM023:00/2019.

Oikeusministeriö. “Maksuhäiriömerkintöjen säilytysaikojen lyhentäminen, lausuntotiivistelmä 2020:19.” Accessed April 29, 2024. https://julkaisut.valtioneuvosto.fi/bitstream/handle/10024/162522/OM_2020_19.pdf?sequence=1&isAllowed=y.

Oikeusministeriö. “Maksuhäiriömerkintöjen säilytysaikojen lyhentäminen OM061:00/2020.” Accessed April 29, 2024, https://oikeusministerio.fi/hanke?tunnus=OM061:00/2020.

Oikeusministeriö. “Positiivisen luottotietorekisterin valmisteleminen, OM022:00/2020.” Accessed April 29, 2024. https://oikeusministerio.fi/en/project?tunnus=OM022:00/2020.

Pormeister, Kärt. “Uus isikuandmete kaitse seadus ja isikuandmed teaduses: kolm näidet probleemsest õigusloomest.” *Juridica* 4 (2019): 239–51.

Rahandusministeerium. “Krediiditeabe jagamise seaduse (nn positiivse krediidiregistri) eelnõu väljatöötamiskavatsus (VTK versioon 2.0).” Published June 2022. https://eelnoud.valitsus.ee/main#BqVdIQFp.

Sein, Karin. “Abusive debt recovery practices in Estonia.” In *Regulation of Debt Collection in Europe. Understanding Informal Debt Collection Practices*, edited by Cătălin Gabriel Stănescu, 101–15. New York: Routledge, 2023.

Stănescu, Catalin-Gabriel. “Is the Unfair Commercial Practices Directive Fit to Effectively Tackle Abusive Debt Collection?” *Journal of European Consumer and Market Law* 9 (2020): 235–47.

Suomen Pankki. “Maksuhäiriömerkintöjen säilytysaikojen lyhentäminen.” Published August 20, 2020. https://api.hankeikkuna.fi/asiakirjat/ddc9031d-084f-4a95-b1cd-519d98b7655a/5230ef37-ce9d-4ca2-b476-2f734b599dbe/LAUSUNTO_20200821064443.PDF.

“Taolusvaliokunnan mietintö 28/2002 vp.” Accessed May 21, 2024. https://www.eduskunta.fi/FI/Vaski/sivut/trip.aspx?triptype=ValtiopaivaAsiakirjat&docid=tavm+28/2002.

Tietosuojavaltuutetun toimisto. “Tietojen täsmällisyys.” Accessed April 29, 2024. https://tietosuoja.fi/tietojen-tasmallisyys.

Uusitalo, Kaisa. “Maksuhäiriömerkinnät poistuvat jatkossa kuukauden kuluttua velan maksamisesta – pitkään valmisteltu lakiuudistus sai lopullisen hyväksynnän.” Published April 16, 2022. https://yle.fi/a/3-12384319.

Varul, Paul, Irene Kull, Villu Kõve, Martin Käerdi, and Karin Sein. *Tsiviilseadustiku üldosa seadus. Kommenteeritud väljaanne*. Tallinn: Juura, 2023.

Virolainen, Anne-Mari, and Jaak Aaviksoo. “Eesti ja Soome tulevikukoostööraport.” Published February 2022. https://um.fi/documents/35732/0/EE-FI+koost%C3%B6%C3%B6raport+EST1+l%C3%B5plik.pdf/8593cee3-f215-bb4b-63f5-f87578ae2883?t=1664801201715.

5 The poor pay more (with data) – strategies and legal solutions in the USA and the EU for credit invisibles and the poorly scored

Ulrich Krüger

1. Introduction[1]

People with no or poor creditworthiness are prevented from participating fully in society by being excluded from financial and other services – or will have to pay more for these services because they are seen as a higher risk. Without doubt, it makes economic sense to check creditworthiness[2] and is, in many cases of consumer credit, a legal requirement.[3] If more and more consumers are excluded from financial services because their creditworthiness is poor or non-existent, it is no longer only a personal and social problem but also a problem for all creditors and the economy as a whole. Particularly in the USA, more than half of the population has a bad or no credit score at all. Therefore, strategies of "credit building" to fight financial exclusion are practiced there, such as credit counselling, the development of new financial products, and the use of "alternative payment data" to improve a poor credit score. All of this raises questions of consumer policy and data protection law, and it is worth taking a comparative look at the situation in the USA and the EU, with the focus on Germany.

2. Credit scores: a trend to exclusion?

The importance of credit checks seems to be growing,[4] especially with the help of "credit scores". These are, in essence, numerical calculations that are supposed to indicate the risk that a borrower will default on repayments. Several factors drive this development. From a technical point of view, it has become increasingly easier to assess creditworthiness based on algorithmic calculations: there is more and more data, which is becoming easier and faster to process.[5] In addition, the integration of scores into digital contracts is simple and cost-effective. Importantly, the use of scores is expanding in general into other business areas, for example, in the insurance sector, which is particularly problematic.[6] But there are more applications for credit scores: more and more landlords are demanding a credit report from prospective tenants as a matter of course. Quick and automatically verifiable credit checks are in use for mobile phone contracts or even energy supply contracts, as well as for a wide range of business models in the sharing economy. Nearly half of U.S. employers check the creditworthiness of applicants as part of the hiring process.[7]

DOI: 10.4324/9781003510406-7

In the USA, in particular, the development towards a credit society is well-advanced. (Fair) access to many areas of life is often dependent on a loan: if buying a house is the norm rather than renting, the use of a mortgage loan becomes essential. If there is no adequate public transport, one will need a car and, therefore, in many cases, also a car loan. Americans owe more than a staggering $1.7 trillion dollars in student loan debt,[8] because they must pay (high) tuition fees for higher education. If health insurance covers only part of the high healthcare costs, you might need to borrow money in case of a special treatment. If everyday consumption relies on credit cards, this form of credit is an everyday requirement as well. The credit score, in turn, is the key to accessing credit in standardised lending. For those who have no or only a poor credit rating, the door to participation in social and economic life often remains closed. The situation in Germany and most of the EU is somewhat different due to more comprehensive social systems, a larger share of rental apartments, better access to public transportation, (higher) education with no substantial tuition fees, etc. Nevertheless, credit reporting agencies and credit scores are gaining more and more importance there as well.

In Germany, the largest credit reporting agency for consumers is SCHUFA (*Schutzgemeinschaft für allgemeine Kreditsicherung*). The scores and reports of SCHUFA are widely used, even for a creditworthiness check in renting an apartment. In the USA, the leading credit score is the FICO score by data analyst Fair Isaac and Company. It is used by the three major credit bureaus in the USA, Experian, TransUnion, and Equifax. The basic structure of all credit-scoring systems is similar. A certain number of points can be achieved, which are assigned to different risk classes. In the FICO score, for example, below 580 points is considered "poor", between 580 and 669 is deemed "fair" (but still "subprime"), 670 and above is considered "good", "very good" starts at 740, and "exceptional" is above 800. Around one-third of American consumers only achieve a "subprime" score.[9] Furthermore, as much as one-fifth of the adult population has no score at all (the so-called "credit invisibles").[10] This highlights a typical vicious cycle: because one has no credit score, they cannot get a loan, and because they cannot get a loan, they have no credit history – and no credit score. So, what can be done when more than half of the population has a poor or no credit score, and this becomes a decisive factor for participation in economic life?[11]

3. Credit building and credit repair: play the game?

As mentioned before, three instruments are in use in the USA: specific credit counselling, the use of special credit products, and the expansion of the data basis eligible for scoring with "alternative payment data". All of this can be criticised for playing the game of the credit reporting agencies because these credit-building strategies, in fact, open up further markets to the credit industry, in which, up to now, it has not been able to employ its risk assessment techniques. On the other hand, these instruments may provide some consumers, who were previously excluded from the credit market, with better access to financial services. If you don't have assets, isn´t credit your only asset? However, the risk of over-indebtedness may increase as well because of the expanded access to credit. All in all, this may pose a dilemma that is difficult to resolve in an advanced credit society. Therefore, it is worth having an overview of the instruments of credit building.

3.1 Credit building through credit counselling

The most important step to empower individuals who do not have reliable access to financial services due to their poor credit scores is education and counselling. For good credit counselling, you will need to explain the scoring system and its significance in general and specifically with regard to the (financial) situation of the clients and make recommendations on how to improve their creditworthiness. For specific advice, you will need specific information. In reality, however, there is a lack of transparency about the algorithms on which the score is based. Without knowing which factors influence the score and to what extent, advice can only be limited. How exactly the scores are calculated and how the algorithm actually works are legally trade secrets in the USA, as it is in Germany, where the Federal Court of Justice (BGH) decided so in 2014.[12] Nevertheless, some disclosure requirements concerning the criteria used in a credit score have been in force, since 2010 in the USA and soon in the EU as well with its new Credit Consumer Directive (see IV.3.). Better information also provides a basis for better financial education of the general public.[13] Better counselling, knowledge, and education concerning the credit score could be problematic from the perspective of the credit bureaus, however. People might learn how to play the system and to tune the score without improving the major underlying economics affecting their creditworthiness.[14]

Good credit counselling to help people repair their credit will, of course, also need all other aspects of "classical" debt counselling:[15] assessment of the financial and social situation, reduction of current expenses and debts, finding money to pay the debts, negotiating with creditors and debt collectors, and considering bankruptcy approaches.[16]

3.2 Credit building with tailored financial products

Various financial products have emerged in the U.S. market to assist affected consumers in building their credit scores for the first time or improving their scores: credit builder loans, secured credit cards, and more recently, (digital) lending circles.

3.2.1 Credit builder loan

From a German and European perspective, the "credit builder loan" is a new and innovative product. The credit builder loan aims to provide a consumer, regardless of their previous credit history, with the opportunity to demonstrate their ability to make regular loan repayments and thus improve their credit score. Although its functioning resembles that of a normal loan, in reality, it is a savings product.[17] Typically, a small "loan" amount is provided, ranging from $300 to $1000, depending on the provider. However, this money is not disbursed directly to the borrower upon completion of the "loan agreement" but is instead "parked" in a locked bank account. During the term, the consumer must then "repay" the amount in fixed instalment rates over 6 to 24 months to the bank. In return, the "borrower" either receives a partial amount each month equal to the "repayment rate" minus the "credit costs" or receives the total amount at the end of the term. This financial product proves its value because the instalment payments are reported to credit bureaus as successful loan repayments, thus improving the credit score. The "lending" banks and the credit reporting agencies contractually agree that the regular instalment payments on a credit builder loan are to be considered just like a regular instalment loan. And for a good reason: even though the credit-building loan is technically a "fake loan", since the customer is essentially giving themselves a loan to "repay", from the perspective of creditworthiness assessment, the proof is provided that a customer is capable of making loan payments regularly.

However, there are also a number of criticisms of this financial product: since the customer pays "interest" on their own money, this can lead to relatively high costs. However, the majority of credit unions in the USA offering such programs to support their customers tend to have costs that are more moderate. Nevertheless, there are, of course, black sheep in the industry, especially when it comes to expensive online offers from FinTechs. Additionally, there are further risks for the customer: if they cannot pay the instalment for the credit builder loan within 30 days, this generates a negative report to the credit bureaus. Also many customers misunderstand this "tricky" product and prefer to pay off the "good" credit builder loan quickly to improve their score quickly. The opposite can be the result, however: if the debtor fails to pay other, more important ongoing instalments and bills, the debt problem increases. Therefore, credit builder loans should not be offered as a "stand-alone product" but only in conjunction with financial counselling.[18] Continuous counselling would, for example, recommend timely closing of the account of the credit builder loan when it becomes foreseeable that the client will not be able to pay the credit builder loan after satisfying ordinary course debt. After termination of the contract, there would be no remaining debt (because there is no real debt), and accordingly, nothing negative needs to be reported to the credit bureaus. Nevertheless, even without corresponding financial counselling, a credit builder loan can be a meaningful solution, namely for the "credit invisibles".[19]

3.2.2 Secured credit cards

In the USA – and prospectively in Germany and the EU – cashless payment via credit card is very popular. Utilising a credit card limit of not more than 30% and paying it off on time will increase a credit score substantially.[20] Although dangerous for those who are not able to follow this rule, a correctly used credit card could be an efficient way to improve a credit score. However, if a consumer already has a poor score, creditors regularly deny consumers a credit card and only offer a debit card. By this, a particular problem arises for credit-building efforts: When the card is only used as a debit card, meaning it is linked to a balance in a checking account, the credit score does not improve while using this card. While there is a strong argument that paying from a positive balance, which must initially be saved, should speak positively for the borrower, in the USA, only successfully managing a (credit) obligation positively influences the score. And there, as we have seen, the vicious circle closes again: those who do not have a sufficient score are not granted a credit line for a credit card. Accordingly, they cannot prove their creditworthiness for the credit score.

One solution is offered to counteract this pitfall is the secured credit card. Payments can only be made from an already deposited amount of money. One could say that this is a "fake credit card" because, technically, the secured credit card is actually a debit card. Nevertheless, payments from this (sometimes quite expensive)[21] card model are considered "real" credit card payments and are reported positively to the credit bureaus. The benefit for the customer is that their secured credit card can be converted into a real credit card after a certain period of use. However, obtaining such a card is not always possible for people with no or a poor score. For this reason, packages are often offered that provide for a secured credit card in a second stage after the successful "repayment" of a credit builder loan.

3.2.3 Lending circles

Both credit builder loans and secured credit cards often come with high costs charged by banks as the intermediaries. Therefore, a product has become quite popular lately in the USA that does not rely on bank loans: lending circles, sometimes referred to as rotational savings clubs. The underlying idea is that a limited group of, for example, 6–12 people, commit to make regular deposits of a certain amount of money until a jointly determined sum is reached. For instance, 10 individuals could agree to deposit $100 each per month. Over the course of 10 months, each member would then receive an interest-free loan of $1,000.[22] The advantage of this form of lending lies mainly in the fact that the monthly payment is reported to credit bureaus to help participants build or repair their credit scores. Such lending circles are traditionally offered by non-profit organisations. In a traditional lending circle, the creditworthiness of the members arises from knowing each other and experiencing social pressure to make payments on time. However, the benefits of this approach and the possibilities of forming digital lending circles on Internet platforms have led a number of FinTech companies, such as Esusu, to offer online lending circles. Recently FinTechs seem to be withdrawing from this business while NGOs continue to use it as a tool to build credit. A regular income is usually required to qualify for online lending circles, and the individual's deposit behaviour is monitored. Although this product may not be suitable for every credit need, the advantages certainly include the low costs, depending on the provider, along with information provided to credit reporting agencies to improve the score. However, this product, too, is not without risk, as lending circles report both on-time payments and late payments, which could have negative effects on the credit score.

3.3 Credit building with "alternative payment data"

The currently most discussed instrument for improving a credit score and thus enabling better credit access for consumers (and more business for providers!) is the use of "alternative payment data". The data is "alternative" because it goes beyond traditional credit (re)payments, for example, it includes rental payments. This instrument to improve credit scores has been popular in the USA for some time[23] and has become a trend in the financial industry in recent years.[24] From the perspective of European and German data protection law, which will be discussed next, this can be questioned in several ways.[25] Nevertheless, corresponding models are also entering the market in Europe, in Germany, for example, at SCHUFA with Bonify.[26] The "alternative payment data" is supposed to prove that the consumer can deal with regular payment obligations, (e.g., rent, cell phone bills, electricity costs), but these may also include, as discussed in the USA, alimony and even foreign remittances from immigrants to their families. Persons disclosing these payments will get a better credit score. Experian has developed the market-leading offering for this in the USA with "Experian Boost".[27] But FinTechs and, of course, BigTechs such as Amazon, Google, and Apple (which are mutating into "BigFins" in Europe) use extended datasets for their own credit-scoring systems. This industry trend also includes the development of "credit builder cards" driven by FinTechs, which allow access to "alternative payment data".[28] All of this is economically at the expense of the banks' previous business area, at the latest when, for example, credit agencies also offer payment accounts in order to merge all data, as Experian is currently doing with its "Experian Smart Money" product as a further development of "Boost".[29]

One may welcome the fact that the credit agencies could make their scores more accurate and better with new data, thus giving consumers better access to financial services. Nevertheless, it remains a double-edged sword, as the "boost" is likely to have both good and bad effects in the long term: if one fails the regular payment obligations, there is a risk that the score will deteriorate. Additionally, contrary to all avowals by providers, there is likely to be indirect pressure on individuals with poor scores: "Those who do not disclose everything have something to hide!" Refusing to disclose data is, therefore, likely to have an additional negative impact on the score algorithm in the short or long term. Of course, this does not apply to those who already have a good score. But people who lack "positive" credit data will have to "pay" more with data from other areas of their lives.[30]

4. A case for political action and legal regulation?

The exclusion of credit invisibles and people with subprime scores as well as the strategies of credit building raises questions. Which measures could be most effective and what is or could be an appropriate legal framework.

4.1 Promotion of meaningful credit-building products

Credit builder loans could provide an opportunity to improve poor creditworthiness in a transparent manner within a foreseeable time. The disadvantage that consumers have to pay "interest" for their own money can be offset by public money or donation. An example of such a model is the so-called "twin account" by the Local Initiatives Support Corporation New York:[31] a credit-building loan can be doubled with (public) funding if the customer successfully pays all instalments.

This provides a good incentive, turns the loan into a good savings product, and can be part of a financial education program. Crucial for a successful and suitable credit builder loan would be a collaboration of credit industry, credit bureaus, and debt counselling in the "product development". The goal is a situation where everyone benefits: banks gain or retain customers who are sensitised to debt and credit issues because they receive a form of financial education through this product. The banking business with these customers can be successful and sustainable in the future. A credit builder loan should thus fit the purpose of banks, in Germany, especially for "Sparkassen" (publicly-owned savings banks) and cooperative banks. Credit bureaus would need to be involved since the contracting and repayment of a credit-building loan must be "scoreable". They could present themselves more credibly as a partner committed to the sustainable inclusion of consumers with previously poor creditworthiness. Lastly, debt counsellors would be involved early on during the emergence of debt problems, contributing to debt prevention through financial counselling that does not merely degenerate into digitally supported help for insolvency procedures. Closer collaboration among these involved stakeholders can help to avoid or manage unproductive over-indebtedness. A credit-building loan could provide a meaningful platform for this stakeholder communication and perhaps cooperation.

4.2 Promotion of financial counselling

People who are threatened with (financial) exclusion need counselling to help them and to enable them to help themselves. In situations of over-indebtedness, multiple social problems occur but one issue is bad creditworthiness and a poor credit score. For this, a form of counselling is also necessary that not only focuses on debt and personal problems but moves towards financial counselling in an early stage. This is the case in the USA. In Germany, debt counsellors see themselves more as social workers. Therefore, counselling to optimise creditworthiness assessments might seem to contradict the self-image of debt counsellors as social workers. One hope to tap the potential of debt counselling organisations in Germany to provide more active independent counselling in a "technical" financial sense has been the legally binding counselling obligation under § 504a of the German Civil Code (*Bürgerliches Gesetzbuch*, BGB) (based on the European Consumer Credit Directive). § 504a (2) BGB requires counselling if the borrower has continuously used the overdraft facility granted to him for a period of six months and has exceeded an amount equivalent to 75% of the agreed maximum amount on average. This hope has not been fulfilled so far. The blame for this certainly does not lie solely with debt counselling but also with the credit industry, which has shown limited interest in the practical development of joint counselling concepts and cooperation. Apparently, the obligation to provide counselling for overdraft loans is understood in such a way that financial counselling for customers, for whom it is still worthwhile, should be exclusively provided by the bank, while the only thing left for debt counsellors is to handle insolvency proceedings.[32]

The USA faces different issues in this sector: it is not uncommon that "credit repair services" actually advance fraudulent business with poverty, meaning high fees for little to no meaningful service. To help in identifying reputable counselling, the U.S. Trustee program at the Department of Justice certifies counsellors as an approved "credit counselling agency". But in addition to being accessible for those affected by financial problems, counselling centres should ideally be free of charge. In Germany and most countries of the EU, the funding of debt counselling comes mainly from public money or social organisations. In the USA, more private funding is needed to offer non-profit counselling. To avoid a conflict of interest in the case that financial services providers fund credit counsellors, the National Foundation of Credit Counselling must be informed about that in the accreditation procedure, and it has to be disclosed to the customers.[33]

Good advice requires independence but also knowledge. To inform people about which behaviours particularly worsen their creditworthiness and which could help, credit counselling needs information about the data in use for the credit score and the weighting assigned to each data point. Furthermore, to prevent discrimination and erase data errors, one will need detailed information about the specific credit-scoring model. There are two different legal approaches to fulfill this need for transparency and consumer protection: as a legal obligation for disclosure in context with the contract or as part of a public data protection law.

4.3 Disclosure requirements for credit scores in consumer credit contracts

The development of consumer credit began in the late 1970s with financial liberalisation, deregulation of interest rates, the use of credit scores, and the increase in use of credit cards.[34] Consumer credit protection law developed from these times of "easy credit" to the nowadays widely accepted principle of "responsible lending". In 2010, the lessons of the financial crisis in the USA were incorporated into the legislation of the Dodd-Frank Act. Because credit assessments frequently missed the mark, a minimum level of transparency is now obligatory by law. The Fair Credit Reporting Act requires the disclosure of the most important criteria of the scoring algorithm for a large number of loans in the event that the credit agreement is not approved or rejected as requested.[35] The four to five most important criteria for the scoring must be disclosed, together with their respective weightings. For the credit score used by Experian, for example, these are: payment history with 35% (on-time payments, late payments, entries in public registers, etc.); amounts owed with 30% (credit utilisation ratio); length of credit history with 15%, new credit 10%, and the credit mix with 10% (e.g., both revolving and instalment credit accounts).[36]

In addition, the U.S. Equal Credit Opportunity Act rules that a creditor must provide a statement of specific reasons in writing if it denies an application for credit, terminates an existing credit account, makes unfavourable changes to the terms of an existing account, or refuses to increase a credit limit.[37] Regulation B prescribes that this information "must be specific and indicate the principal reason(s) for the adverse action".[38] This aims to prevent any creditor from discriminating against an applicant on the basis of race, colour, religion, national origin, sex, marital status, age, because all or part of the applicant's income derives from any public assistance program, or because the applicant has in good faith exercised any right under the Consumer Credit Protection Act.[39] These notice requirements fulfill "the twin goals of consumer protection and education".[40] Consumers and their counsellors need to learn about the reason for the creditor's decision, and the creditors know that they must be able to explain their decision and therefore will be discouraged from discriminatory practices.

The EU, on the other hand, has issued a new Consumer Credit Directive in 2023, which must be transposed into national law by the end of 2026. Pursuant to Article 18 (7), (9) of the Directive, the creditor has to inform the consumer without undue delay and free of charge of the result of the consultation of a database used for assessing the creditworthiness of consumers and of the details of the database consulted as well as the categories of data taken into account. According to Directive recital 57, Member States should in addition

> *ensure that consumers are informed about the registration of any credit repayment arrears in a database in a timely manner and within 30 days of the registration, for instance by sending them a warning via email asking them to access the database to view their own information regarding arrears in repayment of credit.*

The Directive also includes a provision regarding the weighting of criteria, stipulating that the assessment of creditworthiness must not rely solely on the consumer's credit history. All in all, the EU follows the regulation from the Dodd-Frank Act more than 15 years after its passage. The regulation in the USA is still stricter concerning the circumstances under which the creditor has to make disclosures the customer. These circumstances include, for example, even when the creditor is granting or extending the loan but makes "unfavourable changes" like higher interest rates. The Dodd-Frank regulation seems to be a reasonable way of ensuring transparent information to the market and customers.

4.4 Data protection regulation

Whilst, in the USA, the governance function of privacy law can be described as liberal and market-based, in the EU, it is more socially protective, rights-based.[41] After years of negotiation and under considerable lobbying pressure of powerful interest groups, especially from the U.S. digital industries, the General Data Protection Regulation (GDPR) came into force in the EU on May 25, 2018. It applies to the processing of personal data in the context of the activities of a company in the European Union, regardless of whether the processing takes place in the EU or not (Art. 3 GDPR). As a principle, the processing of personal data is generally forbidden unless it is allowed under the exceptions of the law.

The GDPR provides special rules to protect users from the risks of customer profiling (including credit scores), which is defined in Art. 4 (4) GDPR as

> *any form of automated processing of personal data consisting of the use of personal data to evaluate certain personal aspects relating to a natural person, in particular to analyse or predict aspects concerning that natural*

> *person's performance at work, economic situation, health, personal preferences, interests, reliability, behaviour, location or movements.*

In addition, Art. 22 GDPR states that no one should "be subject to a decision based solely on automated processing, including profiling, which produces legal effects concerning him or her or similarly significantly affects him or her". Automated individual decision-making can nevertheless be lawful if it is

> *1. Necessary for entering into, or performance of, a contract between the data subject and a data controller; 2. Authorized by Union or Member State law to which the controller is subject and which lays down suitable measures to safeguard the data subject's rights and freedoms and legitimate interests; or 3. Based on the data subject's explicit consent.*

A landmark decision of the ECJ[42] clarified at the end of 2023 the question of whether the creation of a credit score itself constitutes such an "automated individual decision-making" that would be lawful under one of these three exemptions. In the case, the plaintiff in Germany requested a loan and the bank declined, likely because of plaintiff's subprime SCHUFA credit score. Plaintiff requested SCHUFA to send her information on the personal data registered and to erase some of the data, which was allegedly incorrect. In response to that request, SCHUFA informed her of her score and outlined, in broad terms, the methods for calculating the scores. However, referring to trade secrecy, it refused to disclose the various elements taken into account for the purposes of that calculation and their weighting. The plaintiff complained to the competent supervisory authority to order SCHUFA to grant her request for access to information and erasure, but the supervisory authority rejected. Plaintiff then appealed that decision before the Administrative Court (*Verwaltungsgericht*) Wiesbaden, which decided to refer the question to the European Court of Justice for a preliminary ruling as to whether the creation of a SCHUFA score itself can be a "decision" according to Art. 22 GDPR or not. The ECJ decided:

> *the automated establishment, by a credit information agency, of a probability value based on personal data relating to a person and concerning his or her ability to meet payment commitments in the future constitutes 'automated individual decision-making' within the meaning of that provision, where a third party, to which that probability value is transmitted, draws strongly on that probability value to establish, implement or terminate a contractual relationship with that person.*[43]

A probability value like a credit score affects, "at the very least, the data subject significantly".[44]

The decisions by the Administrative Court and the ECJ have strengths and weaknesses in their interpretation of the Directive. There are indeed good reasons for interpreting only the subsequent decision on the conclusion of the loan contract based on the score as a "decision" within the meaning of Art. 22 GDPR. However, in this case, the Administrative Court in Wiesbaden found that, in reality, even a poor credit score is likely to lead to the refusal of credit in the vast majority of cases. Therefore, the credit score, as automated data processing, in most cases de facto decides already whether a loan contract will be entered into. The ECJ followed that (quite extensive) interpretation of the law and reflected the considerations of the legislator for establishing the rule: statistical probabilities can turn out to be individually wrong and there is always a danger of unfair, manipulative, and discriminatory conclusions. Therefore, no one should be a mere object of data processing that has consequences for the person, which would be the case if the person did not know the underlying data and evaluation criteria and was not able to influence it.[45] The GDPR itself demands in No. 71 of the Recitals a "fair and transparent processing" with "appropriate mathematical or statistical procedures for the profiling" to minimise "the risk of errors" and to prevent "discriminatory effects". In addition, it is worth mentioning that the upcoming EU regulation of artificial intelligence (AI) also categorises credit scores as "high-risk" AI systems, "as they determine the access of these individuals to financial resources or essential services such as housing, electricity, and telecommunications services" (Recital 37 of the AI Act).[46]

As a consequence of this ECJ decision, a credit score is forbidden unless it would be permissible under the three exemptions of Art. 22 (2) GDPR mentioned before. According to Art. 22 (2)(a) GDPR, that could be the case if the score is necessary for entering into, or performance of, a contract. Because (German and European) law provides for a mandatory creditworthiness assessment, it could be argued that the credit score might simply be lawful because it is "necessary" for the contract. However, the law does not require specifically a credit check based on a score. Therefore, it is very doubtful that the score could be justified on this basis. Furthermore, explicit consent from the customer, according to Art. 22 II c GDPR, could justify the scoring, but the information requirements for the creditors will be prohibitively high under GDPR regulation. But, according to Article 22(2)(b) GDPR, credit scoring would be lawful if it is subject to a legal basis at the level of a Member State. In quick response to the ECJ decision, the German federal government has prepared such a new draft law that regulates credit scoring (§ 37a BDSG).[47] According to this national law, the creation and use of a probability value (like a score) shall be permissible as an exception to the prohibition of automated decision-making under specified conditions. Certain datasets are not allowed to be used, such as data from social media activities or, even more relevantly in our case, the mere payment transactions on an account. This would mean that in Germany, it will not be allowed to use "alternative payment data" for a credit score in the future. In the justifications for the proposed law, it is stressed out that these payment data provide extensive insights into personal aspects of life and poses significant risks to the data subject. Payment data is, therefore, particularly sensitive[48] – and strictly regulated.

Besides that, there is another significant consequence of the ECJ decision when the ECJ discusses the heightened information and disclosure obligations of the

GDPR for automated decision-making regarding the "involved logic, as well as the significance and intended effects" involved.[49] The fact that SCHUFA has thus far stonewalled on this issue is now coming back to haunt them. As a response to the ECJ decision, the mentioned German draft law for credit scoring in § 37a (4) BDSG gives everyone the right to be informed of: (i) the personal data used for the creation, (ii) the weighting of categories of criteria and the individual criteria relative to each other that most strongly influence the probability value, (iii) the reliability of the specific probability value, and (iv) the probability values generated and their recipients. In the future, consumers in Germany will have a clearer picture about how the credit score works and financial advisers can counsel people on the basis of this information. This is undoubtedly a step in the right direction towards greater transparency as it has long been the case in the USA. Unlike the situation in the USA, the data basis for the credit scores will not be broadened with "alternative payment data" in Germany and most likely not in the majority of the EU Member States. This kind of data collecting would be forbidden for credit reporting agencies or only possible with very well-informed consent (Art. 22 (2) (c) GDPR).

5. Outlook

The importance of creditworthiness and the use of credit scores seems to increase in the economy and society at large.[50] This carries high risks, especially for the poorly scored and credit invisibles. Providing fair financial advice concerning the building and repairing of credit scores can be essential for self-help of those affected. Credit builder loans and similar products can be helpful under certain circumstances. The use of "alternative payment data" can have inclusive effects but also carries risks. Years ago, David Caplowitz demonstrated in his famous study, "The Poor Pay More"[51] that poorer individuals have to spend more on their consumption than those who are economically in a better situation. In the context of a poor credit score, they may have to pay more for their (financial) services or may not receive loans at all due to poor creditworthiness. To prevent this by building or repairing their credit, they must at least "pay more with data". In doing so, they bear a higher risk that a statistically determined standard discriminates against them or simply imperfectly reflects their actual situation and creditworthiness. In addition, they are more vulnerable in the case that they have any problems fulfilling any payment obligations to anyone. Everything can bring down the credit score.

So, which is the better argument: the criticism that "the Poor Pay More With Data" or Experian's slogan: "Data as a Force for Good"?[52] The answer will depend on how fair and transparent the scores and their use are and what help credit invisibles and the poorly scored can expect. Cooperation between debt counselling and consumer law experts, on the one hand, and financial service providers and credit agencies, on the other, to develop appropriate products and counselling strategies to combat the problem of credit data poverty makes sense and offers opportunities. However, it cannot replace a clear legal framework. The USA has been a pioneer in consumer lending rules, which the EU is now following. Regarding data protection laws, the situation seems to be the other way round. Although the approach is different, the results are converging. Despite all similarities as modern capitalistic economies, there will continue to be differences. This is perhaps most evident in the case of France. Private credit bureaus with credit-scoring systems gained no importance here; only the public Banque de France collects and shares the data concerning payment defaults.[53] This may seem very strange from an U.S. mainstream perspective.[54] Yet, France is not only a well developed economy but also an important financial marketplace with very significant banks in the EU. Banking is obviously possible without ubiquitous credit scorings. In the USA, the use of "alternative payment data" for scoring will continue to be an important trend, while this will become more difficult in the EU due to the recent development in data protection law. The dilemma of including vulnerable consumers by exploiting their data is, in the EU, likely to be decided in favour of data protection – understood as consumer protection, even while it reduces their access to consumer loans. A possible explanation for the different assessment of this trade-off in the EU and Germany as compared to the USA could be that fair access to private financial services seems less relevant where, as in many countries of the EU, there exist better public social security systems.

Notes

1 For this chapter, the author conducted a series of interviews with nonprofit organizations and academics in the USA in the fall of 2022. Special thanks go to Cy Richardson (National Urban League), Ann D. Solomon (Inclusiv), Kim Kaplan (Hebrew Free Loan Society), Jonathan Zinman (Dartmouth College), and the author wishes to express his thanks to each of them and also to Timothy Kautz (Hochschule Mainz) for English language proof-reading. Some results discussed here were presented at the 18th Conference of the International Association of Consumer Law (IACL) in Hamburg, July 19–21, 2023 and have been published in a German-language version in *Verbraucher und Recht*, no. 2 (February 2024): 58–62.
2 Schröder and Taeger, *Scoring im Focus*, 8; Vardi, *Creditworthiness*, 28–71.
3 See for a comparison between the EU and US law, Vardi, *Creditworthiness*, 150–214.
4 Affeldt and Krüger, You Are What You Pay, 74–80.
5 On the various statistical methods and those of AI, compare the review article by Markov, Seleznyova, and Lapshin, "Credit Scoring Methods," 180–201.
6 Sachverständigenrat für Verbraucherfragen, *Verbrauchergerechtes Scoring*, 16–19.
7 Traub, "Establish a Public Credit Registry," 7; Loftsgordon and O'Neil, *Credit Repair*, 29.
8 FRED, "Student Loans Owned and Securitized."
9 DeNicola, "What Is a Good Credit Score?"
10 The problem was examined already in 2015 by the Consumer Financial Protection Bureau (CFPB), which was established in the aftermath of the financial crisis. Brevoort, Grimm, and Kambara, "Data Point: Credit Invisibles."
11 CFPB, *Who Are the Credit Invisibles*.
12 BGH (German Federal Court), Judgment of 28 January 2014, Case no.VI ZR 156/13.
13 CFPB, "Adverse action notification," 3 quoting *Fischl v. Gen. Motors Acceptance Corp.*, 708 F.2d 143, 146 (5th Cir. 1983).
14 Regarding the issue of reactive measurement: Mau, *Das metrische Wir*, 214–18.
15 The term credit or financial counselling refers more to consumer education while debt counselling mainly addresses the situation of a consumer's over-indebtedness.
16 Loftsgordon and O'Neil, *Credit Repair.*

17 Burke et al., "Credit Building or Credit Crumbling?" 1586. CFPB, *Targeting Credit Builder Loans*.
18 Burke et al., "Credit Building or Credit Crumbling?" 1617.
19 CFPB, *Targeting Credit Builder Loans*, 16.
20 Both criteria together equal 65% of the Experian credit score (example see following).
21 For criticism of the costs of this model, see Reifner, *Die Finanzkrise*, 98.
22 Mission Asset Fund (MAF) "Lending Circles."
23 Hurley and Adebayo, "Credit Scoring in the Era of Big Data," 148, 157.
24 CFPB, *Consumer Credit Market Report (2023)*, 169.
25 Affeldt and Krüger, "You Are What You Pay," 87.
26 Schlee and Stoklas, "Bonify."
27 Experian, "Experian Boost."
28 CFPB, *Consumer Credit Market Report (2023)*, 169.
29 Experian, "Experian Smart Money."
30 Nam, "Open Banking," 32–33, showing that people with lower scores tend do share more data.
31 LISC, "Twin Accounts."
32 Weber, "Beratungspflicht," 2.
33 Loftsgordon and O'Neil, *Credit Repair*, 206–7.
34 Vardi, *Creditworthiness*, 215–19.
35 § 609–15 U.S.C. § 1681 ff. FCRA; CFPB, "Adverse Action Notification."
36 DeNicola, "What Is a Good Credit Score?"
37 15 U.S.C. 1691(d)(2)(A), (B); 12 CFR 1002.2(c).
38 12 CFR 1002.9(b)(2).
39 15 U.S.C. 1691(a).
40 CFPB, "Adverse Action Notification," 3 quoting *Fischl v Gen. Motors Acceptance Corp.*, 708 F.2d 143, 146 (5th Cir. 1983).
41 Vardi, *Creditworthiness*, 109.
42 ECJ, Judgment of 7 December 2023 – C-634/21.
43 ECJ, Judgment of 7 December 2023 – C-634/21, operative part of the judgment.
44 ECJ, Judgment of 7 December 2023 – C-634/21, para 49.
45 Affeldt and Krüger, "You Are What You Pay," 85.
46 This assessment is also mentioned in the new consumer credit directive ((EU) 2023/2225) in Recital 56.
47 Bundesregierung, "Gesetzesentwurf," 8–9.
48 Bundesregierung, "Gesetzesentwurf," 23–24.
49 ECJ, Judgment of 7 December 2023 – C-634/21, para 56.
50 Mau, *Das metrische Wir*, 103–34.
51 Caplovitz, *The Poor Pay More*; Silber, "Discovering that the Poor Pay More" explains why that book stimulated the reconstruction of consumer financial protection law in the USA and around the world.
52 Experian, "Data as a Force."
53 Banque de France "Fichiers d'incidents de paiement."
54 Although critical voices in the USA ask for a public credit registry, see Traub "Establish a Public Credit Registry," 1–13.

References

Affeldt, Pauline, and Ulrich Krüger. "You Are What You Pay – Personal Profiling with Alternative Payment Data and the Data Protection Law." *Vierteljahreshefte zur Wirtschaftsforschung des DIW*, no. 89 (2020): 73–89.

Banque de France. "Fichiers d'incidents de paiement." Accessed April 11, 2024. https://www.banque-france.fr/en/node/2567

Brevoort, Kenneth P., Philipp Grimm, and Michelle Kambara (Consumer Financial Protection Bureau). "Data Point: Credit Invisibles." 2015. Accessed April 11, 2024. https://files.consumerfinance.gov/f/201505_cfpb_data-point-credit-invisibles.pdf

Bundesregierung. "Gesetzentwurf zur Änderung des Bundesdatenschutzgesetzes vom 31.01.2024." Accessed April 11, 2024. https://www.bmi.bund.de/SharedDocs/gesetzgebungsverfahren/DE/Downloads/kabinettsfassung/VII4/aendg-bdsg.pdf?__blob=publicationFile&v=2.

Burke, Jeremy, Julian Jamison, Dean Karlan, Kata Mihaly, and Jonathan Zinman. "Credit Building or Credit Crumbling? A Credit Builder Loan's Effects on Consumer Behavior and Market Efficiency in the United States." *The Review of Financial Studies*, no. 36 (2023): 1585–620.

Caplovitz, David. *The Poor Pay More: Consumer Practices of Low-Income Families*. New York: Free Press of Glencoe, 1963.

Consumer Financial Protection Bureau (CFPB). "Adverse Action Notification Requirements in Connection with Credit Decisions Based on Complex Algorithms." Circular 2022-03. Accessed April 11, 2024. https://files.consumerfinance.gov/f/documents/cfpb_2022-03_circular_2022-05.pdf.

Consumer Financial Protection Bureau (CFPB). "Consumer Credit Market Report." 2023. Accessed April 11, 2024. https://files.consumerfinance.gov/f/documents/cfpb_consumer-credit-card-market-report_2023.pdf.

Consumer Financial Protection Bureau (CFPB). "Targeting Credit Builder Loans." 2020. Accessed April 11, 2024. https://files.consumerfinance.gov/f/documents/cfpb_targeting-credit-builder-loans_report_2020-07.pdf.

Consumer Financial Protection Bureau (CFPB). "Who Are the Credit Invisibles." 2016. Accessed April 11, 2024. https://files.consumerfinance.gov/f/documents/201612_cfpb_credit_invisible_policy_report.pdf.

DeNicola, Louis. "What Is a Good Credit Score?." Accessed April 11, 2024. https://www.experian.com/blogs/ask-experian/credit-education/score-basics/what-is-a-good-credit-score/.

Experian. "Data as a Force for Good". Accessed April 11, 2024. https://www.experian.com/corporate/data-for-good/.

Experian. "Experian Boost." Accessed April 11, 2024. https://www.experian.com/consumer-products/score-boost.html.

Experian. "Experian Smart Money." Accessed April 11, 2024. https://www.experian.com/money/experian-smart-money/?cc=van_tvr_smartmoney.

FRED. "Student Loans Owned and Securitized." Accessed April 11, 2024. https://fred.stlouisfed.org/series/SLOAS.

Hurley, Mikella, and Julius Adebayo. "Credit Scoring in the Era of Big Data." *The Yale Journal of Law and Technology*, 18, no. 1 (2016): 148–216.

Krüger, Ulrich. "Kreditdatenarmut – ist Credit Building ein Ausweg." *Verbraucher und Recht*, no. 2 (2024): 58–62.

Local Initiatives Support Corporation (LISC). "Twin Accounts." Accessed April 11, 2024. https://www.foc-network.org/LISC%20Twin%20Accounts%20-%20One%20Pager_V3.pdf.

Loftsgordon, Amy, and Cara O'Neil. *Credit Repair*. Nolo, 2020.

Markov, Anton, Zinaida Seleznyova, and Victor Lapshin. "Credit Scoring Methods: Latest Trends and Points to Consider." *The Journal of Finance and Data Science*, no. 8 (2022): 180–201.

Mau, Steffen. *Das metrische Wir. Über die Quantifizierung des Sozialen*. Suhrkamp, 2017.

Mission Asset Fund (MAF). "Lending Circles." Accessed April 11, 2024. https://www.missionassetfund.org/lending-circles/.

Nam, Rachel. "Open Banking and Customer Data Sharing: Implications for FinTech Borrowers (October 16, 2023)." SAFE Working Paper No. 364. http://dx.doi.org/10.2139/ssrn.4278803.

Reifner, Udo. *Die Finanzkrise*. Springer, 2017.
Sachverständigenrat für Verbraucherfragen. *Verbrauchergerechtes Scoring*, 2018.
Schlee, Nelly, and Jonathan Stoklas. "Bonify: Die neue App der SCHUFA zur digitalen Auskunftserteilung – ein datenschutzrechtliches Sodom und Gomorra?" ZD-Aktuell beck-online (2023): 01325.
Schröder, Michael, and Jürgen Taeger. *Scoring im Focus: ökonomische Bedeutung und rechtliche Rahmenbedingungen im internationalen Vergleich*. BIS-Verlag der Carl von Ossietzky Universität Oldenburg, 2014.
Silber, Norman. "Discovering that the Poor Pay More: Race Riots, Poverty, and the Rise of Consumer Law." *Fordham Urban Law Journal* (2017): 1319–28.
Traub, Amy. "Establish a Public Credit Registry." *DEMOS*, April 3, 2019. https://www.demos.org/policy-briefs/establish-public-credit-registry.
Vardi, Noah. *Creditworthiness and 'Responsible Credit' – A Comparative Study of EU and US Law*. Brill/Nijhoff, 2022.
Weber, Christoph. "Beratungspflicht bei Inanspruchnahme der Überziehungsmöglichkeit § 504a BGB." In *Münchner Kommentar zum Bürgerlichen Gesetzbuch*. Beck, 2023.

Part II

Digitalisation

6 Central Bank Digital Currencies and vulnerable consumers

Risks and opportunities for financial inclusion and access to credit

Noah Vardi

1. Introduction

Central Bank Digital Currencies (CBDCs) are quickly moving towards reality in economies worldwide,[1] and the probability that within the next few years a retail digital euro, released by the European Central Bank, will be available to all citizens is high; whether or not this will induce other economies to follow suit, and whether or not users will actually choose payments with the digital euro over other electronic payment instruments or cash, are among the challenges facing the ECB and central banks.[2]

The projects for the adoption of Central Bank Digital Currencies, currently discussed by *ad hoc* task forces globally, are among the most relevant examples of the process of digitalisation of financial services. Whilst this digitalisation process represents an important opportunity for the development of potential consumer benefits, it also requires special regulatory attention, as part of the broader phenomenon of the so-called financialisation of citizens-consumers.[3]

This chapter focuses on the project for the adoption of a digital euro in the Euro area and its potential impact in terms of financial inclusion. The first part introduces the background for the development of a European CBDC and some of the reasons driving the Eurosystem to undertake the digital euro project. The second part concentrates on the concept and phenomena of financial exclusion and financial vulnerability and their relation to payments (both in cash and digital), as payments indeed will be much affected by the introduction of a digital currency with legal tender status. The specific measures to counter the risks of financial exclusion, as outlined in the projects and Proposal for a Regulation on the establishment of a digital euro, are then examined. Part three adds some considerations on the impact of the digital euro on the two further issues of data protection and access to credit, followed by conclusive remarks.

2. Setting the scene for a European CBDC

Whereas every economy has its own characteristics and monetary policy priorities, the projects for the adoption of CBDCs, initiated globally over the past few years, are driven by a variety of (often common) motivations including, *inter alia*, the

DOI: 10.4324/9781003510406-9

decrease in the use and demand for cash, the competition brought by private digital currencies and stablecoins as well as by third country projects of CBDCs, the availability of distributed ledger technology and the desire to apply it to centralised forms of administration.[4] In the case of the European project for a digital euro, additional motivations include support for the digitalisation processes of the European economy, by providing an official central bank digital means of payment (insomuch as cash alone is insufficient to support the digital economy and currently only private digital means of payment are available); enhancing the development of pan-European and interoperable retail payment solutions; and enhancing the resilience of the European retail payments market and maintaining the role (and market share) of the euro in it.[5] The new Central Bank Digital Currencies are seemingly likely to be designed according to the underlying motivations driving their implementation, so as to meet these different needs. This includes various options, such as the users for whom they are intended; the choice between a retail or a wholesale version of the currency; the modality of access (direct or through supervised intermediaries); the architecture; the technology used for transfer (through an account-based system or as a bearer instrument) and for payments (online only or also offline; as a web-based service or also through dedicated physical devices such as smart cards); the possibility (or limitation) of using the CBDC as an investment instrument; and whether or not the CBDC should have legal tender.[6]

It is interesting to note that from a political and social point of view, the public opinion in the Euro area has been rather lukewarm on the topic of CBDCs, ever since the first discussion of their possible implementation. Concerns have been expressed, more specifically, regarding privacy and data protection as well as the risks of financial exclusion that could ensue from the adoption of a digital euro. The lukewarm attitude is all the more evident when compared with the public attention and the wave of enthusiasm (as well as critical warnings) that have accompanied cryptocurrencies ever since their appearance. It is worth noting, furthermore, how cryptocurrencies and CBDCs each express antithetical conceptions of the monetary phenomenon: the stateless, anarchic, private, de-nationalised currency in the case of cryptocurrencies;[7] a digital currency issued and, above all, guaranteed by central banks in the case of CBDCs.

Since projects for the adoption of CBDCs have been triggered also as a response to the spread of cryptocurrencies, it is not surprising that there are strong references to the secure, official and guaranteed nature of the digital euro in the official documents released by the ECB and its task force – a clear intent to highlight a difference with the risks and uncertainties known to be associated with cryptocurrencies.

These juxtaposed understandings of monetary phenomena emerge clearly in the extensive preparatory documentation accompanying the study and possible configurations of a European CBDC. This study process, furthermore, often through the use of extensive public consultations, has made it possible to emphasise the link between, on the one hand, the needs of monetary policies, protection of the banking system, fair competition and protection of users and, on the other, the possible "design" choices of the digital currency available to legislators. The Proposal for the Regulation for the Establishment of the Digital Euro has for example made clear that several options were considered, following the consultation process with various stakeholders,

> *to achieve the policy objectives while balancing key trade-offs: (i) enabling wide usage while ensuring fair competition with private payment solutions, (ii) protecting privacy while ensuring traceability, (iii) ensuring wide usage while protecting financial stability and credit provision, and (iv) supporting international use while mitigating risks for non-euro countries and the Eurosystem.*[8]

This is a rather unusual element of reflection in the debate surrounding money and payments since the main issues recalled in discussions on official currencies usually concern monetary policy, public confidence and the efficiency of payments (suffice it to recall, once again, albeit in the opposite direction, the different alerts raised by the spread of cryptocurrencies).[9]

In the case of CBDCs, additional "social" and "cultural" needs are taken into account, concerning, among other things, financial exclusion, privacy, and the risk of a potential reduction in available credit. It is particularly with reference to the issue of financial exclusion that some further considerations will be attempted.

3. Financial exclusion, digital payments and vulnerable users

Before any further consideration, it is necessary to try and identify the – far from unanimous – notion of "financial exclusion". Usually defined positively, in terms of financial "inclusion", the notion does not have a single meaning, since often (as is the case, for example, with the World Bank), the concept of financial inclusion also includes access to credit and sustainable finance.[10] Schwarcz and Leonhardt have sought to provide a pragmatic taxonomy that can serve the implementation of the regulatory purposes invoked by various national and supranational institutions.[11] In this functional perspective, financial inclusion has been defined as broad-based deposit-account ownership and access to payments services; access to credit means access to loan funding on reasonable terms, especially for underserved demographics of potential entrepreneurs; while sustainable finance describes a system that continuously provides financial inclusion and access to credit.[12]

Given this conceptual framework of financial inclusion, ever since reflections on CBDCs began, a recurring concern has been that the adoption of an official digital currency (even if alongside cash and not as a substitute for it, as clarified, for example, repeatedly in the ECB's project) may entail specific risks for certain categories of vulnerable users (often defined as the "financially vulnerable consumers").

As with other general parameters identified for consumers, the notion of vulnerable consumers is subject to multiple interpretations.[13] The European Commission has, for example, emphasised that more recent definitions of vulnerability recognise that it is not a static condition, both because depending on the context, consumers may be vulnerable in respect of some categories of transactions but not others and because this condition itself may be transitory, as consumers may move in and out of states of vulnerability. Hence, it has been pointed out that the notion of vulnerability would be best viewed as a spectrum rather than a binary state.[14]

The notion of vulnerability generally implies an *ex ante* assessment, used, for example, by the legislature, about the likelihood of a negative outcome in terms of consumer well-being. Vulnerability in literature is often identified as either a condition that relates to personal characteristics of the consumer or that depends on the transactional context in which consumers find themselves.[15] These two categories of definitions reflect a fundamental change in the approach to the concept of vulnerability, namely the move from the "disadvantaged consumer" (which associates vulnerability with specific groups which are disadvantaged in the marketplace, i.e., due to factors such as income, age, education, race or ethnicity) towards the "vulnerable consumer" (where vulnerability is not limited to specific socio-economic groups but is rather the result of an interaction between internal and external factors).[16]

If the notion of vulnerable consumer, therefore, lends itself to multiple interpretations, with reference to the topic of interest here, it should be noted that two profiles, already identified by literature and by law[17] (and which often originate from the same factors, such as gender, age, level of education, income level, geographical location) come into consideration.[18] The first is that of "digital" vulnerability, (i.e., the socio-economic impact deriving from the digital divide on vulnerable social groups in terms of lower income, education, age, disabilities, minority ethnic groups or residence in remote/isolated geographic areas)[19] and which "describes a universal state of defencelessness and susceptibility to (the exploitation of) power imbalances that are the result of increasing automation of commerce, datafied consumer-seller relations and the very architecture of digital marketplaces".[20] The second is the notion of "financial" vulnerability, which comprises, according to a taxonomy identified by Cartwright, informational vulnerability, pressure vulnerability, supply vulnerability, redress vulnerability and impact vulnerability.[21]

It is with reference to these multifaceted and related categories of vulnerability that the digitalisation of financial services is analysed under the perspective of financial inclusion/exclusion. As previously noted, the projects on CBDCs are amongst the most relevant current processes of this digitalisation. It is, therefore, not surprising that in order to counteract possible negative impacts on financially vulnerable citizens deriving from a future adoption of a centralised digital currency, the project on the digital euro lays down specific measures. Subjects considered to be at risk in this context are the financially fragile (those living in poverty, the homeless, immigrants); those most exposed to the so-called digital divide (for reasons of geography, network infrastructure, access to computing devices); the elderly; people with disabilities or health problems; people with limited digital skills; and those without a bank account (the so-called "unbanked").[22]

"Unbanked" individuals, particularly, are excluded from both the credit system and the cashless payment system; Lupo-Pasini has highlighted the existence of a "monetary exclusion" for these individuals, which intersects the two distinct phenomena of financial exclusion typically recognised in the debate on financial exclusion. On the one hand, access to financial services, (i.e., difficulty in access to credit and savings, hampering access to the formal banking and pension system) and on the other hand, access to payments (i.e., the inability to extinguish pecuniary debts using payment instruments other than cash).[23] The phenomenon of "monetary exclusion" so defined would result from an increasingly cashless society and is "the result of a progressive regulatory shift away from the state-based payment system dominated by cash, in which access to a means of payment is universal, towards a private monetary regime".[24] Individuals who are most exposed to the risks of monetary exclusion resulting from a completely cashless system often fall simultaneously into more than one category of "vulnerable" citizens highlighted earlier; it is not surprising, therefore, that policies of financial inclusion, broadly understood, are accompanied by policies designed to promote, for example, the process of digitalisation of citizenship (both in terms of access to digital services and in terms of education and training in their operation). It is equally understandable, from this perspective – but not only –[25] that the current digital euro project as it stands stresses the fact that cash in the form of coins and banknotes would continue to exist and circulate as legal tender and would not be replaced by a purely digital form.[26]

Alongside this stance by the ECB to maintain the circulation of the euro in its *fiat* form, it may be useful to examine in more detail the policies put in place, at this design stage, to curb the risk that the adoption of the digital euro accentuates existing phenomena of financial exclusion or vulnerability whilst keeping in mind that the groups of people vulnerable to digital-financial inclusion are diverse.

4. Measures for financial and digital inclusion

A useful basis for the analysis of potential measures to counter the risks of financial exclusion that could ensue from the adoption of the European CBDC is constituted by the several reports prepared by the Eurosystem task force and the recent Proposal for a Regulation of the European Parliament and of the Council on the establishment of the digital euro.[27]

In the Final Report on the investigation phase published by the ECB in October 2023, the issue is addressed with a number of specific measures "supporting financial and digital inclusion".[28] Noting that whereas the digital euro does not have the form of a physical coin or banknote, it would still benefit from the most important characteristics of cash as a public good,[29] including its being "inclusive", free for basic use and risk-free, the project envisions a basic form of service accessible to all those who cannot afford a payment card or bank account or cannot make payments online.

The model for implementing a basic service is the one already provided for in the Payment Accounts Directive (so-called PAD Directive).[30] The choice of the PAD is not surprising, if one considers that the PAD Directive was adopted, after a failure of analogous soft law and self-regulation measures, with the aim of promoting access to payment services while taking into account the needs of the most vulnerable consumers (a *ratio* obviously also justified in terms of the broader promotion of the smooth functioning of the internal market as well as the development "of a modern, socially inclusive economy").[31] The choice of the model of the PAD is also supported by the fact that access to payment services *de facto* is almost exclusively contingent on access to a payment account held with a credit institution.[32]

The ECB Report tackles the problem of offering incentives for payment service providers to distribute an accessible form of digital euro (for example, by enhancing opportunities for payment service providers to achieve a European scale), whilst also balancing adequate safeguards for end users by establishing a digital euro compensation model. The compensation model is based on four core principles: a) free basic use by private individuals, comprising all services necessary to enable people to pay and be paid with digital euro in a convenient manner; b) network effects generating economic incentives for acquiring payment service providers and merchants; c) comparable economic incentives for payment service providers that distribute digital euro to private parties; and d) costs of issuance and settlement schemes for the digital euro that remain the responsibility of the Eurosystem, as is already the case for euro cash (with the recommendation that any potential savings that arise from this should benefit end users by reducing their costs).[33]

These principles are supported by the legislative proposals for the digital euro, which, in fact, provide for legal tender status for the digital euro;[34] the definition of the basic services to be provided free of charge for individuals by payment service providers[35] and the provision of caps on fees to be paid on basic digital euro payment services;[36] the intention of the Eurosystem to bear its own costs;[37] and the technical characteristics that the digital euro should have to facilitate its use by the public, including persons who are financially marginalised or at risk of financial exclusion; persons with disabilities, functional limitations or limited digital skills; and older persons.[38]

The implementation of the policy of distribution of basic digital euro payment services for individuals who do not have a non-digital euro payment account or who do not wish to open a digital euro payment account with a credit institution is carried out by designating specific entities (i.e., local or regional authorities or post offices) required to provide such basic payment services (whilst credit institutions have the duty to provide, upon request of their clients, basic digital euro payment services to all natural and legal persons residing or established in the Member States whose currency is the euro). Unlike in the PAD Directive, however, such services should be provided free of charge (as opposed to Article 18 of the PAD which stipulates for the provision of basic payment services "free of charge or for a reasonable charge").[39] Payment service providers thus identified should also provide "digital inclusion support to persons with disabilities, functional limitations or limited digital skills, and elderly persons" including "a dedicated assistance for on-boarding to a digital euro account and using all basic digital euro services".[40]

Further financial accessibility and inclusion measures in the ECB Report comprise a digital euro payment card available for those who are at risk of digital-financial exclusion and prefer a physical card to a digital application (a card that can also be refunded without the necessary use of a smartphone or other device). Onboarding (i.e., the activities that enable the user to access services to pay, be paid, and hold digital euros) should be possible both remotely and in person, as well as the possibility to switch payment service providers easily.[41] The offline functionality of the digital euro also assumes a relevant role in making the digital euro inclusive, especially for areas underserved by network coverage and for persons with no smart devices or who are unaccustomed to using them.

Indeed, within the set of "technical" features designed (also) for inclusive purposes, in addition to ease of use by the public and by categories of people at greater risk of financial marginalisation, the Proposed Regulation for the digital euro prescribes availability for both offline and online payment transactions[42] as well as availability for conditional payment transactions (while it should not be a programmable currency with usage limits).[43] Furthermore, users are not required to hold or open non-digital euro payment accounts or accept other non-digital euro products in their dealings with payment service providers for the provision of digital euro services (with the understanding that each digital euro payment account may be linked to one or more non-digital euro payment accounts designated by the user).[44]

Finally, the ECB Report on the investigation phase on the digital euro suggests the introduction of a Eurosystem app (an application that allows users to interact with their payment service providers) that would ensure the availability of the basic functionalities for the use of the digital euro and support digital inclusion for people with disabilities and low digital skills, in compliance with the European Accessibility Act.[45]

Even a brief overview of advocated measures aiming at promoting access to the use of the digital euro, and currently at a proposal stage, highlights two lines of action. The first is that of ensuring access through substantive regulatory intervention: the measures envisaged along the lines of the PAD to provide a free access to the digital euro with basic functionality (with charges borne by entities specifically identified for this purpose, taking into account appropriate assessments of the entailing risks of distortion in the distribution of costs) fall within this category. The aforementioned offline mode feature of the digital euro, allowing its use regardless of access to the network, also falls within substantive regulation.

The second type of intervention acts upon the technical characteristics of the digital euro, (the "design" features, as termed by the task forces). Here the visible effort is directed towards a simplicity of use, with a choice of "legislative engineering" that can certainly be welcomed since it benefits the entire user base, regardless of its degree of susceptibility to suffer negative impacts from the digitalisation process.[46]

Additional inclusive effects related to the digital euro (although not explicitly taken into account in the Regulation proposal) may also derive from its potential to increase efficiency and reduce costs in the area of cross-border funds transfers, particularly with regard to remittances from cross-border workers.[47]

Indeed, Angeloni points out that facilitating cross-border remittances in terms of cost and time for eurozone workers is a valuable service from an economic and social perspective; where the private financial sector does not efficiently provide it, an active role of central banks would also find justification in terms of inclusive policies. A concrete implementation of such a policy would require interoperability between the digital euro and the CBDCs of the third countries to which remittances are sent and, in any case, bilateral cooperation agreements; the goal could also be pursued through forms of subsidization to the private intermediaries or payment service providers.[48]

5. The digital euro and problems of access to credit

The measures examined so far fall within those policies that expressly aim (as declared in the projects and proposals) at combating phenomena of financial exclusion that could ensue from the adoption of the digital euro. While some of the principal risks are indeed identified and more or less emphatically tackled, there are additional concerns of possible negative effects of a digital euro for vulnerable segments of the population. Issues of data protection and of possible credit contraction, with consequences on access to credit, are often brought up.

Both issues pose questions that are relevant far beyond problems of financial exclusion and, as such, would require a much deeper analysis than what is proposed in this chapter. With this forewarning, the following section will only point out the relevance and interrelation of data protection and access to credit from the perspective of the risks of financial exclusion for vulnerable users.

It should be noted, in the first place, that what emerges from ECB consultations and reports as a constant (and possibly the main) concern in the public opinion on the adoption of a digital euro regards privacy.[49]

Concerns stem mainly from the use that personal data, processed from transactions related to the activation and especially the subsequent use of the digital euro, could be made by both public authorities (the central banks) and private intermediaries. This issue is directly addressed by the legislator in the Proposed Digital Euro Regulation,[50] which defines the tasks for which payment service providers, the ECB and national central banks may process personal data, including, for the latter, the settlement of digital euro payment transactions, and states that the processing of personal data should be based on the use of state-of-the-art security and privacy-preserving measures, such as pseudonymization or encryption, to ensure that payment service providers, the ECB and national central banks cannot directly attribute data to an identified digital euro user.[51]

Data protection also comes into play in the implementation of anti-money laundering and anti-terrorist financing policies and the relevant provisions apply to offline digital euro payment transactions, which have a higher level of privacy protection than online payments (thus theoretically bringing the former, when proximate and low in amount, closer to the characteristics of cash payments).[52]

More in general, however, the relevance of data protection from the perspective of potential consequences in terms of financial exclusion is related to its possible impact on access to credit. Indeed, the data used for payments, particularly on digital platforms, constitute, from the point of view of the variety of users and activities performed, formidable aggregates on the economic behaviour of users/consumers.[53] These data, as is widely known, constitute the basis for algorithmic and big data credit-scoring techniques, which are used to assess the creditworthiness of loan applicants.[54] Hence the strategic importance that data protection of digital euro users assumes as a determining factor for the access to credit, especially for individuals who face higher risks of discrimination.[55] It is also worth noting though, on the other hand, that the use of non-financial data in algorithmic credit scoring could favour individuals with so-called "thin credit history" or who are "credit invisible," whose access to credit may otherwise be jeopardised by an insufficient credit history.[56]

This last aspect is closely related to the second order of issues highlighted earlier, namely the fear that the introduction of the digital euro could provoke a credit crunch. The concern stems from the possible competition of central banks to financial intermediaries on deposit funds, should the digital euro become attractive from a remunerative point of view; this would result in a migration of deposits to central banks, which would dry up the deposits of private credit institutions and reduce the availability for the latter of funds for household and corporate lending.[57] Beyond the measures hypothesised to reduce this risk (including, principally, a cap on the maximum holdings per capita of deposits in digital euros and a possible differentiation of remuneration rates so as to disincentivise large deposits, via so-called "tiering"),[58] it is clear how a potential credit crunch would represent a typical case of disparate impact on the financially vulnerable groups. It is indeed ordinarily the most fragile borrowers who are first affected whenever there is a contraction in available credit, regardless of what provoked the crisis. The financially vulnerable are also often those who then turn to unofficial credit markets, and/or that can become targets of predatory lending and that are more easily subject to over-indebtedness. In cases such as these, there is a vicious cycle in which the vulnerable often cannot access credit because they do not meet creditworthiness requirements, their vulnerability further increases because they cannot access the credit market, and this then compromises their chances of accessing credit in the future. Indeed, the systemic and social dimension of these risks are at the basis of the policies adopted in several legal systems for the promotion of access to credit (under different forms, such as prohibition of discrimination; promotion of loans at "fair" and "safe" conditions; subsidising loans for the purchase of housing, for education, health insurance etc.).[59]

6. Conclusive remarks

The policies analysed above, envisaged as a response to potential problems of financial exclusion deriving from, or amplified by, the proposed digital euro, are indicative of some of the foundational choices that task forces on CBDCs (globally) have to make. The options and related choices emerge during the "design" phase of the digital currency and they concern more than its "social" impact. As this chapter has sought to highlight, often the choices are dictated by priorities in the agendas of central banks and legislators: reducing negative impacts in terms of financial exclusion is one, among multiple concerns, which include increased competitiveness of the currency; attractivity on the international market; temporal priority in implementing the project; stability of the financial system; balancing the role of private credit institutions, payment service providers and financial intermediaries; accelerating the digitalisation of the economy; and encouraging e-commerce. No priority is independent in its implementation from the others; it is interesting, however, to observe a process of "monetary law in the making" that while taking place contemporaneously across very different economies, allows one to identify the cultural, social and, of course, economic factors that influence the tailoring of the projects. There is no "one size fits all" and a comparative functional analysis of the phenomenon seems to yield interesting results.

Notes

1 An updated *tracker* of the progress of CBDCs has been created by the Atlantic Council (https://www.atlanticcouncil.org/cbdctracker/); at the time of writing within 134 Countries/Currency Unions tracked, there are 3 CBDCs launched, 36 pilots, 30 CBDCs at the stage of development and 44 at the stage of research.

2 Where pilot projects have been launched, such as the digital e-yuan (e-CNY) rolled out in China in 2020, the data available for the first period (2022) indicated a slow start, with a much lower percentage of transactions with the official CBDC than with the private sector alternatives (i.e., Alipay and WeChat). See Angeloni, *Digital Euro*, 16; see also the analysis by the Foreign Policy Research Institute, https://www.fpri.org/article/2023/06/china-is-doubling-down-on-its-digital-currency/. Relevant data is also summarised by the Atlantic Council tracker. For a wider review of development of digital banking and the progress of the e-CNY in China, see Allen, Gu, and Jagtiani, "FinTech."

3 The phenomenon is well analysed with reference to European private law by Comparato, *The Financialisation of the Citizen.*

4 For a reconstruction of the reasons and context in which projects on CBDCs have been conceived see, *ex multis*, Barontini and Holden, "Proceeding with Caution"; Bilotta and Botti, *The (Near) Future of Central Bank Digital Currencies*; Bosi, "Taking CBDC Seriously"; Brunnermeier, James, and Landau, "The Digitalization of Money"; Didenko and Buckley, "The Evolution of Currency"; Gnan and Masciandaro, *Do We Need Central Bank Digital Currency?*; Grünewald, Zellweger-Gutknecht, and Geva, "Digital Euro and ECB Powers"; Nabilou, "Central Bank Digital Currencies"; Raskin and Yermack, "Digital Currencies"; Zetzsche et al., "Sovereign Digital Currencies."

5 See Proposal for a Regulation of the European Parliament and of the Council on the establishment of the digital euro, COM (2023) 369 final, of June 28, 2023.

6 See European Central Bank, "Report on a Digital Euro," October 2020, https://www.ecb.europa.eu/pub/pdf/other/Report_on_a_digital_euro~4d7268b458.it.pdf#page=27.

7 Not surprisingly, cryptocurrencies were defined early on as "Hayek Money", with bitcoins considered as a practical implantation of the theories expressed by the Austrian economist in his influential book *The Denationalization of Money* (London: The Institute of Economic Affairs, 1976). See Ametrano, "Hayek Money."

8 See Proposal for a Regulation of the European Parliament and of the Council on the establishment of the digital euro, COM (2023) 369 final, June 28, 2023, 9.

9 Some of the earliest documents issued include: European Central Bank, *Virtual Currency Schemes*, October 2012; European Banking Authority, *Warning to Consumers on Virtual Currencies*, December 12, 2013 [EBA/WRG/2013/01]; European Banking Authority, *Opinion on Virtual Currencies*, July 4, 2014 [EBA/Op/2014/08]; Financial Action Task Force, *Report, Virtual Currencies: Key Definitions and Potential AML/CFT Risks*, FATF/OECD, June 2014; European Securities and Markets Authority, European Banking Authority, European Insurance and Occupation Pensions Authority, *Warning to Consumers on the Risks of Virtual Currencies*, February 12, 2018.

10 According to the World Bank, financial inclusion means that individuals and businesses have access to useful and affordable financial products and services that meet their needs – transactions, payments, savings, credit and insurance – delivered in a responsible and sustainable way. See https://www.worldbank.org/en/topic/financialinclusion/overview.

11 See Schwarcz and Leonhardt, "Scoping and Defining Financial Inclusion," 2, who highlight how international institutions view terms such as "financial inclusion", "access to credit", and "sustainable finance" as describing components of larger targets, such as the United Nations' Sustainable Development Goals (see the UN Global Compact, Scaling Finance for the Sustainable Development Goals: Foreign Direct Investment, Financial Intermediation and Public-Private Partnerships 3 (2019), https://unglobalcompact.org/library/5721#), rather than as independent goals for the existing financial system.

12 See Schwarcz and Leonhardt, "Scoping and Defining Financial Inclusion," 4, who recognise that these definitions correspond to the Vickers Report's "broad functions" of facilitating payments, intermediating funds and managing financial risks.

13 See for example Rabitti, "Il consumatore vulnerabile," 2, who underlines that these notions, as already the case with the notion of the "average consumer", are introduced as general models for an efficient application of European private law, without, however, meeting their scope.

14 See the European Commission, *Consumer Vulnerability Across Key Markets in the European Union Final Report*, 2016, xvii–xviii, 41 and ff.

15 European Commission, *Consumer Vulnerability Across Key Markets in the European Union*, xvii. The Report overviews how academic and grey literature conceptualise vulnerability, with a first category of definitions based on personal characteristics of the consumer which include a) individuals who have diminished capacity to understand the role of advertising, product effects or both; b) individuals who are more susceptible to economic, physical or psychological harm in, or as a result of, economic transactions because of characteristics that limit their ability to maximise their utility and well-being; and c) a difficulty in obtaining or assimilating the information needed for decision-making on goods or services. A second category of vulnerability depends on the overall situation in which consumers find themselves and includes a) consumers who are at a disadvantage in exchange relationships where that disadvantage is attributable to characteristics that are largely not controllable by them; b) consumers' special characteristics and the means or techniques which marketers use that render them especially vulnerable; c) consumers whose circumstances make them vulnerable to suffering consumer disadvantage; d) a state of powerlessness that arises from an imbalance in marketplace interactions or from the consumption of marketing messages and products; and e) the condition in which a consumer is at greater risk of mis-selling, exploitation or being put at a disadvantage in terms of accessing or using a service, or in seeking redress. (European Commission, *Consumer Vulnerability Across Key Markets*, 41–42 and literature cited therein).

16 European Commission, *Consumer Vulnerability Across Key Markets*, 43.

17 The Unfair Commercial Practices Directive (UCPD-Directive 2005/29/EC, in OJ L 149/22, June 11, 2005) provides an explicit legal definition of vulnerability in relation to unfair commercial practices in its Article 5 (3) as "a clearly identifiable group of consumers who are particularly vulnerable to the practice or the underlying product because of their mental or physical infirmity, age or credulity in a way which the trader could reasonably be expected to foresee"; a notion which is related to the concept of the "average" consumer, further recalled in the Directive (art. 8) as the paradigm by which aggressive commercial practices are evaluated. The concept of the "vulnerable" consumer, however, was already known and used, for example, by the European Court of Human Rights as well as in data protection law (with regards especially to minors). See Helberger et al., *EU Consumer Protection 2.0*, 8 and literature cited therein.

18 On the relation between "financial vulnerability" and "digital vulnerability", due, *inter alia*, to the impact of the digital revolution on consumers (and especially data exploitation strategies and the use of artificial intelligence), see Helberger et al., *EU Consumer Protection 2.0*; Barocas and Selbst, "Big Data's Disparate Impact"; Paglietti and Rabitti, "A Matter of Time"; Riefa, "Protecting Vulnerable Consumers." On age-related issues, see Cascione, *Il lato grigio del diritto*, 58 and ff.

19 See, for example, the study by Mazzoni et al., "Implications of the Digital Transformation."

20 Helberger et al., *EU Consumer Protection 2.0*, 5.

21 Moving from the distinction between "vulnerable" and "disadvantaged" consumers, with the latter condition characterised as a persistent characteristic, Cartwright identifies a taxonomy of vulnerability which relates to the way markets operate in classical economic theory. The five forms of vulnerability thus identified are: a) informational vulnerability, deriving from greater information asymmetry; b) pressure vulnerability, deriving from a greater susceptibility to pressure; c) supply vulnerability, deriving from limited or lack of choice of supply, provided by a small number of firms, for certain categories of consumers; d) redress vulnerability, deriving from the difficulty in holding traders accountable for breaches under private law; and e) impact vulnerability, deriving from the greater harm or loss suffered by particular consumers from sub-optimal decisions (with poverty being the principal contributor to impact vulnerability where financial services are concerned). See Cartwright, "Understanding and Protecting Vulnerable Financial Consumers," 121–24.

22 According to the FDIC Survey of 2023, an estimated 4,2% of U.S. households were "unbanked" in 2023, meaning that no one in the household had a checking or savings account at a bank or credit union. See Federal Deposit Insurance Corporation, "National Survey of Unbanked and Underbanked Households," https://www.fdic.gov/household-survey/2023-fdic-national-survey-unbanked-and-underbanked-households-report (The survey is conducted every two years). According to the World Bank *Global Findex Database* of 2021, the average rate of unbanked population in Europe in 2021 was 3.6% with very different percentage rates among States: from Romania, with a 30.88% of unbanked population, and Bulgaria with a percentage rate of 16.03%, to countries like Austria, Belgium, Denmark, Finland, Estonia, Germany, France, Ireland, the Netherlands, Slovenia and Sweden, with less than 1% of unbanked citizens. See the World Bank, "Global Findex Database 2021," https://www.fdic.gov/household-survey/2023-fdic-national-survey-unbanked-and-underbanked-households-report and the analysis by the WSBI-ESBG (European Savings and Retail Banking Group) on the data published in the Findex Database. The lower rate of ownership of bank accounts in countries like Romania and Bulgaria has also been attributed, *inter alia*, to historical-economic factors, such as a heritage from the previous socialist legal framework that discouraged private banking (See Comparato, *The Financialisation of the Citizen*, 91).

23 See Lupo-Pasini, "Financial Inclusion," 20.

24 Lupo-Pasini, "Is It a Wonderful Life?" 166. Lupo-Pasini recalls the growth in the so-called "War on Cash", embraced by governments in the United States, Europe and Asia (justified by anti-money laundering and anti-tax evasion policies) and well exemplified in Kenneth Rogoff's influential book *The Curse of Cash* (Princeton University Press, 2017); a process also visible in the attempts by private "great tech saviours" of financial inclusion (i.e., M-Pesa in Africa, AliPay in China and PayTM in India) to create a digital ecosystem bypassing the constraints of the cash economy. See Lupo-Pasini, "Financial Inclusion," 17–18.

25 The ECB Report, *A Stocktake on the Digital Euro: Summary Report on the Investigation Phase and Outlook on the Next Phase*, October 18, 2023, 5, https://www.ecb.europa.eu/paym/digital_euro/investigation/profuse/shared/files/dedocs/ecb.dedocs231018.en.pdf, cites the findings of the 2022 ECB, *Study on the Payment Attitudes of Consumers in the Euro Area* (SPACE), according to which 60% of Europeans like the option of paying with cash; thus, demonstrating that maintaining the circulation of cash is not driven

only by policies of inclusion. See also Wischnewsky, "Nearly Cashless", for an analysis revealing that the prevailing level of trust (sometimes referred to as social capital) is one of the mechanisms through which culture impacts the adoption of cashless payment methods within a given economy.

26 See, for example, ECB, *A Stocktake on the Digital Euro*, 15, defining the digital euro "As a complement to cash in the digital age, a digital euro would be a public good for people to use in all their everyday digital payments"; but also assuring that it would "exist alongside euro cash" (p. 4), and "would provide an additional payment option to complement cash and current private digital payment solutions (rather than replace them)" (p. 8). See https://www.ecb.europa.eu/paym/digital_euro/investigation/profuse/shared/files/dedocs/ecb.dedocs231018.en.pdf.

27 COM (2023) 369 final.

28 ECB, *A Stocktake on the Digital Euro*, 34 and ff.

29 ECB, *A Stocktake on the Digital Euro*, 3.

30 Directive 2014/92/EU of the European Parliament and of the Council of July 23, 2014 on the comparability of fees related to payment accounts, payment account switching and access to payment accounts with basic features, in OJ L257/214, August 28, 2014. The PAD lays down a right of access to "a payment account with basic features" with credit institutions located in their territory to "consumers legally resident in the Union, including consumers with no fixed address and asylum seekers, and consumers who are not granted a residence permit but whose expulsion is impossible for legal or factual reasons" (Article 16, PAD). The characteristics of a "payment account with basic features" include (at a minimum, but Member States may establish an obligation to provide additional services) services enabling placement of funds in a payment account; cash withdrawals (at a counter or ATM); payment transactions including direct debits; payment through a payment card, including online payments; and credit transfers (Article 17 PAD). As to the fees associated to these services, Article 18 provides that Member States shall ensure that they are offered by credit institutions free of charge or for a reasonable fee, taking into account "at least the following criteria": national income levels and average fees charged by credit institutions in the Member State concerned for services provided on payment accounts.

31 See Recital 3, Directive 2014/92.

32 On the process that led to the adoption of the PAD Directive, including previous self-regulatory and soft law measures, see Comparato, *The Financialisation of the Citizen*, 93–96, 100 and ff. who also highlights the problems and options for promoting financial inclusion through access to basic bank services whilst avoiding possible distortions of competition deriving from the burden of costs for the basic accounts and from the disparity in the percentage rate of "unbanked" citizens in different Member States as well as the sensitive issue of allowing overdraft facilities to be associated with basic payment accounts.

33 ECB, *A Stocktake on the Digital Euro*, 30–31.

34 Article 7 Proposal for a Regulation on the establishment of the digital euro.

35 Article 14 Proposal for a Regulation on the establishment of the digital euro.

36 Article 17(2), Proposal for a Regulation on the establishment of the digital euro which establishes that any merchant service charge or inter-PSP fee in relation to digital euro payment transactions shall comply with the principle of proportionality and are regulated so that they shall not exceed the lowest of the following two amounts: a) the relevant costs incurred by PSPs for the provision of digital euro payments, including a reasonable margin of profit or b) fees or charges requested for comparable digital means of payments. The ECB shall regularly monitor and publish explanatory reports on the relevant information for the purposes of these amounts.

37 Recital 41, Proposal for a Regulation on the establishment of the digital euro.

38 Articles 22–24, Proposal for a Regulation on the establishment of the digital euro.

39 Article 14 (2)(3) and Article 17(1) Proposal for a Regulation on the establishment of the digital euro.

40 Article 14 (4) Proposal for a Regulation on the establishment of the digital euro.
41 ECB, *A Stocktake on the Digital Euro*, 34.
42 See Article 23, Proposal for a Regulation on the establishment of the digital euro, providing that the digital euro held online or offline shall be convertible at par between each other, at the request of the digital euro users; and that payee and payer shall be informed of whether the digital euro payment transaction will be offline or online before initiating the payment transaction in a proximity payment.
43 Article 24 Proposal for a Regulation on the establishment of the digital euro.
44 Article 22 Proposal for a Regulation on the establishment of the digital euro.
45 Directive (EU) 2019/882 of the European Parliament and of the Council of April 17, 2019, on the accessibility requirements for products and services, OJ L 151/70, June 7, 2019. See ECB, *A Stocktake on the Digital Euro*, 29, 35.
46 One can recall at point the concept of vulnerability, famously theorised by Martha Albertson Fineman, as a universal and constant status, inherent in the human condition, which requires a more responsive state and is alternative to the traditional equal protection/discrimination analysis. See for example Fineman, "The Vulnerable Subject."
47 This potential effect has been pointed out by Angeloni, who recalls Eurostat data estimating that over 5% of workers in the EU are non-EU citizens. See Angeloni, *Digital Euro*, 19.
48 Angeloni, *Digital Euro*.
49 This is manifested in the various working documents released by the ECB and in the results of the public consultation phase on the digital euro, https://www.ecb.europa.eu/pub/pdf/other/Eurosystem_report_on_the_public_consultation_on_a_digital_euro~539fa8cd8d.en.pdf; as well as in the impact assessment on the Proposal for a Regulation on the establishment of the digital euro.
50 Chapter VIII (Articles 34–36) of the Proposal for a Regulation on the establishment of the digital euro is titled "Privacy and data protection". For a skeptical view, see Zeno-Zencovich, "Digital Euro as a Platform", 208–9, highlighting that the digital euro, like all other forms of electronic payment, is by its very nature a traceable instrument; and interpreting the inclusion of a data protection Chapter in the regulation proposal as "privacy-washing", with the "function of reassuring the public of an equivalence [between payment in cash and payment in electronic form] that in reality does not exist".
51 Articles 34 and 35 Proposal for a Regulation on the establishment of the digital euro. Furthermore, the Commission is empowered to adopt delegated acts to update the types of personal data processed by PSPs, the ECB and national central banks.
52 See Article 37 of the Proposal for a Regulation on the establishment of the digital euro. For offline digital euro payments, transaction data shall not be retained by PSPs, the ECB and national central banks. PSPs shall retain data of funding and defunding for storing digital euros on payment instruments and shall, upon request, make those data available to the Financial Intelligence Unit (in case of suspect or threat of money laundering and terrorist financing). The Commission can adopt implementing acts setting transaction limits and holding limits for offline digital euro payments.
53 The European Data Protection Supervisor has confirmed these concerns on CBDCs and has highlighted how

> *wrong design choices might worsen data protection issues in digital payments: payment data already reveals very sensitive aspects of a person. Wrong design choices in the underlying technological infrastructure might exacerbate the privacy and data protection issues that already exists in the digital payment landscape. For example, transactional data could be unlawfully used for credit evaluation and cross-selling initiatives.*

The EDPS has also considered as additional negative foreseen impacts on data protection the following: a) concentration of data in the hands of central banks, which could generate incentives for cyberattacks and a high systemic risk of individual or generalised surveillance in case of data breaches or, more in general, unlawful access or b) lack of security in the CBDC infrastructure, which may turn into severe lack of trust from users. See https://www.edps.europa.eu/press-publications/publications/techsonar/central-bank-digital-currency_en.

54 Please see Vardi, *Creditworthiness and Responsible Credit*, 97 and ff. and the literature cited therein.

55 Policies promoting access to credit are, in fact, historically framed first of all as "negative" antidiscrimination regulations (i.e., such as the legislation enacted in the United States in mid-1970s, with the Equal Credit Opportunity Act, the Fair Housing Act, and the Home Mortgage Disclosure Act; or in Europe with the EU Charter of Fundamental Rights and the general Directives prohibiting discrimination (i.e., the Racial Equality Directive; the Goods and Services Directive) applied to access to credit and financial services).

56 See Bruckner, "The Promise and Perils," 5–6.

57 See the considerations by Angeloni, *Digital Euro*, 12–13; and Ahnert et al., "CBDC and Financial Stability" on the relationship between bank fragility and CBDC remuneration. See, however, Abad, Nuño, and Carlos, "CBDC and the Operational Framework of Monetary Policy" predicting that the "deposit crunch" deriving from the adoption of a CBDC has a rather small effect on bank lending (i.e., "credit crunch") to the real economy (differentiating effects according to whether adoption of the CBDC is moderate or larger); and Auer et al., "CBDC and the Banking System," 6, suggesting that individual holding limits and an environment characterised by ample liquidity and stable funding for credit institutions would render the impact of a CBDC on the funding structure of credit institutions manageable.

58 Angeloni, *Digital Euro*, 13.

59 For an overview of some of these policies, see Vardi, *Creditworthiness and Responsible Credit*, 224–28.

References

Abad, Jorge, Galo Nuño, and Thomas Carlos. "CBDC and the Operational Framework of Monetary Policy." Banco de España, Documentos e Trabajo No. 2404, 2024. https://www.bde.es/f/webbe/SES/Secciones/Publicaciones/PublicacionesSeriadas/DocumentosTrabajo/24/Files/dt2404e.pdf.

Ahnert, Toni, Peter Hoffmann, Agnese Leonello, and Davide Porcellaccia. "Central Bank Digital Currency and Financial Stability." ECB Working Paper Series No. 2783. ECB, 2023.

Albertson Fineman, Martha. "The Vulnerable Subject: Anchoring Equality in the Human Condition." *Yale Journal of Law & Feminism* 20 (2008): 1–23.

Allen, Franklin, Xian Gu, and Julapa Jagtiani. "Fintech, Cryptocurrencies, and CBDC: Financial Structural Transformation in China." Working Papers No. 22-12. Federal Reserve Bank of Philadelphia, 2022.

Ametrano, Ferdinando M. "Hayek Money: The Cryptocurrency Price Stability Solution." SSRN, 2016. http://papers.ssrn.com/sol3/papers.cfm?abstract_id=2425270.

Angeloni, Ignazio. *Digital Euro: When in Doubt, Abstain. In-Depth Analysis Requested by the ECON Committee*. European Parliament, April 2023. https://www.europarl.europa.eu/RegData/etudes/IDAN/2023/741507/IPOL_IDA(2023)741507_EN.pdf.

Auer, Simone, Nicola Branzoli, Giuseppe Ferrero, Antonio Ilari, Francesco Palazzo, and Edoardo Rainone. "CBDC and the Banking System." Occasional Papers No. 829. Banca d'Italia, Questioni di Economia e Finanza, 2024.

Barocas, Solon, and Andrew D. Selbst. "Big Data's Disparate Impact." *California Law Review* 104 (2016): 671–732.

Barontini, Christian, and Henry Holden. "Proceeding with Caution: A Survey on Central Bank Digital Currency." BIS Papers No. 101, 2019. https://www.bis.org/publ/bppdf/bispap101.pdf.

Bilotta, Nicola, and Fabrizio Botti, eds. *The (Near) Future of Central Bank Digital Currencies: Risks and Opportunities for the Global Economy and Society*. Bern, Berlin, Bruxelles, New York, Oxford, Warszawa and Wien: Peter Lang, 2021.

Bosi, Giacomo. "Taking CBDC Seriously." *Banca Impresa Società* 39, no. 1 (2020): 67–92.

Bruckner, Matthew Adam. "The Promise and Perils of Algorithmic Lenders' Use of Big Data." *Chicago-Kent Law Review* 93 (2018): 3–60.

Brunnermeier, Markus K., Harold James, and Jean-Pierre Landau. "The Digitalization of Money." NBER Working Paper Series No. 26300. NBER, 2019.

Cartwright, Peter. "Understanding and Protecting Vulnerable Financial Consumers." *Journal of Consumer Policy* 38 (2015): 119–38.

Cascione, Claudia Morgana. *Il lato grigio del diritto. Invecchiamento della popolazione e tutela degli anziani in prospettiva comparatistica*. Turin: Giappichelli, 2022.

Comparato, Guido. *The Financialisation of the Citizen*. Oxford and Portland: Hart, 2018.

Didenko, Anton N., and Ross P. Buckley. "The Evolution of Currency: Cash to Cryptos to Sovereign Digital Currencies." *Fordham International Law Journal* 42 (2019): 1041–94.

Gnan, Ernest, and Masciandaro Donato, eds. *Do We Need Central Bank Digital Currency? Economics, Technology and Institutions*. Vienna: SUERF-Larcier, 2018.

Helberger, Natali, Orla Lynskey, Hans-W. Micklitz, Peter Rott, Marijn Sax, and Joanna Strycharz. *EU Consumer Protection 2.0. Structural Asymmetries in Digital Consumer Markets*. BEUC, 2021.

Lupo-Pasini, Federico. "Financial Inclusion and the 'War for Cash'." *Law and Contemporary Problems* 84, no. 1 (2021): 17–33.

Lupo-Pasini, Federico. "Is It a Wonderful Life? Cashless Societies & Monetary Exclusion." *Review of Banking & Financial Law* 40 (2020–2021): 153–248.

Mazzoni, Leonardo, Marco Botta, Roberta Carlini, Lapo Filistrucchi, Natalia Mendez Gonzalez, and Pier Luigi Parcu. "Implications of the Digital Transformation on Different Social Groups." Requested by the European Parliament's Policy Department for Citizens' Rights and Constitutional Affairs, March 2024. https://www.europarl.europa.eu/RegData/etudes/STUD/2024/760277/IPOL_STU(2024)760277_EN.pdf.

Nabilou, Hossein. "Central Bank Digital Currencies: Preliminary Legal Observations." SSRN, 2019. https://ssrn.com/abstract=3329993.

Neva Grünewald, Seraina, Corinne Zellweger-Gutknecht, and Benjamin Geva. "Digital Euro and ECB Powers." *Common Market Law Review* 58 (2021): 1029–56.

Paglietti, Maria Cecilia, and Maddalena Rabitti. "A Matter of Time: Digital-Financial Consumers' Vulnerability in the Retail Payments Market." *European Business Law Review* 33 (2022): 581–606.

Rabitti, Maddalena. "Il consumatore vulnerabile e la fragilità del diritto. Brevi considerazioni." *Dialoghi di diritto dell'economia* (2023): 1–9.

Raskin, Max, and Yermack, DavidDavid. "Digital Currencies, Decentralized Ledgers, and the Future of Central Banking." NBER Working Paper No. 22238. NBER, 2016.

Riefa, Christine. "Protecting Vulnerable Consumers in the Digital Single Market." *European Business Law Review* 33 (2022): 607–34.

Schwarcz, Steven L., and Theodore L. Leonhardt. "Scoping and Defining Financial Inclusion, Access to Credit, and Sustainable Finance." *Law and Contemporary Problems* 84, no. 1 (2021): 1–15.

Vardi, Noah. *Creditworthiness and Responsible Credit: A Comparative Study of EU and US Law*. Leiden and Boston: Brill-Nijhoff, 2022.

Wischnewsky, Arina. "Nearly Cashless: Digital Transformation or Cultural Transmission?" Universität Trier Research Papers in Economics No. 4/24. https://www.uni-trier.de/fileadmin/fb4/prof/VWL/EWF/Research_Papers/2024-04.pdf.

Zeno-Zencovich, Vincenzo. "Digital Euro as a Platform and Its Private Law Implications." In *European Legal Strategies for Payment Systems in the Open Banking Age*, edited by Alessandro Palmieri, and Giuseppe Versaci. Naples: Edizioni Scientifiche Italiane, 2023.

Zetzsche, Dirk A., Ross P. Buckley, Douglas W. Arner, Anton N. Didenko, and Lucien J. van Romburg. "Sovereign Digital Currencies: The Future of Money and Payments?" *UNSW Law & Justice Research Series* 30 (2023).

7 Open banking and consumer protection

The Canadian perspective

Marc Lacoursière

1. Introduction

The development of an efficient banking system depends on how trustworthy it is in the eyes of consumers. Historical developments, particularly since the creation of the Bank of Venice in the 12th century, bear witness to this. The same is true of the various banking crises that occurred, for example, in the United States in 1907,[1] 1929[2] and 1987,[3] in Argentina in 2001[4] and in Greece in 2009.[5] It must also be added that the percentage of population holding bank accounts (*bancarisation*) rate in Canada is around 99%,[6] whereas it can be as low as around 10% in some developing countries,[7] which shows that Canadians have a great deal of confidence in their banking system.

The role of banks and financial institutions in commercial and consumer transactions is undeniable. Firstly, at the heart of these transactions are the payment transactions carried out by these intermediaries, whether for the issue of a cheque, for a transfer of funds or for other electronic payments. Secondly, financing transactions are carried out by borrowing (credit) or issuing securities (securities). New technologies and artificial intelligence are revolutionising the world of finance.[8] The financial sector is experiencing a metamorphosis with the arrival of commercial companies offering financial products and services to consumers and businesses. In other words, these financial technology companies, commonly referred to as FinTechs, are moving into a territory once reserved for financial institutions, including the big financial technology companies (BigTechs). More recently, and as a result to this phenomenon, has been the emergence of open banking. This new dynamic, which is here to stay, is creating new opportunities (increased competition, improved services and lower costs, financial inclusion), and new risks (operational, cyber-risk, compliance) jeopardising the current state of financial stability.

These new technology companies are at the root of the concept known as "open banking." This is considered as "a framework where consumers and businesses can authorize third party financial service providers to access their financial transaction data, using secure online channels."[9] It can enhance the value that consumers obtain from financial sector products and services, and it can lead to greater financial services competition, to more choice and better prices for consumers.

DOI: 10.4324/9781003510406-10

However, the law is currently in a state of flux and remains a source of profound questions about the content and meaning to be given to it.[10] Financial institutions are different from traditional commercial companies. This is due to their essential role in the functioning of the economy; their greater vulnerability to unforeseen adverse events in the case of high ratios of debt-to-equity (leverage); the serious consequences of a liquidity problem if the confidence of their customers regarding their safety and soundness is affected; the long-term financial commitments of their customers which are based on a high degree of trust; the value of the assets and liabilities of a large number of financial institutions, which can be volatile and difficult to quantify accurately; and the possibility of significant mismatches between the duration of their assets and liabilities, which can lead to major financing risks.[11] The challenges of protecting customers (borrowers, users of payment services, consumers of investment services) and their stakeholders[12] have become central, as demonstrated in Europe by the growing number of statutes adopted to protect them.[13] For these reasons, the regulation of financial institutions is greater and more substantial than the ones regarding commercial companies.

A recent survey conducted in 2023 by the Financial Consumer Agency of Canada (FCAC) revealed Canadians' lack of awareness and concerns about open banking.[14] Canadians' awareness of open banking is excessively low. Only 9% of Canadians had heard of open banking before taking the survey, 87% had never heard of it, and 4% were not sure or declined to answer.[15] Moreover, after hearing the definition, 15% of Canadians said they would participate in an open banking system; 29% said "maybe" and 52% said "no."[16]

The emergence and development of commercial players and new technologies in the financial ecosystem are prompting regulators to reflect on the approach they should adopt. The authorities are assessing the impact of these technologies on the banking and financial sectors. Tremendous work and efforts are being invested on the modernization of the banking system. Given the innovative nature of the subject, we take an exploratory approach to the question of technological impact in the present text, exploring the collaboration between traditional financial institutions and FinTechs (1) and the protection of personal information (2).

2. Metamorphosis of the banking system

The Canadian banking system was structured in the late 19th and early 20th centuries, via several bank mergers, and in the 80s and 90s, through a so-called "decompartmentalisation" of the financial services industry.[17] This led to the acquisition of securities companies, trusts and certain insurance companies by the predominant Canadian banks, characterising the banking ecosystem as an oligopolistic market. The Canadian model, constructed on this approach, has the advantage of being a robust banking system, sheltered from financial turbulences. More specifically, cultural, organisational and regulatory factors contribute to a solid and effective regulatory environment, both in terms of regulation per se and its control and supervision. To illustrate this, Canada came through the 2007–2009 financial crisis almost without a hitch, unlike other industrialised countries, including the United

States, at the heart of the crisis.[18] However, Canada's oligopolistic ecosystem in the banking sector has a number of notable drawbacks, such as higher fees and less innovation. Despite the right to an account, which sets the level of bank penetration in Canada at around 99%,[19] many people find it difficult to access credit and have to turn to alternative, more expensive forms of credit.

This banking oligopoly, therefore, presents an obstacle, given the inability of modest or medium-sized banks to make significant inroads into the Canadian deposit-taking market, which otherwise offers services of as good a quality as the big banks. The entry of financial technology companies (FinTechs) into the banking and financial market, and the emergence of open banking, promises to be a game changer, as demonstrated by the European experience.

Notwithstanding the shortcomings of the regulatory framework, which have been partially resolved, many people are pinning their hopes on this revolution to financially include unbanked or underbanked people. We first present the characteristics and influence of the open banking system (1.1) before discussing financial inclusion (1.2).

2.1 Characteristics and influence of the open banking system

An open banking system allows a customer (or a business) to authorise a third-party financial services provider (non-bank), such as a financial technology company, to obtain their personal data securely via an application programming interface (API) from a bank or another financial institution.[20] In practical terms, this could be a third-party company offering payment services to consumers, which needs to obtain certain banking information, in particular about the adequacy of the provision, in order to transfer the funds. The crux of the problem lies in the fact that the bank must provide this third party with information about its customer. Regardless of this, the consumer or the enterprise can access a wider choice of financial products and services, better suited to their needs.

These new intermediaries offer online banking services similar to those offered by traditional banks and quasi-banks. This new generation of banking activities offers undeniable advantages to consumers, such as a greater control over their financial data, more complete financial picture to improve financial outcomes, enhanced data security and protections for the digital economy, relatively lower costs, more flexible hours, larger markets and, above all, more widespread access. However, these experiences suggest that certain legal obstacles may exist in Canada and hinder the emergence of new forms of intermediation, including the inadequacy of Canadian banking regulations with regard to the advent of new intermediaries. This question is all more legitimate given the importance of new electronic payment issuers. Nevertheless, as we shall see following, this question has been partially resolved, opening the way to a more harmonious development of this concept.

Financial technology companies can be divided into several categories and, depending on their countenance, they can have different effects on the current banks and their ways of operating. In the first place, there are young, small-sized, financial technology companies, known as FinTech, and large financial technology companies, known as BigTech. The latter include global companies that have a clear advantage, can rapidly gain market share and are likely to have a major impact on the financial services market.[21] In the second place, the Basel Committee on Banking Supervision of the Bank for International Settlements has proposed several scenarios that take into account the impact of FinTech companies on banks.[22] First, the current bank is transformed into a "better bank." Second, a digital "new bank" may be created although this will be difficult in some markets, such as Canada, and even drive out of business those banks that cannot adapt. Third, the "distributed bank" involves the fragmentation of financial services amongst relationship between banks and financial technology companies. A collaborative relationship will be formed between these companies, regardless of its nature (joint venture, partnership, consortia, etc.). Fourth, the "relegated bank" scenario occurs when the role of the bank disappears whilst the financial technology company develops a direct relationship with the customer. However, the Basel Committee on Banking Supervision states that "the licensed bank would still need to authenticate the customer to access funds from enrolled payment cards and accounts" when a financial technology company, and especially BigTech, offers a complete service. Peer-to-peer lending (P2P) illustrates this point.[23]

2.2 Financial inclusion

When consumers do not access a traditional or online financial institution, they can be considered financially excluded.[24] Typically, these consumers are financially disadvantaged and/or more vulnerable than the average consumer, or simply less comfortable using online banking services. As Professor Iain Ramsay points out, "Exclusion from access to credit may therefore mean both economic exclusion from markets, such as housing, which may be a key to social mobility, and also exclusion from a central aspect of public expression in modern society."[25] As noted previously, Canada's percentage of population holding bank accounts rate is around 99%, making it one of the highest in the world.[26] At first glance, it may seem difficult to consider that open banking could solve the problem of access to banking services for unbanked or underbanked Canadians. However, the equation is more complex and the possibility of offering access to banking services at lower cost and better access to credit should be considered, arguing in favour of the adoption of an open banking system.

Public policies are aimed more at financial exclusion than financial inclusion. In practice, whether we tackle one or the other, the effect is the same. In Canada, one example of financial inclusion concerns the obligation for a bank to open retail deposit accounts for consumers who present certain identification documents. In 2003, the federal Parliament amended the Bank Act to require banks to offer a right to account.[27] Despite this obligation, some federal financial institutions still charge some fees. Provincial financial institutions, which are not subject to this Act, have no such obligation, although some offer basic accounts free of charge.

Does open banking represent a viable solution to financial inclusion? Certain problems may persist, such as security, information asymmetry and consumer's behavioural biases.[28] On this last point, online financial service providers can more easily identify consumers who are at higher risk and less profitable through the use of financial data and biases.[29] The targeting of more vulnerable consumers is reminiscent of an American technique known as "redlining," or credit rationing.[30] When the decision to grant a loan is determined by an algorithm, more vulnerable consumers can fall victim to bias. Many of these obstacles can be overcome by a better regulation. It should be noted that some people are reticent about open banking, refusing to share their data with a third-party company and preferring to remain anonymous.[31] However, some believe that open banking can help to resolve information asymmetry, given the information sharing required.[32] Other benefits of open banking include more competition, more innovation, more choice and lower fees, as stated earlier. More specifically, the following advantages should not be overlooked: the quality of financial services offered to consumers can better meet their needs;[33] a better financial literacy, "through digital advisors, virtual agent and coaching";[34] and an easy access to temporary workers, freelancers and gig economy workers on variable incomes.[35] In any case, further empirical studies are needed to shed light on this issue.

3. Regulation of the open banking system

Open banking presents a significant number of challenges for regulators. The biggest problem is that FinTechs, which are behind open banking, are far less regulated than financial institutions. In other words, regulators and stakeholders, including consumers, are faced with a double standard that creates legislative injustice.

Because of the regulatory structure, the European approach lends itself better to targeted supervision of FinTechs than the Canadian approach (2.1). In addition to the general principles of regulation, the key to the success of an open banking system lies in the protection of personal information and the notion of consumer consent to data portability (2.2).

3.1 Regulatory framework

The development of the open banking system is particularly promising, offering a range of opportunities for consumers, banks and FinTechs. The legal framework for an open banking system needs to take account of these three stakeholders, as well as consumer data protection.

This has led the European Commission to develop a regulatory framework for this practice. To date, the focus has been on account aggregation and payment mechanisms. The Second Payment Services Directive opens up the payments market to non-banks, known as "payment initiation service providers."[36] It is worth emphasising one important point about regulation: the European regulatory framework is based on what is known as a functional approach, that is, on the basis of the institution's activities.

In Canada, the regulator has adopted the so-called institutional approach, which requires that anyone wishing to carry out banking transactions under the name of a bank must obtain a licence to do so,[37] which has been confirmed by the Supreme Court of Canada.[38] When the time comes to regulate financial technology companies, it is submitted that the regulation based on the institutional approach is not adequate, and it is preferable to opt for regulation based on the activities carried out by the enterprise. A responsiveness towards this approach came in 2016 from Payments Canada, which is responsible for establishing the Canadian payment system. In its Vision, Payments Canada recommended focusing supervision on "functional activity rather than institutional entity."[39] This innovative approach was clearly intended to encourage innovation. As the organisation pointed out,

> *Rather than focusing on the type of service provider (FI vs. non-FI), rules and regulations should be evenly applied to industry participants based on the service provided (for example, holding funds) and associated risks. A fair and balanced oversight model for the payments system better assures the compliance of system participants to rules which safeguard these participants and serve to protect consumers and other users.*[40]

This is certainly an interesting approach, which is also in harmony with the European position.[41]

Following these developments, the legislator has adopted the Retail Payment Activities Act,[42] which is intended to supervise and regulate retail payment activities performed by payment service providers. These payment service providers are required payment to identify and mitigate operational risks, to safeguard end-user funds and to register with the Bank of Canada, Canada's central bank. The Bank of Canada is responsible for monitoring payment service providers' compliance with the various operational and financial requirements under the Act and must maintain a register of regulated payment service providers. The legislation would also include safeguards to address national security risks. Overall, the legislation should foster competition and innovation in payment services by building confidence in the retail payment sector. Accordingly, changes will be made to the *Canadian Payments Act* to expand Payments Canada's membership and to provide access to the payment systems.[43] The Retail Payment Activities Act is in alignment with Canadian Payments Act changes, including the forthcoming "Real-Time Rail."[44]

In addition to the framework structure, the federal regulator is keen to modify three aspects of the Bank Act to enable banks to better compete with new technology companies: powers, networking and investment.[45]

First, the bank may "engage in any activity that relates to the provision of financial services by the bank or any of its affiliates,"[46] which is relatively broad. Banks' powers are also increased to carry on activities relating to the collection, manipulation and transmission of information; the design, development, manufacture and sale of technology; or any other way of dealing with technology, provided that those activities relate to any other activity that is carried on by the bank or any entity in its group or where those activities relate to the provision of financial services by any other entity.[47] Until these 2018 amendments, the bank was required to obtain approval from the Minister of Finance to engage in such operations.[48]

Second, the regulator also amended the provisions governing bank networking. This provision is fundamental when the bank wishes to do business with a financial technology company or, more specifically, when the latter wishes to execute a customer's payment order and needs access to the customer's bank account as is the case of certain mobile payments. Under the new section 411, the bank may act as an agent and enter into arrangements with any person,[49] not just eligible financial institutions, to carry out the activities set out in subsection 410(1), (i.e., computer services) and to provide any service. The new provision also allows banks to refer or recommend any person to any other person, without restriction. In practical terms, this new approach encourages better collaboration between a bank and a non-financial service provider. This is a major breakthrough for banks, which until now have been confined to networking with financial institutions and, in some cases, have had to obtain approval from the Minister of Finance.

Third, the authorised investments regime for banks, set out in section 468 of the Bank Act, is amended as a result of the changes made to sections 410 and 411 of the Act. Thus, a bank may acquire control of, or acquire or increase a substantial investment in, an entity other than a bank (i.e. a FinTech), according to certain limits. If the bank simply wants to invest in the financial technology company, this provision does not seem to pose a problem. However, if the bank wishes to acquire control, the activities of the financial technology company must be "substantial" of the same financial nature as that which the banks can offer, which could be more than the usual requirement of more than 50%. Despite this major stumbling block, it should be noted that this is an improvement on the current situation, which will certainly encourage innovation.[50]

These new developments are likely to change the financial ecosystem's economic concentration structure. The Financial Stability Board has examined the impact of financial technology companies, both small (FinTechs) and large (BigTechs).[51] It states that, in principle, the entry of new companies into the market should increase competition and diversity in payment, lending, brokerage and insurance activities and even create a more efficient and resilient financial system.[52] Competition from small FinTechs is usually limited to a particular niche.[53] However, large FinTechs can offer serious competition to traditional financial institutions, due to their established network and customer base, the ability to use their customers' personal data from non-financial activities, and access to technologies such as artificial intelligence and cloud computing.[54]

In the UK, the Commission & Markets Authority has highlighted the lack of competition in the U.K. banking sector.[55] It states that

> *[e]ssentially, the older and larger banks, which still account for the large majority of the retail banking market, do not have to work hard enough to win and retain customers and it is difficult for new and smaller providers to attract customers.*[56]

It adds that the structure of account charges, and especially bank overdrafts, is complex and disadvantageous for customers and that the possibility of changing institutions would be beneficial in the eyes of many customers. In addition, it notes that

> *older banks have access to cheaper retail deposits from their existing customers which they can use in their lending businesses. This gives such banks an advantage over new banks and the more customer deposits a bank has the bigger that advantage.*[57]

The solution proposed by the Commission & Markets Authority was to develop the open banking system. Consequently, it established the Open Banking Implementation Entity (OBIE) in 2016 to create standards for the open banking ecosystem. The third version of the standards presented by this body aims to comply with the PSD2.[58]

The reflection phase has been underway for some time in Canada. Inspired by the United Kingdom's Commission & Markets Authority,[59] the Canadian Competition Bureau has presented a report on technological innovation in the financial services sector.[60] It states that the development of standards, in which all stakeholders from various horizons must participate,

> *can raise competition concerns; they could create regulatory 'moats' that reduce price and non-price competition, foreclose innovative technologies and restrict firms' ability to compete by denying or providing access on discriminatory terms. Ensuring broad and diverse representation and engagement in the development of standards is critical.*[61]

It adds that these standards will "change the nature of the customer journey," by selling separate products (usually sold together), allowing consumers to move their money to a higher interest account or to a different bank through a single provider.[62] Finally, the Competition Bureau notes that the Commission & Markets Authority concludes that larger established banks have to make less effort than smaller ones to develop a customer base, with the consequence that many customers pay too much and are likely to get less service.[63]

With the aim of encouraging innovation and competition, the Department of Finance Canada suggested, when the budget was tabled in February 2018, "to undertake a review of the merits of open banking in order to assess whether open banking would deliver positive results for Canadians with the highest regard for consumer privacy, data security and financial stability."[64] This took shape, firstly, through the implementation of an Advisory Committee on Open Banking in the fall of 2018[65] and, secondly, through the solicitation of public comment via a consultation paper.[66] The latter sets out the merits and benefits of such a system and addresses the delicate issue of risk management. The framework must be based on three elements: efficiency (competitive prices), usefulness (need for a broad customer base) and stability (a solid, robust financial sector that is resilient to stress).[67] Moreover, this approach by the Department of Finance has undoubtedly acted as a catalyst for reflection on the regulatory framework for the open banking system in Canada. The budget tabled in March 2019 considers these developments to assess the best path to follow in order to "move ahead with open banking, with the highest regard for consumer privacy, security and financial stability."[68]

In the fall of 2023, an Economic Statement from the federal government announced its intention to introduce legislation establishing an open banking framework, re-branded as "consumer-driven banking," that would regulate third-party access to consumers' financial data.[69] The federal government has been considering the merits of an open banking framework for several years. Through the 2023 Economic Statement and Policy Statement, however, the government has committed itself to introducing a new legislation framework through Budget 2024 and fully implementing a consumer-driven banking framework by 2025. The 2024 federal budget followed up on this, with the government moving forward with the introduction of a legislative framework in 2024 in order to frame the "consumer-driven banking."[70] In addition to its intentions, the government has also published the broad outlines of the proposed framework.[71]

The government's approach aims at protecting Canadians who must currently share their banking credentials with financial technology companies. This unsecure, unregulated practice leaves Canadians, using, for instance, screen-scraping techniques, open to security, privacy and liability risks in the event of data breaches or losses.[72] According to the Department of Finance, the new consumer-driven banking framework will provide several advantages: empower Canadians to securely access and share their financial data with a FinTech (financial service providers); ensure free access for Canadians when accessing and sharing their data; phase out Canadians and the financial system from risky practices like screen-scraping; ensure parties at fault are liable for any damages or data breaches; and allow Canadians to safely access innovative products and services that can help them improve their financial outcomes. A main step forward in the Canadian personal data protection is the implement consumer rights to data portability, which is fundamental to the success of consumer-driven banking framework.

The open banking, or consumer-driven banking, framework is framed by three public policy objectives: safety and soundness; consumer financial well-being and protection; and economic growth and international competitiveness.[73] Security is a core element of this policy, alongside governance, scope (types of data and functionalities the system will provide, the participants, and the pace at which the system should expand), accreditation, common rules and technical standards. The FCAC will be mandated to oversee, administer and enforce Canada's consumer-driven banking framework. In particular, regarding the accreditation process, the Department of Finance explains that there will be a formal accreditation framework to ensure Canadians can confidently engage in financial data sharing with trusted entities. This is intended to create trust amongst consumers and participants by validating the merit and financial capability of organisations outside of traditional regulated financial service. Furthermore, with regards to privacy, consent is at the centre of the process, as it will be discussed later.[74]

Following the 2024 budget, the federal legislator adopted the Consumer-Driven Banking Act.[75] It aims "to establish a framework within which consumers, including small businesses, can direct that their data be shared among participating entities of their choice and to ensure that the sharing of data among participating entities is safe and secure."[76] This framework focuses on the essential elements at the heart of an open banking system.

In this first stage, the scope of application is limited to five specific circumstances: a deposit account; registered and non-registered investment accounts; payment products, including credit cards and prepaid payment products; lines of credit, mortgages or hypothecs and other kinds of loans; and other products or services provided for in the regulations.[77] The Act explicitly excludes derivated data,[78] that is, data about a consumer, product or service that has been enhanced by a participating entity to significantly increase its usefulness or commercial value.[79] In other words, open banking service providers, or a participating entity, can only offer services linked to bank accounts, such as account aggregation, as well as payment and credit products. The list remains relatively broad and may be extended by regulation.

In summary, the law provides a number of consumer protection measures. Firstly, a register of participating entities will be kept.[80] Secondly, the law provides for the appointment of a technical standards body responsible for establishing the technical standards that are to be used for the sharing of data by participating entities in accordance with this Act.[81] Thirdly, it is forbidden for an individual or entity other than a participating entity to use the term participating entity, or to present itself as such.[82] More generally, the Act provides for prohibitions and penalties.[83] The FCAC is also responsible for supervising the participating entities, the external complaints body and the technical standards body.[84] For that purpose, the FCAC's Commissioner must appoint an officer, called a Senior Deputy Commissioner, who is to act under the instructions of the Commissioner and who is responsible for consumer-driven banking matters.[85]

As a result, the Bank of Canada is in charge of FinTechs offering simple payments services. However when it comes to implementing an open banking service, the responsibility falls on the shoulders of the FCAC.

With regards to the Canadian constitution, there are federal and provincial financial institutions. It is also important to consider that provincial financial institutions, such as credit unions or *caisses populaires*, might be tempted to take their cue from federal legislative developments in this regard.

3.2 Protection of personal information

At first sight, protecting information is a simple matter, but from a legal point of view, it requires serious thought. In a recent survey conducted in 2023 by the FCAC, 70% of consumers want a "full protection from any losses," including having the ability to revoke consent at any time (63%) as requirements to report data breaches exposing consumer data (63%) were the next most expressed concern by consumers.[86] Canadian banking law recognises that the bank must not intervene in its customer's affairs.[87] However, this principle of non-intervention should not exempt the bank from a duty of care when it is aware, or it suspects, that suspicious or illicit transactions are being carried out through the consumer's bank account.[88] Does this principle prevent banks from sharing customer data with third-party suppliers? *Tournier v National Provincial and Union Bank of England*,[89] which established the basis for the disclosure of customer information by the bank, deserves attention in this instance. In this decision, the bank had revealed personal information about its customer to a third party (a potential employer) without the customer's consent. It turned out that the information was harmful to the customer, who was unable to obtain the job he wanted. The Court of King's Bench stated that four conditions must be met to allow the bank to pass on its customer's information:

> *(a) disclosure is under compulsion by law; (b) where there is a duty to the public to disclose; (c) where the interests of the bank require disclosure; (d) where the disclosure is made by the express or implied consent of the customer.*[90]

Thus, the customer's consent may allow the bank to transfer the data to a third party. In *Tournier*, the third party was a potential employer of the applicant.

Currently, banking contracts contain clauses on the collection and use of customers' personal information. Such clauses stipulate that the bank may communicate this information to credit bureaus (agencies), other financial institutions or even agents or service providers. Although these clauses are part of contracts of adhesion, it must be acknowledged that they have been declared legally valid. By opening a bank account, customers consent to the disclosure of their personal information to third parties, such as agents or service providers. This in no way violates the bank's non-intervention obligation.

Who owns customer bank data? If an analysis of legal sources and banking contracts suggests that the customer could be the owner of his or her data, even though this is not clearly expressed, it is clear that natural persons must have control over his or her own personal data, as expressed in recital 7 of the General Data Protection Regulation.[91] This control is expressed through the consent that the user provides for the use of his or her data.[92] Banking contracts, which are contracts of adhesion by their nature, stipulate that the customer grants the bank the right to use the data in various circumstances, whether for marketing, customer service or financing purposes. Banking contracts allow the customer to refuse the use of their personal data, except in the case of credit services, in which case the customer cannot waive the use of this data by the bank. If the customer refuses, he or she may try to contract with another financial institution, but as the Canadian banking system is an oligopolistic market, the clauses on disclosure of personal information are relatively similar.

If so, what is the value of the customer's consent? Can it be argued that this consent is free and informed? Given that the banking contract is a contract of adhesion, and in view of the foregoing, it is reasonable to doubt the validity of free consent in these circumstances. However, consent remains at the heart of the regulator's concerns, as shown by recent legislative developments. In Europe, the General Data Protection Regulation, in force since 2018, enshrines the principle that

> *[c]onsent should be given by a clear affirmative act establishing a freely given, specific, informed and unambiguous indication of the data subject's agreement to the processing of personal data relating to him or her, such as by a written statement, including by electronic means, or an oral statement.*[93]

This principle permeates the entire regulation. It completes, as it were, a panoply of directives, including the PSD2.[94] Under this directive, a third party initiating a payment may ask the payment service provider managing the account to provide information in order to complete the transaction, provided that strong authentication is applied. Article 98 of PSD2 requires the European Banking Authority to develop regulatory technical standards for payment service providers to specify the requirements for strong authentication under Article 97.[95]

Amongst other things, this regulation provides that an identification code is generated when authentication is based on at least two of the elements belonging to the categories "knowledge," "inherence" and "possession," and control mechanisms must be provided by the payment service provider,[96] which must also ensure the confidentiality and security of the data,[97] and exception measures are provided for.[98] Finally, the payment service provider must provide an interface,[99] which may be dedicated for communicating with the payer.[100] Where applicable, emergency measures must be provided for by payment service providers managing accounts in the event of unavailability or breakdown.[101] Lastly, Article 20 of the General Data Protection Regulation recognises the right of data, subject to data portability, which means "the right to receive the personal data concerning him or her, which he or she has provided to a controller, in a structured, commonly used and machine-readable format and have the right to transmit those data to another controller without hindrance from the controller to which the personal data have been provided."[102]

In this regard, it is worth noting the study undertaken in 2018 by the Canada2020 Policy Lab, which held a focus group with 41 stakeholders from the business, government and academic sectors.[103] A consensus was reached on nine points, the first of which is that consumers must give express consent before their data is shared, and they retain the right to withdraw consent at any time. This is certainly an interesting principle, but can it really be implemented? We have already highlighted the issue of the real value of consent. Should standards, including those of consent, be coercive? This question is absent from the Canada2020 study, as it is from the discussions of other organisations. It seems to us fundamental to consumer protection that future standards should be mandatory, following the example of European law. The new dynamic of the open banking system in the Canadian financial services ecosystem is to be welcomed, subject to consideration of consumer interests.

In its declaration of intent to introduce a new legislation on open banking, the federal government referred to the importance of obtaining consumer consent in the process of transferring their data to a FinTech. These will address the provision of express consent to access data, consent management, and revoking access to data shared by a consumer. It promotes a standardised process for consent and revocation that is done in a clear, simple and transparent manner. These will also be asked to reconfirm consumer consent at specified intervals or following certain events. Entities would also be required to provide consent dashboards to ensure consumers have real-time knowledge of who has access to their data.[104] This is manifested by the appointment of a technical standards body responsible for establishing the technical standards that are to be used for the sharing of data by participating entities in accordance with this Act.[105] The Act provides that data that is shared between participating entities in accordance with this Act is to be shared in a manner that does not enable the participating entity that receives the data to edit the data on servers that are used by the participating entity that provides the data.[106]

4. Conclusion

The banking and financial ecosystem has been in a state of flux for several years now. Traditional financial institutions are being shaken up by new technologies and must either react or give in. The stakes of technological impact are considerable. Three main fronts are vulnerable: the banking system as a whole, payments and credit. By allowing non-financial entities access to the bank accounts of customers of financial institutions, banks must not only collaborate, but above all, they must ensure the security of their customers' data. By way of illustration, the purpose of such access may be to obtain banking information in order to offer account consolidation from various financial institutions or to facilitate a payment transaction.

Whilst the European Union has developed a regulatory environment for open banking, Canadian legislative interventions are more cautious. After a first wave of amendments to the Bank Act and in-depth studies by Payments Canada, a second phase provides a more specific legal framework for open banking. The banking and financial ecosystem is in a state of metamorphosis, and the Canadian regulator is clearly on the move. As the issue of automated financial advice illustrates, Canada is not isolated, even if its reaction seems to be lagging behind that of other countries. Several states and national authorities have made changes to their laws, though no consensus has yet emerged. A quick look at the attitude of the Canadian regulator, nevertheless, shows that serious reflection is underway. Whilst the position of Canadian regulator is being finalised, it must be aware that their work can only be carried out with one objective in mind: to strike a balance between maintaining a certain *laissez-faire* attitude in the industry, likely to support innovation, and consumer protection. The new technologies do not mean that the banking industry is being relieved of its responsibilities, nor do they imply the introduction of excessive paternalism. European inspiration dictates the importance of coordination between the various players in order to develop a legal framework that is mindful of the banking and financial ecosystem of the 21st century.

Notes

1 Mendez and Tutin, "De la crise bancaire à la régulation," 42.
2 Lacoue-Labarthe, "La France a-t-elle connu des paniques bancaires inefficientes?" 633; Henry, *La crise de 1929*.
3 Adam and Szafarz, "Crises boursières," 781.

4 Paddock, "IMF Policy and the Argentine Crisis," 155; Nataraj and Sahoo, "Argentina's Crisis," 1641.
5 Cohen, "La crise grecque," 383.
6 The World Bank Group et al., *The Global Findex Database 2017*, at 123.
7 The World Bank Group et al., *The Global Findex Database 2017*, at 123–26; Yao, "Le rôle de la chambre de compensation dans l'usage du chèque au regard de la bancarisation une étude de droit comparée."
8 Bonneau, *Régulation bancaire et financière européenne et internationale*, 779, para 474.
9 Department of Finance (Canada), "A Review into Merits of Open Banking," See also: Rakotomandimby, "La protection des renseignements personnels du consommateur dans un système bancaire ouvert."
10 On the legal implications of these new technologies, see: Lacoursière and Tchoutourian, "Métamorphose technologique et institutions financières," 737; Bourdeau, Faucher, and Alexandre Brosseau, "Les FinTechs"; Fenwick, Kaal, and Vermeulen, "Regulation Tomorrow," 561.
11 Office of the Superintendant of Financial Institutions Canada, "Corporate Governance – Guidelines," 12, Annex A, September 30, 2018, https://www.osfi-bsif.gc.ca/en/print/pdf/node/592.
12 On the role of stakeholders, see: Mehran, Morrison, and Shapiro, *Corporate Governance and Banks*, 3. See also: European Commission, *Green Paper: Corporate Governance in Financial Institutions and Remuneration Policies*, OM(2010) 284 final (June 2, 2010), 4, https://eur-lex.europa.eu/legal-content/EN/TXT/PDF/?uri=CELEX:52010DC0284.
13 Bonneau, *Régulation bancaire et financière européenne et internationale*, 609, para 388.
14 Financial Consumer Agency of Canada, "Open Banking," 8.
15 Financial Consumer Agency of Canada, "Open Banking," 8.
16 Financial Consumer Agency of Canada, "Open Banking," 10.
17 This was known as the "four pillars". See e.g. Riley, "The Foreign Bank Entry Regime," 27.
18 Booth, "The Secret of Canadian Banking," 1; Dostie, "Le Canada et la crise financière: un retour critique sur la thèse de l'exception canadienne," 27; Lacoursière, "La perspective bancaire canadienne lors de la crise financière de 2007–2009," 271.
19 Canadian Banking Association, "Focus: Banks and Consumers," June 19, 2024, https://cba.ca/banks-and-consumers.
20 Badour and Presta, "Open Banking," 41–42.
21 Western companies include: Google, Amazon, Facebook and Apple, named "GAFA", and Chinese companies: Baidu, Alibaba and Tencent, named "BAT".
22 Basel Committee on Banking Supervision (Bank of International Settlements), "Sound Practices," 14–20.
23 Basel Committee on Banking Supervision (Bank of International Settlements), "Sound Practices," 19.
24 Collard, "Toward Financial Inclusion in the UK," 13. Financial inclusion and open banking were the subject of a qualitative empirical study by two researchers from the UK and Singapore, who interviewed 13 stakeholders (researchers, government, consumer advocates and FinTechs) in 2019 and 2020: Leong and Gardner, "Open Banking in the UK and Singapore," 424.
25 Ramsay, "Consumer Credit Law," 177, 181.
26 The World Bank Group et al., *The Global Findex Database 2017*, 123.
27 *Bank Act*, S.C. 1991, c. 46, s. 627.17 (replacing s. 448.1).
28 Faith Reynolds, "Open Banking: A Consumer Perspective," 1, 17, January 2017, https://home.barclays/content/dam/home-barclays/documents/citizenship/access-to-financial-and-digital-empowerment/Open-Banking-A-Consumer-Perspective-Faith-Reynolds.pdf.
29 Financial Inclusion Centre, "FinTech."

30 On this issue, see: Stiglitz and Weiss, "Credit Rationing in Markets with Imperfect Information," 393; Rice, "Race, Gender, Redlining, and the Discriminatory Access to Loans, Credit, and Insurance," 583; Rheingold, Fitzpatrick, and Hofeld, "From Redlining to Reverse Redlining," 642.
31 Polasik and Kotkowski, "The Open Banking Adoption Among Consumers in Europe," 22, 24.
32 Ariadne Plaitakis and Stephen Staschen, "Open Banking: How to Design for Financial Inclusion," World Bank, Consultative Group to Assis the Poor, Working Paper, 13, October 2020, https://documents1.worldbank.org/curated/en/351881625136775280/pdf/Open-Banking-How-to-Design-for-Financial-Inclusion.pdf?_gl=1*7cm5sf*_gcl_au*NjYwMjkxNTE5LjE3MjU2NzM0ODA.
33 Massimo Preziuso, Franziska Koefer, and Michel Ehrenhard, "Open Banking and Inclusive Finance in the European Union: Perspectives from the Dutch Stakeholder Ecosystem," *Financial Innovation* 9, no. 1 (2023): 1, 5.
34 Preziuso, Koefer, and Ehrenhard, "Open Banking and Inclusive Finance in the European Union," 1, 13.
35 Preziuso, Koefer, and Ehrenhard, "Open Banking and Inclusive Finance in the European Union," 1, 19.
36 *Directive (EU) 2015/2366 of the European Parliament and of the Council of November 25, 2015, on Payment Services in the Internal Market, Amending Directives 2002/65/EC, 2009/110/EC and 2013/36/EU and Regulation (EU) No 1093/2010, and Repealing Directive 2007/64/EC*, [2015] J.O. L 337/35, art. 4(15)(18) (Second (or Revised) Payment Services Directive, Directive 2015/2366 or PSD2).
37 *Bank Act*, s. 983; *Name Use (Foreign Banks) Regulations*, SOR/2008-156. See: Nicholls, "Bank on It," 293.
38 *Canadian Pioneer Management Ltd. et al. v Labour Relations Board of Saskatchewan et al.*, [1980] 1 S.C.R. 433.
39 Payments Canada, "Developing a Vision," 20.
40 Payments Canada, "Developing a Vision," 27.
41 We analyse this issue in more detail in section 2.1, *infra*.
42 S.C. 2021, c. 23, s. 177. See also the regulation: *Retail Payment Activities Regulations*, SOR/2023-229. These regulations are not yet in force.
43 R.S.C. 1985, c. C-21, s. 5. Payments Canada is the organisation responsible for establishing and operating national systems for the clearing and settlement of payments and other arrangements for the making or exchange of payments. This legislation sets out Payments Canada's role and responsibilities, including membership.
44 The Real-Time Rail is Canada's first real-time payment system that supports instant, data-rich payments. It looks forward to transform Canada's economy, giving businesses and consumers more transparency and access to their payments any day, any time, whilst at the same time respecting a safe and secure environment. See: Payments Canada, "The Real-Time Rail: Canada's Fastest Payment System," 2023, https://www.payments.ca/systems-services/payment-systems/real-time-rail-payment-system.
45 *Budget Implementation Act, 2018, No. 1*, S.C. 2018, c. 12, s. 316–319. These modifications are not yet in force.
46 *Bank Act*, s. 410(1)(b.1), mod. by *Budget Implementation Act, 2018, No. 1*, S.C. 2018, c. 12.
47 *Bank Act*, s. 410(c).
48 Subject to certain exemptions: *Information Processing Activities (Banks and Authorized Foreign Banks) Regulations*, SOR/2001-391.
49 *Bank Act*, s. 411(1)(a)(i).
50 However, see: *Information Technology Activities (Banks) Regulations*, DORS/2003-61, s. 3(1), and *Bank Act*, s. 983(5.1).
51 Financial Stability Board, "FinTech."

52 Financial Stability Board, "FinTech," 1, 3.
53 Financial Stability Board, "FinTech," 18.
54 Financial Stability Board, "FinTech," 15.
55 Commission & Markets Authority, "Making Banks."
56 Commission & Markets Authority, "Making Banks," 1.
57 Commission & Markets Authority, "Making Banks," 4.
58 See more recently: *Proposal for a Directive of the European Parliament and of the Council on Payment Services and Electronic Money Services in the Internal Market Amending Directive 98/26/EC and Repealing Directives 2015/2366/EU and 2009/110/EC*, Brussels, June 28, 2023 COM (2023) 366 final, 2023/0209 (COD).
59 Commission & Markets Authority, "Making Banks."
60 Competition Bureau Canada, "Technology-Led Innovation."
61 Competition Bureau Canada, "Technology-Led Innovation," 71.
62 Competition Bureau Canada, "Technology-Led Innovation," 71.
63 Competition Bureau Canada, "Technology-Led Innovation," 71. See also: Commission & Markets Authority, "Making Banks," 4.
64 Department of Finance (Canada), "Equality and Growth: A Strong Middle Class," 355, February 27, 2018, https://www.budget.canada.ca/2018/docs/plan/toc-tdm-en.html (Budget of 2018).
65 Department of Finance (Canada), "Minister Morneau Launches Advisory Committee on Open Banking," *News*, September 26, 2018, https://www.canada.ca/en/department-finance/news/2018/09/minister-morneau-launches-advisory-committee-on-open-banking.html.
66 Department of Finance (Canada), "Review".
67 Department of Finance (Canada), "Review," ii.
68 Department of Finance (Canada), "Investing in the Middle Class," 329, March 19, 2019, https://www.budget.canada.ca/2019/docs/plan/toc-tdm-en.html (Budget of 2019).
69 Department of Finance (Canada), "2023 Fall Economic Statement," 40–41, November 2023, https://www.budget.canada.ca/fes-eea/2023/report-rapport/FES-EEA-2023-en.pdf.
70 Department of Finance (Canada), "Budget 2024: Fairness for Every Generation,"158, April 16, 2024, https://budget.canada.ca/2024/home-accueil-en.html (Budget of 2024). See also: Stephanie Marotta, "Ottawa Makes Federal Consumer Agency the New Oversight Body for Canada's Proposed Open Banking System," *The Globe & Mail*, April 16, 2024, https://www.theglobeandmail.com/business/article-ottawa-makes-federal-consumer-agency-the-new-oversight-body-for.
71 Department of Finance (Canada), "Budget 2024: Canada's Consumer-Driven Banking Framework," April 16, 2024, https://www.canada.ca/en/department-finance/programs/financial-sector-policy/open-banking-implementation/budget-2024-canadas-framework-for-consumer-driven-banking.html.
72 Department of Finance (Canada), "Budget 2024: Canada's Consumer-Driven Banking Framework," 2; Department of Finance (Canada), "2023 Fall Economic Statement," 40.
73 Department of Finance (Canada), "Budget 2024: Canada's Consumer-Driven Banking Framework," 2.
74 See *infra*, subpart 2.2.
75 *An Act to Implement Certain Provisions of the Budget Tabled in Parliament on April 16, 2024*, S.C. 2024, c. 17, sec. 198, subs. 4(1).
76 *An Act to Implement Certain Provisions of the Budget Tabled in Parliament on April 16, 2024*, S.C. 2024, c. 17, sec. 198.
77 *An Act to Implement Certain Provisions of the Budget Tabled in Parliament on April 16, 2024*, S.C. 2024, c. 17, sec. 198.
78 *An Act to Implement Certain Provisions of the Budget Tabled in Parliament on April 16, 2024*, S.C. 2024, c. 17, sec. 198, subs. 4(2).

79 *An Act to Implement Certain Provisions of the Budget Tabled in Parliament on April 16, 2024*, S.C. 2024, c. 17, sec. 198, s. 2.
80 *An Act to Implement Certain Provisions of the Budget Tabled in Parliament on April 16, 2024*, S.C. 2024, c. 17, sec. 198, s. 7.
81 *An Act to Implement Certain Provisions of the Budget Tabled in Parliament on April 16, 2024*, S.C. 2024, c. 17, sec. 198, subs. 8(1).
82 *An Act to Implement Certain Provisions of the Budget Tabled in Parliament on April 16, 2024*, S.C. 2024, c. 17, sec. 198, s. 14.
83 *An Act to Implement Certain Provisions of the Budget Tabled in Parliament on April 16, 2024*, S.C. 2024, c. 17, sec. 198, s. 16–19.
84 *An Act to Implement Certain Provisions of the Budget Tabled in Parliament on April 16, 2024*, S.C. 2024, c. 17, sec. 201, s. 3(4).
85 *An Act to Implement Certain Provisions of the Budget Tabled in Parliament on April 16, 2024*, S.C. 2024, c. 17, sec. 203, subs. 7.2(1).
86 Financial Consumer Agency of Canada, "Open Banking," 14–15.
87 L'Heureux and Lacoursière, *Droit bancaire*, 452–454, nº 629.
88 *124329 Canada inc. v Banque Nationale du Canada/National Bank of Canada*, 2011 QCCA 226.
89 [1924] K.B. 461.
90 [1924] K.B. 461, 473.
91 EU, *Regulation (EU) 2016/679 of the European Parliament and of the Council of 27 April 2016 on the Protection of Natural Persons with Regard to the Processing of Personal Data and on the Free Movement of Such Data, and Repealing Directive 95/46/EC*, [2016] OJ L 119/1, recital nº 7.
92 EU, *Regulation (EU) 2016/679 of the European Parliament and of the Council of April 27, 2016, on the Protection of Natural Persons with Regard to the Processing of Personal Data and on the Free Movement of Such Data, and Repealing Directive 95/46/EC*, [2016] OJ L 119/1, recitals 32, 42, 43, art. 4(11), 7, 20.
93 EU, *Regulation (EU) 2016/679 of the European Parliament and of the Council of April 27, 2016, on the Protection of Natural Persons with Regard to the Processing of Personal Data and on the Free Movement of Such Data, and Repealing Directive 95/46/EC*, [2016] O.J. L 119/1, recital nº 32; art. 4(11°), 7.
94 EU, *Directive (EU) 2015/2366.*
95 EU, *Commission Delegated Regulation (EU) 2018/389 of November 27, 2017, Supplementing Directive (EU) 2015/2366 of the European Parliament and of the Council with Regard to Regulatory Technical Standards for Strong Customer Authentication and Common and Secure Open Standards of Communication*, [2018] O.J. L 69/23.
96 EU, *Commission Delegated Regulation (EU) 2018/389*, art. 2.
97 EU, *Commission Delegated Regulation (EU) 2018/389*, art. 22 ff.
98 EU, *Commission Delegated Regulation (EU) 2018/389*, art. 10 ff.
99 EU, *Commission Delegated Regulation (EU) 2018/389*, art. 30.
100 EU, *Commission Delegated Regulation (EU) 2018/389*, art. 31.
101 EU, *Commission Delegated Regulation (EU) 2018/389*, art. 33. Under Article 33(6), an exemption may be granted to the payment service provider managing accounts under certain conditions. See on this subject: European Banking Authority, "Final Report: Guidelines on the Conditions to Benefit from an Exemption from the Contingency Mechanism Under Article 33(6) of Regulation (EU) 2018/389 (RTS on SCA & CSC), EBA/GL/2018/07," December 4, 2018, https://eba.europa.eu/documents/10180/2250578/Final+Report+on+Guidelines+on+the+exemption+to+the+fall+back.pdf/4e3b9449-ecf9-4756-8006-cbbe74db6d03.
102 EU, *Regulation (EU) 2016/679.*
103 Canada2020 Policy Lab, "Open Banking."
104 Department of Finance (Canada), "Budget 2024: Canada's Consumer-Driven Banking Framework."

105 *An Act to Implement Certain Provisions of the Budget Tabled in Parliament on April 16, 2024*, S.C. 2024, c. 17, sec. 198, subs. 8(1).
106 *An Act to Implement Certain Provisions of the Budget Tabled in Parliament on April 16, 2024*, S.C. 2024, c. 17, sec. 198, subs. 5.

References

Adam, Marie-Christine, and Ariane Szafarz. "Crises boursières: Bulles spéculatives et rationalité économique." *Études Internationales* 20 (1989): 781.

Badour, Ana, and Domenic Presta. "Open Banking: Canadian and International Developments." *Banking and Finance Law Review* 34, no. 1 (2018): 41–47.

Basel Committee on Banking Supervision (Bank of International Settlements). "Sound Practices: Implication of FinTech Development for Banks and Banks Supervisors." February 2018. https://www.bis.org/bcbs/publ/d431.pdf.

Bonneau, Thierry. *Régulation bancaire et financière européenne et internationale*, 4th ed. Bruxelles: Bruylant, 2018.

Booth, Laurence. "The Secret of Canadian Banking: Common Sense." *World Economics* 10, no. 3 (2010): 1–17.

Bourdeau, Sylvie, Nicolas Faucher, and Charles Alexandre Brosseau. "Les FinTechs: Quels sont les enjeux juridiques?" In *Développements récents en droit bancaire (2017)*, vol. 427, edited by Service de la formation continue du Barreau du Québec, 67–102. Montreal: Éditions Yvon Blais, 2017, EYB2017DEV2463.

Canada2020PolicyLab. "OpenBanking: ReportsonBankingandSolutions." July5, 2018. http://canada2020.ca/wp-content/uploads/2018/07/Open-Banking-Report-on-Findings-and-Resolutions-1.pdf.

Cohen, Daniel. "La crise grecque." *Revue économique* 62, no. 3 (2011): 383–94.

Collard, Sharon. "Toward Financial Inclusion in the UK: Progress and Challenges." *Public Money and Management* 27, no. 1 (2007): 13–20.

Commission & Markets Authority. "Making Banks Work Harder for You." August 9, 2016. https://assets.publishing.service.gov.uk/government/uploads/system/uploads/attachment_data/file/544942/overview-of-the-banking-retail-market.pdf.

Competition Bureau Canada. "Technology-Led Innovation in the Canadian Financial Services Sector." December 2017. http://www.bureaudelaconcurrence.gc.ca/eic/site/cb-bc.nsf/fra/04322.html.

Department of Finance (Canada). "A Review into Merits of Open Banking." Consultation Document, January 2019. https://www.canada.ca/en/department-finance/programs/consultations/2019/open-banking.html.

Dostie, Claude. "Le Canada et la crise financière: un retour critique sur la thèse de l'exception canadienne." *Politique et Sociétés* 39, no. 2 (2020): 27–48.

Fenwick, Mark D., Wulf A. Kaal, and Erik P.M. Vermeulen. "Regulation Tomorrow: What Happens When Technology Is Faster Than the Law?" *American Business Law Review* 6 no. 3 (2017): 561–94.

Financial Consumer Agency of Canada. "Open Banking and Consumer Protection: Canadians' Awareness and Expectations." June 2023. https://www.canada.ca/content/dam/fcac-acfc/documents/programs/research-surveys-studies-reports/open-banking-consumer-protection.pdf.

Financial Inclusion Centre. "FinTech – Beware of 'Geeks' Bearing Gifts?" 1–6, January 2018. https://inclusioncentre.co.uk/wp-content/uploads/2018/01/Fintech-Beware-of-geeks-bearing-gifts-FIC-Discussion-Paper-Summary.pdf.

Financial Stability Board. "FinTech and Market Structure in Financial Services: Market Developments and Potential Financial Stability Implications." February 14, 2019. http://www.fsb.org/wp-content/uploads/P140219.pdf.

Henry, Gérard Marie. *La crise de 1929*. Coll. "cursus économie." Paris: Armand Colin, 2000.
Lacoue-Labarthe, Dominique. "La France a-t-elle connu des paniques bancaires inefficientes? Une analyse exploratoire de la crise des années trente." *Revue d'économie politique* 115 (2005): 633–56.
Lacoursière, Marc. "La perspective bancaire canadienne lors de la crise financière de 2007–2009." *Banking and Finance Law Review* 29, no. 2 (2014): 271–319.
Lacoursière, Marc, and Ivan Tchoutourian. "Métamorphose technologique et institutions financières." *Cahiers de Droit* 60, no. 3 (2019): 737–93.
Leong, Emma, and Jodi Gardner. "Open Banking in the UK and Singapore: Open Possibilities for Enhancing Financial Inclusion." *Journal of Business Law* 5 (2021): 424–53.
L'Heureux, Nicole, and Marc Lacoursière. *Droit bancaire*, 5th ed. Montreal: Éditions Yvon Blais, 2017.
Mehran, Hamid, Alan Morrison, and Joel Shapiro. "Corporate Governance and Banks: What Have We Learned from the Financial Crisis?" Federal Reserve Bank of New York Staff Reports No. 502, June 2011. https://www.newyorkfed.org/medialibrary/media/research/staff_reports/sr502.pdf.
Mendez, Julien, and Christian Tutin. "De la crise bancaire à la régulation: l'expérience américaine de 1907." *Économie politique* 48, no. 4 (2010): 42–63.
Nataraj, Geethanjali, and Pravakar Sahoo. "Argentina's Crisis: Causes and Consequences." *Economic and Political Weekly* 38, no. 17 (2003): 1641–44.
Nicholls, Christopher C. "Bank on It: *Bank Act* Restrictions on Use of the Terms 'Bank' and 'Banking', a Case Study on Institutional vs. Functional Financial Services Regulation." *Canadian Business Law Journal* 61, no. 3 (2019): 293–333.
Paddock, John V. "IMF Policy and the Argentine Crisis." *University of Miami Inter-American Law Review* 34, no. 1 (2002): 155–87.
Payments Canada. "Developing a Vision for the Canadian Payment Ecosystem." Draft for Consultation, April 20, 2016.
Polasik Michal, and Radoslaw Kotkowski. "The Open Banking Adoption Among Consumers in Europe: The Role of Privacy, Trust, and Digital Financial Inclusion." May 11, 2022. https://ssrn.com/abstract=4105648.
Rakotomandimby, Lauriane. "La protection des renseignements personnels du consommateur dans un système bancaire ouvert: Étude comparative entre le droit canadien et le droit québécois ainsi que le droit de l'Union européenne et le droit français." PhD diss., Université Laval, 2014.
Ramsay, Iain. "Consumer Credit Law, Distributive Justice and the Welfare State." *Oxford Journal of Legal Studies* 15 (1995): 177–97.
Reynolds, Faith. "Open Banking: A Consumer Perspective." January 2017. https://home.barclays/content/dam/home-barclays/documents/citizenship/access-to-financial-and-digital-empowerment/Open-Banking-A-Consumer-Perspective-Faith-Reynolds.pdf.
Rheingold, Ira, Michael Fitzpatrick, and Al Jr. Hofeld. "From Redlining to Reverse Redlining: A History of Obstacles for Minority Homeownership in America." *Clearinghouse Review* 34 (2000–2001): 642–54.
Rice, Willy E. "Race, Gender, Redlining, and the Discriminatory Access to Loans, Credit, and Insurance: An Historical and Empirical Analysis of Consumers Who Sued Lenders and Insurers in Federal and State Courts, 1950–1995." *San Diego Law Review* 33, no. 2 (1996): 583–699.
Riley, James A. "The Foreign Bank Entry Regime: A Critical Assessment." In *Queen's Annual Business Law Symposium 1996, the Regulation of Financial Institutions – Issues and Perspectives*. Toronto: Carswell, 1997.
Stiglitz, Joseph, and Andrew Weiss. "Credit Rationing in Markets with Imperfect Information." *American Economic Review* 71, no. 3 (1981): 393–410.

The World Bank Group, Asli Demirgü-Kunt, Leora Klapper, Dorothe Singer, Saniya Ansar, and Jake Hess. *The Global Findex Database 2017: Measuring Financial Inclusion and the FinTech Revolution*. Washington, DC: The World Bank, 2018.

Yao, Odile. "Le rôle de la chambre de compensation dans l'usage du chèque au regard de la bancarisation une étude de droit comparée: Canada – France – UEMOA." PhD diss., Université Laval, 2014.

8 Online dispute resolution as a forum for resolving algorithmic trading error disputes in financial markets

Faizal Kurniawan, Harven Filippo Taufik, Izzah Khalif Raihan Abidin, Dinda Ajeng Puspanita, Rizky Amalia, Hilda Yunita Sabrie, and Maradona

1. Introduction

Algorithmic trading has become a popular trading method in the financial market, with its ability to make complex transactions at high speeds with limited human intervention.[1] However, there have been instances where system errors have caused losses for consumers and given rise to legal action against the financial service business actors.[2] These errors can have severe consequences, leading to financial losses. It is important to provide a mechanism for legal action in the event of losses caused by system errors and to regulate provisions to do with the liability of financial service providers.

To ensure consumer protection in cases of system errors, it is crucial to establish a robust mechanism that allows the affected parties to seek legal recourse and obtain appropriate remedies. Such a mechanism should provide a framework for identifying and addressing the liability of financial service business actors when their systems malfunction or generate erroneous outcomes. By establishing clear regulations and guidelines, market participants can understand their rights and responsibilities in case of system errors, contributing to a fair and transparent financial ecosystem.[3]

The emergence of online dispute resolution (ODR) offers a promising avenue for resolving disputes arising from system errors in the financial market. ODR leverages digital platforms and technology to provide an efficient and accessible means of resolving conflicts without the need for physical face-to-face interactions. In the context of resolving disputes between financial service business actors and consumers, ODR can serve as an optimal choice, offering numerous advantages over traditional litigation. By integrating ODR into the legal framework concerning system errors in the financial market, stakeholders can benefit from a more streamlined and cost-effective dispute resolution process. ODR platforms provide a neutral and impartial environment for parties to present their case and engage in negotiation, mediation, conciliation, or arbitration. This online environment allows for greater convenience and flexibility, enabling parties to participate in the dispute resolution process from anywhere, at any time.

DOI: 10.4324/9781003510406-11

ODR provides an opportunity for parties to maintain a cooperative and ongoing relationship rather than engaging in adversarial litigation.[4] By fostering dialogue and promoting collaborative problem-solving, ODR can help preserve the business relationships between financial service providers and their consumers. This approach aligns with the underlying goal of consumer protection, which aims to find fair and mutually beneficial solutions while preserving trust and goodwill in the financial market.[5] Integrating ODR into the resolution of disputes arising from system errors in the financial market can provide an effective and efficient means of addressing consumer losses and ensuring fairness and justice for all parties involved. By harnessing the benefits of digital technology and creating a supportive legal framework, ODR offers an optimal choice for resolving disputes, promoting timely resolutions, and preserving relationships between financial service business actors and their consumers. The utilization of ODR in cases of system error aligns with the evolving nature of the financial market and the need for innovative approaches to consumer protection and dispute resolution.

The primary objective of this research study is to comprehensively examine the liability of financial service business actors when system errors occur, leading to losses for consumers. Additionally, it seeks to identify and propose an appropriate online dispute resolution mechanism that can effectively address and redress these consumer losses. In pursuit of these objectives, this study adopts a normative research approach, employing the statute, conceptual, and comparative approaches to meticulously analyse the regulatory framework and practices in various jurisdictions.

The research findings shed light on a significant gap in Indonesia's existing regulatory provisions concerning the liability of financial service business actors in cases of system errors. Consequently, consumers are often burdened with the potential damages resulting from these errors, as the responsibility for such losses remains ambiguous and ill-defined. Recognising the pressing need for clarity, it becomes imperative to establish robust regulations that definitively outline the responsibilities and accountabilities of the financial service business actors in situations involving system errors. By doing so, the interests and protection of consumers can be significantly enhanced.

Furthermore, this study underscores the substantial potential of online dispute resolution as an effective means of resolving disputes arising from system errors. It gives emphasis to the viability and benefits of mediation, conciliation, and arbitration as alternative dispute resolution mechanisms within the online domain. These mechanisms, supported by the convenience, accessibility, and efficiency of online platforms, offer a compelling avenue for parties to achieve mutually agreeable resolutions to their disputes.

In conclusion, this research endeavour aims to make a meaningful contribution to the existing body of knowledge by delving into the intricate legal implications associated with algorithmic trading system errors and their impact on consumer interests. By critically analysing the liability of financial service business actors and advocating for appropriate online dispute resolution mechanisms, this study seeks to strengthen the legal framework and provide valuable insights for policymakers, market participants, and consumers alike. Ultimately, it endeavours to foster a fair and balanced environment that safeguards consumer rights and promotes trust and confidence in the financial services sector.

2. Liabilities of financial service providers according to Indonesian law in the case of algorithmic errors in their system

2.1 Algorithmic trading and algorithmic trading error

Algorithmic trading has become an increasingly important phenomenon in modern financial markets. With its ability to automate the trading process, algorithmic trading offers solutions to reduce human error and the emotional biases that often affect investment decisions. In this context, algorithmic errors are a major concern, as errors in the code or algorithm logic can lead to significant losses.

Algorithmic trading is a method that uses software to execute trading orders based on a set of pre-programmed instructions. This allows for trade execution at speeds and volumes that human traders cannot achieve. Algorithms can be programmed to consider various factors such as time, price, and volume to determine when and how to execute trades.[6] An algorithmic trading error[7] is a mistake that occurs in the algorithmic trading process, which can arise from various sources, including code errors, data issues, model inaccuracies, or technical disruptions where computers use algorithms to make trading decisions automatically. These errors can have a significant impact, causing financial losses or market disruptions.

As an example of an error case in algorithmic trading in Singapore, the complexity of digital currency disputes has been brought fully into the courtroom. The Singapore International Commercial Court (SICC) facilitates an effective dispute resolution mechanism for disputes in Singapore involving cryptocurrencies, such as Bitcoin and Ethereum. Although the fundamental issue is cryptocurrency trading, the main focus is on the contracts agreed upon by the parties, highlighting the potential dangers of algorithmic trading and the difficulty in applying the doctrine of mistake where the contract was formed without human involvement.

It was highlighted that in disputes regarding digital currencies, the ability of trading parties to reverse transactions might become a crucial issue. In one case in 2019, the UK-registered company B2C2 Ltd, which buys and sells virtual currencies, filed a summary judgment against the Singapore-based currency exchange platform Quoine Pte Ltd before the SICC. B2C2's entire trading process was automated using its algorithmic trading software, which meant that its trades concluded without any direct human involvement. Quoine had a fundamental computer system breakdown that resulted in the conclusion of a certain number of trades by B2C2's algorithmic trading software. When Quoine identified this mistake, it intervened and cancelled the digital contracts. B2C2 sued Quoine alleging breach of contract. Quione claimed it was entitled to cancel the trade because B2C2 had been unjustly enriched due to the mistake, that is, the system error as the cause of the transactions, which could be rectified without detriment to B2C2 or other third parties. However, the SICC ruled in favour of the B2C2.[8]

2.2 Indonesian code on consumer protection and its applicability on financial service providers

Although cases of algorithmic trading in Indonesia have not yet reached a repressive stage, preventive measures have been implemented by law enforcement authorities. In essence, the losses that may be incurred in a series of automated trading activities mean that humans, as legal subjects acting as traders or consumers, have their legal positions normatively regulated by Indonesian Code Number 8 Year 1999 on Consumer Protection (referred to as the Consumer Protection Code). Consumer Protection Code serves as a pivotal legislation in Indonesia, providing a comprehensive legal framework to safeguard the rights and interests of consumers. This Code reflects the nation's commitment to ensuring fair and ethical business practices, product safety, and adequate remedies for consumers. It aims to create a balance of power between businesses and consumers, empowering individuals to make informed choices and protecting them from unfair trade practices. By setting standards for business conduct, product quality, and consumer redress, the Code establishes a robust framework for consumer protection in Indonesia. In this regard, it is essential to examine the provisions of the Consumer Protection Code in greater detail to understand how it regulates and promotes consumer protection, particularly in relation to financial service providers and their responsibilities as producers under the law.

The Consumer Protection Code defines a producer as an individual or entity that produces, assembles, processes, imports, distributes, or provides goods or services. While the definition seems broad, it is crucial to analyse its applicability to financial service providers. Financial service providers typically offer services rather than tangible goods, which might raise questions about whether they can be considered producers under the Consumer Protection Code.

To determine whether a financial service provider falls within the scope of a producer, the provisions of the Code need to be examined in more detail. Article 4 of the Consumer Protection Code stipulates that a producer is responsible for ensuring the quality, safety, and reliability of their products or services. This responsibility includes, but is not limited to, providing accurate information, preventing deceptive practices, and maintaining appropriate standards.

In the case of financial service providers, their "products" can be viewed as the services they offer, such as banking, insurance, or investment services. These services are intangible in nature but hold significant importance to consumers. Therefore, it can be argued that financial service providers fulfill the definition of a producer under the Consumer Protection Law, as they produce and provide services that have an impact on the consumers' financial well-being.

Article 4 paragraph (1) of the Consumer Protection Code states that a producer must ensure the safety of their products or services. Although safety may be more commonly associated with physical products or tangible goods, it can also be applied to financial services; the broader interpretation of the law indicates that financial service providers can, indeed, be considered producers under the Consumer Protection Code. Financial service providers have a duty to operate in a manner that safeguards the interests and financial security of the consumers. This duty includes implementing robust security measures to protect their consumers' personal and financial information as well as ensuring the integrity and reliability of their systems to prevent unauthorised access or fraudulent activities. Therefore, financial service providers can be considered producers, who are, as a result, responsible for ensuring the safety and security of their services.

2.3 Liability of financial service providers under the code

Another relevant aspect to consider is the liability of producers for defects in their products or services. Article 18 of the Consumer Protection Code establishes the liability of producers for defects that cause harm to consumers. It provides consumers with the right to compensation or remedy in cases where the products or services provided by the producer do not meet the required quality, safety, or reliability standards. This provision reinforces the notion that financial service providers can be held liable for any errors, deficiencies, or failures in the services they offer, especially if these errors result in financial loss or harm to consumers.

It is important to note that while financial service providers can be considered producers under the Consumer Protection Code, the specific application of these provisions to the financial services industry may require further interpretation and guidance from the Indonesian courts and regulatory authorities. The evolving nature of financial services and the increasing reliance on digital platforms also necessitates ongoing adaptation and updates to the legal framework to ensure adequate consumer protection. As the United States government includes consumers in the financial services sector, they have established regulations, conduct monitoring, and enforce laws related to security, policies, and trading activities concerning depository, insurance, finance companies, and other financial institutions. Therefore, financial institutions in the United States have made the financial market competitive, efficient, fair, safe, and transparent.[9] This recognition implies that financial service providers have a responsibility to ensure the quality, safety, and reliability of their services. Additionally, they can be held liable for any defects or errors in their services that result in harm or losses to consumers. The specific application of these provisions to the financial services sector may require further clarification through regulations and judicial interpretations. Nonetheless, the Consumer Protection Code serves as an essential tool for protecting consumers and promoting fair and responsible practices in the financial services industry.

Under Consumer Protection Code, the liability of financial service providers for damages caused to consumers as a result of errors in their systems is firmly grounded in the legal framework. Several provisions within the law establish the legal basis for holding financial service providers accountable in such cases.

Article 19 of the Consumer Protection Code specifically regulates the liability of producers regarding defects in their products or services. It stipulates that producers are accountable for damages caused by defects in their goods or services, which includes system errors in the case of financial service providers. This provision serves as a critical legal basis for holding financial service providers liable when errors in their (algorithmic trading) systems result in harm or loss for consumers.

Furthermore, Article 19 of the Consumer Protection Code regulates the consumer's right to compensation for damages suffered due to defects in products or services. This Article provides a legal basis for consumers to seek redress and obtain appropriate remedies when financial service providers' system errors lead to financial loss or harm. It reinforces the principle that financial service providers must be held liable for the consequences of their errors, ensuring that consumers are adequately protected under the law.

2.4 Resolution of consumer disputes and main substantial issues in case of algorithmic trading errors

In line with the previous explanation, consumer disputes are disputes between business actors and consumers that involve claiming compensation for damaged goods or loss caused by or during the consumption of goods and/or utilisation of services.[10] To facilitate dispute resolution in cases involving system errors, the Consumer Protection Code promotes alternative dispute resolution mechanisms. Article 47 encourages parties to resolve disputes amicably through negotiation, mediation, conciliation, or arbitration as regulated in Code Number 30 of 1999 on Arbitration and Alternative Dispute Resolution. These methods offer a legal basis for seeking resolutions outside of formal court proceedings, providing a more accessible and efficient means of addressing disputes arising from system errors in the financial services sector.

As established before, financial service providers are liable for any harm or financial loss resulting from algorithmic system errors under the Indonesian Code on Consumer Protection. Furthermore, alternative dispute resolution mechanisms are applicable to disputes related to system errors. Provisions such as Article 4, Article 7, and Article 19 establish the responsibilities of producers and recognise the rights of consumers to seek compensation for any harm or financial losses resulting from system errors.[11]

Additionally, the law promotes alternative dispute resolution mechanisms as a legal basis for resolving disputes related to system errors. By adhering to these legal provisions, financial service providers can ensure compliance with consumer protection regulations and foster trust and confidence in their services such as mitigating the risk of system errors.

Regarding how the law can evaluate the role of artificial intelligence technology that allows algorithms to form contracts without human assistance, where the validity of a contract typically requires human cognition, it is essential to extend traditional contract law principles. These principles are based on the notion of "two people agreeing to reach an agreement" and should be adapted to current conditions as times evolve. Indonesia can further examine how the Singapore International Commercial Court has adapted the doctrine of unilateral mistake to contracts formed using a deterministic algorithm. A unilateral mistake occurs when one party is mistaken about a fundamental term of the contract and the other non-mistaken party is aware of this. In common-law systems, the non-mistaken party must have

Table 8.1 Provisions establishing the responsibilities of producers under Indonesian Code on Consumer Protection

Article 4 (h) Consumer's rights	*h. mendapatkan kompensasi, ganti rugi, dan/atau penggantian, apabila barang dan/atau jasa yang diterima tidak sesuai dengan perjanjian atau tidak sebagaimana mestinya.* (Receive compensation, indemnity, and or replacement if the goods and/or services received are not by the agreement or as they should be.)
Article 7 (f) and (g) Service provider's obligations	*f. memberi kompensasi, ganti rugi dan/atau penggantian atas kerugian akibat penggunaan, pemakaian, dan pemanfaatan barang dan/atau jasa yang diperdagangkan.* *g. memberi kompensasi, ganti rugi dan/atau penggantian apabila barang dan/atau jasa yang diterima atau dimanfaatkan tidak sesuai dengan perjanjian.* (f. provide compensation, indemnity, and/or reimbursement for losses resulting from using, wearing, and utilising traded goods and/or services. g. provide compensation, indemnity, and/or replacement if the goods and/or services received or utilised are not by the agreement.)
Article 19 paragraph 1 and 2	*(1) Pelaku usaha bertanggung jawab memberikan ganti rugi atas kerusakan, pencemaran, dan/atau kerugian konsumen akibat mengonsumsi barang dan/atau jasa yang dihasilkan atau diperdagangkan.* *(2) Ganti rugi sebagaimana dimaksud pada ayat (1) dapat berupa pengembalian uang atau penggantian barang dan/atau jasa yang sejenis atau setara nilainya, . . . sesuai dengan ketentuan peraturan perundang-undangan yang berlaku.* ((1) Business actors are responsible for compensating for damage, pollution, and/or loss to consumers from consuming goods and/or services produced or traded. (2) Indemnity as intended in paragraph (1) may take the form of a refund or replacement of goods and/or services of the same or equivalent value . . . by the provisions of the applicable laws and regulations.)

actual knowledge of the mistake for the contract to be void. The Singapore Court of Appeal in the case of *Chwee Kin Keong v Digilandmall.com Pte Ltd* also acknowledged the doctrine of unilateral mistake, stating that when the non-mistaken party, who has constructive knowledge of the mistake, engages in unreasonable behavior concerning the mistake, the contract can be voided. This doctrine is frequently applied in common-law jurisdictions.[12]

Banking contracts in Indonesia have undergone significant digital transformation, enabling potential consumers to automatically agree to these terms. However, in the digital contracting process involving the drafting, signing, and executing of agreements, errors can lead to the termination of the contract. The mechanism for terminating the contract due to errors is still relatively new and not fully understood by consumers. Therefore, it is crucial for consumers to understand the processes and regulations governing digital banking contracts to avoid unintended contract termination.[13] Consumers are now fairly educated about the importance of concluding contracts. If an agreement appears detrimental from the outset, it's better not to conclude it. Consumers need to read carefully and think critically by asking about the solutions that would be taken if issues arise in the future. In Indonesia, consumer complaints can be submitted to the National Consumer Protection Agency and the Financial Services Authority. Consumers cannot act independently, making the role of the government essential as both regulator and law enforcer. Consumer protection is crucial, and any violations or issues arising from contracts between parties should be addressed by the appropriate authority.

There are several cases of system error found among the numerous banks in Indonesia. In the Bank Mandiri case of 2019, the bank experienced a system error that caused temporary service disruptions and affected numerous consumers.[14] As a result, consumers were unable to access their accounts, make transactions, or access the necessary banking services. This incident sparked public outcry and drew attention to the potential risks and consequences consumers may face due to system errors in financial institutions.[15] Similarly, the Bank Syariah Indonesia (BSI) case in 2023 involved a system failure that led to the unavailability of banking services for a significant period.[16] The incident caused inconvenience and financial losses for consumers who relied on BSI's services. These cases illustrate the detrimental impact system errors can have on consumers and the importance of robust consumer protection measures in the financial service sector.

In response to such incidents and to strengthen consumer protection, the Financial Services Authority (Otoritas Jasa Keuangan – OJK) has implemented regulations. One notable regulation is "Peraturan Otoritas Jasa Keuangan Nomor 6/POJK.07/2022 tentang Perlindungan Konsumen dan Masyarakat di Sektor Jasa Keuangan", which translates to "Financial Services Authority Regulation Number 6/POJK.07/2022 on Consumer and Public Protection in the Financial Services Sector".[17] By implementing this regulation, the Financial Services Authority aims to create a more transparent and accountable environment in the financial services sector, promoting consumer confidence and ensuring adequate protection for consumers.[18]

The Regulation sets out guidelines and requirements for financial service providers to establish robust systems, implement risk management measures, and address the potential impacts of system errors on consumers. The regulation points up the need for financial service providers to have contingency plans in place to mitigate the consequences of system failures and minimise disruptions to consumer services. Furthermore, the regulation emphasises the importance of providing clear and accurate information to consumers regarding the risks associated with financial services, including the potential for system errors. It mandates that financial service providers must disclose all relevant information about their system's reliability, security measures, and contingency plans to enable consumers to make informed decisions.

The Bank Mandiri case, the BSI case, and the implementation of Financial Services Authority Regulation Number 6/POJK.07/2022 on Consumer and Public Protection in the Financial Services Sector underscore the significance of consumer protection in the context of system errors in financial services in Indonesia. These incidents highlight the need for financial service providers to establish robust systems, adopt risk management measures, and prioritise consumer protection. The Regulation by the Financial Services Authority serves as a crucial step in promoting fair treatment, transparency, and accountability in the financial services sector, thereby safeguarding the interests of consumers in Indonesia.

2.5 Burden of proof

In principle, producers are indeed responsible for defects in their products or services. However, in practice, the burden of error risk is often placed more heavily on the consumer. Generally, providers who offer algorithmic trading create and enforce standard agreements that include exoneration clauses which release the provider from liability in the event of product errors.

Although such exoneration clause are prohibited under Article 30(5) of Financial Services Authority Regulation Number 6/POJK.07/2022 on Consumer and Public Protection in the Financial Services Sector, the clause might still be permitted by other regulations. For example, "Peraturan Nomor III-K tentang Fasilitas Pesanan Langsung dan/atau Penerapan Automated Ordering Oleh Anggota Bursa Efek", which translates to "Indonesia Stock Exchange Regulation Number III-K on Direct Order Facility and/or Implementation of Automated Ordering by Stock Exchange Members", stipulates the inclusion of certain clauses in the agreement between securities companies providing automated ordering facilities and consumers as consumers. According to Section III.2.15.1.6 of this Regulation, one of the clauses that must be included is that "transactions made by customers are valid and binding, which is the customer's responsibility". In this case, this provision can be interpreted as imposing absolute responsibility on the customer, without any exceptions, even in the event of errors in the automated ordering system during the transaction.

The inclusion of provisions in Regulation Number III-K on Direct Order Facility and/or the Implementation of Automated Ordering by Stock Exchange Members is not surprising, considering that producers or service providers in the financial market should be responsible for defects in their products or services but only if it can be proven that such defects arise due to the fault, negligence, and/or actions of the producers or providers. This is stipulated in Article 8(1) of Financial Services Authority Regulation Number 6/POJK.07/2022 on Consumer and Public Protection in the Financial Services Sector.

2.6 Application to algorithmic trading errors

The issue is that the existing theories and liability provisions are difficult to apply in markets that employ algorithmic trading systems. This is because unforeseen errors in algorithmic trading systems are considered "endemic" to the operating system.[19] The functioning of algorithmic trading systems is not always predictable, and it cannot be entirely ensured from the initial programming stage.

Unforeseen algorithmic errors beyond human and securities firms' control can still occur.[20] In fact, mistakes may arise even when securities firms have exercised caution and attempted to ensure the safe operation of their algorithmic trading systems.[21] Consequently, it becomes challenging to establish the element of fault on the part of the company when pursuing liability claims or attributing liability for system errors if the applied concept is *liability based on fault*.

In order to achieve a balanced legal protection between producers or providers and consumers, the *presumption of liability* concept is more suitable to be applied. Under this framework, producers or providers are presumed to always be liable for consumer losses unless they can prove that the losses were not their own fault. In this case, the burden of proof is on the producers or providers to demonstrate their lack of fault in order to be exempted from liability for the losses.[22] This is what distinguishes it from the *liability based on fault* concept, where the burden of proof lies on the affected consumer to prove the fault of the producer or provider.

Focusing on the responsibilities of banking application owners when customer service is affected and hindered due to system errors, impacting the consumers' access to their material wealth and potentially resulting in loss, there is often no clear and strong legal recourse for consumers to prove their losses if they genuinely experience them (not necessarily in the form of money, as time and other aspects are important) and now banking applications also facilitate purchases of shares, mutual funds, and money markets that consumers can make in real-time. The management of consumers' money by banking institutions on digital platforms is the output of an agreement where consumers agree to use digital banking platforms. In practice, terms and conditions are also signed by consumers online. In such cases, if a banking institution mismanages the system, it can also be considered negligence, since consumers cannot benefit from the contract during the system error.[23]

In short, it is necessary to anticipate and prevent errors involving IT by accommodating clauses that mutually benefit both parties, particularly regarding how to handle system errors and other adverse situations that disadvantage consumers. These standard clauses must also be formulated by the legislator, in this case the government. So that the limitation of liability that is detrimental to consumers must be proven and imposed on the service provider.

What should be the mechanism for resolution? Is it effective to bring the matter directly to court? Court proceedings require strong evidence to first be justified in order to assess the contract. The essence of the unilateral mistake rule in cases of algorithmic trading errors is the importance of financial digital platform users obtaining information. Therefore, if they suffer losses resulting from errors related to financial or economic aspects, proof must be provided and not just based on assumptions, because the term 'unilateral mistake' will be used to announce a decision to enforce the promise.[24]

In situations involving unilateral mistakes, the affected party must demonstrate that the mistake significantly altered the terms or implications of the agreement and that it was fundamental to the contract's validity. Under Indonesian contract law, an error in the understanding or representation of crucial terms could lead to rescission or modification of the contract if it is proven that the other party did not share or was not aware of the mistake.[25] However, if the mistake results solely from one party's negligence or assumption without due diligence, courts may be reluctant to relieve them of contractual obligations.

Within the fault-based liability under Indonesian consumer protection law, it is important to determine the presence of 'fault' which is caused by the provider or another party under the provider's supervision before they can be held legally accountable. This is based on the liability based on fault principle, where a person or party can only be held legally responsible if the element of fault is proven.[26] In cases of unilateral mistake, this assessment may involve analysing whether the mistake was avoidable or whether it was caused by a failure to disclose relevant information, especially in digital trading platforms, where transparency and data accuracy play key roles.[27]

3. Settlement of algorithmic error disputes through online dispute resolution

3.1 Key aspects and benefits of online dispute resolution

The emergence of online dispute resolution (ODR) offers a promising avenue for resolving disputes arising from system errors in the financial market. ODR leverages digital platforms and technology to provide an efficient and accessible means of resolving conflicts without the need for physical face-to-face interactions. In the context of resolving disputes between financial service providers and consumers, ODR can serve as an optimal choice, offering numerous advantages over traditional litigation.[28]

By integrating ODR into the legal framework concerning system errors in the financial market, stakeholders can benefit from a more streamlined and cost-effective dispute resolution process. ODR platforms provide a neutral and impartial environment for parties to present their case and engage in negotiation, mediation, conciliation, or arbitration. This online environment allows for greater convenience and flexibility, enabling parties to participate in the dispute resolution process from anywhere, at any time.

Furthermore, ODR can facilitate timely resolutions, particularly in cases involving system errors where immediate action may be necessary to mitigate potential financial losses or restore access to services. Traditional court proceedings can often be time-consuming and burdensome, causing further delays and exacerbating the impact on consumers. In contrast, ODR offers a more expedient alternative, allowing parties to address their concerns promptly and efficiently.

Additionally, ODR provides an opportunity for parties to maintain a cooperative and ongoing relationship rather than engaging in adversarial litigation. By fostering dialogue and promoting collaborative problem-solving, ODR can help preserve the business relationships between financial service providers and their consumers. This approach aligns with the underlying goal of consumer protection, which aims to find fair and mutually beneficial solutions while preserving trust and goodwill in the financial market. ODR is a significant component of the alternative dispute resolution (ADR) process, leveraging Internet technology to enhance dispute resolution methods. Following are detailed the key aspects and benefits of ODR.[29]

Firstly, ODR provides a more convenient and accessible platform for dispute resolution compared to traditional ADR methods. In cases involving system errors, the affected parties may be geographically dispersed, making it impractical to convene in person for face-to-face meetings. ODR eliminates this physical constraint by utilising digital technology, enabling parties to participate in the resolution process remotely. Through online platforms, parties can present their arguments, exchange information, and engage in negotiations without the need for travel or to have a physical presence. This accessibility makes ODR a more practical and cost-effective option, especially when dealing with complex financial disputes involving multiple parties.[30]

Secondly, ODR offers greater efficiency and expediency in resolving system error disputes. Traditional ADR methods often involve time-consuming processes such as scheduling meetings, coordinating availability, and conducting lengthy negotiation sessions. In contrast, ODR allows for real-time communication and immediate access to relevant information, expediting the resolution process. Parties can engage in discussions and negotiations at their own pace, without being bound by the constraints of scheduling conflicts or limited timeframes. As a result, ODR enables faster resolutions, which is particularly crucial in cases involving system errors where swift action is necessary to mitigate financial losses or restore access to services.

ODR enhances the transparency and accountability of the dispute resolution process. Digital platforms used in ODR can facilitate the documentation and tracking of communications, ensuring a comprehensive record of the proceedings. This transparency not only promotes fairness and procedural integrity but also assists in evaluating the merits of each party's arguments and evidence. Additionally, ODR platforms often have built-in safeguards to protect the integrity of the process, such as secure data encryption and authentication mechanisms. These features contribute to instilling trust and confidence in the resolution process, assuring parties that their concerns will be addressed in a transparent and accountable manner.

Furthermore, ODR can accommodate the complexities associated with system errors in the financial market. System errors may involve intricate technical details, data analysis, or complex algorithms, making it necessary to have experts or specialists participate in the dispute resolution process. ODR platforms can facilitate the inclusion of such experts through video conferencing, virtual presentations, and secure document sharing. This enables the involved parties to benefit from the expertise of professionals without incurring additional costs or logistical challenges, ensuring that the dispute resolution process adequately addresses the intricacies involved.

In conclusion, when it comes to resolving disputes arising from system errors in the financial market, ODR emerges as the best choice compared to traditional ADR methods. ODR's convenience, accessibility, efficiency, transparency, and capacity to handle complex technical matters make it particularly well-suited for addressing disputes related to system errors. By leveraging digital platforms and technology, ODR provides an optimal solution that overcomes geographical constraints, expedites the resolution process, enhances transparency, and accommodates the intricacies associated with system errors. Ultimately, ODR offers a more practical and cost-effective means of resolving disputes in the evolving landscape of the financial industry.

3.2 A real-world example

One notable case that highlights the relevance and effectiveness of ODR in the resolving of disputes arising from system errors in the financial market is the Knight Capital Group incident. In 2012, Knight Capital, a prominent U.S. trading firm, experienced a technical glitch in its trading system, leading to a series of erroneous trades and substantial financial losses. This case serves as an illustrative example of how ODR can be an optimal choice for resolving such disputes.

Following the incident, Knight Capital faced numerous legal challenges from affected parties seeking compensation for their losses.[31] Recognising the need for an efficient and fair resolution process, Knight Capital engaged in ODR by establishing an online portal for affected traders to submit their claims and engage in settlement discussions. The ODR platform provided a user-friendly interface, allowing traders to present their evidence, exchange information, and negotiate potential settlements in a transparent and structured manner.

By opting for ODR, Knight Capital was able to handle a large volume of claims efficiently and mitigate the costs and time associated with traditional litigation. The use of digital technology streamlined the claims process, enabling prompt communication and collaboration between the trading firm and affected parties. This approach facilitated a more expeditious resolution, reducing the financial burden and uncertainty experienced by the affected traders.

The Knight Capital case also highlights the benefits of ODR in fostering transparency and accountability. The online platform provided a centralised repository for evidence, allowing all parties involved to access and review relevant documents. This transparency not only facilitated a better understanding of the technical glitch and its impact but also enabled the involved parties to evaluate the strength of their claims and engage in informed negotiations. The availability of an online trail of communication and evidence further enhanced the integrity and fairness of the resolution process.

Furthermore, the Knight Capital incident showcases how ODR can contribute to maintaining business relationships and preserving market reputation. By engaging in collaborative negotiations and settlements through the ODR platform, Knight Capital demonstrated its commitment to addressing the concerns of affected traders and finding mutually agreeable solutions. This cooperative approach helped to minimise the adversarial nature of the dispute and fostered goodwill between the trading firm and its consumers, mitigating potential long-term damage to their business relationship.

The success of ODR in the Knight Capital case highlights its potential as an optimal choice for resolving disputes arising from system errors in the financial market. By leveraging digital platforms and technology, ODR offers an efficient, cost-effective, and accessible means of addressing consumer losses and promoting fair outcomes. It not only expedites the resolution process but also fosters transparency, accountability, and the preservation of business relationships.

The Knight Capital case serves as a compelling real-world example of how ODR can be successfully utilised in resolving disputes arising from system errors in the financial market. By embracing ODR, financial service providers can effectively address consumer losses, enhance transparency and accountability, and maintain positive business relationships. The lessons learned from this case underscore the potential of ODR as an optimal choice for settling disputes in the ever-evolving landscape of algorithmic trading and the financial industry.

When considering the resolution of disputes arising from system errors in the financial market, ODR stands out as the best choice compared to traditional ADR methods. While ADR methods like mediation, conciliation, and arbitration have been valuable in resolving various types of conflicts, ODR offers unique advantages that make it particularly suitable for addressing disputes related to system errors in the financial sector.

3.3 Construction of evidence tools and easing the burden on consumers

There are three types of developing ODR systems, namely:[32]

(i) *Fully Automated Cyber Negotiation:* An ODR service provider with this system operates using software that can automatically match the complainant's request with the respondent to reach an agreement.

(ii) *Using Software and Facilitator*: Mediation using software and a third party as a facilitator. Thus, the ODR services will be conducted through two processes: a) the parties appoint a third party to assist each party in determining a suitable negotiation model and making requests to be submitted as part of the ODR process then b) the software system will automatically compare the desires of each disputing party, and an agreement can be reached.

(iii) *Using Online Technology*: The use of technology in dispute resolution can utilise mediums such as email, instant messaging, chat rooms, and video conferences as supporting media for the dispute resolution process.

Therefore, in line with the development of ODR systems, the construction of evidence tools in electronic dispute resolution becomes crucial. This is because Indonesian Civil Procedural Code does not comprehensively regulate the position of evidence tools in the trial's evidentiary agenda despite these provisions holding a central position in the evidentiary agenda.[33] In Indonesia, there is currently no recognition of online alternative dispute resolution. However, development in this area has led to the introduction of electronic trials as a digital dispute resolution method. Specifically, during the evidentiary stage of electronic civil trials, Article

22 of Supreme Court Regulation Number 1 of 2019 regulates that documentary evidence is presented online by uploading documents or proof in the form of letters to the E-Court application. Other regulations regarding documentary evidence in electronic trials are not detailed but the importance of documentary evidence in civil cases, which prioritises formal truth (truth based on documents), remains essential.[34]

The user discusses the ability to obtain witness testimony through audiovisual communication media, which allows a witness to be present remotely when they cannot attend the trial in person. They also note that Supreme Court Regulation Number 1 of 2019 only addresses witness examination in Article 24, highlighting the need for more comprehensive regulations in electronic trials, especially regarding supervision mechanisms for witnesses undergoing examination. They express concern about potential interference or guidance from third parties during witness examinations conducted via teleconferencing technology, which could violate the principle of fair trial.[35]

3.4 Safeguarding consumer protection

The solution is to create implementing regulations that specifically address protection against system errors in banking while still referring to Code 8/1999 and Code 30/1999 as the main regulations on consumer protection and alternative dispute resolution methods in Indonesia.[36] These regulations should include specific procedures for handling claims due to system errors, including stages of compensation and loss mitigation to prevent further harm to consumers and to maintain trust in banking institutions. With clear regulations in place, when a case goes to court or non-court dispute resolution, judges will have primary reference points for sanctions that can be imposed on service providers when they are legally held negligent.

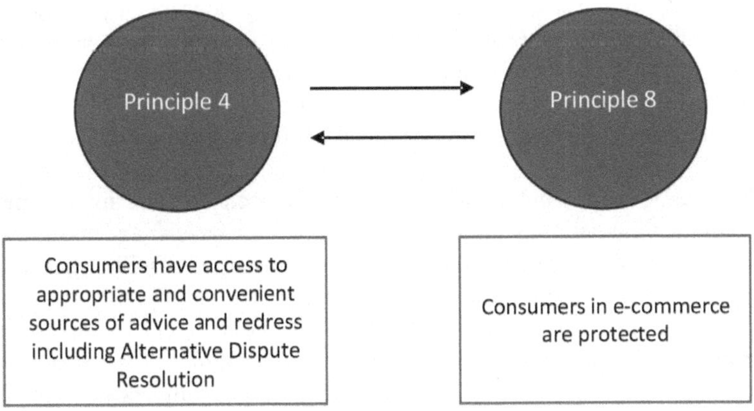

Figure 8.1 Two principles regarding consumer protection.

Source: Author's resume from ASEAN Guidelines on Online Dispute Resolution (ODR).

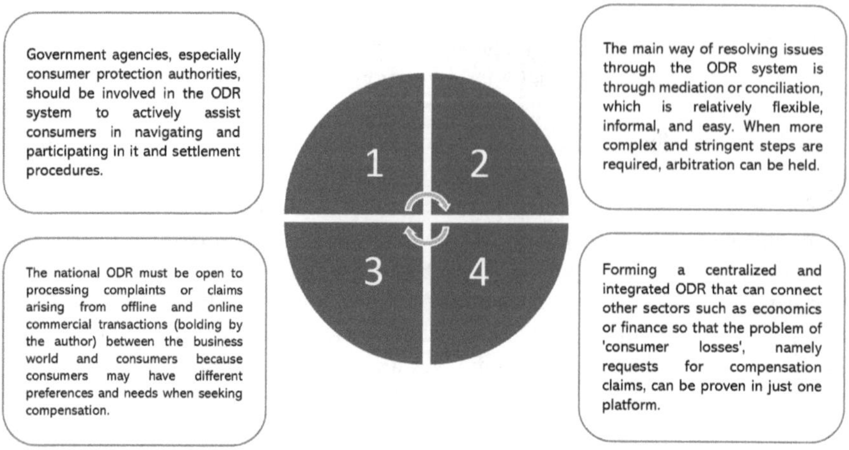

Figure 8.2 ODR's main characteristics.

Source: Author's resume from ASEAN Guidelines on Online Dispute Resolution (ODR).

This approach ensures that decisions are no longer fully reliant on judges' interpretations derived from international cases, given that in the civil law system, jurisprudence only serves as a reference for judges in crafting their arguments.[37]

The enactment of Supreme Court Regulation Number 1 of 2019 is Indonesia's effort to achieve efficiency when handling cases in order to meet the ASEAN High-Level Principles on Consumer Protection (AHLPCP):[38]

In addition to the two principles mentioned here, ASEAN has classified the "Main characteristics of ODR" as shown in the following table:[39]

As previously explained, it can be understood that handling algorithmic trading cases in Indonesia can be resolved through ODR by considering the nature of the contract made by the involved parties as well as the concept of presumption of liability instead of the concept of liability based on fault. This can be further outlined in written legislation as a concrete commitment to navigate and participate in the ODR system and dispute resolution procedures.

Best practices in other countries include the following examples:

(i) China, an Asian country known for its advanced use and management of electronics, already has three Internet courts, e-tribunals, and more than 30 online arbitration institutions.[40] Even after China initially facilitated its citizens through the online platform of the China International Economic and Trade Arbitration Commission in 2009, the Chinese government has opened up to several institutions and private entities to launch ODR platforms, such as the Supreme People's Court in 2019 and Benchmark Chambers International & Benchmark International Mediation Center in 2019.[41] This rapid expansion was made possible because the government established ODR Guidelines, which serve as the foundation for any institution wishing to offer ODR legal services.

(ii) Thailand, as one of the ASEAN countries advocating for ODR, established the Thailand Arbitration Center, which introduced an arbitration, mediation, and negotiation platform for the Thai people called "Talk DD". This platform has been officially accessible on its official website since January 2021. The online platform specifically handles certain types of cases, such as copyright, patent, and trademark infringements.[42] The main goal of the Talk DD platform is to facilitate and support out-of-court dispute resolutions as well as to reduce the number of cases submitted to the Intellectual Property and International Trade Court. Inspired by the spirit of these two countries, which prioritise consumer satisfaction and trust, Indonesia, through the BANI Arbitration Center, will pursue a similar effort to quickly develop its national ODR system, focusing on time and cost efficiency in the resolution of consumer protection cases.

Currently, Indonesia has Supreme Court Regulation Number 1 of 2019, and in response to this regulation, the Ministry of Trade is developing a national ODR system for Indonesian consumers. Additionally, the BANI Arbitration Center will soon launch an ODR program in line with Arbitration and Alternative Dispute Resolution Code, which accommodates the use of electronic media in the arbitration process.

Thus, the choice of ODR as a medium for resolving civil disputes becomes one of solutions, where the ODR paradigm prioritises efficiency while maintaining the principles of dispute resolution, being easy, quick, and thorough. It is important to agree that bank consumers, classified as 'consumers,' certainly look forward to a dispute resolution process that is straightforward, with time and efficiency in mind. Consequently, the costs are also lower, minimising the burden of accommodation and mobility for the parties involved, as the dispute resolution process can be conducted online. Therefore, customer protection is a banking challenge that directly impacts a large portion of society. Legal protection for consumers must be prioritised given their vulnerable position, which should not be overlooked.[43]

Thus, integrating ODR into the resolution of disputes arising from system errors in the financial market can provide an effective and efficient means of addressing consumer losses and ensuring fairness and justice for all parties involved. By harnessing the benefits of digital technology and creating a supportive legal framework, ODR offers an optimal choice for resolving disputes, promoting timely resolutions, and preserving relationships between financial service business actors and their consumers. The utilization of ODR in cases where there are system errors aligns with the evolving nature of the financial market and the need for innovative approaches to consumer protection and dispute resolution.[44]

4. Conclusion

The liability of financial service providers for algorithmic errors in their systems, as regulated by Indonesian Code Number 8 Year 1999 on Consumer Protection, underscores the importance of consumer protection in the financial services sector. While financial service providers primarily offer intangible services, they can be considered producers under the law, responsible for ensuring the quality, safety, and reliability of their services. Financial service providers must also ensure the safety and security of their systems, implementing robust measures to protect the consumers' information and prevent unauthorised access or fraudulent activities. The law establishes the liability of producers for defects in their products or services, including system errors, thus providing consumers with the right to compensation for damages or losses by adhering to the concept of presumption of liability concept, which is more suitable to be applied where producers or providers are presumed to always be liable for consumer losses unless they can prove that the losses were not caused by their own fault. However, there is a need for regulatory changes regarding algorithmic errors by implementing the concept of presumption of liability instead of the concept of liability based on fault. The implementation of Financial Services Authority Regulation Number 6/POJK.07/2022 further strengthens consumer protection by setting guidelines for financial service providers to help them establish robust systems, disclose relevant information, and have contingency plans in place to mitigate the consequences of system failures. In cases of disputes arising from system errors, ODR offers an efficient and accessible alternative to traditional litigation. ODR leverages digital platforms to facilitate timely resolutions, maintain cooperative relationships, and provide a transparent and accountable environment for parties to negotiate, mediate or arbitrate their disputes. The Knight Capital Group incident in the United States serves as a notable example of successful ODR implementation for resolving disputes arising from system errors in the financial market. By integrating ODR into the legal framework and embracing digital technology, financial service providers can enhance consumer protection, promote fair resolutions, and maintain positive business relationships.

Notes

1 Schmidt-Kessen, Eenmaa, and Mitre, "Machines," 2.
2 Staff, "U.S. Stocks."
3 Lenglet, "Conflicting," 46.
4 Cortes, *Online Dispute Resolution*, 54.
5 Petrauskas and Kybartienė, "Consumer Disputes," 5.
6 Halls-Moore, *Step Guide*, 7.
7 In this work, the terms 'algorithmic trading error' and 'system error' are used interchangeably.
8 *vide* Suit No 7 of 2017 *B2C2 Ltd v Quoine Pte Ltd* [2019] SGHC(I) 03.
9 Kaliski, *Encyclopedia of Business*, 315.
10 Subagyono et al., "Enforcement," 684.
11 Wulandari, "Aspek Perlindungan Hukum," 95–97.
12 Fu, "Algorithmic Contracts," 1.
13 Takasenseran, "Perjanjian Antar Bank," 46.
14 Tektona and Listiyapuji, "Perlindungan Hukum," 68.
15 Tektona and Listiyapuji, "Perlindungan Hukum."
16 Mukhtar, "Evaluation," 29–30.
17 Sunaryo and Utomo, "Perlindungan Hukum Preventif," 4.
18 Astutik and Soerodjo, "The Role," 439.
19 Yadav, "How Algorithmic," 1653.
20 Yadav, "The Failure of Liability," 1082.
21 Yadav, "The Failure of Liability," 1083.

22 Massie, Pandaag, and Soewikromo, "Tanggung Jawab Perusahaan," 249.
23 Zhou, "An Economic Perspective," 9.
24 Rasmusen and Ayres, "Mutual and Unilateral Mistake," 312.
25 Article 1320, Indonesian Civil Code.
26 Umboh, "Tanggung Jawab," 47.
27 Indonesian Consumer Protection Code Number 8 of 1999.
28 Katsh, *Online Disputes Resolution*, 9.
29 Nenstiel, "Online Dispute Resolution," 313.
30 Goodman, "The Pros and Cons," 4.
31 Lynch, *The Worst Computer Bugs*.
32 Lynch, *The Worst Computer Bugs*, 29.
33 Kurniawan et al., "Evidence of Contract," 22.
34 Kurniawan et al., "Evidence of Contract."
35 Kurniawan et al., "Evidence of Contract," 23–25.
36 Indonesian Consumer Protection Code Number 8 of 1999 and Indonesian Arbitration Code Number 30 of 1999.
37 Wijaya, "Weakness," 42.
38 ASEAN, *ASEAN Guidelines*, 1.
39 ASEAN, *ASEAN Guidelines*, 4–5.
40 Online Dispute Resolution Guide.com, "ODR in China," www.odrguide.com.
41 Cao, "Online Dispute Resolution Mechanism," 30–35.
42 Thailand Arbitration Center, "THAC Online Dispute Resolution System."
43 Dewi et al., "Legal Protection," 3.
44 Kharisma and Nadzya Tanazal, "Online Dispute Resolution," 144.

References

Astutik, Sri, and Irawan Soerodjo. "The Role of The Financial Services Authority in Setting the Interest Rate for Financial Technology Loans as Consumer Protection of Financial Services." *Yuridika* 38, no. 2 (2023): 431–42.

Cao, Zhixun. "Online Dispute Resolution Mechanism in China: Principle of Proceedings and Impact of Technologies." *China and WTO Review* 8, no. 1 (2022): 29–61.

Cortes, Pablo. *Online Dispute Resolution for Consumers in the European Union*. Abingdon: Routledge, 2011.

Dewi, Sri, Miftah Hulazannah, Maria Panggabean, Riki Afri Rizki, and Sriono Sriono. "Legal Protection Against Bank Customers in Review of Banking Laws." *International Journal of Educational Research & Social Sciences* 1, no. 1 (2020): 1–6.

Fu, Journe. "Algorithmic Contracts: Who Is to Blame?" *Singapore Law Review Juris Illuminae* 12 (2020): 1–8.

Goodman, Joseph W. "The Pros and Cons of Online Dispute Resolution: An Assessment of Cyber-Mediation Websites." *Duke Law and Technology Review* 2 (2003): 1–16.

Halls-Moore, Michael L. *A Step-by-Step Guide to Quantitative Strategies: Successful Algorithmic Trading*. vissionforex Ebook, 2015.

Kaliski, Burton S., ed. *Encyclopedia of Business and Finance*. Thomson Gale, 2007.

Katsh, E. Rifkin. *Online Disputes Resolution: Resolving Conflicts in Cyberspace*. Jossey Bass, 2001.

Kharisma, Dona Budi, and E.A. Nadzya Tanazal. "Online Dispute Resolution as an Alternative Model for Dispute Settlement in the Financial Technology Sector." *Pandecta* 17, no. 1 (2022): 136–45.

Kurniawan, Faizal, Erni Agustin, Xavier Nugraha, Rahajeng Dzakiyya Ikbar, and Stefania Arshanty Felicia. "Evidence of Contract Dispute Settlement in Electronic Trials in Indonesia in the Construction of the Ius Contitutum and Ius Constituendum." *UiTM International Conference on Law & Society* 7, no. SI11 (2021).

Lenglet, Marc. "Conflicting Codes and Codings: How Algorithmic Trading Is Reshaping Financial Regulation." *Theory, Culture & Society* 28, no. 6 (2011): 44–66.

Lynch, Jamie. *The Worst Computer Bugs in History: Losing $460m in 45 Minutes*. SmartBear Bugsnag, September 14, 2017. https://www.bugsnag.com/blog/bug-day-460m-loss.

Massie, Epafras Nyong Eli, Hendrik Pandaag, and Suriyono Soewikromo. "Tanggung Jawab Perusahaan Ekspedisi Muatan Kapal Laut Atas Kerusakan dan Kehilangan Barang Dengan Menggunakan Transportasi Laut." *Lex Privatum* IX, no. 3 (2021): 247–57.

Mukhtar, M. "Evaluation of Bank BSI Error Service Quality in Increasing Customer Satisfaction." *West Science Journal Economic and Entrepreneurship* 1, no. 2 (2023): 28–34.

Nenstiel, Andra Leigh. "Online Dispute Resolution: A Canada-United States Initiative." *Cana-United States Law Journal* 32, no. 1 (2006): 313–29.

Online Dispute Resolution Guide.com. "Online Dispute Resolution in China: The Ultimate Guide of ODR Platforms and E-Courts." https://odrguide.com/online-dispute-resolution-in-china-the-ultimate-guide-of-odr-platforms/#google_vignette.

Petrauskas, Feliksas, and Eglė Kybartienė. "Online Dispution Resolution in Consumer Disputes." *Jurisprudence* 18, no. 3 (2011): 921–41.

Rasmusen, Eric, and Ian Ayres. "Mutual and Unilateral Mistake in Contract Law." *The Journal of Legal Studies* 22, no. 2 (1993): 309–43.

Reuters Staff. "U.S. Stocks Regulator Increases Scrutiny of Algorithmic Trading." *Reuters.com*. https://www.reuters.com/article/us-regulations-sec-algotrading/u-s-stocks-regulator-increases-scrutiny-of-algorithmic-trading-idUSKCN0X42RR.

Schmidt-Kessen, Maria José, Helen Eenmaa, and Maya Mitre. "Machines That Make and Keep Promises – Lessons for Contract Automation from Algorithmic Trading on Financial Markets." *Computer Law & Security Review* 46 (2022): 1–17.

Southeast Asian Nations (ASEAN). *ASEAN Guidelines on Online Dispute Resolution (ODR)*. Jakarta: ASEAN Secretariat, 2022.

Subagyono, Bambang Sugeng Ariadi, Zahry Vandawati Chumaida, and Mochamad Kevin Romadhona. "Enforcement of Consumer Rights Through Dispute Settlement Resolution Agency to Improve the Consumer Satisfaction Index in Indonesia." *Yuridika* 37, no. 3 (2022): 673–96.

Sunaryo, Sidik, and Jatminko Wahyu Utomo. "Perlindungan Hukum Preventif Oleh OJK Dalam Mencegah Kebocoran Data Pribadi Konsumen Pinjaman Online Berdasarkan Peraturan OJK Nomor 06/POJK.07/2022 Tentang Perlindungan Konsumen dan Masyarakat di Sektor Jasa Keuangan." *Civilia* 3, no. 2 (2023): 1–9.

Takasenseran, Mauritz Pray. "Perjanjian Antar Bank dan Nasabah Menurut Undang-Undang Nomor 10 tahun 1998." *Lex et Societatis* IV, no. 7 (2016): 41–48.

Tektona, Rahmadi Indra, and Fona Kartika Listiyapuji. "Perlindungan Hukum Nasabah Bank Mandiri Atas Perubahan Saldo Pada Rekening Nasabah Akibat Kesalahan Sistem Teknologi Informasi." *Res Judicata* 3, no. 1 (2020): 66–82.

Thailand Arbitration Center. "THAC Online Dispute Resolution System." https://thac.or.th/talk-dd/.

Umboh, Arnando. "Tanggung Jawab Pelaku Usaha Dalam Pemenuhan Hak Konsumen Menurut Hukum Positif Indonesia." *Lex Privatum* VI, no. 6 (2018): 45–52.

Wijaya, Made Hendra. "Weakness of Judges Thinking in Civil Law Systems." *Sociological Jurisprudence Journal* 4, no. 1 (2021): 39–44.

Wulandari, Bernadetta Tjandra. "Aspek Perlindungan Hukum Pengguna Fasilitas Financial Technology di Indonesia." *Jurnal Paradigma Hukum Pembangunan* 2, no. 1 (2017): 93–107.

Yadav, Yesha. "The Failure of Liability in Modern Markets." *Virginia Law Review* 102, no. 4 (2016): 1031–100.

Yadav, Yesha. "How Algorithmic Trading Undermines Efficiency in Capital Markets." *Vanderbilt Law Review* 6, no. 6 (2015): 1607–71.

Zhou, Qi. "An Economic Perspective on the Doctrine of Unilateral Mistake in English Contract Law: A Remedy-Based Approach." *Northern Ireland Legal Quarterly* 59, no. 3 (2008): 1–18.

Part III

Over-indebtedness

9 The 2021 reform of the Brazilian Consumer Code in consumer credit and over-indebtedness

Effectiveness and unanswered questions[1]

Claudia Lima Marques

1. Introduction

On 2 July 2021, the president of Brazil adopted the long-awaited Reform of the 1990 Brazilian Consumer Code (Braz.CC), through Law 14.181/2021,[2] aiming to increase consumer protection in the credit market and to combat financial hardship, consumer social exclusion (new Art. 4, X Braz.CC) and over-indebtedness.[3] It was the sole great victory for Brazilian civil society and the consumer movement to achieve this approval of the Reform during the Bolsonaro regime.

The Reform Act 14.181/2021 has its origins in the 2012 Senate Bill 283, made by a Commission of Jurists under the leadership of Antonio Herman Benjamin.[4] And it was approved at the Senate in 2015 (PL 3515) and, after the pandemic, in July 2021 in the Deputy House. Its objective was to update the 1990 Brazilian Consumer Code, to introduce in Brazil the principle of responsible lending[5] (or responsible credit in Portuguese: '*crédito responsável*') and the treatment of consumer over-indebtedness ('*tratamento do superendividamento*') adapted from the French system.[6]

During debates at the Brazilian parliament and especially with the revisions and vetoes of the Bolsonaro regime, the final version was heavily changed; for example, the wage credit cooling-off period of seven days and the percentage limitation of payday loans to preserve the existential minimum were vetoed.[7] It was a two-step reform, with a second Bill to adapt the Brazilian Consumer Code to the digital world, including in the digital credit market (Bill 3514/2015), but this second step is still pending approval.[8] So this chapter aims, at the first part, to introduce the main features of the new discipline of consumer credit in Brazil, what we will call 'responsible credit, *à brasileira*'. The second part of the chapter aims to introduce the new treatment system of consumer over-indebtedness, analysing the new 'global extrajudicial conciliation audience' and the five-year payment plan without debt discharge. The focus of our analysis will be the new role of the judges in this conciliation part (Art. 104-A of the Braz.CC) but also at the final judicial part (Art. 104-B of the Braz.CC) of the treatment. Their role will be analysed in light of two different empirical research studies by the UFRGS Observatory of Credit and Over-indebtedness.[9] The central question here is if this adaptation of the

DOI: 10.4324/9781003510406-13

French system will work in an emergent country like Brazil that has no usuary laws or ceiling of interest rates, but it has strong financial lobbies and easy capture of the financial and controlling agencies.

2. Reform of the Braz.CC to prevent and regulate consumer credit and over-indebtedness: adapting the French model through Act 14.181/2021

The 2021 Reform is a significant advancement in combating the widespread irresponsible lending practices in Brazil.[10] Article 4 of the Reformed Brazilian Consumer Code, new number 'X', aims at the "prevention and treatment of over-indebtedness as a means of avoiding the social exclusion of the consumer". Indeed, as we saw during the COVID-19 pandemic, financial distress can be a factor of social exclusion, so the Brazilian Parliament decided to regulate responsible lending.[11]

At the 2015 Revision of the UN Guidelines on Consumer Protection (UNGCP),[12] new rules on financial services (J, Guidelines 66 to 68) were introduced, aiming to enhance "fair treatment and proper disclosure, ensuring that financial institutions are also responsible and accountable for the actions of their authorized agents" (GL 66, 'e'). These are also the objectives of the amended Brazilian Consumer Code (CDC) by Act 14.181/2021. Now we will highlight the main changes of this new responsible lending 'à brasileira' (without mandatory consumer counselling and without debt discharge after five years of payment), with focus on disclosure and the role of intermediaries.

2.1 Amendments to the Braz.CC (Act 14.181/2021) and the 'responsible credit à brasileira': disclosure and focus at the intermediaries

Since the COVID-19 pandemic, over-indebtedness and financial hardship in Brazil have grown exponentially: in February 2023, 79,5% of all active consumers in Brazil had one or more debts in default.[13] In May 2023, the default rate reached 70,71 million Brazilians (43,43% of the population over 18 years).[14] In April 2024, 78,5% of all active consumers in Brazil had one or more debts in default, and 49,7% have a default longer than 90 days.[15] In June 2024, the Serasa Experian Credit base shows that 72,50 million Brazilians were in default (43,99% of the population over 18 years).[16]

Rules to prevent over-indebtedness and financial consumer protection are more than a necessity in Brazil.[17] The 'easy access to consumer credit' as mainstream ideology imported by the US has had a strong impact on the Brazilian consumer market, especially because of poor financial education, high interest rates and the inapplicability of usury law to banks and credit card companies.[18] The purpose of the update was to prevent or treat consumer ruin/over-indebtedness, to reduce the systemic risk that this mass "bankruptcy" of consumers would mean and to allow the re-inclusion of over-indebted individuals in society and the market,[19] through good faith cooperation between creditors and consumers.

The new chapter of the Braz.CC (from Art. 54-A to 54-G), titled "Prevention and Treatment of Over-indebtedness", provides for preventing over-indebtedness of natural persons, responsible credit and financial education of consumers. Art. 54-A para. 1 Braz.CC defines consumer over-indebtedness as: "the manifest impossibility of the consumer, as a natural person, in good faith, to pay all his/her consumer debts, due and falling due, without compromising his/her existential minimum ('mínimo existencial'), under the terms of the regulations".[20]

The debt referred to in this provision "encompasses any financial commitments assumed arising from consumer relations, including credit operations, instalment purchases and services provided on an ongoing basis" (Art. 54-A para. 2). However, Art. 54-B para. 3 excludes "consumers whose debts have been contracted by fraud or have arisen from contracts entered into maliciously with the purpose of not making payment or have arisen from the acquisition or contracting of high-value luxury products and services".

New information duties (Art. 54-B), complementary to Art. 52 Braz.CC, are in the new chapter imposed at the same level to intermediaries and credit providers for consumer credits in general and for instalment sales. The focus on the intermediary role is a very positive novelty of this Reform, although Art. 34 Braz.CC has, since 1990, had a rule about intermediaries, the Reform specifies the same information and cooperation duties to the main credit providers and all its intermediaries (Art. 54-B and Art. 54-D).

So, Art. 54-B imposes "that the supplier or intermediary shall inform the consumer, previously and adequately, at the time of the offer, about . . . the term of validity of the offer, which must be of at least 2 (two) days". This 'prior/cooling' offer period of two days is inspired by the European Union, but the seven days cooling-off period for wage credit (Art. 54-E) was vetoed by President Bolsonaro.[21] The Brazilian parliament has not accepted a general consumer credit cooling-off period but only the possibility to withdraw the wage or payroll credit, and anyway, the Bolsonaro regime has vetoed this 'small' cooling-off-period, which could be seen as a sign that the Reform should not grant "too much rights" to consumers.

One of the great novelties is the notion of consumer harassment, also inspired by the European Union Unfair Practices Directive 2005/29/EC (amended by Directive 2019/2161) but generalised to all aggressive practices as consumer harassment.[22] Art. 54-C para. 4 states that by the "offer of credit to the consumer, it is forbidden, expressly or implicitly" to "[harass] or pressure the consumer to contract the supply of a product, service or credit, especially if the consumer is elderly, illiterate, ill or in a state of aggravated vulnerability or if the case of offers involving prizes". Although the Braz.CC recognise all consumers as vulnerable (Art. 4 para. 1), the recognition of the special aggravated vulnerability of these groups (elderly, illiterate, sick people or with dis-capacity) is an important step.[23]

The most important article concerning responsible lending is Art. 54-D, which brings a judicial sanction at the "Single Paragraph" as follows:

Art. 54-D. When offering credit, prior to contracting, the supplier or intermediary shall, among other conducts:

I – adequately inform and clarify the consumer, taking into consideration his/her age, about the nature and type of credit offered, all costs incurred, pursuant to the provisions of Articles 52 and 54-B of this Code, and the generic and specific consequences of default.

II – assess, in a responsible manner, the consumer's credit conditions, through the analysis of information available in credit protection databases, pursuant to the provisions of this Code and the legislation on data protection.

III – inform the identity of the funding agent and deliver to the consumer, guarantor and other co-obligors a copy of the credit agreement.

Single Paragraph. Failure to comply with any of the duties provided for in the main Section of this Article and in Articles 52 and 54-C of this Code may result in a court order to reduce interest, charges or any additional charges to the main obligation and to extend the payment term provided for in the original contract, depending on the seriousness of the supplier's conduct and the consumer's financial means, without prejudice to other sanctions and compensation for losses and damages, both pecuniary and moral, to the consumer.[24]

The prevention of over-indebtedness will not work if the Code does not provide a sanction to the violation of good faith and the duties to information and clarification (Art. 54-D para. 1), to deliver the copy of the contract (Art. 54-D para. 2), to conduct itself and the intermediaries in a responsible manner (Art. 54-D para. 3), without any harassment (Art. 54-C para. 4) and not concealing or making "it difficult to understand the burden and risks of contracting credit or sales on credit terms" (Art. 54-C para. 3). It must be also mentioned that the Reform assures the right to identify errors and frauds in Art. 54-G and allows the chargeback. So "the supplier of products or services involving credit is prohibited" to "prevent or hinder, in the event of fraudulent use of the credit card or similar, the consumer from requesting and obtaining, where applicable, the cancellation or immediate blocking of the payment, or the refund of amounts unduly received".

It is important to repeat that Brazil has no usuary law applicable to banks as well as to credit cards and has no ceiling on interest rates. Our emergent country deals with high interest rates,[25] with a strong financial lobby at the parliament and very easy capture of administrative agencies. Also, our interest rate spread is number one in the world, so over-indebtedness is a current phenomenon. The Reform introduces a global conciliation audience to try to renegotiate all consumers debts in a new payment plan.

2.2 *Adaptation of the French system of consumer over-indebtedness: global conciliation without discharge and the five-year payment plan*

Act 14.181/2021 updated the Braz.CC by introducing two new proceedings. The first proceeding could be held extrajudicially and was called "debt renegotiation proceeding" (Art. 104-A). This can be a pre-lawsuit proceeding if it is held at a "Conciliation Center and Alternative Dispute Resolution of the Judiciary" (so-called "CEJUSC"). However, it also could be a "parajudicial" proceeding under the terms of Art. 104-C if it is carried out by administrative consumer agencies, the so-called "PROCONS", or directly at the public defender's office, at the University Consumer Counters (*'Balcão do Consumidor'*) and other public bodies of the National Consumer Defence System. The second proceeding is to be held in Courts and with a special procedure called "over-indebtedness proceedings for the review and integration of contracts and renegotiation of remaining debts" under Article 104-B of the CDC.

The Reform was inspired by the French model but with many adaptations. There is no 'Commission' but the establishment of a global conciliation hearing between the consumer and all their creditors to achieve a payment plan of a maximum of five years. The goal is to preserve the consumer existential minimum (or *rester à vivre*), but the plan does not allow any debt relief (also not for NINA – non-income, non-assets – debtors) and the procedure does not see any special order of payments or specific rules about the real estate property of the consumer.[26] Also no counselling is foreseen, but the consumer can participate in the audience conciliation only if in good faith.[27]

The focus of the Reform is on the extrajudicial conciliation, but if no agreement is achieved in one or more debts, the consumer can go to the judicial phase (but the payments will be made only after the first payment plan in another five years). In both phases (extrajudicial and judicial) the "treatment of consumer over-indebtedness" is made by a global conciliation audience to elaborate a payment plan for a maximum of five years, without mandatory consumer counselling and without debt discharge, only discounts and moratorium. However, the judicial phase (Art. 104-B) begins with a previous revision of the contracts that did not achieve conciliation, to see if it was concluded irresponsibly, with violation of the good faith or to Articles 54-B to 54-G or contains abusive clauses.[28] Only after this revision, the judge will impose a compulsory payment (of the non-abusive contracts and debts), also a plan of a maximum of five years payments. Article 104-B provides for a six-month moratorium and the payment should begin after the conciliation payment plan has been finalized. An 'existential minimum (*restre à vivre*)' should be kept during all the payment plans (Art. 6 para. 12),[29] but a Bolsonaro Presidential Decree nr. 11.150/2022, now challenged by the Supreme Court, tries to impose one *restre à vivre* of 110 euros monthly for all consumers. Decree 11.150/2022 is currently not used by the Brazilian judges who have diffused constitutional control.[30]

Long before the 2021 Reform, since 2007, under the leadership of Judges Clarissa Costa de Lima and Karen Bertoncello, Brazil has already had pilot projects[31] to conciliate over-indebted consumers and all their creditors at the Conciliation Centers (CEJUSCs) in the country.[32] The Observatory of Credit and Over-indebtedness at the Federal University (UFRGS) conducted a five-year empirical research study about these pilot projects.[33] In order to analyse the effectiveness of the Reform, we would like to compare the empirical research conducted by Observatory of Credit and Over-indebtedness at the Federal University (UFRGS) in Porto Alegre (CEJUSC *Foro Central* and CEJUSC *Foro Partenon*) before and after the 2021 reform.

3. Effectiveness of the 2021 consumer code reform in the light of empirical research and unanswered questions

To point out the challenges and the effectiveness of the new system, this part will analyse the new conciliatory role of judges at the Judicial Centers for Solution and Conciliation of Conflicts (CEJUSC)[34] based on empirical research, two of which were already published,[35] and the initial 134 cases of consumer over-indebtedness conciliation audiences in the first year of the Act 14.181/2021 in Porto Alegre. These findings were presented in Hamburg during the 18th International Association of Consumer Law Conference.[36] Following, we will compare the data of 6.125 consumer conciliation cases before the Act (from five years, 2007–2012) at the sole 'Over-indebtedness Pilot-Project' at the AJURIS Center for Conciliation in Porto Alegre, with the data after the Act (from three years, 2021–2024) in two Centers of Conciliation-CEJUSC in Porto Alegre (*Foro Central* and *Foro Partenon*). It must be noted that since the Act 14.181/2021 entered into force, consumers can reach conciliation in all six CEJUSCs and at the very popular Administrative Agencies PROCONs and by the public defender, without any cost.

So, the sample of this 2021–2024 research, made with the help of LLM candidates Lissandra Lopes and Alyane Dornelles and PhD candidate Maria Luiza Targa and supervised by Judge Karen Bertoncello, is significantly smaller: 308 cases and only 201 global audiences from July 2021 to July 2024 will be analysed, focusing at the special vulnerabilities of elderly over-indebted consumers. Act 14.181/2021 came into force in 2 July 2021, so three years of conciliation audiences in two centralised Centers of Conciliation-CEJUSC in Porto Alegre (*Foro Central* and *Foro Partenon*) have been analysed.

3.1 Comparing conciliation cases before and after the Act 14.181/2021 and its reform of the Braz.CC

The core of the inquiry surrounding the effectiveness of the 2021 Consumer Code Reform will be answered with resources from two empirical research studies conducted by our Observatory. This chapter analyses the lessons of this empirical research about the profile and characteristics of Brazilian consumer over-indebtedness. Also, the results of these two empirical research studies made before and after the Reform will be compared in order to verify whether the current legislation is enough to regulate consumer over-indebtedness, especially the over-indebtedness of women and elderly consumers.

First, 2012 (2007–2012) research made before the Act with 2024 (2021–2024) research made after the reform will be compared. The analysis of 6.165 cases of consumer over-indebtedness global conciliation in Porto Alegre, Rio Grande do Sul, at the Conciliation Center of the Judge School-AJURIS, collected between 2007 and 2012 before the Consumer Code Reform, with the first 308 cases at two Conciliation Centers in Porto Alegre, collected from July 2021 and June 2022 after entry in force of the 2021 Consumer Code Reform, will be the main material and subject. The aim is to determine whether the adaptation of the French model of the treatment of consumer bankruptcy through global conciliation has been effective enough.

The new empirical research of three years analysing all cases of global audiences at the same CEJUSC Porto Alegre (*Foro Central* and *Foro Partenon*), from July 2021, when the Act 14.181/2021 came into force, until July 2024 indicates that consumers are using more and more the administrative conciliation at the PROCON and less the judiciary conciliation as before. In 2021, after the Act came into force, there were 87 cases; in 2022, there were 137 cases in 2023, 63 cases were closed; and in 2024, until July, there were only 21 cases. It should be noted that the Conciliation Center was closed for one month due to a major flood in May 2024 in Porto Alegre. In total, the research involves 308 cases.

The comparison will highlight four aspects: gender, civil status, causes of debts and success rate of the conciliation in the extrajudicial phase. In the longitudinal research from 2007 to 2012, before the Act, 6.165 over-indebtedness cases of voluntary global conciliation at the CEJUSC Porto Alegre were analysed, and the audience to conciliate were required primarily female consumers (61,8%).[37] In the 2024 empirical research, after the Reform, there were only 308 global conciliation audiences to analyse, but the female consumers constituted, again, the majority: male 45,1%; female 54,9%.

According to the Brazilian Central Bank, most of the indebted consumers are men,[38] but the risk of becoming over-indebted is greater for women.[39] Indeed, with the Reform, proceedings involving male consumers increased; nevertheless, the majority remained involving female consumers. This can be understood as a failure of the financial education of women or as a general incapacity of the bank system to renegotiate with women, so they need the help of the official system to achieve renegotiation or a global payment plan. The number of females with over-indebtedness remains the majority but not significantly so in the 2024 research. This can be seen as a positive result of the Act 14.181/2021: the new cooperation duty to renegotiate imposed by the Consumer Code is now used by males and females equally. In any case, following the 2019 data from the Government of Rio Grande do Sul, where Porto Alegre is, the occupied female in the work force represents only 44,8% of the population,[40] and they are the majority of the over-indebtedness consumers (54,9%), so the cause of this unbalance must be further analysed by academia. The data from 2021–2024 shows that the majority of these consumers have one to two dependents at home (52,3%), and 10,7% have two to four dependents at home, but 37% of the over-indebted consumers live all by themselves. The 2012 research has no information about the dependents, but a comparison based on age is possible.

Of the 308 cases, the majority were 40 to 59 years of age (46,9%), but elderly people, from 60 to 85 years of age, represent 31,8%. The age group from 20 to 39 was only 21,3% of the over-indebted consumers. In the 2012 research, most of the consumers were 40 to 59 years of age (41,7%), followed by elderly people from 60 to 79 years of age (17,5%), with those more than 80 at 1,0%. Hence, 18,5% of over-indebted consumers were older than 60 years.[41] Comparing the two research studies, it is very significant that the number of the elderly now is 31,8% of the sample, when only 14,1% of the population of Rio Grande do Sul[42] is older than 60 years! After the COVID-19 pandemic, the number of elderly who were older than 80 years dropped significantly.

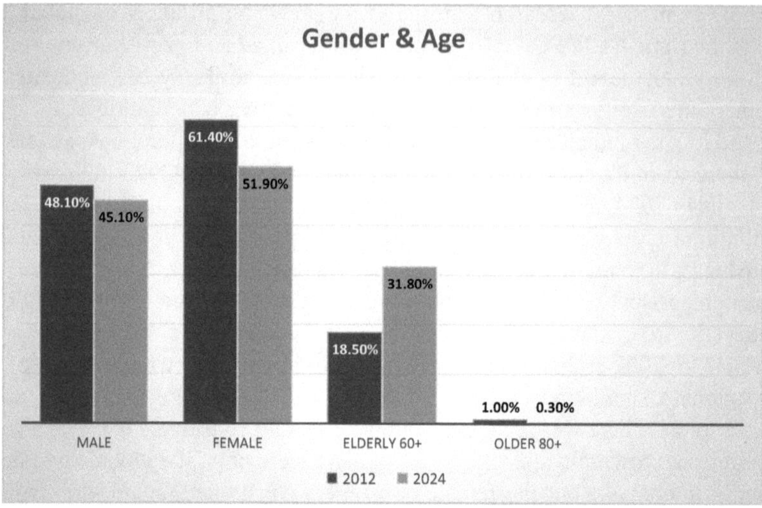

Figure 9.1 Gender and age.

Source: Graphic illustration by the author.

About civil status:[43] those who were married were 33,70% in the 2012 research and 38,80% in 2024; single consumers were 40,90% in the 2012 research and 37,10% in 2024 research. Those who were divorced were 12,30% in 2012 and 12,90% in 2024, and widowed were 7,80% in 2012 and 7,10% in 2024, almost the same data. Those who were separated rose from 0,60% to 3,10%. The majority of the over-indebted consumers were not married, widowed, divorced or separated persons (60,2%).

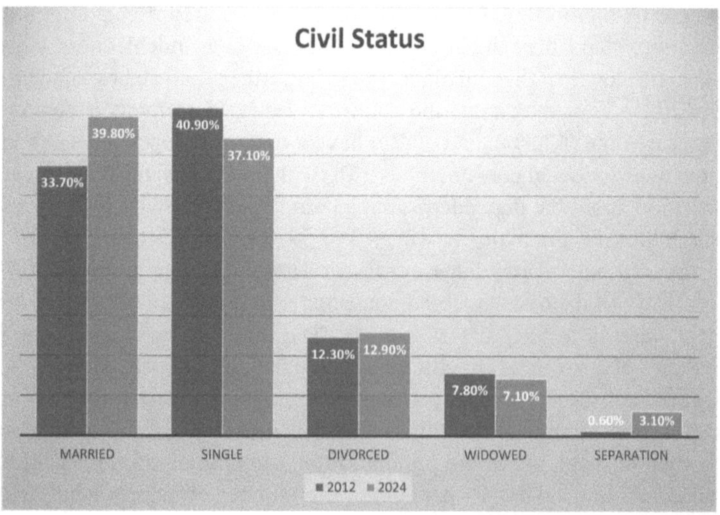

Figure 9.2 Civil status.

Source: Graphic illustration by the author.

About the activities and professions, the 2024 research provides the following results: retired and pensioners were 35,6%, public servants 20,3% and unemployed (receiving help from the Brazilian government) were 7,7%, but 17,5% were persons that did not have formal employment and work at platforms like Uber, Cabify and in seasonal small jobs. Only 18,1% are officially employed by the private or liberal professions, and 0,3% identified themself as entrepreneurs or students. The 2012 data provides the following results: retired and pensioners were 23,2% (now 35,6%!), public servants 6,9% (now 20,3%, which shows the rise of payday loans!) and unemployed (receiving help from the Brazilian government) were 9,3%.[44] Officially employed at the private sector (33,8%) and liberal professionals (13,4%) were almost half of the sample: 47,2%. Students (1,5%) and entrepreneurs (0,8%) were not a significant group of the sample.

The overall results of the research show the flexibility of employment after the pandemic crisis and the rise of the elderly over-indebtedness in Brazil.

The causes of the over-indebtedness in the 2024 research, which includes 2021 and 2022 of the COVID-19 pandemic, were the following: 39,8% reduction of income; 26,4% personal illness or in the family; 14,7% unemployment; 10,4% divorce, dissolution of the union, separation; 6,5% death in the family; 2,2% has spent more than earned. Together illness and death achieve the impressive figure of 32,9% of the causes of over-indebtedness in Porto Alegre.

Comparing the causes of over-indebtedness, the reduction of income was the first cause in 2012 (26,5%), but after the COVID pandemic, it is 39,8% of the causes. Also, the pandemic had an effect on the rise of the number of divorces and separations from 4,8% to double, 10,40%. Also, the rise of illness or death as a cause of over-indebtedness must be noted: from 20,50% to 32,90%. Unemployment and "expend more than earn" have decreased considerably: unemployment from 26,50% to 14,70% and consumers that inform that the cause is that they expend more money than they earn, from 24% to 2,2%.[45]

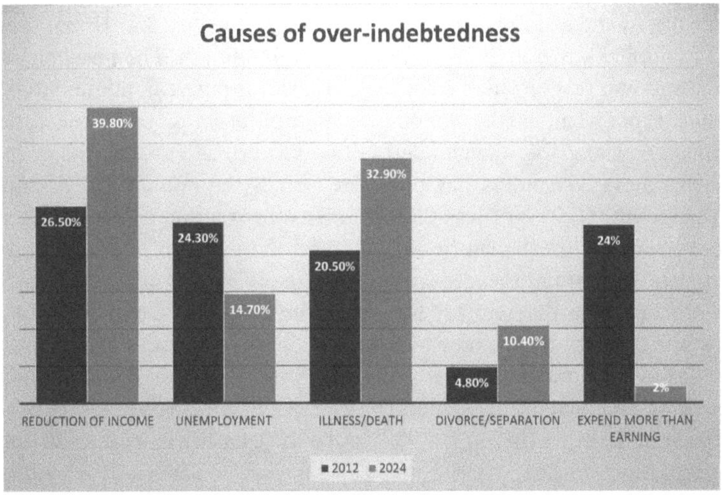

Figure 9.3 Causes of over-indebtedness.

Source: Graphic illustration by the author.

Indeed, the COVID-19 pandemic has been a stress test for all countries, economies and political systems like never before, but Brazil had devastating outcomes with more than 699.000 deaths,[46] due to the insufficient pandemic response of the Bolsonaro government. This unprecedented economic and social crisis increased unemployment by 14,4% and reduced household incomes in 38% of the population,[47] which correlates with the data from our last research from 2021 to 2024.

However, the pandemic impact has not helped with the openness of the creditors to conciliate. All the parties were present in only 70% of the audiences, and in these, the success rate of the global audience was only 30,3%. It is to be noted that in 10,7% of the cases, the consumer has dropped the conciliation tentative plan and in 19,3% of the cases, one of the creditors was not present, so the conciliation plan could not be reached in its totality. So, at 69,7% of the cases, the judicial part of the treatment needed to be used. It is to be noted that Brazil does not have a high rate of conciliation in civil matters, about 12%, but in family matters, the amount can reach 70%.[48] In 2012 research, before the Act, the success rate of conciliation and payment plans were from 64,3% in general and 65,7% with women![49] In this five-year long research, in 19,1% of the cases, the consumer has dropped the conciliation tentative audience, and in 22,4%, one of the creditors was not present. After the Act, a higher number of audiences can be noted, but there was a significant drop in the numbers of successful conciliations (from 64,3% to 30,3%!), less than half. It is, nevertheless, significantly higher than the general conciliation rates.

In 2024, 36,1% of the over-indebted consumers were paying their debts, and 63,9% were in default and in the negative credit-scoring database. In the 2012 research, 72,9% were in default and in the negative credit-scoring database and only 27,1% were paying the debts.[50] This difference may mean that consumers are now asking to renegotiate and organise a payment plan before going to bankruptcy, but it may also show the rise of the payday loans, which allow the banks to collect their payment before the consumer is able to do anything, so the debt is paid under any circumstances.

About the financial information, it is necessary to note that Brazil raised the national minimum wage in 2024 to 263,3 euros per month. The research uses this national minimum wage, which equals to 3.423 euros per year, taking into account 13 payments per year as the national legislation assures, or 3.160 euros with 12 payments.[51] The 2024 research shows that in Porto Alegre the majority of the over-indebtedness consumers has only three times the amount of the minimum wages per month (60,2%) or less than 800 euros per month. In the 2012 research, this group were the great majority 81,7%, and the group of consumers that had between 3 and 5 minimum wages were 12,1% (in 2024, this group rose to 20,1%). This difference means that with the Reform of the Consumer Code, the poor middle class has begun to ask for the new over-indebtedness procedure. The other data are very similar in both studies. In 2024, consumers with less than one minimum wage represent only 11,1% of the consumers (in 2021, 13,5%), also only 4,71% have more than 10 minimum wages (in 2012, 4,9%), and only 0,4% has more than 20 minimum wages per month (in 2012, 0,9%). We can say that consumer over-indebtedness in Brazil remains a subprime and poor middle-class phenomenon. The challenge of addressing the situation of the NINA (non-income, non-assets) debtors was not made by the Reform and that perhaps can explain the great number of consumers (more than 10%) that are not present at the conciliation hearing.

So, it is interesting to note that in the 2024 research, 45,1% of the consumers owned their home and 10% of the consumers paid alimonies. In the 2012 research, we did not have these data. Modern bankruptcy systems, as in France, agree that the debtor must not be stripped of all his assets.[52] Brazilian law exempts one piece of real estate as the 'family home' ('Bem de família', Act 8.009, 1990), but this exemption, perhaps, is causing difficulties to achieve consensus at the extrajudicial hearings.

In 2024, the number of creditors was one to three in 62,1% of the cases (in 2012, in 68,3% of the cases, the consumer had only one creditor, and in 88,4% of the cases, there were one to three creditors).[53] This limited number of creditors could be a positive factor for the re-negotiation. Instead, the success rate has diminished. The success rate of the global audience was, in 2024, only 30,3% compared to the 64,3% success rate in 2012. This drastic drop in the conciliation rate shows that Law 14.181/2021 has not yet reached great success, and the consumers must ask to the judiciary for a mandatory payment plan. The judicial treatment allows urgent measures to be decided by the judge, such as the full stop of interest for irresponsibly given credits (Art. 54-D) or the end of wage credit or payroll discounts to assure the monthly existence minimum (*restre à vivre*) at the beginning of the procedure (Art. 6, paras. X and XI), so perhaps because of these possibilities, it has been more attractive to be an over-indebted consumer in Brazil.

3.2 Judicial treatment of over-indebtedness

Only in December 2021 did the Brazilian National Justice Council (CNJ) make its Resolution n. 125 to recommend the adaptation of all Centers of Dispute Resolution (CEJUSC) to the new Law.[54] In 2022, the new judicial writ on the treatment of consumer over-indebtedness began to be registered at the DATAJUD.[55] So we have only the data from 2023 and 2024 about new cases of judicial over-indebtedness lawsuits where consumers ask the judges to proceed with the revision of debts and to organise a mandatory payment plan. The DATAJUD from CNJ indicates that in 2023, consumers initiated 18.592 cases of judicial treatment of over-indebtedness and in 2024, through May, 5.766 cases.[56]

Art. 104-B of the Braz.CC provides for a special procedure, as follows:

> *"If there is no successful conciliation in relation to any creditors, the judge, at the request of the consumer, will initiate proceedings for over-indebtedness for the review and integration of contracts and renegotiation of remaining debts through a compulsory judicial plan and will proceed to summons all creditors whose claims have not integrated the agreement that may have been concluded."*

Paragraph 1 allows that the "documents and information provided in a hearing shall be considered in the over-indebtedness proceedings, if applicable". Paragraph 2 of Art. 104-B of the Braz.CC imposes fifteen (15) days, for "the creditors who have been served shall attach documents and the reasons for their refusal to agree to the voluntary plan or to renegotiate". Following para. 3, the judge has the possibility to

> *"appoint an administrator, provided that this does not burden the parties, who, within thirty (30) days, after fulfilling the steps that may be necessary, shall submit a payment plan that contemplates measures for temporizing or mitigating the charges."*

The judges use the Judicial Fund for Experts to pay the administrators, but there is now an academic app (Concilia Super App), created by UFRGS (Prof. Claudia Lima Marques) and UPF (Prof. Liton Pilau), that can help the mediator or judge compute the discounts and offers made during the global audience. The Brazilian National Justice Council-CNJ is now testing the Concilia Super App to be used by all judges and CEJUSCs.

Art. 104-B para. 4 is very controversial because it imposes on one side that the "compulsory judicial plan shall assure the creditors of at least the amount of the principal due, monetarily restated by official price indexes" but also that this judicial payment plan provides the "settlement of the debt, after the consensual payment plan under Article 104-A of this Code has been settled, in a maximum of five (5) years" and gives a moratorium so "the first installment of which shall be due in a maximum term of one hundred and eighty (180) days, as from its judicial ratification". So, on one hand, paragraph 4 ties the hand of the judge but, on the other hand, gives precedent for the conciliation payment plan, which can assure within 10 years a resolution of the consumer's debts.

The judicial treatment of the consumer over-indebtedness introduced in Brazil has not yet achieved great effectiveness. And the five-year compulsory payment plan without debt relief at the end can be a difficult task for judges.

4. Final remarks

The Brazilian Consumer Code, after the 2021 reform, tries to achieve effective consumer protection on consumer credit and over-indebtedness. It is not clear that this objective to introduce credit fairness and to incentivise a new conciliatory role of judges at the Centers for Conciliation and Alternative Dispute Resolution was successful. This chapter has shown the main features of the new discipline of consumer credit in Brazil and critically analysed these new rules on responsible lending 'à brasileira' and the Brazilian over-indebtedness treatment (without mandatory consumer counselling and without debt discharge after five years of payment). We must recognise that for an efficient treatment system in an emergent economy like Brazil, the debt discharge should be included.

The chapter compared two empirical research studies to point out the challenges and the effectiveness of the new system. Research before the law, analysing 6.125 consumer conciliation cases in a pilot project in Porto Alegre; one with the initial 308 cases of consumer over-indebtedness conciliation audiences at the first three years of Law 14.181/2021 and its conciliation audiences in the two Centers of Conciliation-CEJUSC in Porto Alegre (*Foro Central* and *Foro Partenon*).

The treatment of the consumer over-indebtedness introduced in Brazil has not yet achieved great effectiveness in the conciliation part. The new global conciliation audience and the five-year payment plans without debt relief are a very *sui generis* adaptation of the French system. Also, the judicial part is not an easy task for judges and needs, perhaps, new instruments and chances to be more effective.

As the European Union has done with the New Consumer Credit Directive,[57] there is also a task to be fulfilled: the existing rules for consumer lending need to be tailored for the online lending environment. So, for digital credit, there is a need to complete the Reform. These unanswered questions are in the Reform Bill 3515/2015, not yet approved by the Brazilian parliament.

Notes

1 Paper presented at the 18th IACL Congress in Hamburg, 19–21 July 2023, organised by the Institute for Responsible Finance (*iff*), updated with new empirical data in July 2024. The author thanks Maria Luiza Targa and Lorenzo Nicoletti for the English corrections and Dr. Karen Bertoncello, Lissandra Lopes, Alyanne Dornelles and the CNPq-UFRGS Consumer Law Research Group for the decisive help at the empirical research. It is a pleasure to participate in this book, so well organised by our former IACL president Professor Dr. Michelle Kelly-Louw and Dr. Duygu Damar-Blanken on financial inclusion law and over-indebtedness.

2 For the English translation, see Marques and Nicoletti, "Translation Offered by the IACL."

3 Marques, de Lima and Vial, "Nota à atualização," 517.

4 Senado Federal, "Relatório Final," 73 ff.; Marques and Benjamin, "Consumer Over-Indebtedness in Brazil," 55 ff.

5 Called the principle of responsible lending by Ramsay, "Regulation of Consumer Credit," 55; Whitford, *Consumer Credit, Debt and Bankruptcy*, 371.

6 Se Marques, "Superendividamento e as mudanças de paradigma," 32 ff. On the French System see Paisant, "A reforma do procedimento de tratamento," 239; Paisant, "El tratamiento del sobreendeudamiento," 9.

7 Marques, "Do crédito responsável," 231–35.

8 on PL 3514,2015 to update the CDC to the digital world Marques, "Perspectives," 73.

9 Marques, de Lima, and Bertoncello, "Dados da pesquisa empírica," 411 ff.; Marques, "Primeiro 134 casos," 17–40.

10 Benjamin, "Breve Nota sobre a atualização," 22.

11 Agencia Brasil, "Over 70 Million Brazilians in Default," May 10, 2024, accessed April30,2024,https://agenciabrasil.ebc.com.br/economia/noticia/2023-05/over-70-million-brazilians-in-default.

12 The UNGCP were first adopted by the General Assembly in Resolution 39/248 of 16 April 1985, expanded in 1999 and now revised by the General Assembly in Resolution

70186 of 22 December 2015. Available in: General Assembly Resolution 70/186 on Consumer protection, Adopted on December 22, 2015 (unctad.org) or ditccplp-misc2016d1_en.pdf (unctad.org) or United Nations guidelines for consumer protection | UNCTAD.

13 Thais Carrança, "Brasil bate recorde de endividados," *BBC News Brasil*, May 10, 2023, accessed April 30, 2024, https://www.bbc.com/portuguese/brasil-57019777.

14 Agência Brasil, "Brasil tem 70 milhões de inadimplentes,' May 10, 2023, accessed April 30, 2024, https://www.brasil247.com/economia/brasil-tem-70-milhoes-de-inadimplentes-43-da-populacao.

15 See CNC, "Pesquisa Nacional de Endividamento e Inadimplência do Consumidor (Peic)," Abril 2024, accessed May 13, 2024, www.Relatorio_Peic_abr24.pdf (portal-bucket.azureedge.net).

16 See SERASA EXEPERIAN, "Mapa de inadimplência e renegociação de dívidas no Brasil da Serasa," accessed August 25, 2024. In the Province of Rio Grande do Sul, were Porto Alegre is the capital, the default rate it was 35,08%, Source: Serasa Experian Map, accessed August 1, 2024, www.assets/b212bb18f00a40869a6cd42f77cbeefc/320df5376d774dca86dc117e12f47f09 (builder.io).

17 Marques and Benjamin, "Consumer Over-Indebtedness in Brazil," 55.

18 See also Micklitz, "Access," 62–63.

19 So the Statement "Enunciado 1 da II Jornada do CDEA. A Lei 14.181/21 é de ordem pública e de interesse social, e reconhece que o fenômeno do superendividamento do consumidor pessoa natural é estrutural da sociedade de crédito e consumo, constituindo grave risco sistêmico e de exclusão social, que deve ser prevenido e tratado através do princípio da boa-fé e práticas de crédito responsável." Accessible in Marques and Rangel, "Enunciados das I e II Jornadas de Pesquisa CDEA," 400 ff. See also Marques, "Consumo como igualdade," 405.

20 Marques and Nicoletti, "Translation Offered by the IACL," 410.

21 Marques and Pfeiffer, "Art. 54-E," 579–80: "Law No. 14 181 introduced to Brazilian legislation the institutionalization of combating harassment of consumers, identifying harassing and overly aggressive marketing strategies focused on certain groups, such as the elderly and illiterate . . . The option of the Brazilian legislator was to consider consumer harassment ('assédio de consumo') to categorise all aggressive commercial practices that limit freedom of consumer choice."

22 See Art. 8 and 9 of the Directive 2005/29/EC of the European Parliament and of the Council of May 11, 2005 concerning unfair business-to-consumer commercial practices in the internal market as amended by the Directive (EU) 2019/2161. Art. 8 defines aggressive commercial practices in three different categories (use of harassment, coercion and undue influence Art. 9), but the Brazilian Reform use the definition 'consumer harrassment' as a general term for all three forms of aggressive practices (Art. 8). See Marques and Pfeiffer, "Dissemination of Consumer Law and Policy in Brazil," 34.

23 So Marques and Pfeiffer, "Dissemination of Consumer Law and Policy in Brazil," 33.

24 Marques and Nicoletti, "Translation Offered by the IACL," 413.

25 The official interest rate is determined by the Central Bank of Brazil (Selic rate) at 10.50% in July 2024. See Selic interest rate (bcb.gov.br). However, at the official banks, Banco Caixa Economica Federal, the monthly rate on credit cards is 10,35%, which equals to an annual interest of 226,13%, Banco do Brazil, monthly 12,44% and annual 308,36%. At the official Bank of the State Rio Grande do Sul, BANRISUL, the monthly rate is 16,51%, and annual 525,85%. See Central Bank table of rates: Taxa de juros (taxas anuais) (bcb.gov.br).

26 See about the French Model and its characteristics, Bazin-Beust and Guérin-Seysen, *Droit de la consummation*, 265–70.

27 So Marques and Pfeiffer, "Dissemination of Consumer Law and Policy in Brazil," 34.

28 Marques, "Dever de cooperação no tratamento do superendividamento dos consumidores," 149.
29 Bertoncello, *Superendividamento do Consumidor*, 10 ff.; de Carvalho and Silva, "Superendividamento e mínimo existencial," 363.
30 Bertoncello, "O processo judicial de repactuação das dívidas," 17 ff.
31 de Lima and Bertoncello, "Conciliação aplicada ao superendividamento," 106.
32 Bertoncello and de Lima, "Overindebtedness in Mercosul Countries," 403.
33 Marques, de Lima, and Bertoncello, "Dados da pesquisa empírica," 411.
34 See the Directive for judges to conciliation in over-indebtedness, organised by the Brazilian National Justice Council-CNJ, cartilha-superendividamento.pdf (cnj.jus.br).
35 Marques, de Lima, and Bertoncello, "Dados da pesquisa empírica," 411ff.
36 Marques, "Primeiros 134 casos," 17–40.
37 Marques, "Dados das pesquisa empíricas," 376; Marques, "Conciliação em matéria de superendividamento dos consumidores," 264.
38 Banco Central, "Endividamento de Risco no Brasil," 15.
39 Banco Central, "Endividamento de Risco no Brasil," 13.
40 See Government of Rio Grande do Sul, https://planejamento.rs.gov.br/upload/arquivos/201903/27175806-mulheres-27-03-final.pdf.
41 Marques, "Dados das pesquisa empíricas," 376.
42 See Censo 2022, in Censo 2022: Rio Grande do Sul, Rio de Janeiro e Minas Gerais têm maior percentual de idosos | CNN Brasil.
43 Marques, "Dados das pesquisa empíricas," 377.
44 See the data of the 2012 research in Marques, "Dados das pesquisa empíricas," 378.
45 Marques, "Dados das pesquisa empíricas," 376.
46 See Brazil – COVID-19 Overview – Johns Hopkins (jhu.edu) and Brazil COVID – Coronavirus Statistics – Worldometer (worldometers.info).
47 See Coronavirus: How Brazil became the second worst affected country in the world (theconversation.com).
48 See data from 2023, Brazilian National Justice Council-CNJ, acessible 12% dos processos de 2023 foram resolvidos por meio de conciliação (conjur.com.br). Data from 2022, 11% CNJ, https://www.cnj.jus.br/estudos-apresentam-dados-sobre-eficiencia-do-uso-mediacao-e-conciliacao-na-justica-brasileira/.
49 Marques, "Dados das pesquisa empíricas," 385.
50 Marques, "Dados das pesquisa empíricas," 380.
51 See Brazil National Minimum Wage – NMW 2024 | countryeconomy.com.
52 See French Consumer Code Article L-732–111 in Bazin-Beust and Guérin-Seysen, *Droit de la consummation*, 270.
53 Marques, "Dados das pesquisa empíricas," 379.
54 See Brazilian National Justice Council-CNJ, Recomendação CNJ n. 125/2022, original-1456372022010761d854a59e2f5.pdf (cnj.jus.br).
55 See Brazilian National Justice Council-CNJ, DATAJUD – Portal CNJ.
56 See Brazilian National Justice Council-CNJ, "Justiça em Números, Brasília, 2023," accessible in English, cnj.jus.br/wp-content/uploads/2024/02/justice-in-numbers-2023.pdf.
57 Cherednychenko, "On the Bumpy Road to Responsible Lending," 241.

References

Banco Central. "Endividamento de Risco no Brasil – Atualização: impacto no Sistema Financeiro Nacional e qualificação dos indicadores." Série cidadania financeira: Estudos sobre educação, proteção e inclusão, No. 8. Brasília, 2023. https://www.bcb.gov.br/cidadaniafinanceira.

Bazin-Beust, Delphine, and Dorothée Guérin-Seysen. *Droit de la consummation.* Lextenso, 2023.

Benjamin, Antonio Herman. "Breve Nota sobre a atualização do CDC pela Lei 14.181/2021: A dimensão constitucional protetiva do microssistema do CDC." In *Superendividamento dos consumidores: Aspectos materiais e processuais*, edited by Marco Aurélio Gastaldi Buzzi, Claudia Lima Marques, Trícia Navarro Xavier Cabral, and Juliana Loss de Andrade. Foco, 2023.

Benjamin, Antonio Herman, Claudia Lima Marques, Clarissa Costa de Lima, and Sophia Vial, eds., *Comentários à Lei 14.181/2021: A atualização do CDC em matéria de superendividamento.* RT, 2021.

Bertoncello, Káren Rick Danilevicz. "O processo judicial de repactuação das dívidas: Modelo brasileiro de mínimo existencial instrumental." *Revista de Direito do Consumidor* 144 (2022): 17–35.

Bertoncello, Káren Rick Danilevicz. *Superendividamento do Consumidor - Mínimo Existencial - Casos Concretos.* RT, 2015.

Bertoncello, Káren Rick Danilevicz, and Clarissa Costa de Lima. "Overindebtedness in Mercosul Countries: An Overview." In *Consumer Law and Socioeconomic Development*, edited by Claudia Lima Marques and Dan Wei. Springer, 2017.

Bertoncello, Káren Rick Danilevicz, and Maria Claudia Felten. *Núcleo Multidisciplinar de atendimento ao superendividado – Um ano de cooperação acadêmica e extensão à comunidade.* Tirant lo Blanch, 2023.

Buzzi, Marco Aurélio Gastaldi, Trícia Navarro Xavier Cabral, and Juliana Loss de Andrade. *Superendividamento dos consumidores: Aspectos materiais e processuais.* Foco, 2024.

Cherednychenko, Olga O. "On the Bumpy Road to Responsible Lending in the Digital Marketplace: The New EU Consumer Credit Directive." *Journal of Consumer Policy* 47, no. 1 (2024): 241–70.

de Carvalho, Diógenes Faria, and Frederico Oliveira Silva. "Superendividamento e mínimo existencial: Teoria do restre à vivre." *Revista de Direito do Consumidor* 118, no. 27 (2018): 363–86.

de Lima, Clarissa Costa, and Karen Rick Danilevicz Bertoncello. "Conciliação aplicada ao superendividamento: Estudo de casos." *Revista de Direito do Consumidor* 71, no. 18 (2009): 106–41.

de Lima, Clarissa Costa, and Karen Rick Danilevicz Bertoncello. *Superendividamento aplicado: Aspectos doutrinários e experiência no Poder Judiciário.* GZ, 2010.

Marques, Claudia Lima. "Consumo como igualdade e inclusão social." *Revista Jurídica da Presidência* 101, no. 13 (2011): 405–24.

Marques, Claudia Lima. *Decreto 11.150/22: A inconstitucional tentativa de esvaziar a lei 14.181/21 e retroceder o dever do Estado de proteção do consumidor.* Informativo Migalhas, 2022.

Marques, Claudia Lima. "Conciliação em matéria de superendividamento dos consumidores. Principais resultados de um estudo empírico de 5 anos em Porto Alegre." In *Direitos do Consumidor endividado II: Vulnerabilidade e inclusão*, edited by Claudia Lima Marques, Rosângela Lunardelli Cavallazzi, and Clarissa Costa de Lima. RT, 2016.

Marques, Claudia Lima. "Dever de cooperação no tratamento do superendividamento dos consumidores: Evitar a ruína através da conciliação ou revisão-sanção dos contratos." In *Superendividamento dos consumidores: Aspectos materiais e processuais*, edited by Marco Aurélio Gastaldi Buzzi, Claudia Lima Marques, Trícia Navarro Xavier Cabral, and Juliana Loss de Andrade. Foco, 2024.

Marques, Claudia Lima. "Notas sobre a lei 14.181/2021: A noção de mínimo existencial e sua aplicação imediata." *Revista de Direito do Consumidor* 137 (2021): 387.

Marques, Claudia Lima. "Perspectives for Consumer Protection in the XXI Century." *Macau Journal of Brazilian Studies* 4, no. 1 (2021): 73–86.

Marques, Claudia Lima. "Primeiro 134 casos de conciliação no superendividamento da Lei 14.191/2021: Comparação com os dados anteriores do observatório do crédito e superendividamento da UFRGS." *Revista de Direito do Consumidor* 145 (January–February 2023): 17–40.

Marques, Claudia Lima. "Sugestões para uma lei sobre o tratamento do superendividamento de pessoas físicas em contratos de crédito ao consumo: Proposições com base em pesquisa empírica de 100 casos no Rio Grande do Sul." *Revista de Direito do Consumidor* 55, no. 14 (2005): 11–52.

Marques, Claudia Lima. "25 Years to Celebrate: Horizons of the 1990s Brazilian Protection Code and New Horizons, Especially on the Protection of Consumers." In *Consumer Law and Socioeconomic Development*, edited by Claudia Lima Marques and Dan Wei. Springer, 2017.

Marques, Claudia Lima, and Antônio Herman Benjamin. "Consumer Over-Indebtedness in Brazil and the Need of a New Consumer Bankruptcy Legislation." In *Consumer Credit, Debt and Bankruptcy – Comparative and International Perspective*, edited by Joana Niemi, Iain Ramsay, and William C. Whitford. Hart Publishing, 2009.

Marques, Claudia Lima, Antonio Herman Benjamin, and Bruno Miragem. *Comentários ao Código de Defesa do Consumidor*, 7th ed. RT, 2021.

Marques, Claudia Lima, Káren Rick Danilevicz Bertoncello, and Clarissa Costa de Lima. "Exceção Dilatória para os Consumidores frente à Força Maior da Pandemia de COVID-19: Pela Urgente Aprovação do PL 3.515/2015 de Atualização do CDC e por uma Moratória aos Consumidores." *Revista de Direito do Consumidor* 129 (2020): 47–72.

Marques, Claudia Lima, Clarissa Costa de Lima, and Káren Rick Danilevicz Bertoncello. "Dados da pesquisa empíricas sobre o perfil dos consumidores superendividados da Comarca de Porto Alegre nos anos de 2007 a 2012 e notícia sobre o Observatório do Crédito e Superendividamento UFRGS-MJ." *Revista de Direito do Consumidor* 99, no. 24 (2015): 411–36.

Marques, Claudia Lima, and Bruno Miragem. "Art. 104-A, Art. 104-B e Art. 104-C." In *Comentários ao Código de Defesa do Consumidor*, 7th ed., edited by Claudia Lima Marques, Antonio Herman Benjamin, and Bruno Miragem. RT, 2021.

Marques, Claudia Lima, and Roberto Augusto Castellanos Pfeiffer. "Art. 54-E." In *Código Brasileiro de Defesa do Consumidor comentado pelos autores do Anteprojeto*, edited by Ada Pellegrini Grinover, Antonio Herman de Vasconcellos e Benjamin, Daniel Roberto Fink, José Geraldo Brito Filomeno, Kazuo Watanabe, Nelson Nery Júnior, Roberto Pfeiffer, and Zelmo Denari. GEN, 2022.

Marques, Claudia Lima, and Roberto Augusto Castellanos Pfeiffer. "Dissemination of Consumer Law and Policy in Brazil: The Impact of EU Law." *Journal of Consumer Policy* 45 (2022): 27–48. https://doi.org/10.1007/s10603-022-09503-w.

Marques, Claudia Lima, and Andréia Fernandes Rangel. "A Enunciados das I e II Jornadas de Pesquisa CDEA: Superendividamento e proteção do consumidor, UFRGS-UFRJ-Brasilcon-PUCRS-UNINOVE-PROCON-SP." *Revista de Direito do Consumidor* 139 (2022): 400.

Marques, Claudia Lima, and Lorenzo Bittencourt Nicoletti. "Law 14,181, of July 1, 2021 – Amends Law No. 8,078 of September 11, 1990 (Consumer Protection Code) and Law No. 10,741 of October 1, 2003 (Statute of the Elderly) to Improve the Discipline of Consumer Over-Indebtedness – Translation Offered by the IACL – International Association of Consumer Law." *Revista de Direito do Consumidor* 140 (2022): 409–16.

Marques, Claudia Lima, Clarissa Costa de Lima, and Sophia Vial. "Nota à atualização do Código de Defesa do Consumidor para 'aperfeiçoar a disciplina do crédito', para a prevenção e o tratamento do superendividamento e proteção da pessoa natural." *Revista de Direito do Consumidor* 136 (2021): 517.

Mendes, Gilmar Ferreira. "A ampliação dos direitos subjetivos do cosnumidor superendividado: Reflexões sobre a Lei 14.181/2021." In *Superendividamento dos consumidores: Aspectos materiais e processuais*, edited by Marco Aurélio Gastaldi Buzzi, Claudia Lima Marques, Trícia Navarro Xavier Cabral, and Juliana Loss de Andrade. Foco, 2024.

Micklitz, Hans-W. "Access to, and Exclusion of European Consumers from Financial Markets." In *International Responses to Issues of Credit and Over-Indebtedness in the Wake of Crisis*, edited by Therese Wilson. Ashgate, 2013.

Paisant, Gilles. "A reforma do procedimento de tratamento do superendividamento pela lei de 29 de julho de 1998 relativa à luta contra as exclusões." *Revista de Direito do Consumidor* 55 (2005): 239.

Paisant, Gilles. "El tratamiento del sobreendeudamiento de los consumidores en derecho francés." *Revista de Direito do Consumidor* 42 (2002): 9–26.

Pellegrin Grinover, Ada, Antonio Herman de Vasconcellos e Benjamin, Daniel Roberto Fink, José Geraldo Brito Filomeno, Kazuo Watanabe, Nelson Nery Júnior, Roberto Pfeiffer, and Zelmo Denari. *Código Brasileiro de Defesa do Consumidor comentado pelos autores doAnteprojeto*. GEN, 2022.

Ramsay, Iain, ed. *Consumer Law in the Global Economy*. Ashgate, 1997.

Ramsay, Iain. *Personal Insolvency in the 21st Century: A Comparative Analysis of the US and Europe*. Hart Publishing, 2017.

Ramsay, Iain. "Regulation of Consumer Credit." In *Handbook of Research in International Consumer Law*, edited by Geraint Howells, Iain Ramsay, and Thomas Wilhelsson. Edward Elgar Publishing, 2010.

Roscoe Bessa, Leonardo. *Código de Defesa do Consumidor*, 2nd ed. GEN-Forense, 2022.

Senado Federal. *Relatório Final: Comissão de Juristas de Atualização do Código de Defesa do Consumidor*. Senado Federal, 2012.

Whitford, William C., ed. *Consumer Credit, Debt and Bankruptcy – Comparative and International Perspective*. Hart Publishing, 2009.

10 The *in Duplum* rule in South Africa and Kenya

A tool to protect over-indebted consumers or regulate banking?

Michelle Kelly-Louw

1. Introduction

At the height of the COVID-19 pandemic, there was a marked increase in applications for consumer credit globally and, as a consequence, also an increase in consumer over-indebtedness after the COVID-19 financial crisis.[1] In South Africa, inflation is high ranging from 4,4 per cent to about 5,2 per cent,[2] and living costs (i.e., the prices for food, fuel and utilities) and interest rates have spiraled in recent years, particularly post-pandemic. This is not unique to South Africa as many countries are still reeling from the aftereffects of the pandemic.

The South African National Credit Act (NCA)[3] came into full effect in 2007[4] and is an all-encompassing piece of legislation. It not only regulates consumer credit, interest rates and other costs of credit but aims also to encourage responsible borrowing, avoid over-indebtedness and provide debt relief to over-indebted consumers.

Prior to the NCA, the Usury Act of 1968[5] mostly regulated money lending to consumers of up to a maximum of ZAR500,000 (presently around £21,979)[6] and capped the interest rates for these loans only. The Exemption Notices of 1992[7] and 1999,[8] respectively, issued in terms of section 15A of the Usury Act, provided that certain small loans (micro-loans) up to certain amounts and payable in a maximum number of instalments were exempted from the provisions of the Usury Act and the capped interest rates. It caused various micro-lenders to regularly offer the same consumer different micro-loans. This meant that lenders could grant various loans, tallying up to large amounts of money, outside the provisions of the Usury Act, at exorbitantly high, uncapped and unregulated interest rates. So, accessing credit in the micro-lending sector was extremely expensive.

Therefore, a severely dysfunctional South African credit market existed that was characterised *inter alia* by discrimination and high interest rates, particularly on micro-loans and other costs of credit, and offered limited consumer protection. The mechanisms to prevent over-indebtedness in place at the time could also not properly promote the rehabilitation of consumers, and the available debt relief could also not assist already over-indebted consumers to deal with their debt. As a necessity, the NCA was introduced.[9]

DOI: 10.4324/9781003510406-14

To make credit more affordable in South Africa, the NCA capped the interest rates and other costs of credit (non-interest costs), such as initiation fees and service fees, irrespective of the amount borrowed by consumers (individuals/natural persons). These provisions limiting the interest rate charges and other costs of credit are found in the NCA read with the National Credit Regulations.[10]

To cater for the inadequate debt-relief mechanism that existed in South Africa prior to the NCA, the NCA also made provision for a formal debt rearrangement/restructuring of debts by a court or the National Consumer Tribunal, or voluntarily by a consent order based on an agreement made between the relevant parties.[11] These measures are all direct debt-relief measures, but the NCA went a step further and also introduced an indirect debt-relief mechanism, namely the statutory *in duplum* rule set out in section 103(5). The NCA modeled this statutory rule on its existing common-law *in duplum* rule that has its origin in Roman-Dutch law.

The common-law *in duplum* rule in its very essence, prevents unpaid (arrear) interest from running when it reaches the outstanding unpaid capital amount when a consumer is in default. The NCA adapted this common-law *in duplum* rule and incorporated it into its provision to function as a potent rule against the accumulation of further interest and expanded the rule to also bar against the further accumulation of other costs of credit and operates for as long as a consumer is in default ("statutory *in duplum* rule"). Although the statutory *in duplum* rule has its origin in the common-law rule, it differs drastically from the common-law rule.[12] Both these rules operate as powerful indirect debt-relief mechanisms rather than preventing over-indebtedness occurring.[13] At their core, both rules provide a moratorium on the further accumulation of interest for a consumer while he is in default. To simplify, the rules offer a "payment holiday for further interest" presenting a consumer an opportunity to catch up on his outstanding arrears. The common-law rule was not abolished by the NCA and still frequently applies to certain agreements, while, in contrast, the statutory rule applies to nearly all credit agreements concluded with consumers (natural persons/individuals) in South Africa. Both rules find application often where consumers default on payments that carry interest with them.

Over time, the South African common-law *in duplum* rule, its operation and vast benefits to consumers led to Kenya also adopting a similar rule. The Kenyan rule was legislated and contains a mixture of the statutory and common-law rule, respectively. As the rule in Kenya has its origin in the South African common-law rule, South African jurisprudence is used to interpret the rule and its application in Kenya. This chapter aims to selectively discuss, compare and distinguish the South African *in duplum* rules with the statutory *in duplum* rule in Kenya.

2. The *in duplum* rules in South Africa

2.1 Common-law **in duplum** *rule*

The common-law *in duplum* rule has its roots in Roman law and was later received into the Roman-Dutch law.[14] It is a very old form of consumer protection that still forms part of South African law.[15]

Fundamentally the common-law rule bars the amount of interest recoverable in terms of a loan or credit agreement, but only when a debtor[16] is in default. The rule mainly prevents all interest (contractual and *mora* (default) interest) from further accumulating when the unpaid or, rather, arrear interest equals the outstanding capital amount. When the total amount of unpaid interest has accumulated to an amount equal to the outstanding capital sum, the debtor in default has to first start making payments on his loan again (and so decrease the interest amount), whereafter interest may then again increase to an amount equal to the outstanding capital sum.[17] The rule, therefore, prevents unpaid interest from growing further the minute it reaches the unpaid capital sum. For the purposes of applying the rule, even where interest is capitalised (meaning interest was charged on interest), the capitalised interest never loses its character as interest and become part of the capital amount.[18] The rule does not affect, prevent, prohibit or cap interest or compound interest being charged in terms of contracts generally and in the ordinary course (that is, where there is no default).

The rule provides that "arrear" interest that is lawfully/legally claimable in terms of the agreement between the parties may not surpass the outstanding capital amount on which interest is due and, for purposes of this calculation, what has already been paid by way of interest is not taken into consideration.[19] It is important to understand that the rule does not imply that a creditor/lender is generally prevented from collecting more than double the unpaid (or paid) capital amount in interest, as long as he, at no time, allows the unpaid/arrear interest to reach the unpaid/outstanding capital sum. However, if this escalation occurs, the interest would then merely stop running. The rule prevents interest from running only on a temporary basis. If the defaulting debtor starts making payments again and the interest element of the total amount owed is decreased, the interest may start running again until it yet again equals the outstanding capital sum. Hence, the rule only momentarily prevents the interest from accumulating when a consumer is in default, but does not set a maximum amount of interest that may be charged otherwise by a credit provider.[20] Unless the agreement provides differently, the common law provides that payments are appropriated first to interest and then to capital.[21]

The common-law rule operates despite a creditor instituting legal proceedings against a defaulting consumer.[22] However, once a judgment has been granted against a consumer, the interest begins to run afresh on the judgment debt again. The insolvency (sequestration) of a consumer has no effect on the operation of the *in duplum* rule, and during insolvency, the credit provider's claim against the insolvent estate will still be limited to what is permitted under the rule.

The *in duplum* rule is founded on public policy, as its main goal is to protect the debtor from exploitation by the creditor.[23] It operates as a tool to assist debtors who experience financial difficulties[24] and are unable to service their debts and to protect them from an ever-increasing accumulation of interest. "[T]he purpose of [*in duplum*] is to protect debtors from being crushed by the never-ending accumulation of interest on an outstanding debt".[25] However, it provides the debtor with interim relief only, as the escalation of the ever-continuing interest is simply tempered by the rule.[26] The rule provides an indirect form of debt relief/mechanism to alleviate over-indebtedness for a consumer, as it does not prevent him from becoming over-indebted.[27] The rule also aims to prevent a situation where a creditor is slack in enforcing his debt.[28] It permits the creditor to insist on "regular servicing of the loan without interfering with his right to recovery of interest" while concurrently forcing him not to "allow a burdensome amount of interest to accrue against the debtor, should the credit provider, 'tolerate fiscal indiscipline'".[29] Public policy is thus served by two basic underlying principles of the *in duplum* rule. First, to protect debtors from being exploited by unscrupulous creditors who allow interest to accumulate to an unacceptably high level and, secondly, to urge creditors to issue summons and claim payment of debt quickly.[30] The application of the rule is limited to unpaid arrear interest because the principle underlying this constraint is the policy consideration that debtors whose financial affairs were declining should not be entirely drained, while persons who continue to look after their interest have no need for such protection.[31] Credit providers should, in order to avoid the *in duplum* rule leading to a capping of its interest, ensure they enforce their credit agreements within a reasonable time when a debtor defaults.

The common-law *in duplum* rule is not limited to interest on money-lending transactions and also applies to all type of contracts in terms of which a capital sum is due by a debtor to a creditor and on which amount a specific rate of interest is payable.[32]

2.2 *Statutory* **in duplum** *rule*

Prior to the NCA, consumers of credit agreements could rely only on the common-law *in duplum* rule to protect them from exploitation by their credit providers. Nowadays, consumers of credit agreements that are governed by the NCA are able to rely on the protection afforded by the statutory *in duplum* rule in section 103(5) of the NCA. The statutory rule is somewhat of an adaptation of the common-law rule.[33] Though the statutory rule has its origins in its common-law predecessor, it is not its twin; the statutory rule expands considerably upon the common-law rule, operates in a somewhat different manner and offers much better consumer protection.[34]

Unlike the common-law rule that has wider application to agreements than just money lending or credit agreements, the statutory rule applies only to consumer-credit agreements that fall within the NCA's ambit.[35] The statutory rule set out in section 103(5) generally protects only consumers that are natural persons (individuals).[36] So, if the borrower is a juristic person like a company, the common-law rule is the applicable rule. Furthermore, the statutory rule does not apply to credit agreements that were already in existence when section 103(5) came into operation on June 1, 2007.[37] However, the common-law rule will still apply to such pre-existing credit agreements concluded before June 1, 2007 as well as to contracts where a capital sum is due by a debtor to the creditor and upon which a specific rate of interest is payable falling outside the ambit of the NCA. As a result, the common-law rule is still relevant today.

The NCA and its Regulations place strict caps on interest rates and other costs of credit (that is, non-interest costs) for the different type of credit agreements falling within the parameters of the Act. The Act also provides that the interest rate applicable to an amount in default or an overdue payment under a credit agreement (that is, default interest) may not exceed the highest interest rate applicable to any part of the principal debt under that agreement.[38] The NCA read with its Regulations prescribe the type of fees or charges that a credit provider is permitted to charge a consumer for credit.[39] These provisions generally apply only if the consumer involved is a natural person. A credit agreement is not allowed to require payment by the consumer of any money or other consideration except the principal debt, initiation fee,[40] service fees, interest, the cost of credit insurance, default administration charges and collection costs. A credit provider who contravenes these provisions of the NCA is guilty of an offence.[41]

The statutory *in duplum* rule in section 103(5) provides that, when a consumer of credit is in default, all the combined amounts set out in section 101(1)(b) to (g) (i.e., initiation fees, service fees, interest (both contractual and default); costs of any credit insurance,[42] default administration charges[43] and collection costs) cease to run when they reach the outstanding balance of the consumer's principal debt (basically the capital amount originally lent)[44] at the time of the default. Collection costs refer to an amount that a credit provider may charge "in respect of enforcement of a consumer's monetary obligations under a credit agreement, but does not include a default administrative charge".[45] Regulation 47 also limits some of the collection costs that may be recovered. In *University of Stellenbosch Law Clinic v National Credit Regulator*,[46] the court held that the collection costs include legal fees, which a credit provider may charge a defaulting consumer incurred by the credit provider to enforce "the monetary obligations of the consumer under a credit agreement charged before, during and after litigation".[47] Initially it was uncertain if *all* the legal costs of the credit provider indeed formed part of "collection costs". The Western Cape Division of the High Court, Cape Town in *University of Stellenbosch Law* declared it included *all* legal fees. However, the Supreme Court of Appeal in *Bayport Securitisation Limited v University of Stellenbosch Law Clinic*[48] disagreed and made a distinction between collection costs and legal fees (i.e., in essence, fees that start when the summons is issued), thus effectively meaning that the statutory rule does not include *all* legal costs.[49]

Like with the common-law rule, the interest and other costs of credit which are charged to a consumer in the ordinary course, while he is not in default, are not subject to or capped by the statutory rule.[50] Also, the statutory *in duplum* rule is not a tool that may be used to put blanket ceilings on the prescribed caps of interest rates or other costs of credit. Given the policy considerations the rule is based on, it is strictly aimed at capping the interest (contractual and default) and other costs of credit only for as long as a consumer is in default and the arrears has accumulated equal to the outstanding balance of the consumer's principal debt. The rule or its possible application in a scenario is not factored in when credit is granted to a consumer or the interest rate applicable to granted credit is set. Interest rates, as mentioned, are capped at maximums by legislation, but it remains a credit provider's own prerogative to set the interest rate of each consumer based on his own risk and affordability assessments, provided it falls within the maximum set parameters. The rule, therefore, plays no role in responsible lending tests as that is not the rule's objective.

The core difference between the two rules is that under the common-law rule, it is only the interest that ceases to run if it equals the outstanding capital amount, while, in contrast, under the statutory rule, it is the interest plus all the other listed non-interest costs that cease to run if they jointly exceed the outstanding principal debt. The statutory rule will, therefore, find application much quicker than the common-law rule in the same scenario (that is, where both the terms and the interest of the loan are the same as seen in the practical example further below). The unpaid and accrued interest and non-interest costs jointly, in case of the statutory rule, will reach the *in duplum* ceiling much earlier than merely the unpaid and accrued interest as in the case of the common-law rule.[51] Still, both rules have in common that they operate only if a consumer is in default/in arrears with his payments. The two simplified figures (Figures 10.1 and 10.2) show the difference between the two rules.

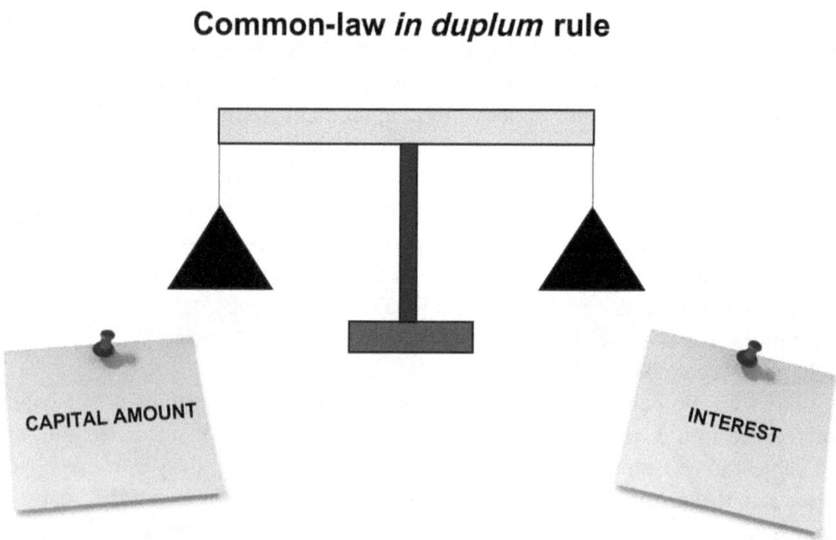

Figure 10.1 Common-law *in duplum* rule.

Source: Graphic illustration by the author.

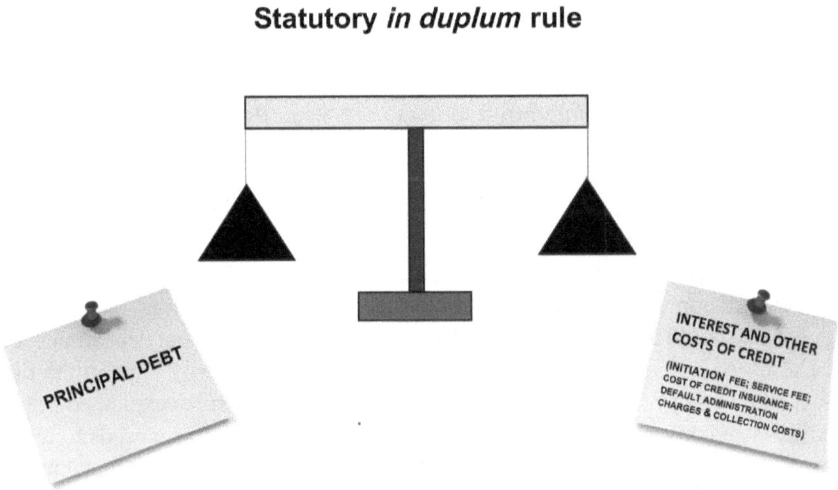

Figure 10.2 Statutory *in duplum* rule.

Source: Graphic illustration by the author.

In terms of the statutory rule, the interest and other listed non-interest costs of credit may not exceed in aggregate the unpaid balance of the principal debt during the time that the consumer is in default, and once those charges and interest equal the principal debt, no further charges and interest may accrue at all *for as long as the consumer is in default.*[52] So, when the maximum amount has been reached no further charges may accrue during the period of default, even if the consumer were to make any payments reducing these costs of credit and interest. This means that once the unpaid interest and costs of credit reaches the outstanding balance of the principal debt (once the *in duplum* ceiling has been reached), the credit provider is not permitted to charge any further interest and other costs of credit while such default persists. Interest or the other costs of credit may only start running again once the consumer is no longer in any default.[53] Therefore, "a consumer, providing the credit provider does not institute legal action against him of course, actually has a real opportunity to pay off the arrear interest and other costs of credit and not to remain in a debt trap forever".[54] In *University of Stellenbosch,*[55] the court held that the statutory rule operates "from the date of default to the date of collection of the final payment owing in order to purge his default, irrespective of whether judgment in respect of the default has been granted or not during this period".[56] Thus, neither a summons nor a judgment suspends the operation of the statutory rule and the rule can thus operate for as long as the consumer is in default.[57] Contrary to this, the Supreme Court of Appeal in *Bayport* made it clear that once a credit provider obtains a judgment against the consumer, a new cause of action comes about.[58] The court held:[59]

> *After a judgment has been granted against a consumer usually, save for necessary disbursements and charges allowed in terms of the relevant tariff, only*

> *interest accrues on the judgment debt. The remaining charges contemplated in s 101(1)(b) to (g) [eg, initiation, service fees] are thus not post-judgment charges. The judgment entered is thus for the capital sum fixed at a particular date together with interest. It follows that . . . s 103(5). . .[do] not apply post-judgment.*

In short, it means is that after judgment, the debt/amount owed is no longer based on a credit agreement regulated in terms of the NCA but on a new cause of action (a judgment debt), thus the statutory rule no longer applies, but the common-law *in duplum* rule may still apply to the judgment debt in such an instance (meaning, the outstanding interest should not equate to more than the outstanding judgment debt amount).

The following simplistic example may be used to practically explain the difference in the application of the common-law and statutory rules explained previously. Say, a consumer borrows ZAR60 000 from his bank and succeeds to repay ZAR30 000 of this amount but then starts to default on his monthly instalments. During his default, the interest and other costs of credit due on the outstanding capital amount of ZAR30 000 continues to accrue each month. Ultimately, the consumer ends up owing arrear interest to the amount of ZAR50 000 and other costs of credit (for instance, initiation fees, service fees, costs of credit insurance, default administration fees and collection costs) amounting to ZAR20 000. If the common-law rule found application, the maximum amount that the bank could recover would be the unpaid/outstanding capital amount of ZAR30 000 plus a maximum amount of arrear interest of ZAR30 000 for the outstanding interest (that is, the amount of arrear interest equal to the outstanding capital amount) together with the non-interest related costs of credit amounting to ZAR20 000. Thus, in total, the bank may claim ZAR80 000, consisting of ZAR30 000 (capital still outstanding) plus interest of ZAR30 000 plus ZAR20 000 for the other non-interest related costs of credit. The other ZAR20 000 due for arrear interest still owed the bank may not claim. While the unpaid interest still equals the outstanding capital amount, the bank can also not add any further interest. However, should the consumer then start paying off the arrear interest amount of ZAR30 000 (permitted amount of interest), the credit provider may again add further interest to the point where it once again equals the outstanding capital amount (that is, ZAR30 000). Realistically the common-law rule works against the consumer who cannot afford to settle his arrear interest instantly or in one or two payments.[60] "The smaller payments that he can afford to make only succeed in setting off the interest again, which means that he can never really manage to pay off the arrear interest".[61] Effectively with no legal action, the consumer can thus remain in this debt trap and the bank can simply let the consumer continue to try and repay this debt in this see-saw manner.

If the statutory rule were to apply to the same set of facts, the maximum amount that the credit provider could recover would be the unpaid capital/principal amount of ZAR30 000 plus the maximum amount for any of the *arrear interest and other costs of credit combinedly* of ZAR30 000 (the amount equal to the outstanding capital amount) equalling a total maximum amount of ZAR60 000. The shortfall on the arrear amounts owed for the interest and other costs of credit *combinedly* amounting to ZAR40 000 the bank may not claim. While the unpaid interest and other costs of credit still equal the outstanding principal debt amount, the bank cannot add any further interest or other costs of credit. But, should the consumer then start paying off the arrear interest and other costs of credit amounting to ZAR30 000 (amount equal to the outstanding capital amount), the credit provider may *still not* add any further interest or other costs of credit so that they again equal the outstanding principal debt amount (that is, ZAR30 000) for as long as the consumer remains in arrears. The statutory rules in this sense provides the consumer with a tangible option to repay the arrears and get out of arrears, while the bank is prohibited from adding more interest and other costs of credit during this period. Of course, this is only provided the bank does not take legal action and successfully enforce the agreement and end the matter. Clearly, the statutory rule provides greater consumer protection and also finds much quicker application than the common-law rule in the same scenario.[62] This is so because the unpaid and accrued interest and statutory costs of credit in accordance with the statutory rule will equal the outstanding principal debt much faster than just unpaid and accrued interest in terms of the common-law rule.

The statutory rule is a useful mechanism to provide debt relief, but it is certainly not perfect. For instance, it is unclear when dealing with the statutory rule whether the word "default" refers to any contractual default (e.g., being in breach of any term in the credit agreement) or whether it refers only to "payment default". In my view, the term refers to an instance where a consumer is in default regarding his payment in terms of the credit agreement. It does not refer to default by a consumer in general. Ideally the word "default" in section 103(5) should be limited to "payment default". Another difficulty with applying the statutory rule is in determining the moment upon which the consumer is no longer in default. In other words, when will the consumer purge his default? It is important to provide guidance on what is meant by "during the time that a consumer is in default under a credit agreement" given that the rule will operate for this duration. Kelly-Louw proposes that a consumer will no longer be in default when he has repaid all the arrear interest and other costs of credit that a credit provider may be entitled to demand in terms of the statutory rule, as well as all the arrears owed on the outstanding capital amount (put differently, the capital amount he would have repaid, if he had never defaulted).[63] Therefore, once said payments are made the consumer will no longer be in default and the interest and other costs of credit can start accruing on the account again.

Section 126(3) of the NCA is prescriptive of the order any payments that are made should be appropriated. Firstly, to due or unpaid interest charges; secondly, to due or unpaid fees or charges; and lastly to the principal debt. No distinction is made between payments before and payments after default and all payments must be appropriated as such.[64]

From the description, it is clear that there are some differences between the different *in duplum* rules. Another important difference is whether a court can raise the defence of the *in duplum* rule on its own accord, for instance, in a case where a credit provider has instituted debt collecting proceedings against a defaulting consumer and the consumer, for some reason, fails to raise the defence that the credit provider has contravened one of the rules. Regarding the common-law rule, the Supreme Court of Appeal in *F & I Advisors (Edms) Bpk v Eerste Nasionale Bank van Suidelike Afrika Bpk*[65] held that a court would not order interest in contravention of the *in duplum* rule in cases where it is clear. However, this does not mean that a court is forced to act, on its own accord, to raise such a defence on the consumer's behalf or must manufacture it from fragments of evidence if a consumer fails to raise it as a defence or argues the rule has been contravened. Hence, a court will not merely act on a suspicion of a contravention.[66] In contrast, since the NCA and its Regulations are prescriptive of the type of fees or charges that a credit provider may charge a consumer, a court is obliged to always consider whether the statutory rule has been contravened, irrespective of whether it was raised as a defence by the consumer.[67]

Despite the rules' differences, both place a moratorium on the further escalation of interest and also cap the amount a judgment may be granted for.

3. The *in duplum* rule under Kenyan law

The introduction of the South African common-law *in duplum* rule in Kenya was already advocated for in 2000 in the Kenyan case *Pelican Investment Ltd v National Bank of Kenya Ltd.*[68] In this case, Onyango-Otieno J said such a legal proposition could be ideal in Kenya, as it would ensure that debtors do not suffer the requirements upon them to pay extra-large interest caused by the apathy and lapse or deliberate failure by the creditors so as to let the unserviced loans accumulate interest to unimaginable levels. It would protect the debtors while also ensuring that the creditors get their money back.

Later Kenya modelled its own statutory *in duplum* rule based on both the South African common-law and statutory *in duplum* rule, respectively.[69] The rule found its way into the legal framework of the financial service sector when section 44A of the Kenya Banking Act (Chapter 488) was inserted by section 17 of the Bank Amendment No 9 of 2006.[70] Kenya's history does not show any application of the *in duplum* rule prior to the amendment made to its Banking Act, it is, therefore, assumed that all references to the *in duplum* rule in the Kenyan context refer to the statutory *in duplum* rule.[71] The statutory rule set out in section 44A of the Banking Act provides:[72]

> *44A. (1) An institution shall be limited in what it may recover from a debtor with respect to a non-performing loan to the maximum amount under subsection (2)*
>
> *(2) The maximum amount referred to in subsection (1) is the sum of the following-*
>
> *(a) the principal owing when the loan becomes non-performing;*
> *(b) interest, in accordance with the contract between the debtor and the institution, not exceeding the principal owing when the loan becomes nonperforming; and*
> *(c) expenses incurred in the recovery of any amounts owed by the debtor*
>
> *(3) If a loan becomes non-performing and then the debtor resumes payments on the loan and then the loan becomes non-performing again, the limitation under paragraphs (a) and (b) of subsection (1) shall be determined with respect to the time the loan last become non-performing.*

The rule not only directly determines "when interest on a non-performing loan ought to stop running, but it also outlines the elements that comprise the recoverable sum from the debtor".[73] The rule ensures that "borrowers are not extorted into paying back more than double the principal amount accorded to them by credit-rendering institutions".[74] Despite the Kenyan *in duplum* rule having the same objective of the South African rule – the simultaneous protection of the debtor and safeguarding of the creditor's interests – concerns were expressed that the application of the *in duplum* rule in the Kenyan context could yield different results from those intended. One reason being that while the rule stemmed from the South African jurisdiction, it was not fully adapted to the Kenyan context.[75] It has even been asked, because of some differences between the South African rules and the Kenyan rule, if the Kenyan rule "is indeed the codification of the *in duplum* rule *stricto senso* or whether it is a mere semblance of the same".[76]

As with the South African statutory rule, the Kenyan statutory rule also has ambiguities. For instance, it is unclear what payment is meant by "*any expenses* incurred in the recovery of any amounts owed by the debtor", and it has been stated that this can be very widely interpreted to encompass a wide array of "expenses". Ndegwa argues that, in that sense, the South African rule is more descriptive and clearer on the matter of costs the rule aims to stop accruing further.[77] Furthermore, the South African NCA and its Regulations also provide distinct definitions of the different costs and set out limits/caps of the interest rates and other costs of credit (non-interest related) that fall within the scope of its *in duplum* rule.[78] The South African rule is more detailed, therefore, leaving fewer grey areas regarding its interpretation.[79]

The Kenya Banking Act defines an institution to mean a bank or financial institution or a mortgage finance company[80] and describes a loan to include any advance, credit facility, financial guarantee or any other liability incurred on behalf of any person.[81] Therefore, it is believed that the Kenyan *in duplum* rule is intended to govern the banking sector solely.[82] The Kenyan *in duplum* rule only finds application to contracts that involve financial institutions such as bank as lenders, and it does not also cover microfinance institutions. However, there are a few misperceptions as to which institutions fall under the ambit of section 44A and if it extends the application of the rule to non-bank lending businesses.[83] For instance, in *Mugure & 2 Others v Higher Education Loans Board*,[84] the High Court in Nairobi (Milimani Commercial Courts Commercial and Tax Division) declared that the rule would apply to those lending monies as it does to banks. In *Mugure*, the court had to decide *inter alia* whether the statutory rule was applicable to money loaned out by the Higher Education Loans Board. However, the court did not discuss the meaning of those involved in the "lending business".[85] The same High Court, in a more recent case, in *Momentum Credit Limited v Kabuiya*,[86] had to again decide on a similar matter. The *Momentum* case, in short, involved a matter where the lender was a microfinance institution. Here the consumer (debtor) had successfully argued before the small claims court that the credit provider was subject to the statutory *in duplum* rule as per the Banking Act. The small claims court agreed and found that the credit provider could not recover the shortfall in view of the exorbitant and unconscionable interest rates charged. However, on appeal the High Court overturned these findings and held:[87]

> *For purposes of section 44, it must be established that the appellant is a bank or financial institution. It is not in dispute that the appellant is neither a bank nor mortgage finance company. In order to qualify as a financial institution, the appellant must either be gazetted as such by the Minister or be one that carries on or proposes to carry on financial business as defined under the Banking Act. In order to qualify as a financial institution, it must accept money on deposit from members of the public and employ that money or part of it for lending or investment as contemplated under the Act.*

From the *Momentum* case, it thus follows that the statutory *in duplum* rule only applies to financial institutions as defined by the Banking Act. The court concluded that the rule governs only the banking sector and not also other entities that offer other forms of loans or financial facilities; therefore, the rule does not apply to microfinance institutions operating in terms of the Microfinance Act 2006.[88] Waigwa states:[89]

> *Therefore, while the* in duplum *rule is embedded into the Kenyan jurisdiction, its application is limited to the banking sector as per section 44 of the Banking (Amended) Act. This rule protects the debtors from unfair practices imposed by banks within the definition of the Act.*

From the opposing court cases described, it appears there is, at times, confusion amongst the courts in Kenya as to who the *in duplum* rule applies to.[90] In contrast, the South African common-law rule not only relates to money lending transactions involving financial institutions but rather to all contracts where a capital amount that is subject to interest at a fixed rate is owed. In contrast, the South African statutory rule applies only to all consumer-credit agreements falling within the scope of the NCA, irrespective of whether the credit provider is a financial institution or a bank. It has been argued, correctly, that the Kenyan rule should be expanded to cover all borrowers,[91] as "equity must apply to all".[92] Gichuhi states the Kenyan statutory rule offered "much needed reprieve for bank creditors in eliminating exploitation by ensuring banks were motivated to recover debts owed at the earliest and were limited in how much they could recover".[93] He adds that prior to the statutory rule, the situation was "dire" in Kenya.[94] "While bank borrowers have found reprieve, the majority of borrowers are still suffering under oppressive and exploitative credit arrangements daily," so Gichuhi, too, supports the expansion of the rule to protect all borrowers.[95] One of his reasons advanced for this support relates to the fact that many Kenyans still make use of other lenders, besides banks. He also petitioned the Kenyan parliament to consider enacting legislation to "expand the scope of the *in duplum* rule to all credit arrangements, be they formal or informal, oral or written, and with individuals or organisations".[96] Time will tell if the petition will bear fruit.

The whole premise of the South African common-law and its statutory rule is that it would be utterly unfair and somewhat counterproductive to restrict the application of the rules to money-lending transactions to which financial institutions (banks) are party to because the objective of both rules is the protection of debtors from exploitation.[97]

It has not been settled in Kenya whether the *in duplum* rule will continue to operate once the creditor institutes legal proceedings against a defaulting consumer, but it has been argued that the same position as prevailing in South Africa will be followed.[98] Thus, the rule will not cease to operate where legal action has been instituted/taken.[99]

In contrast to the two South African *in duplum* rules, the Kenya statutory rule does not apply to judgment debts. Section 44(A) (4) provides that the rule "shall not apply to limit any interest under a court order accruing after the order is made". In such instance, it is thus possible "that the interest on a judgment debt can accrue such as to surpass the original judgment debt".[100]

4. A few comments and conclusion

One may very well ask how an antiquated rule that developed in Roman times and later evolved under Roman-Dutch law could still be relevant today? The answer is a simple one. Agreements where money (debts) were owed and interest charged often resulted in unbalanced and unequal relationships. The debtors (consumers) were often placed in vulnerable positions and were exploited by the creditors/lenders. Consumers (debtors) were also over-indebted back in ancient times. Consumers struggle with the same issues today. They are still in unequal bargaining positions, over-indebted and get exploited, irrespective of legislation providing consumer protection. The common-law *in duplum* rule, the solid public policies it is based on and the laudable objectives it aims to achieve still hold water today and the need for the rule is more prevalent than ever. Hence, the whole idea behind incorporating adaptations of the common-law *in duplum* rule into legislation is based on the notion that protection is needed for the weaker party of a contract, like a consumer, against the stronger party, like the credit provider (for instance, a bank).

The rule was adapted for more modern times, and both South Africa and Kenya have legislated the rule to not only reinforce but also clarify some uncertainties under the common-law rule and increase consumer protection. The South African *in duplum* rule has also influenced the law of other African countries; for instance, the rule still forms part of the law of Zimbabwe. However, Zimbabwe has, similar to South Africa, also legislated the rule and that is found in section 9 of the Moneylending and Rates of Interest Act.[101] Like South Africa, Zimbabwe also kept the common-law rule that has its roots in the South African common-law rule. Therefore, the South African jurisprudence on the common-law rule is also important for Zimbabwe.[102] The rule is, therefore, of significant importance to a number of African countries.

The South African statutory rule clearly provides much better debt relief for an over-indebted consumer, than its common-law counter-part. The statutory rule provides interim debt relief to a consumer that has insufficient financial resources and is willing to repay his arrears but just needs a "temporary moratorium on the further accumulation of interest and other costs of credit to be able to be in a situation where he can properly service his account again".[103] However, both South African *in duplum* rules balance the rights of the parties. On the one hand, they ensure that debtors whose financial affairs are not in a healthy state do not find themselves in an "insufferable position" and, on the other hand, that the creditor/lender are "not slack in enforcing" their debts.[104]

In South Africa, it was argued over many years, including by the South African Law Reform Commission in the 1970s already, that the common-law *in duplum* rule was fundamentally inequitable, despite attempts to justify it, towards a creditor and accordingly attempts to limit its application should be welcomed.[105] It was even argued that the rule was "arbitrary and inappropriate" towards credit providers.[106] Edmunson, more recently goes as far as saying that:[107]

> *[t]he [common-law]* in duplum *rule sought, in its original form, to prevent the greedy creditor from taking not only his pound of flesh, but any blood, muscle or other body parts – to prevent the greedy Shylock from punishing Antonio by death when he failed to repay his lender. This rule dates back so long ago that it is hard for most of us to read it in its original form, let alone understand it in the electronic marketplace, and in the global village. The fact is that not all debtors are 'stout-boned', and not all creditors are financial institutions; not all debtors are ignorant, naïve and preyed on; and not all creditors are wealthy.*

It is, of course, important for any rule protecting a consumer, particularly when it comes to credit or debts owed, that the rights of the parties should be fairly balanced. One of the objectives of the NCA is aimed at "balancing the respective rights and responsibilities of credit providers and consumers".[108] The NCA is not only focused on the protection of consumers. In the end, the South African legislator considered concerns raised by creditors, banks and others arguing for the abolishment of the common-law rule when it drafted the NCA. However, the high levels of over-indebtedness, lack of appropriate debt-relief mechanisms and level of exploitation by credit providers prevailing at the time of drafting seemed to rather support keeping the common-law rule, but there was an obvious need to legislate it and to ensure a better understanding of the rule. The statutory rule has "an important role to play in alleviating over-indebtedness of consumers". The statutory *in duplum* rule has "become the single most important measure to limit the excessive cost of small credit . . . and to protect consumers from entrapment by debt".[109] Credit providers may also benefit from the rule, in that, if they permit vulnerable consumers of small credit amounts to use the rule to pay off the arrear interest and other costs of credit they will be better off financially, instead of taking expensive legal action against consumers that will yield no results in recovering the debt due to their lack of having any attachable assets.[110]

As mentioned, the Kenyan statutory rule has its roots in South Africa's common law. By accepting and incorporating the *in duplum* rule specifically into Kenyan legislation, the Kenyan legislator affirms the usefulness and importance of the rule for consumers, particularly in Africa.[111]

The statutory rule in South Africa is better explained in the NCA than it is in Kenya's Banking Act. The South African statutory rule caters for various amounts falling within the rule, whilst the Kenyan statutory rule is less clear, leaving more room for (mis)interpretations and determinations regarding the precise costs included in the rule. In particular, if one considers the vague phrase in Kenya's Banking Act "*expenses* incurred in the recovery of any amounts owed by the debtor". However, it does not automatically mean that the South African rule is perfect either as discussed and alluded to before. The one major flaw in the South African rule is determining when a consumer is no longer in default. However, the Kenyan rule refers to "non-performing" loans, but it is also unclear what that exactly means and section 44A(3) sheds little light to when a loan is no longer a "non-performing" loan. At face value, the subsection creates the impression that the moment the consumer pays, it no longer is a "non-performing" loan. Nevertheless, despite various uncertainties and vagueness, the importance of the rules remains.

In the application of an *in duplum* rule, it is vital that the correct unpaid (outstanding) principal debt/capital amount is taken into consideration when a calculation is done to determine whether the arrear (unpaid) interest and other costs of credit (if catered for under the rule) equal the unpaid principal debt/capital amount (the *in duplum* ceiling has been reached) so there is no further accrual of interest and other costs.[112] An unfortunate weakness of *in duplum* rules in South Africa and the statutory rule in Kenya (also under the Zimbabwe rule) is that the calculations required to determine whether a rule applies in a scenario are very complex.[113] It is highly probable that an expert will be needed to assist a consumer, court and even the credit provider itself to determine whether the unpaid interest, especially where it has been capitalised, and the other costs, if permitted under a specific rule, equal the outstanding principal debt/capital outstanding.[114] If these calculation costs are passed on to the consumer who is already cash-strapped and has limited financial means, it will unnecessarily overburden the consumer.[115] These calculation problems will undoubtedly bring "about the need for expert evidence to be adduced".[116] "The complexity of the calculations which in itself is a laborious task, stands to prolong trials as evidence as to the sum of the debt will need to be adduced".[117] Furthermore, "practitioners who do not understand how to do the calculation or even the rule itself may thus confound the confusion of their ill-educated clients, marring the whole process with imprecision".[118] Another issue is that there will also be some variances in the calculations presented as interest rates fluctuates and the exact dates the calculations were made may have an impact in the amounts derived at. So, in both jurisdictions considered here, there should be a simplification of how these calculations should be done to mitigate some of these practical application challenges, at least in the legislated versions of the *in duplum* rule.[119]

Scholars have argued that the Kenyan rule ought to apply to all transactions involving an advancement of credit, instead of maintaining the *status quo* that only allows for the rule's application to loans issued by financial institutions as defined by the Banking Act. Seen from that perspective, it may be said that the Kenyan rule is focused more on the rule to be used as tool to regulate banking instead of being focused on the rule to operate as a tool providing debt relief to all consumers irrespective of where they borrowed money from.[120] Interestingly and, perhaps, relevant here to further illustrate that the rule in some other countries are used as a tool to regulate banking is that in Zimbabwe, the statutory *in duplum* rule, in contrast to the Kenyan rule, excludes banks from its ambit, while the common-law *in duplum* in Zimbabwe rule applies to banks.[121] It has been argued that Zimbabwe should consider including the banking sector within the ambit of its statutory *in duplum* rule as the banking sector is the largest registered credit provider in that country.[122] In South African, both the *in duplum* rules have, at their crux, the protection of over-indebted consumers irrespective of whether the creditor involved is a financial institution or not. In South Africa, where the common-law rule originated from, neither of the rules are used as tools to regulate banking and both rules may apply to banks. Therefore, it is important to take cognisance of the roots of the *in duplum* rule and what it aims to achieve – provide consumer protection to all debtors irrespective of the type of creditor, debt or debtor involved. The ancient ("original") rule was way ahead of its time as it is one of the earliest forms of a debt-relief (albeit indirect) mechanism and a tool for protecting all debtors, not only natural persons. Consumer protection ranked very low in ancient times, and although the rule is antiquated, the rule has not only stood the test of time but has even been magnified and incorporated into other African countries that do not necessarily share a common history with South Africa.

Notes

1 Kelly-Louw, "Recent Developments," 24–25.
2 Inflation decreased only recently. For instance, in May 2024, it still stood at 5,2 per cent and, in August 2024, it stood at 4,4 per cent, see accessed October 12, 2024, https://www.statssa.gov.za/?p=17330 and https://www.statssa.gov.za/?p=17656.
3 Act 34 of 2005 (hereinafter "the NCA").
4 Proc 22 in *Government Gazette* 28824 of May 11, 2006.
5 Act 73 of 1968.
6 See accessed October 12, 2024, https://www.xe.com/currencyconverter/convert/?Amount=500000&From=ZAR&To=GBP.
7 Notice 73 in GN R3451 in *Government Gazette* 14498 of December 31, 1992.
8 GN 713 in *Government Gazette* 20145 of June 1,1999, as amended by GN 910 in *Government Gazette* 20307 of July 16, 1999.
9 For a detailed discussion of the background to the NCA, see Kelly-Louw, "Prevention".
10 GN R489 in *Government Gazette* 28864 of May 31, 2006, as amended by GN R1209 in *Government Gazette* of November 30, 2006, GN R604 in *Government Gazette* 30713 of March 29, 2008, GN R202 in *Government Gazette* 38557 of March 13, 2015, and GN 1080 in *Government Gazette* 39379 of November 6, 2015 (hereinafter "the Regulations").
11 See sections 83 and 85–88 of the NCA.
12 For more, see Kelly-Louw, "Better."

13 For more, see Kelly-Louw, "Statutory *in Duplum.*"
14 *LTA Construction Bpk v Administrateur, Transvaal* 1992 1 SA 473 (A); Schulze, "In Duplum," 487; Otto, *National Credit Act*, 95; Scholtz, *Guide*, para 10.6.4.
15 See, e.g., *Union Government v Jordaan's Executor* 1916 TPD 411; *Van Coppenhagen v Van Coppenhagen* 1947 1 SA 576 (T); *Stroebel v Stroebel* 1973 2 SA 137 (T); *LTA Construction Bpk v Administrateur, Transvaal* 1992 1 SA 473 (A); *ABSA Bank Ltd v Leech* 2001 4 SA 132 (SCA); *Standard Bank of SA Ltd v Oneanate Investments (Pty) Ltd (in liquidation)* 1998 1 SA 811 (SCA); *Margo v Gardner* 2010 6 SA 385 (SCA); *Silvermoon Investments 278 CC v Slip Knot Investments 777 (Pty) Ltd* [2012] ZAECGHC 58 (July 23, 2012) *Silvermoon Investments 278 CC v Slip Knot Investments 777 (Pty) Ltd* [2012] ZAECGHC 106 (December 28, 2012); *Paulsen v Slip Knot Investments* 2014 4 SA 253 (SCA); *Paulsen v Slip Knot Investments 777 (Pty) Limited* 2015 3 SA 479 (CC); Vessio, "In Duplum and the Lump-Sum," 466–78.
16 As the common-law rule applies even in instances where the debtor may not necessarily be a consumer, the term "debtor" is used. Later when the discussion moves to the statutory rule, the term "consumer" is used, as generally the statutory rule finds application only to consumers (natural persons) and the focus of the book is on consumers.
17 *Sanlam Life Insurance Ltd v South African Breweries Ltd* 2000 2 SA 647 (W) 652H-J; *Stroebel v Stroebel* 1973 2 SA 137 (T); Vessio, "Short" 727.
18 *Standard Bank v Oneanate* 827–829. For comprehensive discussion of the rule, its history and application, see Vessio, "Effects."
19 *Sanlam Life Insurance Ltd v South African Breweries Ltd* 2000 2 SA 647 (W) 652H-J; Vessio, "Short," 727.
20 Kelly-Louw, "Better" and the authorities listed there; Vessio, "Limit," 36.
21 *Standard Bank v Oneanate* 832E–F.
22 For how the rule continues to apply after legal action commences, see *Paulsen v Slip Knot Investments 777 (Pty) Limited* 2015 3 SA 479 (CC); and *Paulsen v Slip Knot Investments* 2014 4 SA 253 (SCA) para 21. *Paulsen v Slip* is very contentious in that it overturned the long-held view by the Supreme Court of Appeal in *Standard Bank of South Africa Ltd v Oneanate Investments (Pty) Ltd (in liquidation)* 1998 (1) SA 811 (SCA) at 834 that if a creditor had instituted legal proceedings against a defaulting consumer by issuing and servicing a summons, the common-law *in duplum* rule was suspended and the interest could once again accrue on the outstanding amount (for severe criticism of the Constitutional Court in the *Paulse*n case, see Edmunson, "Interested," 38–40).
23 *Standard Bank v Oneanate* 828D. For a detailed discussion of the role of public policy and consumer protection in justifying keeping the rule, see Vessio, "Limit," 35–36.
24 *LTA Construction Bpk v Administrateur, Transvaal* 1992 1 SA 473 (A) 482E–F.
25 *Paulsen v Slip Knot Investments 777 (Pty) Limited* 2015 3 SA 479 (CC) in para [44].
26 Vessio, "Limit," 36; Kelly-Louw, "Better," 338.
27 Kelly-Louw, "Statutory *in Duplum*," 352.
28 Scholtz, *Guide*, para 10.6.4.
29 Kelly-Louw, "Statutory *in Duplum*," 358 and authorities cited; Vessio, "Effects," 38.
30 *Standard Bank v Oneanate* 828D; *Margo v Gardner* para 12.
31 *Bellingham NO v Clive Ferreira & Associates CC* 1998 (4) SA 382 (W).
32 Schulze, "In Duplum," 487; Vessio "Limit," 26–27; Kelly-Louw, "Better," 338–39.
33 South African Department of Trade and Industry, "*Consumer Credit Law Reform*" para 6.17. For a discussion of both rules, see Vessio, "In Duplum Rule," chapter 31.
34 Vessio, "Short Discussion," 728.
35 See sections 4–6 and 8 of the NCA.
36 For a detailed discussion of the statutory rule, see Scholtz, *Guide*, para 10.6.4.
37 See Sch 3 item 4(2) of the NCA.
38 Section 103(1) of the NCA.
39 Sections 100–106 of the NCA and regulations 39–48 of the Regulations.
40 For example, an initiation fee may never exceed 15 per cent of the principal debt.

41 Section 100(3).
42 These costs pertain specifically to credit insurance and not also to costs relating to insurance generally.
43 This refers to a charge that a credit provider may impose to cover administration costs incurred because of the consumer having defaulted under the credit agreement.
44 For a definition and what the amount includes, see section 1 read with section 101(1)(a) of the NCA plus the value of any item listed in section 102. In brief, if the credit agreement is a mortgage agreement (home loan), a secured loan, an instalment agreement, lease, the next may be added to the principal debt: any initiation fee, cost of an extended warranty agreement, delivery, installation or fuelling charge, connection fee, or insurance premium.
45 See section 1 for the definition.
46 2020 3 SA 307 (WCC).
47 In para 42.
48 2022 2 SA 343 (SCA).
49 For the actual costs included and its parameters under "collection costs" see the full judgment.
50 Scholtz, *Guide*, para 10.6.4; and Campbell, "In Duplum," 5.
51 Kelly-Louw, "Statutory *in Duplum*," 371.
52 *National Credit Regulator v Nedbank Ltd* 2009 6 SA 295 (GNP).
53 *Nedbank Ltd v National Credit Regulator* 2011 3 SA 581 (SCA).
54 Kelly-Louw, "Statutory *in Duplum*," 371.
55 2020 3 SA 307 (WCC).
56 In para 42.
57 *University of Stellenbosch Law Clinic v National Credit Regulator* 2020 3 SA 307 (WCC).
58 2022 2 SA 343 (SCA) in paras 24 and 26.
59 In para 26.
60 Kelly-Louw, "Statutory *in Duplum*," 370.
61 Kelly-Louw, "Statutory *in Duplum*."
62 Kelly-Louw, "Statutory *in Duplum*," 371.
63 Kelly-Louw, *Consumer Credit*, footnote 257 at 260.
64 *Nedbank Ltd v National Credit Regulator* 2011 3 SA 581 (SCA) para 48.
65 1999 (1) SA 515 (SCA) at 525E–F and authorities cited there.
66 Campbell, "In Duplum," 10; Kelly-Louw, "Statutory *in Duplum*," 369.
67 Kelly-Louw, "Statutory *in Duplum*," 369 and authority listed.
68 [2000] 2 EA 488.
69 Ndegwa, "In Duplum," 2, 6.
70 Ndegwa, "In Duplum."
71 Ndegwa, "In Duplum," 11.
72 Section 44A (1)–(3), Banking Act (Chapter 488, Laws of Kenya).
73 Ndegwa, "In Duplum," 8.
74 Ndegwa, "In Duplum," 8.
75 Ndegwa, "In Duplum," 8.
76 Ndegwa, "In Duplum," 9.
77 Ndegwa, "In Duplum," 13.
78 Ndegwa, "In Duplum," 14.
79 Ndegwa, "In Duplum," 14.
80 Section 2, *Banking Act* (Chapter 488, Laws of Kenya).
81 Section 44A (5), *Banking Act* (Chapter 488, Laws of Kenya).
82 Ndegwa, "In Duplum," 15.
83 Ndegwa, "In Duplum," 15.
84 (Petition E002 of 2021) [2022] KEHC 11951 (KLR) (Civ) (August 19, 2022).
85 Waigwa, "In Duplum."
86 (Civil Appeal E035 of 2022) [2022] KEHC 13705 (KLR) (October 7, 2022).

87 In para 13.
88 Waigwa, "In Duplum."
89 Waigwa, "In Duplum."
90 KN Law LLP, "Application."
91 Ndegwa, "In Duplum," 16.
92 Gichuhi, "In Duplum."
93 Gichuhi, "In Duplum."
94 Gichuhi, "In Duplum."
95 Gichuhi, "In Duplum."
96 Gichuhi, "In Duplum."
97 Ndegwa, "In Duplum," 16.
98 Ndegwa, "In Duplum," 18.
99 See footnote 20 for the South African common-law position, and note that under South African law, the statutory rule will operate for as long as a consumer is in default, irrespective of whether legal action is taken/instituted.
100 Ndegwa, "In Duplum," 17.
101 Moneylending and Rates of Interest Act [Chapter 14:14] (Law of Zimbabwe).
102 Reserve Bank of Zimbabwe, *Consumer Education*, 5–7; for a discussion of the Zimbabwe position, see Madzokere, *Codification*.
103 Kelly-Louw, "Statutory *in Duplum*," 372.
104 Scholtz, *Guide*, para 10.6.4; Kelly-Louw, "Statutory *in Duplum*," 372.
105 Kelly-Louw, "Statutory *in Duplum*," 372–73 and the authorities and reports listed.
106 Vessio, "Limit," 36.
107 Edmunson, "Interested," 40.
108 Section 3(d) of the NCA.
109 Campbell, "In Duplum," 1.
110 Kelly-Louw, "Statutory *in Duplum*," 374.
111 Kelly-Louw, "Statutory *in Duplum*," 373.
112 Kelly-Louw, "Statutory *in Duplum*," 363.
113 Kelly-Louw, "Statutory *in Duplum*," 372.
114 Kelly-Louw, "Statutory *in Duplum*."
115 Kelly-Louw, "Statutory *in Duplum*," 372; Campbell, "In Duplum," 10.
116 Madzokere, *Codification*, 24.
117 Madzokere, *Codification*, 24 (footnote omitted).
118 Madzokere, *Codification*, 24.
119 Campbell, "In Duplum," 10; Madzokere, *Codification*, 24–25.
120 Ndegwa, "In Duplum," 22.
121 Madzokere, *Codification*, 43.
122 Madzokere, *Codification*, 42.

References

ABSA Bank Ltd v Leech 2001 4 SA 132 (SCA).

Banking Act (Chapter 488, Laws of Kenya).

Bayport Securitisation Limited v University of Stellenbosch Law Clinic 2022 2 SA 343 (SCA).

Bellingham NO v Clive Ferreira & Associates CC 1998 (4) SA 382 (W).

Campbell, Jonathan. "The in Duplum Rule: Relief for Consumers of Excessively Priced Small Credit Legitimised by the National Credit Act." *The South African Mercantile Law Journal* 22 (2010): 1–11.

Edmunson, Kerron. "Interested About the Interest in Debt? The in Duplum Rule Revisited." *De Rebus* (August 2015): 38–40.

F & I Advisors (Edms) Bpk v Eerste Nasionale Bank van Suidelike Afrika Bpk 1999 (1) SA 515 (SCA).

Gichuhi, Allen Waiyaki. "In Duplum Law Must Be Expanded to Cover All Borrowers." *Legal Update: Wamae & Allen LLP*, February 15, 2022. Accessed July 31, 2024. https://wamaeallen.com/in-duplum-law-must-be-expanded-to-cover-all-borrowers/.

GN 713 in *Government Gazette* 20145 of June 1,1999, as amended by GN 910 in *Government Gazette* 20307 of July 16,1999.

LTA Construction Bpk v Administrateur, Transvaal 1992 1 SA 473 (A).

Madzokere, T.D. "The Codification of the in Duplum Rule in South Africa and Zimbabwe." LLM diss., North West University, 2018.

Margo v Gardner 2010 6 SA 385 (SCA).

Microfinance Act, 2006 (Laws of Zimbabwe).

Momentum Credit Limited v Kabuiya (Civil Appeal E035 of 2022) [2022] KEHC 13705 (KLR) (7 October 2022).

Moneylending and Rates of Interest Act [Chapter 14:14] (Law of Zimbabwe).

Mugure & 2 others v Higher Education Loans Board (Petition E002 of 2021) [2022] KEHC 11951 (KLR) (Civ) (August 19, 2022).

Kelly-Louw, Michelle. "Better Consumer Protection Under the Statutory *in Duplum* Rule." *The South African Mercantile Law Journal* 19 (2007): 337–45.

Kelly-Louw, Michelle. *Consumer Credit Regulation in South Africa*. Contributions by Philip N. Stoop. Claremont: Juta & Co. Ltd, 2012.

Kelly-Louw, Michelle. "The Prevention and Alleviation of Consumer Over-Indebtedness." *The South African Mercantile Law Journal* 20 (2008): 200–26.

Kelly-Louw, Michelle. "Recent Developments Regarding Administration Orders." In *De Serie Legenda: Developments in Commercial Law: Insolvency Law*, vol. IV, edited by Jani Van Wyk, 23–42. Johannesburg: LexisNexis (Pty) Ltd, 2023.

Kelly-Louw, Michelle. "The Statutory *in Duplum* Rule as an Indirect Debt Relief Mechanism." *The South African Mercantile Law Journal* 23 (2011): 352–75.

KN Law LLP. "Application of the In Duplum Rule in Kenya." April 6, 2023. Accessed July 31, 2024. https://kn.co.ke/applicatiwaion-of-the-in-duplum-rule-in-kenya/.

National Credit Regulations published in GN R489 in *Government Gazette* 28864 of May 31, 2006, as amended by GN R1209 in *Government Gazette* of November 30, 2006, GN R604 in *Government Gazette* 30713 of March 29, 2008, GN R202 in *Government Gazette* 38557 of March 13, 2015, and GN 1080 in *Government Gazette* 39379 of November 6, 2015.

National Credit Regulator v Nedbank Ltd 2009 6 SA 295 (GNP).

Ndegwa, Christopher. "In Duplum Rule in Kenya: A Critical Analysis of the Unaddressed Aspects of section 44A of the Banking Act (January 16, 2016)." *Strathmore Law Review* 1 (2016): 1–23.

Nedbank Ltd v National Credit Regulator 2011 3 SA 581 (SCA).

Notice 73 in GN R3451 in *Government Gazette* 14498 of December 31, 1992.

Otto, J.M., and Otto, R.-L. *The National Credit Act Explained*. Durban: LexisNexis (Pty) Ltd, 2010.

Paulsen v Slip Knot Investments 2014 4 SA 253 (SCA).

Paulsen v Slip Knot Investments 777 (Pty) Limited 2015 3 SA 479 (CC).

Pelican Investment Ltd v National Bank of Kenya Ltd [2000] 2 EA 488.

Proc 22 in *Government Gazette* 28824 of May 11, 2006.

ReserveBank of Zimbabwe. "Consumer Education & Awareness." Accessed July 29, 2024. https://rbz.co.zw/documents/consumer_protection/consumer-education-awareness-bulletin.pdf.

Sanlam Life Insurance Ltd v South African Breweries Ltd 2000 2 SA 647 (W).

Scholtz, J.W., J.M. Otto, E. Van Zyl, C.M. Van Heerden, and N. Campbell. *Guide to the National Credit Act*. Durban: LexisNexis (Pty) Ltd, 2008 et seq and loose-leaf.

Schulze, W.G. "The in Duplum Rule: A Short List of Some Unresolved Issues." *The South African Mercantile Law Journal* 18 (2006): 418–29.

Silvermoon Investments 278 CC v Slip Knot Investments 777 (Pty) Ltd [2012] ZAECGHC 58 (July 23, 2012).
Silvermoon Investments 278 CC v Slip Knot Investments 777 (Pty) Ltd [2012] ZAECGHC 106 (December 28, 2012).
South African Department of Trade and Industry. *Consumer Credit Law Reform: Policy Framework for Consumer Credit.* South African Department of Trade and Industry, August 2004.
Standard Bank of South Africa Ltd v Oneanate Investments (Pty) Ltd (in liquidation) 1998 (1) SA 811 (SCA).
Stroebel v Stroebel 1973 2 SA 137 (T).
Union Government v Jordaan's Executor 1916 TPD 411.
University of Stellenbosch Law Clinic v National Credit Regulator 2020 3 SA 307 (WCC).
Usury Act 73 of 1968.
Van Coppenhagen v Van Coppenhagen 1947 1 SA 576 (T).
Vessio, Monica L. "The Effects of the in Duplum Rule and Clause 103(5) of the National Credit Bill 2005 on Interest." LLM diss., University of Pretoria, 2006.
Vessio, Monica L. "In Duplum and the Lump-Sum Loan: The Common Law and Section 103(5) of the National Credit Act." *South African Law Journal* 136 (2019): 463–88.
Vessio, Monica L. "The in Duplum Rule." In *Banking Law and Practice*, edited by J. Moorcroft and M.L. Vessio. Johannesburg: LexisNexis (Pty) Ltd, 2009 et seq and loose-leaf.
Vessio, Monica L. "A Limit on the Limit on Interest? The in Duplum Rule and the Public Policy Backdrop." *De Jure* 39 (2006): 25–26.
Vessio, Monica L. "A Short Discussion on the Effects of the in Duplum Rule Upon Commencement of Litigation and After Judgment: A View Both 'Inside' and 'Outside' the National Credit Act." *Obiter* (2010): 725–34.
Waigwa, Ambrose. "The in Duplum Rule Does Not Apply to Microfinance Institutions." CMSME Club (Blog), April 30, 2024. Accessed July 29, 2024. https://cmsmeclub.com/blog/the-in-duplum-rule-does-not-apply-to-microfinance-institutions.
Web pages (all last accessed July 11, 2024):
https://www.statssa.gov.za/?p=17330.
https://www.xe.com/currencyconverter/convert/?Amount=500000&From=ZAR&To=GBP.

11 Buy now, pain later? Over-indebtedness of young individuals*

Duygu Damar-Blanken

1. Introduction

The newest and, perhaps, the most widespread micro-lending scheme, namely Buy Now, Pay Later (BNPL), has become increasingly popular worldwide within the last half decade. Germany poses no exception to the widespread use of BNPL in e-commerce: whereas in 2016 the use of BNPL amounted to only 3 percent of all e-commerce transactions, after continuously increasing, it reached 23 percent in 2022. See Figure 11.1[1]

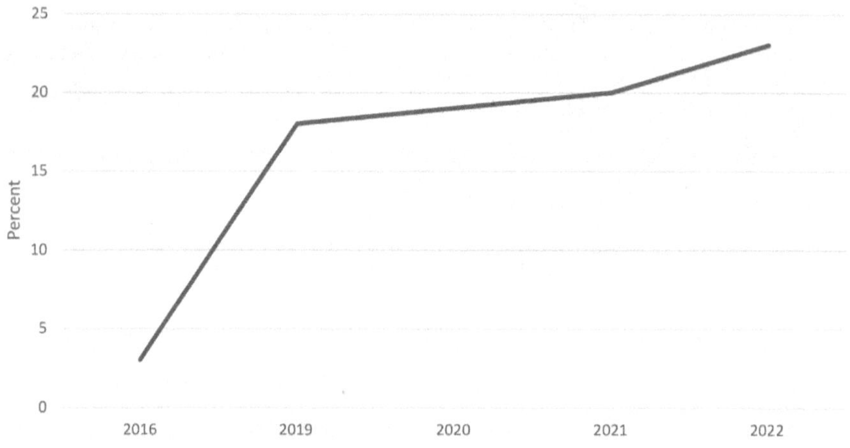

Figure 11.1 Market share of BNPL in e-commerce in Germany.

The rapidly increasing popularity of BNPL services is accounted for not only by digitalisation and the initial interest-free character of such purchases but also the increasing need (alas dependency) of consumers and households on small credit lines for meeting their needs or making ends meet.[2] It is important to stress that BNPL-users are typically consumers who do not have access to regular credit or lack savings and/or planning ability.[3]

DOI: 10.4324/9781003510406-15

The biggest difference to options directly offered by sellers[4] is that a third party is involved in BNPL-schemes, called a payment service provider in European law.[5] The most well-known providers of BNPL services in Europe are Clearpay, PayPal and Klarna. In the meantime, other payment services providers, including some banks, have started to offer BNPL on the European market.[6] In a BNPL-scheme, a consumer purchases a product or a service (in most cases online) and can, among other options, choose payment by BNPL. In this case, the BNPL-provider will pay the purchase price (minus the commission) to the seller or service provider. The consumer is then obliged to pay the full purchase price to the BNPL-provider.

2. Is it really a zero-cost product?

In order to fulfill his/her payment obligation to the BNPL-provider, the consumer can choose among several payment options, for example, instant payment or deferred payment or payment in instalments. If the instant payment option is chosen, the amount will be debited either from the bank account or the credit card – depending on the payment source the consumer has previously chosen – without any costs for the consumer (other than the credit card charges). If the deferred payment option is chosen, the amount will normally be debited from the bank account of the consumer in 30 days – again without any additional costs for the consumer. On or before the date of the deferred payment, the consumer can once more postpone the payment for another 30 or 60 days, this time in exchange for a small "deferral fee". Payment in instalments option generally comes at a cost, especially if the number of instalments is greater than four or five, depending on the BNPL-provider.[7]

One of the most important advantages of the BNPL-option is that it allows the costs of purchases to be delayed or spread out without having to apply for credit or a credit card.[8] This aspect, among others, allows consumers to bridge a temporary money shortage in a quick, simple way. Furthermore, consumers are not forced to share their bank account or credit card information with different online stores. Instead, the information is saved only by the BNPL-provider.

So far so good.

Irrespective of whether deferred payment or payment in instalments is chosen, late fees must be paid if payment is not performed on the due date. In fact, one of the most important revenue sources of BNPL-providers is the late fees and/or interest stemming from late payments.[9] In a majority of the cases, pre-contractual information about the fees for late payment or default is – presumably intentionally – far from clear.[10] Thus, the marketing strategy claiming that BNPL-services are zero-cost products does not reflect the whole picture and is misleading.[11]

The problem is aggravated by the method used by BNPL-providers to calculate late fees, with fees accruing for each small instance of credit rather than all outstanding payments being consolidated into a single written warning. If, for instance, a person makes ten purchases for 20 euros on a single day and cannot perform the payment of 200 euros total on the due date, this person would be subject to paying a late fee of, for example, 1.20 euros for each purchase, in total 12 euros; this instead of 1.20 euros for a consolidated outstanding payment amount of 200 euros even though the purchase date and due date are the same for all payment obligations – and even though a single purchase of 200 euros would have been subject to only the 1.20 euro fee.

Additionally, failure to pay may result in a notification being sent to a credit database,[12] when the legal requirements for such a notification are fulfilled. According to sec. 31 para. 2 of the German Federal Data Protection Act, in the absence of a court decision, outstanding payments can be notified to a credit database only if (1) the consumer has explicitly acknowledged the debt, or (2) (a) the consumer has received at least two written warnings after the due date, with an intervening interval of at least four weeks, and (b) the consumer has been informed, in at least one of these warnings, of possible referral to a credit database, and (c) the consumer has not contested the payment claim. Once this notification is made and registered in the database, it is known as a negative indicator (*Negativmerkmal*). The credit database will share this negative indicator with the bank of the consumer and, if inquired, with other banks as well as other service providers (e.g., payment service providers, telecommunication companies or retail service providers).

When the information regarding an outstanding payment reaches banks, it generally results in the cancellation of the existing credit card and/or the overdraft facility.[13] When other banks or service providers are informed of the outstanding payment(s), access to credit on regular terms[14] or conclusion of new contracts for goods and services on a deferred payment basis will be nearly impossible.

Additionally, individuals may subsequently face challenges in the housing and employment markets. In Germany, most homeowners/lessors require a certificate from a credit database stating that the potential tenant has no outstanding payment obligations. An inability to provide this certificate will regularly result in the tenancy application being disregarded. Especially in the big cities of Germany, renting a flat without such a certificate is extraordinarily difficult. The same applies to securing jobs in certain areas of work. Companies in sensitive lines of work, such as those offering security or financial or transport services, consider outstanding payment obligations to be a source of vulnerability and potential blackmail. Just as homeowners/lessors, such employers will, therefore, require a certificate establishing the applicant's unblemished credit status. An inability to provide this certificate will typically result in the job application being disregarded.

As evident from this picture, an inability to make scheduled payments, including BNPL-payments, can have devastating consequences. Persons who are further along in their career and who have a regular income will usually have resources that allow them to overcome these consequences. Young persons, on the other hand, will either still be students or at the beginning of their careers and will not in general have any or much savings. Hence, a negative indicator registered in a credit database will constitute a significant hurdle which could, in the worst-case scenario, prevent them from having access to the employment market which should, in the first place, give them the financial means to overcome such hurdles.

3. Pitfalls for a debt spiral

One of the biggest achievements of BNPL-services is that they very successfully mask their character as short-term, small-scale credit and present themselves as a convenient means of payment,[15] since such services are not associated with banks and offer easy access without a burdensome application procedure.[16] Their concept is based on the premise that consumers are not provided money by a third party but that they are borrowing "from their future selves."[17] Consumers are, thus, provided with an illusionary sense of increased purchasing power.[18] It is, therefore, not surprising that BNPL-services promote impulse buying.[19] Additionally, BNPL-services create a high number of small credit obligations with a high number of due dates, increasing the risk that one will lose track of upcoming payment obligations. This could even lead to over-indebtedness.[20]

Using BNPL-services without falling into its pitfalls requires a certain level of financial literacy and the ability to control one's impulses,[21] both of which are often missing in young persons, at least to a certain degree. A study conducted by the Institute for Responsible Finance[22] confirms that the perception of BNPL-services as a non-credit product is widely held among young persons. For the purposes of the study "Credit Competence of Young Adults in Germany", a survey was conducted among persons aged from 16 to 20 years. The question, whether BNPL is a credit product was answered in the affirmative by only one-third of the survey participants (Figure 11.2).

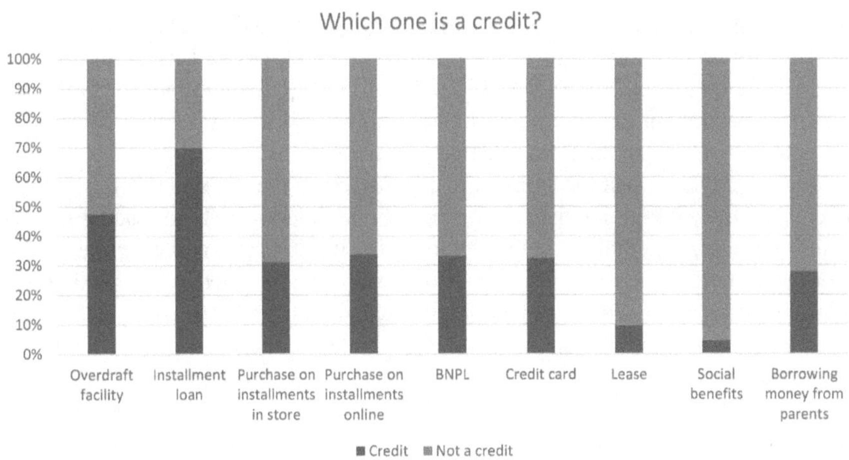

Figure 11.2 Test question on the types of credit.

Furthermore, especially young people have difficulties in reflecting on and controlling their impulses. Combined with the illusionary sense of increased purchasing power, it leads young individuals to overspend.[23] The high number of impulse purchases creates a high number of deadlines, which increases the risk of losing track of one's payment obligations and even over-indebtedness among young individuals.[24]

The result of a survey conducted by the biggest credit database among young persons in Germany confirms that these pitfalls indeed have a big impact: 82 percent of survey participants agree that BNPL-services lead to quick purchases of unnecessary products; 88 percent of survey participants think that there is a risk or a high risk of losing track of their finances and expenses due to the use of BNPL-services. Every tenth survey participant was surprised when their bank account was debited for a deferred payment since they were not expecting it, for example, they had forgotten about the due date. Also, 47 percent of survey participants had forgotten about a payment deadline at least once. While – luckily – this was rarely the case for 35 percent of the respondents, 12 percent of the survey participants almost always or often forgot about payment deadlines and received a payment reminder. In addition, 19 percent of those who rarely missed a payment deadline also lacked the financial means to make the payment.[25]

There are also cases where BNPL-debt leads to the over-indebtedness of a young person. The Institute for Responsible Finance works closely with debt counselling offices, which share the view that particularly young people are affected by the payment difficulties associated with BNPL. Statistics from the German Federal Statistics Office for 2021 confirm this impression. It shows that almost a third (28 percent) of those seeking advice from debt counselling offices were indebted to online or mail-order shops. This figure had been 25 percent in 2016 – thus indicating a 3 percent raise in five years. A large proportion of these individuals tended to be younger people, with 38 percent being between 20 and 24 years old.[26]

A case communicated by a debt counselling office offers a prime example of how quickly young people can fall into a debt spiral under BNPL-schemes: A young individual who did not yet have a regular income and was still living in parents' house conducted a total of 50 BNPL-purchases for PlayStation vouchers within 3 months. The amount of the vouchers varied between 4 and 100 euros. Thus, s/he had taken out a loan, in the form of deferred payments, totalling almost 2,000 euros in 3 months. Due to lack of an income, s/he deferred those payments for another 30 days on their initial due date, incurring second deferral costs for each payment position. It was, nonetheless, not possible for the individual to make payment after the second deferral period; thus, part of the loan was converted into instalments – again incurring costs. Yet these payments could similarly not be made; as a result, a debt collection agency stepped in, which generated additional costs. As the young person had no source of income, the case landed in a debt counselling office.

4. Are there any safeguards?

4.1 Status quo

Owing to the over-indebtedness risk posed by the BNPL-schemes, especially for young people, it is necessary to examine the safeguards that have been provided by current legal regulations. At present, the national rules of European Member States on consumer credit are based on the Consumer Credit Directive of 2008.[27] This instrument is applicable on credit contracts concluded between a creditor and a consumer, also in the form of deferred payment (art. 3 lit. c). However, the Directive is not applicable to credit contracts having a total amount of credit of less than 200 euros (art. 2 para. 2 lit. c) [i.e., small credit], nor is it applicable to credit contracts under the terms of which the credit must be repaid within three months and only insignificant charges are payable (art. 2 para. 2 lit. f) [i.e., short-term credit]. Consequently, the legal safeguards provided by the Consumer Credit Directive of 2008, such as the duty to provide pre-contractual and contractual information or the obligation to assess the creditworthiness of the consumer, are not applicable to BNPL-services since they generally fall under the scope of small and short-term credit agreements within the meaning of the Consumer Credit Directive of 2008.[28]

Germany's national legislation reflects the rules of the Directive of 2008 on small and short-term credit agreements: Sec. 491 para. 2 nos. 1 and 3 of the German Civil Code exempts small and short-term credit agreements from the definition of consumer credit contract. Accordingly, legal safeguards provided for consumer credit contracts are not applicable to small and short-term credit contracts.

Nevertheless, one would assume that providers of BNPL-services would like to prevent their customers from falling into a debt spiral and/or missing the deadlines for their payments. Therefore, they should be assessing in advance whether small and short-term credit agreements will be repaid according to the terms of the contract. Yet a study conducted by Finance Watch confirmed that in more than half of the cases, a proper creditworthiness assessment is not conducted.[29]

For credit risk management purposes, some BNPL-providers conduct a *credit check*, using either data directly available to them or data found on one or several credit databases or a combination of both. In contrast to a *creditworthiness assessment*, where the repayment likelihood in relation to a specific application is assessed, a credit check (in other words, checking the credit score) addresses only a person's general ability to make payments on time and in full. For a proper creditworthiness assessment, at the very least, information on the regular income and expenses of the person applying for a credit is necessary in order to determine debt sustainability. However, according to the information on the websites of the two largest BNPL providers in Germany, they carry out instead a credit check based on the data stored by numerous credit databases.[30] Thus, whereas the general payment behaviour is particularly important for BNPL-providers, the applicant's regular income and expenses are not taken into consideration. The process of conducting a credit check and the decision-making process of BNPL-providers are fully automated.[31]

Some other BNPL-providers, on the other hand, work with credit limits in order to manage credit risks. For a new customer, a lower credit limit is established upon initial registration, and this limit may be increased depending on the purchase and repayment behaviour of the consumer. If the customer cannot make a payment or a certain number of payments, s/he will have restricted access to the remainder of the credit limit.[32] Alternatively, the limit will not be set initially but only after the customer is unable to fulfill payment obligations.[33] In this model, neither regular income nor regular expenses nor a credit score is considered in granting access to BNPL-services; the determination depends solely on the personal repayment behaviour and history of the consumer with that specific BNPL-provider.

4.2 New Consumer Credit Directive

4.2.1 Extended scope

Due to several reasons, such as an imprecise wording of certain articles and digitalisation, the Consumer Credit Directive of 2008 proved to be only partially effective in the protection of consumers. Especially the market developments linked to digitalisation were not foreseen at the time of the adoption of Directive of 2008. Therefore, in 2023, the European legislature adopted a new and improved Consumer Credit Directive (CCD).[34] It entered into force on November 20, 2023, (art. 49 CCD) and is to be implemented into national laws by November 20, 2025. Its new rules are to be applicable by November 20, 2026 (art. 48 CCD). On that same day, the 2008 Directive will be repealed (art. 47 CCD).

Small and short-term credit contracts, which were excluded from the scope of the 2008 Directive, have been included into the scope of application of the new Directive. According to art. 3 no. 3, the term "credit agreement" includes credit in the form of a deferred payment, and the exception of the 2008 Directive regarding small and short-term credit agreements has been removed. The Directive, in its recital 16, even specifies BNPL-credit as short-term credit agreements falling within its scope. However, the extension of the scope of application to small and short-term credit agreements, unfortunately, does not entail that all of the CCD safeguards are applicable to BNPL-credit. In order to avoid an unnecessary burden for creditors (recital 15 CCD), the CCD gives Member States a regulatory option to exclude the application of certain provisions related to advertisement, pre-contractual and contractual information for, *inter alia*, BNPL-credit (art. 2 para. 8 CCD). It remains to be seen how many Member States will make use of this option. Nevertheless, there is no reference to art. 18 in art. 2 para. 8 CCD; thus, a creditworthiness assessment should be conducted in all cases of BNPL-credit without any exception.

4.2.2 Deferred payments directly offered by suppliers

Deferred payments free of interest and without any charges are offered not only by third-party BNPL-providers but also directly by suppliers of goods and services. This business practice is commonly used and allows consumers to pay only after the receipt of the goods or services. The CCD excludes such deferred payments from its scope of application, provided that

(1) there is no third party, such as a BNPL-provider, involved in it (art. 2 para. 2 lit. h CCD), and
(2) the payment is to be executed free of interest and without any other charges, and

(3) the payment is to be entirely executed within 50 days of the delivery of the good or service, if the supplier is a micro, small or medium-sized enterprise,[35] or
(4) the payment is to be entirely executed within 14 days of the delivery of the good or service, if it is a large online supplier.

The difference in the deferral period for large online suppliers and small and medium-sized suppliers reflects concerns that large online suppliers, considering their financial capacities, would otherwise be able to offer deferred payment in a very extensive way and weaken fair competition with other suppliers of goods or providers of services (recital 17).[36] Hence, if large online suppliers would like to provide for deferred payments exceeding the 14-day period, those deferred payments will be subject to CCD regulations. Accordingly, if a deferred payment with a 30-day period is offered by a large online supplier, it is a credit contract within the meaning of CCD; and if it is a small or short-term credit agreement within the meaning of art. 2 para. 8 CCD, the Member States' regulatory choice will determine whether the provisions related to advertisement as well as pre-contractual and contractual information will be applicable in full or in part.

4.2.3 Pre-contractual and contractual information duties as a prevention tool?

One of the prevention tools the CCD employs for financial consumer protection is the duty to provide certain information to consumers, be it in the pre-contractual phase or at the beginning of the contractual phase. As addressed before, especially pre-contractual information about late payment or default fees is not presently clear. Against this background, it is a welcome development that providers of small and short-term credit agreements will have to inform consumers in the pre-contractual phase and at the beginning of the contractual relationship about the costs in the event of late payments and about charges incurred for default (art. 10 para. 3 lit. g, art. 11 para. 2 lit. g, art. 21 para. 1 lit. l CCD). Still, the business model employed by BNPL-credit providers can bypass these provisions quite easily, veiling the consequences until it is too late for consumers. Namely, costs are incurred not only in the case of late payments and default but also in the case of second or third deferral options or where several payment obligations are bundled and converted into payment in instalments. Since these options are not technically late payments or instances of default, BNPL-providers are not required to inform the consumers as to the fees for utilising these options.

Furthermore, and unfortunately, the information duties do not solve the problems that result when there are a multiple number of small and short-term credit agreements, which generally lead to the individual losing track of upcoming payment obligations and missing deadlines. The provisions whereby the creditor must provide information on "the amount, number and frequency of payments to be made by the consumer" (art. 10 para. 3 lit. h, art. 11 para. 2 lit. h, art. 21 para. 1 lit. h CCD) relate to payments to be made within a single credit contract (cf. art. 23 para. 1, recital 38 CCD). As such, they are not applicable to several small and short-term credit contracts with multiple due dates, that is, to different credit obligations in the form of deferred payments independent from one another.

4.2.4 Creditworthiness assessment as a prevention tool?

The obligation to assess the creditworthiness of the consumer (art. 18 CCD) is applicable to small and short-term credit agreements without any limitation. Therefore, creditors, including BNPL-providers, are required to carry out a thorough assessment of the consumer's creditworthiness before concluding the credit contract. Rather than serving the risk management of the creditor, this assessment aims to protect the interests of consumers and to prevent over-indebtedness – and thus to prevent irresponsible lending practices (art. 18 para. 1 CCD). It is apparent that the CCD attaches much importance to creditworthiness assessment as a tool for ensuring responsible lending practices.

Creditors are allowed to grant credit to the consumer only if the result of the creditworthiness assessment indicates that the consumer will likely repay the credit in the manner required under the credit contract (art. 18 para. 6 CCD). In this respect, art. 18 para. 3 CCD dictates that the creditworthiness assessment is to be carried out on the basis of relevant and accurate information on the consumer's income and expenses and other financial and economic circumstances. As has been addressed earlier (see 4.1), information on the regular income and expenses of the consumer is not considered under the current credit limits or credit-check-schemes of BNPL-providers. Furthermore, art. 18 para. 11 provides that the creditworthiness assessment cannot be based exclusively on the consumer's credit history as registered in a credit database. Consequently, current methods employed by BNPL-providers, that is, making a credit decision based on a credit score or credit limits, will not satisfy the requirements for a proper creditworthiness assessment under the CCD since neither the credit score nor the information processed by the credit databases include regular income and all regular expenses. Therefore, the creditworthiness assessments for BNPL-credit will have to become more comprehensive.[37]

Yet all is not well.

The CCD might have created – intentionally or unintentionally – an important gap in the protection of consumers via the creditworthiness assessment. Art. 18 para. 3 CCD, after stating that the creditworthiness assessment is to be carried out on the basis of relevant and accurate information on the consumer's income and expenses and other financial and economic circumstances, provides that the information to be collected for the assessment should be "necessary and proportionate to the nature, duration, value and risks of the credit for the consumer". BNPL-credit is generally small ("value of the credit") and short-term ("duration of the credit") credit. Thus, there is a legitimate concern that national legislators will, during the implementation of the CCD into national laws, focus on the "duration" and "value" of the loan, particularly for small and short-term credit agreements in the form of BNPL, and not on the increased risk of over-indebtedness posed by these credit contracts for consumers ("risks of the credit for the consumer").[38] A focus on the value and duration of the extended credit would lead to a watered-down creditworthiness assessment.

In order to prevent this outcome, the objective of the creditworthiness assessment as expressed in art. 18 para. 1 CCD should be taken into account: the creditworthiness assessment is to be carried out in the interest of consumers in order to prevent irresponsible lending practices and over-indebtedness. In this respect, the prevention of over-indebtedness should be given priority when the requirements for the creditworthiness assessment for BNPL-credit are implemented, and the focus should not be upon the value or duration of the credit.[39] It remains to be seen, how the Member States transpose the obligation to conduct a creditworthiness assessment for BNPL-credit into their national laws.

Furthermore, already existing small and short-term credit agreements should be incorporated into the creditworthiness assessment before the conclusion of any new contracts on small and short-term credit. Currently, it is not clear whether the BNPL-providers notify credit databases of small and short-term credit agreements although they do notify credit databases of outstanding payment obligations. According to the study of the European Commission, small and short-term credit agreements are either not reported to credit databases or the credit databases do not provide information on them.[40] Therefore, BNPL-providers, like other creditors, lack the necessary information for a thorough creditworthiness assessment in the event a consumer has been making use of offers of (several) BNPL-providers.

5. Monitoring features as responsible lending practices

BNPL-providers seem to be somewhat aware of the difficulties which their business model is causing in practice. Therefore, some of them have already started to adopt certain features which should help consumers to keep track of their upcoming payment obligations. One such feature is the reminders sent by the BNPL-providers about upcoming payments.[41] Such reminders are generally sent by e-mail or SMS a couple of days before the payment is due and will be debited from the consumer's bank account. Yet these reminders are sent after the consumer has already concluded the credit contract. If a consumer concludes several small and short-term credit contracts within a short period of time, these reminders will not prevent the consumer from falling into over-indebtedness.

Some BNPL-providers insert personalised shopping limits as a risk management tool, which, at the same time, should serve as a monitoring tool for consumers. Such limits would be a useful prevention tool if they were based on regular income and expenses. However, as addressed earlier (see 4.1), this is not the case in BNPL-practice. Indeed, there are reported incidents in which the available limit is disproportionately high in relation to the consumer's regular income. According to the informal reports of debt counselling offices in Germany, not a small number of consumers obtain "limits" from BNPL-providers that they never would have received as an overdraft facility or as a regular line of credit from a bank. Therefore, a shopping limit that is set without due regard for regular income and expenses is neither a feature nor an example of responsible lending practice.

The higher risk of over-indebtedness, especially among young persons, caused by BNPL-credits is the result of individuals failing to control their impulses and losing track of upcoming payments. Currently, each BNPL-user can visit their account on the website or app and see the list of upcoming payments. Nevertheless, most consumers do not check the list of upcoming payments in advance, that is, before they initiate a purchase process via BNPL-credit. Therefore, an overview of this nature needs to be integrated into the BNPL-process, meaning that consumers will be prompted or even required to review their upcoming obligations before agreeing to the next purchase using a BNPL-credit.

For example, if a person would like to initiate a BNPL-credit via Klarna or PayPal, s/he will be redirected to the website or app of the BNPL-provider. Here, consumers will first decide whether the amount should be directly debited from their bank account or credit card or whether they would like to defer payment for 30 days. In the event the deferred payment option is chosen, before agreeing to the deferred payment, the consumer should be shown a list of upcoming payment obligations in the next 30 or 60 days. The new yet-to-be-agreed deferred payment obligation should also be listed. This overview could also provide further details, for example, identifying in red those payments that have already been deferred twice. This way, consumers would have a clear picture of which payments obligations they must fulfill in the next 30 or 60 days and see how the new intended BNPL-credit fits into their individual financial picture. Such a monitoring feature will not only protect consumers from the accumulation of payment obligations which they cannot meet but also improve the financial literacy of consumers, especially young individuals.

6. Conclusion

It is to be welcomed that the European legislature decided to include small and short-term credit agreements into the scope of application of the CCD. As discussed before, BNPL-services as small and short-term credit contracts create an increased risk of over-indebtedness in general and pose such a risk, in particular, to young individuals, a demographic commonly needing to improve their financial literacy and exercise better control over their impulses.

However, pre-contractual and contractual information duties can prove ineffective in the case of BNPL-credit. Furthermore, Member States have been conferred discretion in terms of the implementation of the creditworthiness assessment into their national laws as relates to small and short-term credit agreements. Where a Member State decides to adopt rules that make a creditworthiness assessment for BNPL-services depend on the value and duration of these services rather than the risk of over-indebtedness, the protection that the CCD intends to give against the risk of over-indebtedness posed by the BNPL-credits will be watered down. Additionally, information on a high number of existing BNPL credit agreements might not be available for a creditworthiness assessment, especially if a consumer uses services of several BNPL-providers.

One of the gravest problems regarding BNPL-credit is that consumers quickly lose sight of "the big picture" in terms of their upcoming obligations. This cause of over-indebtedness is not entirely eliminated by payment reminders or by a generally available overview of upcoming payments. An overview mechanism which is integrated into the BNPL-credit process, on the other hand, would be more effective in preventing over-indebtedness and improving the financial literacy of young individuals.

Notes

* The title is in reference to the panel discussion "Buy Now Pain Later? The consumer payment journey" at the event "Back to the Future – The promises and perils of digital finance", held on November 23, 2023, and organised by BEUC.

1 Damar-Blanken et al., "Kreditwürdigkeitsprüfung," 16; see also Engelbrecht et al., *Buy Now, Pay Later*, 42–43.

2 Cook et al., "Buy Now Pay Later," 246; European Commission, *Consumers' Over-Indebtedness*, 211; Machura-Urbaniak and Lupinu, "'Buy Now, Pay Later' (BNPL) Payment Services," 185, 187; for more information, Engelbrecht et al., *Buy Now, Pay Later*, 44–45.

3 Finance Watch, "Causes of Over-Indebtedness," 9; European Banking Authority, "Non-Bank Lending," 41.

4 Sellers can also directly offer payment in instalments or deferred payment or a lay-by sale (also known as layaway sales), see Cook et al., "Buy Now Pay Later," 246.

5 Directive (EU) 2015/2366 of the European Parliament and of the Council of November 25, 2015 on payment services in the internal market, OJ L 337 23.12.2015, p. 35. From a regulatory point of view, some of the payment service providers also have a banking licence, especially for payment in instalment schemes.

6 European Banking Authority, "Non-Bank Lending," 42–43; Cherednychenko, "Responsible Lending."

7 See also Engelbrecht et al., "Buy Now, Pay Later," 37–38.

8 European Banking Authority, "Non-Bank Lending," 41; for further information, see Schufa, "Jugend-Finanzmonitor 2023."

9 Cherednychenko, "Responsible Lending"; Machura-Urbaniak and Lupinu, "'Buy Now, Pay Later' (BNPL) Payment Services," 186.

10 Finance Watch, "Causes of Over-Indebtedness," 10.

11 Machura-Urbaniak and Lupinu, "'Buy Now, Pay Later' (BNPL) Payment Services," 187.

12 See e.g., PayPal, "Datenschutzerklärung," No. 12; Klarna, "Datenschutzerklärung," No. 7.3.1.

13 In fact, most consumers learn of a wrongful notification to a credit database when their bank informs them of the cancellation of their credit card and/or overdraft facility; for an example, see the decision of the Hamburg Court of Appeal (OLG Hamburg) of January 10, 2024, Case no. 13 U 70/23.

14 In Germany, some providers offer credit without making inquiry of a credit database. However, these lines of credit are offered at prices which are considerably higher than the average market prices.

15 Cook et al., "Buy Now Pay Later," 246–47, 252–54; Engelbrecht et al., "Buy Now, Pay Later," 56; Schufa, *Risiko- und Kreditkompass 2023*, 5; Machura-Urbaniak and Lupinu, "'Buy Now, Pay Later' (BNPL) Payment Services," 187–88.

16 Cook et al., "Buy Now Pay Later," 253.

17 Cook et al., "Buy Now Pay Later," 254; see also Engelbrecht et al., *Buy Now, Pay Later*, 61–62.

18 Finance Watch, "Causes of Over-Indebtedness," 9; Machura-Urbaniak and Lupinu, "'Buy Now, Pay Later' (BNPL) Payment Services," 187.

19 European Commission, *Consumers' Over-Indebtedness*, 204; European Banking Authority, *Non-Bank Lending*, 41; Roggemann et al., *Chancen und Risiken*, 20; Machura-Urbaniak and Lupinu, "'Buy Now, Pay Later' (BNPL) Payment Services," 187.

20 European Banking Authority, *Non-Bank Lending*, 41; Krüger, "Believe Now – Regret Later," 401; Machura-Urbaniak and Lupinu, "'Buy Now, Pay Later' (BNPL) Payment Services," 188.
21 Schufa, *Risiko- und Kreditkompass 2023*, 5.
22 https://www.iff-hamburg.de/en/.
23 Roggemann et al., *Chancen und Risiken*, 20.
24 Roggemann et al., *Chancen und Risiken*, 21.
25 Schufa, "Jugend-Finanzmonitor 2023."
26 Statistisches Bundesamt, "Überschuldete."
27 Directive 2008/48/EC of the European Parliament and of the Council of April 23, 2008 on credit agreements for consumers and repealing Council Directive 87/102/EEC, OJ 2008 L 133/66.
28 Judgment of the CJEU of October 17, 2024, C-409/23 (*Riverty*), ECLI:EU:C:2024:895, para 36–52.
29 Finance Watch, *Causes of Over-Indebtedness*, 10.
30 PayPal, "Nutzung Ihrer persönlichen Daten"; Klarna, "Bonitätsprüfung."
31 Klarna, "Datenschutzerklärung," No. 6.2; PayPal, "Datenschutzerklärung," No. 11; Buck-Heeb, "Rechtsrisiken," 143.
32 Machura-Urbaniak and Lupinu, "'Buy Now, Pay Later' (BNPL) Payment Services," 185, 188.
33 Klarna, "Wie viel kann ich ausgeben?"
34 Directive (EU) 2023/2225 of the European Parliament and of the Council of October 18, 2023, on credit agreements for consumers and repealing Directive 2008/48/EC, OJ L, 2023/2225, October 30, 2023.
35 To be determined according to Commission Recommendation of May 6, 2003, concerning the definition of micro, small and medium-sized enterprises, OJ 2003 L 124/36.
36 The European Consumer Organisation BEUC criticised this exception since the CCD itself created a loophole to circumvent its own application. Thanks to this exception, large online suppliers or small or medium-sized enterprises can themselves offer deferred payment options without resorting to BNPL-providers. This does not eliminate the risk of over-indebtedness for consumers. See BEUC, "Consumer Credit Directive," 5–6.
37 Damar-Blanken et al., "Kreditwürdigkeitsprüfung," 36; cf. Cherednychenko, "Responsible Lending."
38 Damar-Blanken et al., "Kreditwürdigkeitsprüfung," 36–37.
39 Damar-Blanken et al., "Kreditwürdigkeitsprüfung," 37.
40 European Commission, *Consumers' Over-Indebtedness*, 211.
41 Machura-Urbaniak and Lupinu, "'Buy Now, Pay Later' (BNPL) Payment Services," 188.

References

BEUC. "Consumer Credit Directive: BEUC Recommendations for Trilogues." Accessed April 24, 2024. https://www.beuc.eu/sites/default/files/publications/BEUC-X-2022-091_Members_consultation_CCD_position_paper_for_trilogues.pdf.

Buck-Heeb, Petra. "Rechtsrisiken bei automatisierter Kreditwürdigkeitsprüfung und Kreditvergabe." *Zeitschrift für Bank-und Kapitalmarktrecht* 23, no. 3 (2023): 137–45.

Cherednychenko, O.O. "On the Bumpy Road to Responsible Lending in the Digital Marketplace: The New EU Consumer Credit Directive." *Journal of Consumer Policy* 47, no. 1 (2024), Open Access. https://doi.org/10.1007/s10603-024-09564-z.

Cook, Julia, Kate Davies, David Farrugia, Steven Threadgold, Julia Coffey, Kate Senior, Adriana Haro, and Barrie Shannon. "Buy Now Pay Later Services as a Way to Pay: Credit Consumption and the Depoliticization of Debt." *Consumption Markets & Culture* 26, no. 4 (2023): 245–57. https://doi.org/10.1080/10253866.2023.2219606.

Damar-Blanken, Duygu, Anne Riechert, Hanne Roggemann, Ingrid Größl, Helena Klinger, and Sally Peters. "Kreditwürdigkeitsprüfung – Zwischen Überschuldungs-und Datenschutz: Perspektiven zur nationalen Umsetzung der Verbraucherkreditrichtlinie." 2024. https://www.vzbv.de/sites/default/files/2024-05/24-05-14_Gutachten_iff_Kreditw%C3%BCrdigkeitspr%C3%BCfung.pdf.

Engelbrecht, Laura, Philippe Krahnhof, and Alexander Zureck. "'Buy Now, Pay Later' – Kritische Analyse der potenziellen Schuldenfalle." 2024. https://www.researchgate.net/publication/378913491_Buy_now_pay_later_-Kritische_Analyse_der_potenziellen_Schuldenfalle.

European Banking Authority. "Final Report on Response to the Non-Bank Lending Request from the CfA on Digital Finance." 2022. https://www.eba.europa.eu/sites/default/files/document_library/Publications/Reports/2022/1032199/Report%20on%20response%20to%20the%20non-bank%20lending%20request%20from%20the%20CfA%20on%20Digital%20Finance.pdf.

European Commission. *Study on European Consumers' Over-Indebtedness and Its Implications – Final Report*. European Commission, 2023.

Finance Watch. "Tackling Causes of Over-Indebtedness in the EU Consumer Credit Market." 2022. https://www.finance-watch.org/policy-portal/retail-inclusion/over-indebtedness-eu-consumer-credit-market-ccd/.

Klarna. "Führt Klarna eine Bonitätsprüfung bei mir durch und wirkt sich das auf meine Kreditwürdigkeit aus?" Accessed April 19, 2024. https://www.klarna.com/de/kundenservice/fuehrt-klarna-bonitaetspruefung-wirkt-sich-das-auf-meine-kreditwuerdigkeit-aus/.

Klarna. "Klarnas Datenschutzerklärung." Accessed April 19, 2024. https://cdn.klarna.com/1.0/shared/content/legal/terms/0/de_de/privacy.

Klarna. "Wie viel kann ich ausgeben?" Accessed April 21, 2024. https://www.klarna.com/de/kundenservice/wie-viel-kann-ich-ausgeben/.

Krüger, Ulrich. "Believe Now – Regret Later." *Verbraucher und Recht* 37, no. 11 (2022): 401–2.

Machura-Urbaniak, Anna, and Pier Mario Lupinu. "'Buy Now, Pay Later' (BNPL) Payment Services: Opportunities and Legal Challenges for EU Consumers and Businesses." *Journal of European Consumer and Market Law* 12, no. 5 (2023): 184–93.

PayPal. "Nutzung Ihrer persönlichen Daten durch Kreditauskunfteien in Deutschland." Accessed April 19, 2024. https://www.paypal.com/de/webapps/mpp/ua/creditref.

PayPal. "PayPal-Datenschutzerklärung." Accessed April 19, 2024 https://www.paypal.com/de/webapps/mpp/ua/privacy-full#11.

Roggemann, Hanne, Sally Peters, Duygu Damar-Blanken, Helena Klinger, Ingrid Größl, and Maximilian Päsler. "Chancen und Risiken des Kreditmarktes für Junge Erwachsene." 2023. https://www.iff-hamburg.de/wp-content/uploads/2023/03/studie-chancen-risiken-kreditmarkt-junge-erwachsene_2023_sally-peters_hanne-roggemann.pdf.

Roggemann, Hanne, Sally Peters, Duygu Damar-Blanken, Helena Klinger, Ingrid Größl, and Maximilian Päsler. "Kreditkompetenz junger Menschen in Deutschland." 2023. https://www.iff-hamburg.de/wp-content/uploads/2023/03/studie-kreditkompetenz-junge-menschen-finanzielle-bildung_2023_sally-peters_hanne-roggemann.pdf.

Schufa. "Der neue SCHUFA Jugend-Finanzmonitor 2023: Viele jungen Menschen nutzen Buy Now Pay-Later-Angebote, ihnen sind aber auch die Risiken bewusst." Accessed April 18, 2024. https://www.schufa.de/themenportal/jugend-finanzmonitor-buy-now-pay-later/index.jsp.

Schufa. *Risiko-und Kreditkompass 2023*. Schufa, 2023.

Statistisches Bundesamt. "28% der Überschuldeten hatten 2021 Schulden bei Onlinehändlern." Accessed April 18, 2024. https://www.destatis.de/DE/Presse/Pressemitteilungen/2023/01/PD23_N001_63511.html.

Conclusion

Duygu Damar-Blanken and Michelle Kelly-Louw

As the contributions in this book clearly demonstrate, causes of financial exclusion and over-indebtedness are manyfold and eliminating them requires combined efforts of both specific legislation and the broader legal framework. The European Union legislation on consumer credit contracts and on unfair terms in consumer contracts present a good example. For instance, two European directives, namely the Consumer Credit Directive[1] and the Mortgage Credit Directive,[2] indirectly promote financial inclusion by fostering transparency and responsible lending. Additionally, the Unfair Contract Terms Directive (UCTD)[3] is also applicable to consumer credit contracts.

Having said that, strict application of general norms in cases of financial services might result in unfavourable outcomes for consumers. For instance, if a clause in a mortgage credit is considered invalid according to the UCTD, this could result in the invalidity of the whole mortgage contract. This would mean that the consumer would have to repay the (rest of the) capital he or she received under this agreement. What if, however, the consumer is required to pay interest on that amount according to the national rules? In her contribution, Jagna Mucha examined this and similar questions in the light of recent case law of the Court of Justice of the European Union (CJEU) and illustrated the Court's consumer-friendly approach.

Digitalisation, which creates a new type of information asymmetry, poses new challenges in consumer protection regarding data protection, transparency, and fairness.[4] Consumer protection in financial services is not an exemption. Difficulties in keeping up with increasing digitalisation could lead to digital-financial exclusion of certain consumer groups, such as the elderly. Currently, many existing legal frameworks do not always offer an adequate solution for such cases of financial exclusion. Adequate solutions, including legal intervention, require, *inter alia*, a solid scientific basis. As set forth in the contribution by Anne-Marie Weber, Weronika Herbet-Homenda, and Helena Kordasiewicz on elderly consumers and digital-financial exclusion, certain general barriers could be identified despite the heterogeneity of this consumer group being occasionally overlooked in scientific research. From a legal political perspective, further research is necessary on all negatively affected consumer groups and cases of digital vulnerability so that legislative incentives could be initiated in order to alleviate digital-financial exclusion.

DOI: 10.4324/9781003510406-16

Doubtlessly, increasing financial literacy of consumers is one of the key aspects in financial inclusion. However, as the literacy level of consumer substantially varies from country to country or even from one consumer group to another,[5] the European legislator introduced the requirement that banking staff should have an adequate level of knowledge and competence in relation to credit agreements.[6] In her contribution, Joana Farrajota examined this requirement and concluded, on the basis of the Portuguese implementation, that the requirement does not ensure the desired outcome since the Member States are not required to evaluate and measure the adequacy of the level of knowledge and competence. As it pertains to every legal requirement, lack of supervision and/or sanctions rather result in paper tigers also in financial consumer protection and in inclusionary measures in financial services.

Anu Kaup and Karin Sein contemplated fully how credit registries and credit-scoring companies deal with the practices and rules regarding the disclosure of information about payment defaults in credit information registers and their impact on the privacy of consumers specifically under Estonian law and Finnish law. A particular focus was how these respective jurisdictions dealt with the disclosure of defaults on old, prescribed, and even already paid debts. They compared these two jurisdictions to the position set out in the EU's General Data Protection Regulation[7] (GPDR) providing Member States with a discretion in the matter. They concluded that the application of the EU's GPDR and the Finnish rules and practices on the length of time of storage of payment default data is much more mindful of consumer privacy, unlike the Estonian rules and practices that provide for undue lengthy periods of storage before the payment default information is removed from the credit information register. They highlighted some of the tension that exists between consumer protection and data protection in Estonian law on the matter. They conclude that the periods related to the publication of payment defaults under Estonian law are too long and therefore not desirable. They further argue the Estonian regulation permitting extremely long publication periods does not conform with the GDPR. In their view, the Estonian domestic data protection regulation is not in conformity with the EU GPDR, and the Estonian legislature should accordingly amend the law as soon as possible. Their contribution exposes the differences in the application of Member States of the GDPR.

Ulrich Krüger concentrated on the financial exclusion of consumers with no credit scores, the so-called credit invisibles, and those with poor credit scores, specifically in the USA and EU. Krüger unpacked how credit scores can lead to financial exclusion and that credit invisibles and consumers with poor credit scores end up not only paying more for credit, financial services, and consumables but also more with data. He considers a number of strategies for credit building proposed in the USA and EU. For example, he looked at specific credit counselling, the use of special credit products (for example, credit-builder loans, secured credit cards, and more recently, (digital) lending circles), and the expansion of the data basis eligible for scoring with "alternative payment data" (for example, payment of rent, cell phone bills, utility costs). He agrees that some of these strategies are useful but also shows that others are flawed and/or others even carrying some risk. He concludes fittingly that to genuinely enhance financial inclusion of credit invisibles and poorly scored consumers, real political action and legal reform are required relating to the promotion of credit-building products, promotion of financial counselling, the disclosure requirement for credit scores (e.g., how algorithms work, not only prohibiting the information that may be used) and for data protection.

As opposed to its challenges for financial consumer protection and financial inclusion, digitalisation offers innovative solutions to financial exclusion. New technologies and artificial intelligence have and will continue to revolutionise the world of finance and add to financial inclusion. However, in order to fully unlock this potential, built-in consumer protection measures are indispensable.

We have entered an era of increased digital payments and the digitalisation of financial services. Digitalisation in the financial sector brings with it many new opportunities for advancing financial inclusion but also brings the possibility that many consumers, particularly the more vulnerable ones, may become financially digitally excluded. It inevitably also places more strain on consumers and duties of financial regulators and others to ensure that consumers become digital-financially literate. This is indeed a big challenge for the vulnerable consumer groups, like the elderly and the ones that are struggling with just becoming generally financially literate. Even for consumers with high levels of financial literacy, it is becoming more difficult to keep up with the fast pace of technological advancements and digitalisation in the financial sector.

There is a global drive to reduce the use of cash and move towards a more cashless society. The reality, though, is that some countries or portions of society still continue to be cash driven and use cash – particularly the poor, low, and middle market segments. Many of these consumers still face access and/or utilisation barriers and are unable to access, or fail to utilise, financial services and products. It is very possible that if retail Central Bank Digital Currency (CBDC) is designed at the outset with the goal of promoting financial inclusion, it can bridge the gap between cash and digital payments. Noah Vardi wisely considered CBDCs and explored their risks (e.g., data protection issues and lack of consumer protection) and opportunities for financial inclusion and access to credit, particularly for vulnerable consumers. She correctly identifies some key problems with CBDCs, proposes some solutions, and shows that it is also possible that retail CBDC, if designed and adopted in a responsible and inclusive manner, may successfully grow the number of consumers using digital payment methods, reduce cash usage, and provide a more inclusive financial sector. Appropriately, she did not focus on CBDCs as payment instruments or the electronic equivalent to cash here but rather on their potential for financial inclusion and how access to credit can be achieved if CBDCs were accepted. It is doubtful that CBDCs will soon replace cash entirely, and it is likely to rather co-exist with it. If properly designed, retail CBDC can certainly complement existing financial inclusion initiatives and grow the number of consumers who have access to digital payments. It may, depending on their design, even offer low-cost, easily accessible, fast, and secure digital payments in future.

Open banking undoubtedly has the potential to grow financial inclusion but also poses valid challenges concerning the protection of consumers' data and privacy.

Like many other new innovations, proper rules are required that will protect consumers. For instance, a consumer should be able to control the access to their financial data, consent to the specific aspects of data to be shared, and the parties the data may be shared with. There should also be a way for a consumer to opt out of open banking or revoke the sharing of her or his data. Marc Lacoursière illustrates the benefits of open banking, for instance, creating new opportunities such as increased competition, improved services, lower costs, and advancement of financial inclusion, but he also stresses the potential and new risks it brings, such as operational, cyber-risk, and compliance, that may jeopardise the current state of financial stability. He also dealt with the impact of open banking on consumer protection and the current legal banking law framework in Canada. He tracked the recent legislative and other developments in Canada in this area and the willingness and efforts so far to create a legal framework for open banking. He concludes that a more inclusive banking model is needed in Canada if open banking is to work. He further proposes various amendments to the banking and finance regulatory framework in Canada that will improve inclusivity for consumers and offer better protection to consumers of open banking.

Faster conflict resolution, is, without any doubt, one of the greatest potentials of digitalisation. In their contribution, Faizal Kurniawan et al. explored the potential of online dispute resolution systems for the settlement of consumer claims in cases of algorithmic trading errors in Indonesian law. Their analysis demonstrates that the main issues regarding adequate protection of consumers in online dispute resolution systems concern the liability regime based on fault (as opposed to presumed liability); lack of clear, specific regulation regarding system errors; burden of proof; and evidence tools. As demonstrated by these loopholes in Indonesian law, certain consumer protection measures must be implemented so that the digital systems provided by financial institutions do not serve only their interests but a balance between their interests and consumer interests is struck.

Measures to prevent and tackle over-indebtedness play a vital role in financial inclusion. Some national laws enable private insolvency of over-indebted consumers combined with a debt relief. In her contribution, Claudia Lima Marquez illustrated the reform of the Brazilian Consumer Code as well as the judicial and extrajudicial proceedings provided for over-indebted consumers. Having compared the empirical data from the extrajudicial proceedings before and after the reform, she concludes that the reform cannot unlock its potential unless debt relief is also introduced in Brazilian law for over-indebted consumers. Debt relief (subject to certain conditions under insolvency proceedings) gives over-indebted consumers the possibility of a fresh start in life and, thus, facilitates their financial re-inclusion.

However, the task should be, first and foremost, to prevent over-indebtedness. For this purpose, different countries and legal systems take different approaches, especially regarding consumer credits.

Proper indirect debt-relief measures to deal with over-indebtedness are also important to assist consumers experiencing financial difficulties. For instance, sometimes all a consumer really needs to recover from a temporary financial set-back is to merely have the interest due on the debt not to accumulate further during the period the consumer is in default. The statutory *in duplum* rule in South

Africa and the rule in Kenya both guard against an excessive and further accumulation of interest while a consumer is in default, and both constitute a type of indirect debt-relief mechanism assisting defaulting consumers to be able to repay their debt. Michelle Kelly-Louw conducted compared research regarding the rule in both jurisdictions. After her comparative analyses, she concluded that under the South African law, the rule aims to operate as a tool to protect consumers irrespective of the type of lender of the money (thus to cover all borrowers), while under Kenyan law, the rule is aimed firstly to operate as a tool to regulate banking and, secondly, to function as a tool to protect only selective consumers, namely those that borrowed money from financial institutions, such as banks. She argues that the interest rule should operate as a tool providing debt relief to all consumers irrespective of where they borrowed the money from.

Lately, "Buy Now, Pay Later" (BNPL) credits, or small and short-term credits, proved to be an emerging problem for consumer over-indebtedness, in particular, for young consumers. In order to tackle this problem, the European legislature decided to include small and short-term credit agreements into the scope of the new Consumer Credit Directive. In her contribution, Duygu Damar-Blanken welcomed this decision as pre-contractual and contractual information duties and the duty to assess the creditworthiness of the consumer will be applicable to small and short-term consumer credits as well. She indicated, however, that these measures might not prove as effective as the legislature anticipates since the over-indebtedness based on small and short-term credits is generally caused by the fact that consumers quickly lose sight of "the big picture" in terms of their upcoming obligations. As this cannot be entirely eliminated by the pre-contractual and contractual information duties as well as the creditworthiness assessment, she proposed that an overview mechanism should be integrated into the BNPL-credit process. This would not only be more effective in preventing over-indebtedness, but also in improving the financial literacy of young individuals.

Notes

1 Directive 2008/48/EC of the European Parliament and of the Council of April 23, 2008 on credit agreements for consumers and repealing Council Directive 87/102/EEC, OJ 2008 L 133/66. This Directive will be repealed on November 20, 2026, by the Directive (EU) 2023/2225 of the European Parliament and of the Council of October 18, 2023, on credit agreements for consumers and repealing Directive 2008/48/EC, OJ of October 30, 2023, L 2023/2225.

2 Directive 2014/17/EU of the European Parliament and of the Council of February 4, 2014 on credit agreements for consumers relating to residential immovable property and amending Directives 2008/48/EC and 2013/36/EU and Regulation (EU) No 1093/2010, OJ 2014 L 60/34.

3 Council Directive 93/13/EEC of April 5, 1993 on unfair terms in consumer contracts, OJ 1993 L 95/29.

4 For more information see Helberger et al., *EU Consumer Protection 2.0.*

5 OECD, *2023 International Survey*, 14, 66.

6 Art. 9 Mortgage Credit Directive (Directive 2014/17/EU of February 4, 2014 on credit agreements for consumers relating to residential immovable property, OJ 2014 L 60/34); Art. 33 Consumer Credit Directive 2 (Directive (EU) 2023/2225 of the European

Parliament and of the Council of October 18, 2023, on credit agreements for consumers and repealing Directive 2008/48/EC, OJ L, 2023/2225, October 30, 2023).

7 Regulation (EU) 2016/679 of the European Parliament and of the Council of April 27, 2016 on the protection of natural persons with regard to the processing of personal data and on the free movement of such data, and repealing Directive 95/46/EC (General Data Protection Regulation), OJ 2016 L 119/1.

References

Helberger, Natali, Orla Lynskey, Hans-W. Micklitz, Peter Rott, Marjin Sax, and Joanna Strycharz. "EU Consumer Protection 2.0 – Structural Asymmetries in Digital Consumer Markets." March 2021. Accessed December 17, 2024. https://www.beuc.eu/sites/default/files/publications/beuc-x-2021-018_eu_consumer_protection_2.0.pdf.

OECD. *OECD/INFE 2023 International Survey of Adult Financial Literacy*. OECD, 2023. Accessed December 18, 2024. https://www.oecd.org/en/publications/oecd-infe-2023-international-survey-of-adult-financial-literacy_56003a32-en.html.

Index